W9-BUF-962

The Best AMERICAN ESSAYS 1993

Edited and with an Introduction by JOSEPH EPSTEIN

ROBERT ATWAN, Series Editor

TICKNOR & FIELDS • NEW YORK • 1993

ISSN 0888-3742
ISBN 0-395-63649-3
ISBN 0-395-63648-5 (pbk.)

Printed in the United States of America

AGM 10 9 8 7 6 5 4 3 2 1

The Best
AMERICAN
ESSAYS
1993

GUEST EDITORS OF
THE BEST AMERICAN ESSAYS

1986   ELIZABETH HARDWICK
1987   GAY TALESE
1988   ANNIE DILLARD
1989   GEOFFREY WOLFF
1990   JUSTIN KAPLAN
1991   JOYCE CAROL OATES
1992   SUSAN SONTAG
1993   JOSEPH EPSTEIN

Contents

Foreword by Robert Atwan   ix

Introduction by Joseph Epstein   xiii

MARCIA ALDRICH. *Hair*   1
from Northwest Review

JOSEPH BRODSKY. *Collector's Item*   8
from The New Republic

ANTHONY BURGESS. *Mozart and the Wolf Gang*   47
from The Wilson Quarterly

JACOB COHEN. *Yes, Oswald Alone Killed Kennedy*   66
from Commentary

GERALD EARLY. *Their Malcolm, My Problem*   87
from Harper's Magazine

JEAN ERVIN. *Afterthoughts*   101
from Iowa Woman

LAWRENCE OTIS GRAHAM. *Invisible Man*   114
from New York

DANIEL HARRIS. *Cuteness*   131
from Salmagundi

BARBARA GRIZZUTI HARRISON. *P.C. on the Grill*   141
from Harper's Magazine

DIANE JOHNSON. *Rolex* 158
from The Missouri Review

WARD JUST. *When It's Over Over There* 176
from GQ

PAUL R. McHUGH. *Psychiatric Misadventures* 187
from The American Scholar

SHAUN O'CONNELL. *A Memory of Two Fathers* 203
from The Massachusetts Review

CYNTHIA OZICK. *Alfred Chester's Wig* 214
from The New Yorker

THOMAS PALMER. *The Case for Human Beings* 254
from The Atlantic Monthly

JAMES SALTER. *You Must* 266
from Esquire

SCOTT RUSSELL SANDERS. *Wayland* 296
from The Gettysburg Review

ROBERT SHERRILL. *The Truth About Growing Old* 311
from Esquire

FLOYD SKLOOT. *Trivia Tea: Baseball as Balm* 326
from The Gettysburg Review

SHELBY STEELE. *The New Sovereignty* 341
from Harper's Magazine

LEWIS THOMAS. *Crickets, Bats, Cats, & Chaos* 355
from Audubon

PHILIP WEISS. *How to Get Out of a Locked Trunk* 362
from Harper's Magazine

Biographical Notes 369

Notable Essays of 1992 373

Foreword

APROPOS OF POSTAGE STAMPS, I received a letter from Pakistan recently that arrived in an airmail envelope decorated on both sides with an impressive array of stamps. I never saw an envelope bearing so many stamps. It was addressed in a fine script to "The Respectable Mr. Robert Atwan," and I was pleased to consider myself for one fleeting moment in that exalted fashion.

The writer thanked me for the "marvellous" editions of *The Best American Essays* he had found in a Lahore library and wanted me to know that they "were, indeed, the best introduction of America, ever." Each year as I work on the series, I find myself reflecting on the various meanings of "best," but I hadn't yet considered the possibility that aside from their literary or intellectual merits, essays are also one of the best means of forming a close acquaintance with a culture. With few exceptions, the essays that have appeared so far in these volumes offer readers (both foreign and domestic) an annual portrait of our nation. They represent the attempts of many of our best writers and thinkers to come to honest terms with the varieties of American experience.

This year's book is true to form. Though it visits a few European cities, it keeps returning home to examine our present affairs, big ones as well as small: endangered species, sex-change operations, the comforts of baseball trivia, the discomforts of grievance groups, racial prejudice at a Connecticut country club, the Kennedy assassination, a meditation on Malcolm X, an outrageous writer's wig, a bogus Rolex, a West Point education, our preoccupations with hair, cuteness, and politically correct food. There is even some good advice for anyone who ever gets locked inside the trunk of a car.

But good essays do more than introduce us to a culture's current or recurrent themes and topics; they introduce us to its dominant styles of thinking as well. An understanding of America in our time isn't simply a matter of knowing what topics are being discussed but of knowing *how* they're discussed. This is what the essay does best and why it penetrates deeper into the surface of society than journalism. If you want a record of what happened today, you pick up a newspaper; if you're interested in a timely or trendy topic, you read a magazine article; but if you want to get closer to the dynamics of a culture's thinking, you need essays. "Literature is news that stays news," Ezra Pound once said. And the essay — as this volume makes abundantly clear — is still the most "newsy" of literary forms.

This is mainly because the essayist is usually serving two masters: truth and imagination. The essay's commitment to truth — historical or personal — keeps it closely in touch with the world of reasoned ideas and plausible occurrences. Essayists usually inhabit a familiar world. But we shouldn't forget that the essay is also a literary genre, one of the forms of imaginative literature. The essayist creates, shapes, projects a presence, fashions metaphors, imagines what happens when one idea collides with another.

The essayist's world is not imaginary, though it *is* imaginative. Look at how Philip Weiss straddles both worlds — the familiar and the imaginative — in "How to Get Out of a Locked Trunk." What could be more familiar, or even more mundane, than the different kinds of automobile trunks Weiss personally examines? Even his title suggests the type of service article that fills the pages of our popular magazines. But *why* does Weiss become obsessed with locked trunks? That's where the imagination comes in. Anyone who doubts the essay's imaginative capacity should read Joseph Brodsky's "Collector's Item," an intricately woven meditation on international espionage inspired by a very peculiar foreign postage stamp.

Besides introducing us to a particular cultural moment, this year's collection also invites us to meet an exciting range of individual voices, many of them new to the series. That is another pleasure of the essay; it is permeated by the presence of its writer. Sometimes the presence is decidedly personal, almost physical; at other times, it is shy, tentative, or ruminative; or it may be powerfully aggressive and disputatious. The article may be impersonal, but the essay isn't. Genuine essays always bear the imprint of an individual writer, like those letters Cynthia Ozick used to receive from Alfred Chester: "The French stamps running helter-skelter on the envelope had been licked into displacement by a wild tongue and pounded down by a furious fist." An individual presence, undeniable, right down to the message conveyed by the stamps themselves.

The Best American Essays features a selection of the year's outstanding essays, essays of literary achievement that show an awareness of craft and a forcefulness of thought. Hundreds of essays are gathered annually from a wide variety of national and regional publications. These essays are then screened and turned over to a distinguished guest editor, who may add a few personal favorites to the list and who makes the final selections.

To qualify for selection, the essays must be works of respectable literary quality, intended as fully developed, independent essays (not excerpts) on subjects of general interest (not specialized scholarship), originally written in English (or translated by the author) for publication in an American periodical during the calendar year. Publications that want to make sure their contributors will be considered each year should include the series on their subscription list (Robert Atwan, *The Best American Essays*, P.O. Box 416, Maplewood, New Jersey 07079).

This year I'd like to thank a good friend, Peter Lushing, for all the advice and assistance (not to mention magazines!) he has generously given me since the inception of the series. I appreciate, too, the invaluable help I received this year from my research assistant, David Harris. It was a great pleasure to work on this volume with Joseph Epstein, one of our preeminent essayists. A few years ago, he wrote that "it's a sweet time to be an essayist." He's right. And he's also one of the chief reasons it is a "sweet time."

Introduction

MORE THAN THIRTY years ago, I spent six or seven months in the army at Fort Hood in Texas, where, in the same barracks, lived an amiable fellow from Brooklyn named Freddy Schindler. We were a headquarters company. This was back in the days of the cold war, and I personally fought communism as the movie reviewer and cultural news reporter for the *Fort Hood Armored Sentinel*. It was a dirty job, but someone had to do it. Freddy, though Jewish, was the assistant to the base's Catholic chaplain, whom he never referred to as other than Big Daddy. I was later transferred to Little Rock, Arkansas, to type the results of physical examinations in a recruiting station, and Freddy and I fell out of touch.

Three or four years later, though, I ran into Freddy Schindler on lower Fifth Avenue in New York. When I asked how things were going, he said that they were going terribly in general, and even worse in particular. Just this past weekend, he reported, he had been at a family wedding where he was seated, a bachelor of twenty-seven, at the children's table. "My goddamned cousin, knocked up and married at eighteen," Freddy said, "she gets to sit with the grownups, while I, because I'm unmarried, I am put at the children's table."

I hope it won't seem too much of a stretch, but I thought of Freddy as I was thinking about my introduction to *The Best American Essays 1993*, because it occurred to me that the position of the essay in relation to literature is a little like my friend Freddy Schindler at the family wedding — the essay, even though of age, is still, alas, assigned to the children's table. Poor essay, a versatile but never a major form, except in the hands of a very few magnificent practitioners: Montaigne, of course, Hazlitt, too; but after that things thin out a good bit, and from Charles Lamb to Max Beerbohm to Virginia Woolf to E. B. White, the quality of modesty becomes part of the job description for the essayist, as if a certain smallness were built into the form.

As someone who takes some pride in being known as "Joseph Epstein, an essayist" — or, even better, "the essayist Joseph Epstein" — who takes the term "essayist" as an honorific, I have both an interest and a stake in the form. I hate to see it put down, defamed, spat upon, even mildly slighted. The best luck that any writer can have is to find his or her form, and I feel fortunate in having found mine some twenty years ago in the familiar essay. It happened quite by luck: I was not then a frequent reader of Montaigne and Hazlitt; in those days I was even put off by Charles Lamb, who sometimes seemed to me a bit precious. For me the novel was the form of forms, and easily the one I most admired and should most have liked to master. Although I have published a dozen or so short stories, I have not yet written a novel — nor have I one in mind to write — and so I have to conclude that despite my enormous regard for that form, it just isn't mine. Perhaps it is quite useless for a writer to search for his perfect form; that form, it may well be, has to find him.

Over the years, I have come to think more and more of the history and of the contemporary standing of the essay, the form that is apparently mine. I recently had occasion to read through Montaigne, who was the first modern essayist. It is a deep tribute to call a man modern who began writing in 1572, but the first thing one notices in reading Montaigne is how contemporary he feels. The essay, his own chosen form — he all but invented it, really — made it possible for him to speak to us person to person, with an intimacy hitherto unknown in literature. In this magical form Montaigne could dilate upon his subject, deliberately digress, or do anything he pretty much damn well pleased. The slender silver thread that holds a Montaigne essay together is the man Montaigne himself. He was the first essayist to talk about himself: "not to dare to talk roundly of yourself betrays a defect of thought," he felt. In his hands, the essay became an instrument of discovery — self-discovery, chiefly. "I study my-self more than any other subject," Montaigne wrote. "That is my metaphysics; that is my physics."

As there is no standard human type who writes essays, so is there no standard essay: no set style, length, or subject. But what does unite almost all successful essays, no matter how divergent the subject, is that a strong personal presence is felt behind them. This is so even if the essayist never comes out to tell you his view of the matter being discussed, never attempts directly to assert his personality, never even slips into the first-person singular. Without that strong personal presence, the essay doesn't quite exist; it becomes an article, a piece, or some other indefinable verbal construction. Even when the subject seems a distant and impersonal one, the self of the writer is in good part what the essay is about.

Milan Kundera once wrote that he thought the novel one of the great European inventions for discovery. By this I take Kundera to mean that through the form of the novel, writers can study their society — or other societies — with aesthetic distance and through the force of imagination, learning many things they hadn't conceived before their novels, which in composition raised many fresh questions about human nature and existence generally, were written. The essay, too, is an invention for discovery. But it works differently from the novel; what the essayist seeks to discover is himself. This would end in simple and dreary egotism if the essayist didn't take things a step further and through study of himself gain a great grasp of the world beyond this self. The essayist investigates the world by looking first into his own heart. The essay, in this view, becomes an epistemology — a way of coming to knowledge — through which the essayist, beginning always with his own reactions to people and things, studies the world from the inside out. In an extreme case, such as Montaigne's, the essayist, by studying himself, studies the world; just as often, though, the essayist, beginning by studying the world, ends up studying himself.

I happen also of late to have been reading Theodore Dreiser, a novelist whom I much admire, and while doing so the unoriginal thought occurred to me that the novel, though it often gains through style, is far from dependent upon style. A strong case in

point is Dreiser — of whom his friend and literary supporter
H. L. Mencken once said that he had "an incurable antipathy to
the *mot juste.*" Dreiser is in the line of Balzac and Dostoyevsky,
all three being novelists who took on such large subjects as to
make matters of style seem rather beside the point. When you
are reading them you may notice crudities of style, but these
don't destroy their work or even long delay your surging forward in your reading. People of greatly refined — or narrowly
snobbish — sensibilities may be so put off by crudities of style
as to make reading such writers painful to them, but most of
us, caught up in the large sweep of the imaginative worlds these
writers present, scarcely notice.

An essayist, on the other hand, could not long survive a crude
style. To no one does Buffon's famous aphorism about the style
and the man being the same thing apply with greater pertinency
than to the essayist. Style is said to be the preservative of literature (Dreiser, Dostoyevsky, Balzac & Company excluded), but
without style the essayist can hardly be said to exist. While there
is no firmly set, single style for the essayist, styles varying with
each particular essayist, the best general description of essayistic
style was written in 1827 by William Hazlitt in his essay "Familiar Style." "To write a genuine familiar or truly English style,"
Hazlitt wrote, "is to write as any one would speak in common
conversation who had a thorough command and choice of
words, who could discourse with ease, force, and perspicuity,
setting aside all pedantic and oratorical flourishes." The style of
the essayist is that of an extremely intelligent, highly commonsensical person talking, without stammer and with impressive
coherence, to him- or herself and to anyone else who cares to
eavesdrop. This self-reflexivity, this notion of talking to oneself,
has always seemed to me to mark the essay off from the lecture.
The lecturer is always teaching; so, too, frequently is the critic. If
the essayist does so, it is usually only indirectly.

Apart from Montaigne and Bacon — and, well before them,
Plutarch — the development of the essay is, historically, a subset
of the development and prosperity of the magazine. The essay's
true history, that is to say, begins in the eighteenth century with
the beginning of the periodical press in Europe. The essay came
to the fore in England under the reign of Queen Anne, when

Joseph Addison and Richard Steele emerged in the pages of such periodicals as the *Tatler,* the *Spectator,* and the *Guardian.* Different magazines seemed to encourage different styles, and a mini-history of the essay could best be discovered in publications as various as the *Edinburgh Review* through the *American Mercury* through *The New Yorker* to the magazine that is still a gleam in the eye of some young man or woman not yet out of college but with impressive plans for a magazine that will be like no other that has been published before.

Every age produces its own kind of essay. E. B. White, for example, whose powerful reputation is owing to his essays in *Harper's* and *The New Yorker* from the twenties until his death in 1985, might not find it so easy to publish his kind of essay today in *Harper's, The New Yorker,* or anywhere else. *Best American Essays* will doubtless one day serve a cultural historian well who studies these volumes closely with an eye toward understanding the age in which they were written. These volumes will show, I would guess, the preoccupations of the day, styles of thought, literary tastes and manners, interesting eccentricities, and much more.

As editor of *The Best American Essays 1993,* reading through the few hundred essays published in 1992 that were serious candidates for this volume, I quickly enough discovered some of the main preoccupations of the past year. Multiculturalism was certainly one, political correctness another. A number of essays, almost all of them of real interest, were about Malcolm X, both the man and the phenomenon, a subject in good part pushed into prominence by the movie *Malcolm X.* Although essays touching on these subjects appear in this volume, the subjects themselves do not, I am pleased to be able to report, dominate the book.

I say I am pleased to report this because I think the essay is at its characteristic best when it is not too strongly bullied into being by current events and the intellectual trends of the day. I especially delight in the essay when it allows for a considerable distance from the news and even, for that matter, from the new. I prefer the essay when it is ruminative yet playful, commonsensical yet idiosyncratic, raising lots of questions yet under no strong obligation to provide many answers. I prefer it when the essay takes a small, very particular subject and, through the force of the essayist's artistically controlled maunderings, touches on un-predictably large general matters, makes hitherto unexpected connections, tells me things I hadn't hitherto known, or reminds me of other things I have always known but never thought to formulate so well as has the essayist I am reading at the moment. I believe that many of the essayists in this book provide many of these services — and extremely well.

If *The Best American Essays 1993* has a general character or quality, it is in its display of the impressive variety of which the essay, as a form, is capable. Essays deeply personal, comically idiosyncratic, patently polemical, essays reportorial, memoiristic, socially significant, essays dark in mood and light in touch, essays experimental, historical, analytical, and essays happily eluding all general categories appear in this book. Some among the book's contributors are not essayists primarily but novelists, jour-nalists, poets, psychiatrists, oncologists, and I am not sure what all else. But what I am sure of — and I hope you will be, too, when you have finished reading this book — is that each of them has served the essay well, while the essay, that wondrously form-less form, has lent them all some of its quiet but powerful magic.

JOSEPH EPSTEIN

The Best
AMERICAN
ESSAYS
1993

MARCIA ALDRICH

Hair

FROM NORTHWEST REVIEW

I'VE BEEN AROUND and seen the Taj Mahal and the Grand
Canyon and Marilyn Monroe's footprints outside Grauman's
Chinese Theater, but I've never seen my mother wash her own
hair. After my mother married, she never washed her own hair
again. As a girl and an unmarried woman — yes — but, in my
lifetime, she never washed her hair with her own two hands.
Upon matrimony, she began weekly treks to the beauty salon
where Julie washed and styled her hair. Her appointment on
Fridays at two o'clock was never canceled or rescheduled; it was
the bedrock of her week, around which she pivoted and
planned. These two hours were indispensable to my mother's
routine, to her sense of herself and what, as a woman, she should
concern herself with — not to mention their being her primary
source of information about all sorts of things she wouldn't
otherwise come to know. With Julie my mother discussed mo-
mentous decisions concerning hair color and the advancement
of age and what could be done about it, hair length and its effect
upon maturity, when to perm and when not to perm, the need
to proceed with caution when a woman desperately wanted a
major change in her life like dumping her husband or sending
back her newborn baby and the only change she could effect was
a change in her hair. That was what Julie called a "dangerous
time" in a woman's life. When my mother spoke to Julie, she
spoke in conspiratorial, almost confessional, tones I had never
heard before. Her voice was usually tense, on guard, the laughter forced, but with Julie it dropped much lower, the timbre

darker than the upper-register shrills sounded at home. And most remarkably, she listened to everything Julie said.

As a child I was puzzled by the way my mother's sense of self-worth and mood seemed dependent upon how she thought her hair looked, how the search for the perfect hair style never ended. Just as Mother seemed to like her latest color and cut, she began to agitate for a new look. The cut seemed to have become a melancholy testimony, in my mother's eyes, to time's inexorable passage. Her hair never stood in and of itself; it was always moored to a complex set of needs and desires her hair couldn't in itself satisfy. She wanted her hair to illuminate the relationship between herself and the idea of motion while appearing still, for example. My mother wanted her hair to be fashioned into an event with a complicated narrative past. However, the more my mother attempted to impose a hair style pulled from an idealized image of herself, the more the hair style seemed to be at odds with my mother. The more the hair style became substantial, the more the woman underneath was obscured. She'd riffle through women's magazines and stare for long dreamy hours at a particular woman's coiffure. Then she'd ask my father in an artificially casual voice: "How do you think I'd look with really short hair?" or "Would blonde become me?" My father never committed himself to an opinion. He had learned from long experience that no response he made could turn out well; anything he said would be used against him, if not in the immediate circumstances, down the line, for my mother never forgot anything anyone ever said about her hair. My father's refusal to engage the "hair question" irritated her.

So too, I was puzzled to see that unmarried women washed their own hair, and married women, in my mother's circle at least, by some unwritten dictum never touched their own hair. I began studying before and after photographs of my mother's friends. These photographs were all the same. In the pre-married mode, their hair was soft and unformed. After the wedding, the women's hair styles bore the stamp of property, looked constructed from grooming talents not their own, hair styles I'd call produced, requiring constant upkeep and technique to sustain the considerable loft and rigidity — in short, the antithesis of anything I might naively call natural. This was hair no one

touched, crushed, or ran fingers through. One poked and prodded various hair masses back into formation. This hair presented
obstacles to embrace, the scent of the hair spray alone warded
off man, child, and pests. I never saw my father stroke my
mother's head. Children whimpered when my mother came
home fresh from the salon with a potent do. Just when a woman's life was supposed to be opening out into daily affection, *the*
sanctioned affection of husband and children, the women of my
mother's circle encased themselves in a helmet of hair not unlike
Medusa's.

In so-called middle age, my mother's hair never moved, never
blew, never fell in her face: her hair became a museum piece.
When she went to bed, she wore a blue net, and when she took
short showers, short because, after all, she wasn't washing her
hair and she was seldom dirty, she wore a blue plastic cap for the
sake of preservation. From one appointment to the next, the
only change her hair could be said to undergo was to become
crestfallen. Taking extended vacations presented problems sufficiently troublesome to rule out countries where she feared no
beauty parlors existed. In the beginning, my parents took over-
nighters, then week jaunts, and thereby avoided the whole hair
dilemma. Extending their vacations to two weeks was eventually
managed by my mother applying more hair spray and sleeping
sitting up. But after the two-week mark had been reached, she
was forced to either return home or venture into an unfamiliar
salon and subject herself to scrutiny, the kind of scrutiny that
leaves no woman unscathed. Then she faced Julie's disapproval,
for no matter how expensive and expert the salon, my mother's
hair was to be lamented. Speaking just for myself, I had difficulty
distinguishing Julie's cunning from the stranger's. In these years
my mother's hair looked curled, teased, and sprayed into a
waved tossed monument with holes poked through for glasses.
She believed the damage done to her hair was tangible proof she
had been somewhere, like stickers on her suitcases.

My older sisters have worked out their hair positions differently. My oldest sister's solution has been to fix upon one hair
style and never change it. She wants to be thought of in a singular fashion. She may vary the length from long to longer, but
that is the extent of her alteration. Once, after having her first

baby, the "dangerous time" for women, she recklessly cut her hair to just below the ear. She immediately regretted the decision and began growing it back as she walked home from the salon, vowing not to repeat the mistake. Her signature is dark, straight hair pulled heavily off her face in a large silver clip, found at any Woolworth's. When one clip breaks, she buys another just like it. My mother hates the timelessness of my sister's hair. She equates it with a refusal to face growing old. My mother says, "It's immature to wear your hair the same way all your life." My sister replies,

"It's immature to never stop thinking about your hair. If this hair style was good enough when I was twenty, it's good enough when I'm forty, if not better."

"But what about change?" my mother asks.

"Change is overrated," my sister says, flipping her long hair over her shoulder definitively. "I feel my hair."

My other sister was born with thin, lifeless, nondescript hair: a cross she has had to bear. Even in the baby pictures, the limp strands plastered on her forehead in question marks wear her down. Shame and self-effacement are especially plain in the pictures where she posed with our eldest sister, whose dark hair dominates the frame. She's spent her life attempting to disguise the real state of her hair. Some years she'd focus on style, pulling it back in ponytails so that from the front no one could see there wasn't much hair in the back. She tried artless, even messy styles — as if she had just tied it up any old way before taking a bath or bunched it to look deliberately snarled. There were the weird years punctuated by styles that looked as if she had taken sugar water and lemon juice and squeezed them onto her wet hair and then let them crystallize. The worst style was when she took her hair and piled it on the top of her head in a cone shape and then crimped the ponytail into a zigzag. Personally, I thought she had gone too far. No single approach solved the hair problem, and so now, in maturity, she combines the various phases of attack in hope something will work. She frosts both the gray strands and the pale brown, and then perms for added body and thickness. She's forced to keep her hair short because chemicals do tend to destroy. My mother admires my sister's determination to transform herself, and never more than in my sister's latest assault upon middle age. No one has known for many years nor does anyone remember what the untreated color or texture of either my mother's or my sister's hair might be.

As the youngest by twelve years, there was little to distract Mother's considerable attention from the problem of my hair. I had cowlicks, a remarkable number of them, which like little arrows shot across my scalp. They refused to be trained, to lie down quietly in the same direction as the rest of my hair. One at the front insisted on sticking straight up while two on either side of my ears jutted out seeking sun. The lack of uniformity, the fact that my hair had a mind of its own, infuriated my mother and she saw to it that Julie cut my hair as short as possible in order to curtail its wanton expression. Sitting in the swivel chair before the mirror while Julie snipped, I felt invisible, as if I was unattached to my hair.

Just when I started to menstruate, my mother decided the battle plan needed a change, and presto, the page boy replaced the pixie. Having not outgrown the thicket of cowlicks, Mother bought a spectrum of brightly colored stretch bands to hold my hair back off my face. Then she attached thin pink plastic curlers with snap-on lids to the ends of my hair to make them flip up or under, depending on her mood. The stretch bands pressed my hair flat until the very bottom, at which point the ends formed a tunnel with ridges from the roller caps — a point of emphasis, she called it. Coupled with the aquamarine eyeglasses, newly acquired, I looked like an overgrown insect that had none of its kind to bond with.

However, I was not alone. Unless you were the last in a long line of sisters, chances were good that your hair would not go unnoticed by your mother. Each of my best friends was subjected to her mother's hair dictatorship, although with entirely different results. Perry Jensen's mother insisted that all five of her daughters peroxide their hair blonde and pull it back into high ponytails. All the girls' hair turned green in the summer from chlorine. Melissa Matson underwent a look-alike "home perm" with her mother, an experience she never did recover from. She developed a phobic reaction to anything synthetic, which made life very expensive. Not only did mother and daughter have identical tight curls and wear mother-daughter outfits, later they had look-alike nose jobs.

In my generation, many women who survived hair bondage to

their mothers now experiment with hair styles as one would test a new design: to see how it works, what it will withstand, and how it can be improved. Testing requires boldness, for often the style fails dramatically, as when I had my hair cut about a half inch long at the top, and it stood straight up like a tacky shag carpet. I had to live with the results, bear daily witness to the kinks in its design for nine months until strategies of damage control could be deployed. But sometimes women I know create a look that startles in its originality and suggests a future not yet realized.

The women in my family divide into two general groups: those who fasten upon one style, become identified with a look, and are impervious to change, weathering the years steadfastly, and those who, for a variety of reasons, are in the business of transforming themselves. In my sister's case, the quest for perfect hair originates in a need to mask her own appearance; in my mother's case, she wants to achieve a beauty of person unavailable in her own life story. Some women seek transformation, not out of dissatisfaction with themselves, but because hair change is a means of moving along in their lives. These women create portraits of themselves that won't last forever, a new hair style will write over the last.

Since my mother dictated my hair, I never took a stand on the hair issue. In maturity, I'm incapable of assuming a coherent or consistent philosophy. I have wayward hair: it's always becoming something else. The moment it arrives at a recognizable style, it begins to undo itself, it grows, the sun colors it, it waves. When one hair pin goes in, another seems to come out. Sometimes I think I should follow my oldest sister — she claims to never give more than a passing thought to her hair and can't see what all the angst is about. She asks, "Don't women have better things to think about than their hair?"

I bite back: "But don't you think hair should reflect who you are?"

"To be honest, I've never thought about it. I don't think so. Cut your hair the same way, and lose yourself in something else. You're distracted from the real action."

I want to do what my sister says, but when I walk out into shop-lined streets, I automatically study women's hair and always with the same question: How did they arrive at their hair? Lately,

I've been feeling more and more like my mother. I hadn't known how to resolve the dilemma until I found Rhonda. I don't know if I found Rhonda or made her up. She is not a normally trained hairdresser: she has a different set of eyes, unaffected. One day while out driving around to no place in particular, at the bottom of a hill, I found: "Rhonda's Hair Salon — Don't Look Back" written on a life-size cardboard image of Rhonda. Her shop was on the top of this steep orchard-planted hill, on a plateau with a great view that opened out and went on forever. I parked my car at the bottom and walked up. Zigzagging all the way up the hill, leaning against or sticking out from behind the apple trees, were more life-size cardboard likenesses of Rhonda. Except for the explosive sunbursts in her hair, no two signs were the same. At the bottom, she wore long red hair falling below her knees and covering her entire body like a shawl. As I climbed the hill, Rhonda's hair gradually became shorter and shorter, and each length was cut differently, until when I reached the top, her head was shaved and glistening in the sun. I found Rhonda herself out under one of the apple trees wearing running shoes. Her hair was long and red and looked as if it had never been cut. She told me she had no aspirations to be a hairdresser, "she just fell into it." "I see hair," she continued, "as an extension of the head and therefore I try to do hair with a lot of thought." Inside there were no mirrors, no swivel chairs, no machines of torture with their accompanying stink. She said, "Nothing is permanent, nothing is forever. Don't feel hampered or hemmed in by the shape of your face or the shape of your past. Hair is vital, sustains mistakes, can be born again. You don't have to marry it. Now tip back and put your head into my hands."

JOSEPH BRODSKY

Collector's Item

FROM THE NEW REPUBLIC

> If you sit long on the bank of the river, you may see the body of
> your enemy floating by.
> — Chinese proverb

GIVEN THE LUNACY this piece deals with, it ought to be written
in a language other than English. The only option available to
me, however, is Russian, which is the very source of the lunacy
in question. Who needs tautology? Besides, several of the assertions I am going to make are, in their turn, quite loony, and best
checked by a language that has a reputation for being analytical.
Who wants to have his insights ascribed to the vagaries of some
highly inflected language? Nobody, perhaps, save those who
keep asking what language I think or dream in. One dreams in
dreams, I reply, and thinks in thoughts. A language gets into the
picture only when one has to make those things public. This, of
course, gets me nowhere. Still (I persevere) since English isn't
my mother tongue, since my grip on its grammar isn't that tight,
my thoughts, for example, could get quite garbled. I sure hope
that they don't; at any rate I can tell them from dreams. And
believe it or not, dear reader, this sort of quibbling, which normally gets one nowhere, brings you straight to the core of our
story. For no matter how its author solves his dilemma, no matter
what language he settles for, his very ability to choose a language
makes him, in your eyes, suspect; and suspicions are what this
piece is all about. Who is he, you may wonder about the author,
what is he up to? Is he trying to promote himself to the status of
a disembodied intelligence? If it were only you, dear reader,

inquiring about the author's identity, that would be fine. The trouble is, he wonders about his identity himself — and for the same reason. Who are you, the author asks himself in two languages, and gets startled no less than you would upon hearing his own voice muttering something that amounts to "Well, I don't know." A mongrel, then, ladies and gentlemen, this is a mongrel speaking. Or else a centaur.

II

This is the summer of 1991, August. That much at least is certain. Elizabeth Taylor is about to take her eighth walk down the aisle, this time with a blue-collar boy of Polish extraction. A serial killer with cannibalistic urges is apprehended in Milwaukee; the cops find three hard-boiled skulls in his fridge. Russia's Great Panhandler makes his rounds in London with cameras zeroing in, as it were, on his empty tin. The more it changes, the more it stays the same: like the weather. And the more it tries to stay the same, the more it changes: like a face. And judging by the "weather," this could easily be 1891. On the whole, geography (European geography in particular) leaves history very few options. A country, especially a large one, gets only two. Either it's strong or it's weak. Fig. 1: Russia. Fig. 2: Germany. For most of the century, the former tried to play it big and strong (at what cost is another matter). Now its turn has come to be weak: by the year 2000 it will be where it was in 1900, and about the same perimeter. The latter, Germany, will be there, too. (At long last it dawned on the descendants of Wotan that saddling their neighbors with debt is a more stable and less costly form of occupation than sending in troops.) The more it changes, the more it stays the same. Still, you can't tell time by weather. Faces are better: the more one tries to stay the same, the more it changes. Fig. 1: Miss Taylor's. Fig. 2: one's own. The summer of 1991, then, August. Can one tell a mirror from a tabloid?

III

And here is one such, of humble strikebreaking origins. Actually it is a literary paper, *The London Review of Books* by name, which came into existence several years ago when the London *Times* and its Literary Supplement went on strike for a few months. In order not to leave the public without literary news and the benefits of liberal opinion, *LRB* was launched and evidently blossomed. Eventually the *Times* and its Literary Supplement resumed operation, but *LRB* stayed afloat, proof not so much of the growing diversity of reading tastes as of burgeoning demography. No individual I know subscribes to both papers, unless he is a publisher. It's largely a matter of one's budget, not to mention one's attention span or one's plain loyalty. And I wonder, for instance, which one of these — the latter, I should hope — prevented me from purchasing a recent issue in a small Belsize Park bookstore, where I and my young lady ventured the other day on our way to the movies. Budgetary considerations as well as my attention span — alarming as it may be of late — must be ruled out: the most recent issue of the *LRB* sat there on the counter in full splendor, its cover depicting a blown-up postal stamp: unmistakably of Soviet origins. This sort of thing has been enough to catch my eye since I was twelve. In its own turn, the stamp depicted a bespectacled man with silver neatly parted hair. Above and underneath the face, the stamp's legend, in now-fashionable Cyrillic, went as follows: "Soviet Secret Agent Kim Philby (1912–1988)." He looked indeed like Alec Guinness, with a touch perhaps of Trevor Howard. I reached into my pocket for two one-pound coins, caught the salesboy's friendly glance, adjusted my vocal chords for some highly pitched, civilized "May I have . . . ," and then turned ninety degrees and walked out of the store. I must add that I didn't do it abruptly, that I managed to send the boy at the counter a "just changed my mind" nod and to collect, with the same nod, my young lady.

IV

As we had some time to kill before the show, we went into a nearby café. "What's the matter with you?" my young comrade-in-arms asked me once we sat down. "You look like . . ." I didn't interrupt her. I knew how I felt and actually wondered what it might look like. "You look, you look . . . sideways," she continued hesitantly, tentatively, since English wasn't her mother tongue either. "You look as if you can't face the world any longer, can't look straight in the world's eye," she managed finally. "Something like that," she added just in case, to widen the margin of error. Well, I thought, one is always a greater reality for others than for oneself, and vice versa. What are we here for but to be observed. If that's what "it" really looks like from the outside, then I am doing fine — and so, perhaps, is the bulk of the human race. For I felt like throwing up, like a great deal of barf was welling up in my throat. Still, while I wasn't puzzled by the situation, I was surprised by its intensity. "What's the matter?" asked my young lady. "What's wrong?" And now, dear reader, after trying to figure out who the author of this piece is and what its timing, we've got to find out also who is its audience. Do you remember, dear reader, who Kim Philby was and what he did? If you do, then you are around fifty and thus, in a manner of speaking, on your way out. What you are going to hear, therefore, will be of little import to you, still of lesser comfort. Your game is up, you are too far gone; this stuff won't change anything for you. If, on the other hand, you've never heard of Kim Philby, this means that you are in your thirties, life lies ahead, all this is an ancient history and of no possible use or entertainment value for you, unless you are some sort of a spy buff. So? So where does all this leave our author, the question of his identity still hanging? Can a disembodied intelligence rightfully expect to find an able-bodied audience? I say, hardly, and I say who gives a damn.

V

All of this leaves our author at the close of the twentieth century with a very bad taste in his mouth. That, of course, is to be expected in a mouth that is in its fifties. But let's stop being cute with each other, dear reader, let's get down to business. Kim Philby was a Briton, and he was a spy. He worked for the British Intelligence Service, for MI5 or MI6, or both — who cares about all that arcana and whatever it stands for — but he spied for the Russians. In the parlance of the trade, he was a mole, though we are not going to use that lingo here. I am not a spy buff, not an aficionado of that genre, and never was; neither in my thirties nor even in my fifties, and let me tell you why. First, because

espionage provides a good plot, but seldom palatable prose. In
fact, the upsurge of spy novels in our time is the byproduct of
modernism's emphasis on texture, which left literature in practically all European languages absolutely plotless: the reaction
was inevitable, but with few exceptions, equally execrable. Still,
aesthetic objections are of little consequence to you, dear reader,
aren't they, and that in itself tells the time as accurately as the
calendar or a tabloid. Let's try ethics, then, on which everyone
seems to be an expert. I, for one, have always regarded espionage as the vilest human pursuit, mainly, I guess, because I grew
up in a country the advancement of whose fortunes was incon-
ceivable to its natives. To do that, one indeed had to be a foreigner; and that's perhaps why the country took such pride in its
cops, fellow travelers, and secret agents, commemorating them
in all manner of ways, from stamps to plaques to monuments.
Ah, all those Richard Zorges, Pablo Nerudas, and Hewlett Jon-
sons, and so on, all that pulp of our youth! Ah, all those flicks
shot in Latvia or in Estonia for the "Western" backdrop! A foreign surname and the neon lettering of "Hotel" (always put
vertically, never horizontally), sometimes the screeching brakes
of a Czech-made motorcar. The goal was not so much verisimili-
tude or suspense as the legitimization of the system by the exploits on its behalf outside of it. You could get a bar scene with a
little combo toiling in the background, you could get a blonde
with a tin-can taffeta skirt and a decent nose job looking positively non-Slavic. Two or three of our actors, too, looked sufficiently gaunt and lanky, the emphasis being always on a thor-
oughbred beak. A German-sounding name for a spy was better
than a French one, a French one was better than a Spanish one,
a Spanish one was better than an Italian one (come to think of it,
I can't recall a single Italian Soviet secret agent). The English
were tops, but hard to come by. In any case, neither English
landscapes nor street scenes were ever attempted on our big
screens, as we lacked vehicles with steering wheels on the right.
Ah, those were the days — but I've digressed.

VI

Who cares what country one grows up in, and whether it colors
one's view of espionage? Too bad if it does, because then one is

robbed of a source of entertainment — perhaps not of the most delectable kind, but entertainment nonetheless. In view of what surrounds us, not to mention what lies ahead, this is barely forgivable. Dearth of action is the mother of the motion picture. And if one indeed loathes spies, there still remains spy-catching, which is as engrossing as it is righteous. What's wrong with a little paranoia, with a bit of manifest schizophrenia? Isn't there something recognizable and therefore therapeutic to their paperback and Bakelite video versions? And what's any aversion, including this aversion toward spies, if not a hidden neurosis, an echo of some childhood trauma? First therapy, then ethics.

VII

The face of Kim Philby on that stamp. The face of the late Mr. Philby, Esq., of Brighton, Sussex, or of Welwyn Garden, Herts, or of Ambala, India — you name it. The face of an Englishman in the Soviet employ. The pulp writer's dream come true. Presumably, the rank of general, if the poor sod cared for such trifles; presumably, highly decorated, maybe a Hero of the Soviet Union. Though the snapshot used for the stamp shows none of that. Here he appears in his civvies, which is what he donned for most of his life: the dark coat and the tie. The medals and the epaulets were saved for the red velvet cushion of a soldier's funeral, if he had one. Which I think he did, his employers being suckers for top-secret solemnity. Many moons ago, reviewing a book about a chum of his for the *TLS*, I suggested that, considering his service to the Soviet State, this now aging Moscow denizen should be buried in the Kremlin wall. I mention this since I've been told that he was one of the few *TLS* subscribers in Moscow. He ended up, though, I believe, in the Protestant cemetery, his employers being sticklers for propriety, albeit posthumously. (Had Her Majesty's government been handling these matters, it could hardly have done better.) And now I feel little pangs of remorse. I imagine him interred, clad in the same coat and tie shown on the stamp, wearing this disguise — or was it a uniform? — in death as in life. Presumably he left some instructions concerning this eventuality, although he couldn't have been fully certain whether they would be followed. Were they? And what did he want on his tombstone? A line of English poetry,

perhaps? Something like "And death shall have no dominion"?
Or did he prefer a matter-of-fact "Soviet Secret Agent Kim
Philby (1912–1988)"? And did he want it in Cyrillic?

VIII

Back to hidden neurosis and childhood trauma, to therapy and
ethics. When I was twenty-four, I was after a girl, and in a big
way. She was slightly older than I, and after a while I began to
feel that something was amiss. I sensed that I was being deceived,
perhaps even two-timed. It turned out, of course, that I wasn't
wrong, but that was later. At the time I simply grew suspicious,
and one evening I decided to track her down. I hid myself in an
archway across the street from her building, waited there for
about an hour, and when she emerged from her poorly lit entrance, I followed her for several blocks. I was tense with excitement, but of an unfamiliar nature. At the same time I felt
vaguely bored, as I knew more or less what I might discover.
The excitement grew with every step, with every evasive action I
took; the boredom stayed at the same level. When she turned to
the river, my excitement reached its crescendo, and at that point
I stopped, turned around, and headed for a nearby café. Later I
would blame my abandoning the chase on my laziness and re-
proach myself, especially in the light — or, rather, in the dark —
of this affair's dénouement, playing an Actaeon to the dogs of
my own hindsight. The truth was less innocent and more absorbing. The truth was that I stopped because I had discovered the
nature of my excitement. It was the joy of a hunter pursuing his
prey. In other words, it was something atavistic, primordial. This
realization had nothing to do with ethics, with scruples, taboos,
or anything of the sort. I had no problem with conferring upon
the girl the status of prey. It's just that I hated being the hunter.
A matter of temperament, perhaps? Perhaps. Perhaps had the
world been subdivided into the four humors, or at least boiled
down to four humor-based political parties, it would be a better
place. Yet I think that one's resistance to turning into a hunter,
the ability to spot and to control the hunting impulse, has to do
with something more basic than temperament, upbringing, social values, received wisdom, ecclesiastical affiliation, or one's

concept of honor. It has to do with the degree of one's evolution, with the species' evolution, with reaching the stage marked by one's inability to regress. One loathes spies not so much because of their low rung on the evolutionary ladder, but because betrayal invites you to descend.

IX

Dear reader, if this sounds to you like an oblique way of bragging about one's own virtues, so be it. Virtue, after all, is far from being synonymous with survival; duplicity is. But you will accept, dear reader, won't you, that there is a hierarchy between love and betrayal. And you also know that it is the former that ushers in the latter, not vice versa. What's worse, you know that the latter outlasts the former. So there is not much to brag about, even when you are absolutely smitten or besotted, is there? If one is not a Darwinist, if one still sticks to Cuvier, it is because lower organisms seem to be more viable than complex ones. Look at the moss, look at algae. I understand that I am out of my depth here. All I am trying to say is that to an advanced organism duplicity is, at worst, an option; for a lower one, however, it is the means of survival. In this sense, spies don't choose to be spies any more than a lizard chooses its pigmentation: they just can't do any better. Duplicity, after all, is a form of mimicry; it is this particular animal's maximum. One could argue with this proposition if spies spied for money, but the best of them do it out of conviction. In their pursuit, they are driven by excitement, better yet by instinct unchecked by boredom. For boredom interferes with instinct. Boredom is the mark of a highly evolved species; a sign of civilization, if you will.

X

Whoever it was who ordered this stamp's issue was no doubt making a statement. Especially given the current political climate, the warming of East-West relations and all. The decision must have been made on high, in the Kremlin's own hallowed chambers, since the Foreign Ministry would have been up in arms against it, not to mention the Ministry of Finances, such as they are. You don't bite the hand that feeds you. Or do you? You do if your teeth are those of the CSS — the Committee for State Security (a.k.a., the KGB) — which is larger than both those ministries to begin with, not only in the number of employees but in the place it occupies in the conscience and the subconscious of the powerful and the powerless alike. If you are that big, you may bite any hand you like, and, for that matter, throats too. You may do it for several reasons. Out of vanity: to remind the jubilant West of your existence. Or out of inertia: you're used to biting that hand anyway. Or out of nostalgia for the good old days, when your diet was rich in the enemy's protein because you had a constant supply of it in your compatriots. Still, for all the grossness of the CSS's appetite, one senses behind this stamp initiative a particular individual: the head of a directorate, or perhaps his deputy, or just a humble case officer who came up with the idea. He might simply have revered Philby, or wanted to get ahead in his department; or, on the contrary, he may have been approaching retirement and, like many people of that generation, truly believed in the didactic value of a postage stamp. None of these things contradicts one another. They are fully compatible: vanity, inertia, nostalgia, reverence, careerism, naïveté; and the brain of the CSS's average employee is as good a place for their confluence as any, including a computer. What's puzzling about this stamp, however, is the promptness with which it has been issued: only two years after Mr. Philby's demise. His shoes, as well as the gloves that he always wore on account of a skin allergy, were, so to speak, still warm. Issuing a stamp in any country takes a hell of a lot of time, and normally it is preceded by national recognition of its subject. Even if one skips this requirement (the man was, after all, a secret agent), the speed with which the stamp was produced is amazing, given the thick of bureaucratic hurdles it ought to have gone through. It obviously didn't; it was evidently rushed into production. Which leaves you with this sense of personal involvement, of an individual will behind this four-centimeter-square piece of paper. And you ask yourself about the motive behind that will. And you understand that somebody wanted to make a statement. *Urbi et orbi,* as it were. And, as a part of the orbus, you wonder what sort of statement that was.

XI

The answer is: menacing and spiteful, also profoundly pro-
vincial. One judges an undertaking, I'm afraid, by its result. The
stamp subjects the late Mr. Philby to the ultimate ignominy, to
the final slight: it proclaims a Briton to be Russia's own, not so
much in spirit — what's so special about that? — but precisely in
body. No doubt Philby asked for that. He spied for the Soviet
Union for a good quarter of a century. For another quarter of a
century he simply lived in the Soviet Union, and wasn't entirely
idle either. On top of that, he died there, and was interred in
Russian soil. The stamp is essentially his tombstone's replica.
Also we shouldn't discount the possibility that he might have
been pleased by his masters' posthumous treatment: he was stupid enough, and secrecy is a hotbed of vanity. He could even
have approved (if not initiated himself) the stamp project. Yet
one can't help feeling some violation here, something deeper
than the desecration of a grave: a violation that is elemental. He
was, after all, a Briton, and the Brits are used to dying in odd
places. What's revolting about this stamp is its proprietary sentiment; it's as though the earth that swallowed the poor sod licks
its lips with profound satisfaction and says, he is mine. Or else it
licks the stamp.

XII

Such was the statement that a humble case officer, or a bunch of
them at CSS, wished to make, and did, and that a liberal literary
paper of humble strikebreaking origins has found so amusing.
Well, let's say point taken. What should be done about it, if
anything? Should we try to disinter the unholy remains and
bring them back to Britain? Should we petition the Soviet government or offer it a large sum? Or should Her Majesty's Postmaster issue perhaps a counterstamp, with a legend something
like "English Traitor, Kim Philby, 1912–1988," in English, of
course, and see whether some Russian paper reprints it? Should
we try to retrieve the idea of this man, despite himself, from the
collective psyche of his masters? And anyway who are these "we"
who provide your author, dear reader, with such rhetorical com-

fort? No, nothing of the sort could, or for that matter should, be done. Philby belongs there, body and soul. Let him rot in peace. But what one — and I emphasize this "one" — can do, and therefore should do, is rob the aforementioned collective psyche of its ownership of that unholy relic, rob it of the comfort it thinks it enjoys. And in fact it's easy to do this. For, in spite of himself, Kim Philby wasn't theirs. Considering where we are today, and especially where Russia is, it is obvious that, for all its industry, cunning, human toil, and investment of time and currency, the Philby enterprise was a bust. Were he a British double-agent, he couldn't inflict a greater damage on the system whose fortunes he was actually trying to advance. But double or triple, he was a British agent through and through, for the bottom line of his quite extraordinary effort is a sharp sense of futility. Futility is so hideously British. And now for the fun part.

XIII

In the few spy novels that I read as a child, the role of the postage stamp was as grand as the item itself was small, and would yield only to that of a torn photograph, the appearance of the other half of which often would clinch the plot. On the stamp's sticky side, a spy in those novels would convey in his chicken scrawl, or on a microfilm, the secret message to his master, or vice versa. The Philby stamp is thus a fusion of the torn man with the medium-is-the-message principle; as such, it is a collector's item. To this we might add also that the priciest things in the stamp-collecting world are those issued by political or geographical ephemera — by short-lived or defunct states, negligible potentates or specks of land. (The most sought-after item in my childhood, I recall, was a stamp from Pitcairn Island — a British colony, as it happens, in the South Pacific.) So, to use this philatelist logic, the issue of the Philby stamp appears to be a cry from the Soviet Union's future. At any rate, there is something in its future that, in the guise of the CSS, asks for that. Actually, this is a fine time for philatelists, and in more ways than one. One even can speak of philatelist justice here — the way one speaks of poetic license. For half a century ago, when the CSS warriors were deporting people from the Baltic states that the USSR invaded and rendered defunct, it was precisely philatelists who clinched the list of social categories subject to removal. (In fact, the list ended with the Esperantists, the philatelists being the penultimate category. There were, if memory serves me right, sixty-four such categories; the list began with the leaders and active members of political parties, followed by university professors, journalists, teachers, businessmen, and so on. It came with a highly detailed set of instructions as to how to separate the provider from his family, children from their mothers, and so forth, down to the actual wording of sentences like "Your daddy went to get hot water from the station boiler." The whole thing was rather well thought through and signed by CSS General Serov. I saw the document with my own eyes; the country of application was Lithuania.) This, perhaps, is the source of a retiring case officer's belief in the didactic power of a stamp. Well, nothing pleases the tired eyes of an impartial observer so much as the sight of things coming full circle.

XIV

Let's not dismiss, though, the didactic powers of the stamp. This one at least could have been issued to encourage the CSS's present and future employees, and was no doubt distributed among the former for free, a modest fringe benefit. As for the latter, one can imagine the stamp doing rather well with a young recruit. The establishment is big on visuals, on iconography, its monitoring abilities being justly famous for their omniscience, not to mention omnivorousness. When it comes to didactic purposes, especially among its own brethren, the organization readily goes the extra mile. When Oleg Pen'kovsky, a GRU man who betrayed Soviet military secrets to the British in the 1960s, was finally caught, the establishment (or so I was told) filmed his execution. Strapped to a stretcher, Pen'kovsky is wheeled into the Moscow city crematorium's chamber. An attendant opens the furnace door and two other attendants start to push the stretcher and its contents into the roaring furnace; the flame is already licking the screaming man's soles. At this point a voice comes over the loudspeaker interrupting the procedure because another body is scheduled for this time slot. Screaming but un-

able to kick, Pen'kovsky is pulled back; another body arrives and
after a small ceremony is pushed into the furnace. The voice
comes over the loudspeaker again: now it's Pen'kovsky's turn,
and in he goes. A small but effective skit. Beats Beckett hands
down, boosts morale, and can't be forgotten: it brands your wits.
A kind of stamp, if you will: for intramural correspondence.

                                XV

Before we set out for the fun part in earnest, dear reader, let me
say this. There is a distinction between the benefit of hindsight
and having lived long enough to see heads' tails. This is not a
disclaimer; quite the contrary, most of your author's assertions
are borne out by his life, and if they are wrong then he blew it, at
least partially. Still, even if they are accurate, a good question
remains. Is he entitled to pass judgment upon those who are no
longer around — who have lost? Outlasting your opponent gives
you the sense of membership in a victorious majority, of having
played your cards right. Aren't you then applying the law retro-
actively? Aren't you punishing the poor buggers under a code of
conscience foreign to them and to their times? Well, I am not
troubled by this, and for three reasons. First, because Kim Philby
kicked the bucket at the ripe age of seventy-six; as I write this, I
am still twenty-six years behind him in the game, my catching-
up prospects being very dim. Second, because what he believed
in for most of his life, allegedly to its very end, has been utter
garbage to me at least since the age of sixteen, though no benefit
of foresight can be claimed here, let alone obtained. Third,
because the baseness of the human heart and the vulgarity of the
human mind never expire with the demise of their most gifted
exponents. What I must disclaim, however, is any pretense to
expertise in the field I am wading through. As I say, I am no spy
buff. Of Philby's life, for instance, I know only the bare bones, if
that. I've never read his biography, in English or in Russian, nor
do I expect I ever will. Of the options available to a human being,
he chose the most redundant one: to betray one set of people to
another. This sort of subject is not worthy of study; intuition will
suffice. I am also not terribly good with dates, though I normally
try to check them. So the reader should decide for himself at this

stage whether he is going to proceed with this stuff any further.
I certainly will. I suppose I should bill the following as a fantasy.
Well, it isn't.

XVI

On Marchember umpteenth, Nineteen Filthy Fine, in Brooklyn,
New York, agents of the FBI arrested a Soviet spy. In a small
apartment filled with photo equipment, on a floor strewn with
microfilm, stood a little middle-aged man with beady eyes, an
aquiline profile, and a balding forehead, his Adam's apple moving busily: he was swallowing a scrap of paper containing some
top-secret information. Otherwise the man offered no resistance. Instead he proudly declared: "I am Colonel of the Red
Army Rudolph Abel, and I demand to be treated as such in
accordance with the Geneva Convention." Needless to say, the
tabloids went ape, in the States and all over the place. The
colonel was tried, got donkey years, and was locked up, if I
remember correctly, in Sing-Sing. There he mostly played pool.
In Nineteen Sissy Through or thereabouts he was exchanged at
Checkpoint Charlie in Berlin for Gary Powers, the unlucky U-2
pilot who made headlines for the last time just a few years ago
when he went down again, this time near L.A., in a helicopter,
and for good. Rudolph Abel returned to Moscow, retired, and
made no headlines, save that he became the most feared pool
shark in Moscow and its vicinity. He died in Nineteen Cementy
and was buried, with scaled-down military honors, at Novodevi-
chie Cemetery in Moscow. No stamp was issued for him. Or was
one? I may have missed it. Or the British literary paper of
humble origin missed it. Perhaps he didn't earn a stamp: what's
four years in Sing-Sing to a lifelong record? And besides, he
wasn't a foreigner, just another displaced native. In any case, no
stamp for Rudolph Abel, just a tombstone.

XVII

But what do we read on this tombstone? We read: "Willie
Fischer, a.k.a. Rudolph Abel, 1903–1971," in Cyrillic, of course.
Now that's a bit too long for a stamp's legend, but not for us.

(Ah, dear reader, look at what we've got here: spies, stamps, cemeteries, tombstones! But wait, there's more: poets, painters, assassinations, exiles, Arab sheikhs, murder weapons, stolen cars, and more stamps!) But let's try to make this long story short. Once upon a time — in 1936–39 in Spain, to be precise — there were two men: Willie Fischer and Rudolph Abel. They were colleagues and they were close friends. So close that other employees of the same enterprise called them "Fischerabel." But nothing untoward, dear reader, they were simply inseparable, partly because of the work they did. They were a team. The enterprise for which they toiled was the Soviet intelligence outfit that handled the messy side of the Spanish Civil War's business. That's the side where you find bullet-riddled bodies miles away from the trenches. Anyway, the outfit's boss was a fellow by the name of Orlov, who prior to his Spanish assignment headed the entire Soviet counterintelligence operation for Western Europe out of an office in the Soviet Embassy in the French capital. We'll play with him later — or, as the case may be, he will play with us. For the moment let's say that Orlov was very close with Fischerabel. Not as close as they were with each other, but very close. Nothing untoward there either, since Orlov was married. He was just the boss, and Fischerabel were his right and his left hand at once. Both hands were dirty.

XVIII

But life is cruel, it separates even the best of friends. In 1938 the Spanish Civil War is ending, and Fischerabel and Orlov part ways. They check out of the Hotel Nacional in Madrid, where the entire operation was run, and travel — some by air, some by boat, still others by the submarine that carried the Spanish Gold Reserve, which was handed over to the Soviets by Juan Negrin, the Republican government's finance minister — in opposite directions. Orlov disappears into thin air. Fischerabel return to Moscow and continue to work for the old establishment, filing reports, training new recruits — the kind of thing that field men do when they are out of the field. In 1940, when Rudolph Abel gets transferred to the Far East, where trouble is brewing on the Mongolian border, he makes a wrong move, and gets killed.

Then comes World War II. Throughout it Willie Fischer remains in Moscow, trains more recruits — this time perhaps with
greater gusto, since German is his father tongue — but he generally feels fallen by the wayside, bypassed for promotion, aging.
This fretful state of affairs ends only in Nineteen Faulty Ape,
when he's suddenly taken out of mothballs and given a new
assignment. "The kind of assignment," he remarks cryptically on
the eve of his departure to one of his former sidekicks from the
old Spanish days, "the kind of assignment that a field man's
entire life is the preparation for." Then he takes off. The next
time his pals hear of him is X years later when, nabbed by the
feds in that Brooklyn apartment, good old Willie sings, "I am
Colonel of the Red Army Rudolph Abel, and I demand . . ."

XIX

Of the many virtues available to us, dear reader, patience is best
known for being rewarded. In fact, patience is an integral part
of every virtue. What's virtue without patience? Just good temper. In a certain line of work, however, that won't pay. It may, in
fact, be deadly. A certain line of work requires patience, and a
hell of a lot of it. Perhaps because it is the only virtue detectable
in a certain line of work, those engaged in it zero in on patience
with a vengeance. So bear with us, dear reader. Consider yourself a mole.

XX

The twang of a guitar, the sound of a shot fired in a poorly lit
alley. It's Spain, shortly before the end of the Civil War (not
ending through neglect on the part of Orlov's good offices, of
course, but in Moscow they may see things differently). On this
night Orlov has been summoned to see a certain official from
Moscow aboard a ship lying at anchor in Barcelona. As the head
of Soviet intelligence in Spain, he reports only to Stalin's own
secretariat: directly. Orlov senses a trap and runs. He grabs his
wife, takes the elevator down, tells a bellboy in the lobby to get
him a taxi. Cut. Panorama of the ragged Pyrenees, roar of a two-
engine airplane. Cut. Next morning in Paris, sound of an accor-

dion, panorama of, say, the Place de la Concorde. Cut. An office in the Soviet Embassy on the rue de Varennes. Stalin's whiskers above the door of a Mosler safe flung wide open; a pin-striped wrist with cuffs stuffing a satchel with French bank notes and files. Cut. Blackout.

XXI

Sorry, no close-ups. Orlov's disappearing act offers none. Still, if one stares at the blackout intently enough, one can make out a letter. This letter is addressed to Comrade Stalin, and it says something to the effect that he, Orlov, now severs his links with godless communism and its hateful, criminal system; that he and his wife choose freedom, and should a single hair fall from the heads of their aging parents, who are still in the clutches of this system, then he, Orlov, will spill *urbi et orbi* all the dirty top-secret beans in his possession. The letter goes into an envelope, the address on that envelope is that of the offices of *Le Monde,* or maybe *Figaro.* At any rate, it's in Paris. Then the pen dips into the ink pot again: another letter. This one is to Leon Trotsky, and it goes something like this: I, the undersigned, am a Russian merchant who just escaped with my life from the Soviet Union via Siberia to Japan. While in Moscow and staying in a hotel, I overheard, by pure chance, a conversation in the next room. The subject was an attempt on your life, and through the crack in the door I even managed to espy your would-be assassin. He is young, tall, and speaks perfect Spanish. I thought it my duty to warn you. The letter is signed with an alias, but Don Levin, the Trotsky scholar and biographer, has positively identified its author as Orlov, and, if I am not mistaken, the scholar has received Orlov's personal confirmation. This letter is post-marked Nagasaki and the address on it is in Mexico City. It, too, however, ends up in a local tabloid *(La Prensa Latina? El Pais?),* since Trotsky, still smarting from the second attempt on his life (in the course of which his American secretary was murdered by a would-be world-famous muralist — David Alfaro Siqueiros — with the assistance of a would-be world-famous, indeed a Nobel Prize–winning, poet, Pablo Neruda), habitually forwards all threats and warnings he receives to the press. And Orlov must

be aware of this, if only because for the last three years he has
been in the habit of perusing quite a few periodicals in Spanish.
While having his coffee, say. In the lobby of the Nacional, or in
his suite there on the sixth floor.

XXII

Where he used to entertain all sorts of people. Including Ramon
Mercader, Trotsky's third and successful assassin. Who was simply Orlov's employee, much the same as Fischerabel, working
for the same outfit. So if Orlov really wanted to warn Trotsky, he
could have told him a lot more about Ramon Mercader than that
he was young, tall, handsome, and spoke perfect Spanish. Yet
the reason for the second letter was not Trotsky, the reason was
the first letter, whose addressee wasn't Stalin. To put it more
neatly, the Stalin letter, printed in *Le Monde,* addressed the West,
while the Trotsky letter, though it went literally to the Western
Hemisphere, addressed the East. The purpose of the first was to
win Orlov good standing abroad, preferably in the intelligence
community. The second was a letter home, informing his pals in
Moscow headquarters that he was not spilling the beans, though
he could: about Mercader, for instance. So they, the pals, could
go ahead with the Trotsky job if they cared to. (They did, though
no tear should be shed, since Trotsky, who drowned the only
genuine Russian Revolution that ever took place — the Kron-
stadt Uprising — in blood, wasn't any better than the spawn of
hell who ordered his assassination. Stalin, after all, was an oppor-
tunist. Trotsky was an ideologue. The mere thought that they
could have swapped places makes one wince.) Moreover, should
the authorship of the second letter ever come to light, as it did in
Don Levin's research, it could only enhance Orlov's credentials
as a true anti-Stalinist. Which is precisely what he wasn't. He had
no ideological or any other disagreement with Stalin. He was
simply running for his dear life, so he threw the dogs a bone to
munch on. They munched on it for a couple of decades.

XXIII

Blackout. Time for the credits. Ten years ago an émigré Russian
publishing house in France published a book called *A Hunter*

Upside Down. The title suggests one of those cartoon puzzles in which you have to look for the hidden figures: hunters, rabbits, farmers, birds, and so on. The author's name was Victor Henkin. He was Willie Fischer's sidekick from the good old Spanish days, and the Fischerabel story is what the book is all about, although it aims to be an autobiography. Some of the Orlov tidbits also hail from there. The book should have been a hit, if only because people in the know on the longer side of the Atlantic still believed that they had Rudolph Abel. By the same token, they still believed that Orlov, who had joined them, truly worked for that side whose decorations one may see proudly displayed on his chest in one of Orlov's rare close-ups, in a book published with great fanfare in the States well after Orlov's death in 1972. But no fanfare for Henkin's book. When an American publisher tried to get a contract for it, he ran into a copyright wall. There were also some minor scandals over alleged plagiarism in the German or French edition, it was in the courts, and for all I know Henkin lost. Now he works for a radio station in Munich that broadcasts into Russia — almost the flip side of the job he had for donkey years at Radio Moscow broadcasting in French. Or else he is retired. A Russian émigré, with a highly checkered record. . . . Not trustworthy, presumably paranoid. . . . Living in the past, ill-tempered. . . . Still, he is free now, he's got the right papers. He can go to the Gare de Lyon, board a train, and just like fifty years ago, after a night-long journey, he can arrive in Madrid, the city of his youth and adventure. All he has to do is to cross the large station square and he'll be standing in front of the Nacional; he could do it with his eyes closed. Still with his eyes closed he can enter a lobby that teemed fifty years ago with Orlovs, Fischers, Abels, Hemingways, Philbys, Orwells, Mercaders, Malrauxs, Negrins, Erhenburgs, and lesser lights like himself: with all those who have taken part in our story thus far or to whom we, one way or another, owe credits. Should he open his eyes, however, he'll discover that the Nacional is closed. It's been closed, according to some — mostly the young — for the last ten years; according to others, for the last fifty. Neither the young nor the old seem to know who pays the property tax, but maybe in Spain they do things differently.

XXIV

And in case you think, dear reader, that we've forgotten him, let's extract Kim Philby from the crowd in the lobby, and let's ask him what he's doing there. "I'm with the paper, actually," we'll hear. "Covering the war." Let's press him as to whose side he's on, and let's imagine that, just for an instant, he'll talk straight. "Switching at the moment. Orders." He may as well motion slightly upward with his chin, toward the sixth floor of the Nacional. For I am absolutely convinced that it was Orlov who told Kim Philby in 1937 in Madrid or thereabouts to change his tune in the *Times* from pro-Republican to pro-Franco, for reasons of deeper cover. If, as the story goes, Philby was meant to be a long shot aimed at the *sancta sanctorum* of British intelligence, he had better go pro-fascist. It's not that Orlov foresaw which way the Spanish show might go, though he could have had an inkling; he simply thought, or knew, that Philby should be played for keeps. And he could think this way, or know this, only if he were privy to the file that the Russians by then had on Philby, who was recruited in 1933, or to the actual recruitment of Philby. The first is certain, the second is possible. In any case Orlov knew Philby personally, which is what he tried to tell the hapless FBI man who interviewed him in 1944, in Iowa I think, where he then dwelled, having immigrated to the United States from Canada. At that point, it seems, Orlov was finally ready to spill the beans; but the FBI man paid no attention to the mention of some Englishman with a stutter who worked for the Soviet Union, which, on top of everything, was at that time an American ally. So Orlov decided not to press this any further, and Kim Philby headed for the stamp.

XXV

With these beans still intact in his hippothalamus on the one hand, and on the other having penned a couple of novels filled with the standard field-man yarn, but of the Russian variety, Orlov was no doubt of some interest to the budding CIA in the late 1940s. I have no idea, dear reader, who approached whom: I haven't studied Orlov's life, or its available record. Not my line of work. I am not even an amateur; I am just piecing all these things together in my spare time, not out of curiosity even, but to quell the sensation of utter disgust caused by the sight of that literary paper's cover. Self-therapy, then, and who cares about sources so long as it works. At any rate, regardless of who approached whom, Orlov seems to have been retained by the CIA from the 1950s onward. Whether he was on the payroll or just free-lancing is hard to say; but to judge by his decorations, as well as by the marginal evidence of his subsequent penmanship, it's a fair assumption. Most likely, he was engaged by the agency in an advisory capacity; nowadays this sort of thing is called consultancy. A good question would be whether the fellows back in Moscow knew of his new affiliation. Assuming, for Orlov's sake, that he didn't notify them himself, for that would still be suicidal, and assuming that the newly born agency couldn't be penetrated — if only for the sake of definitions — the fellows in Moscow were in the dark. Still, they had reason to believe that Orlov was around, if only as an aspiring thriller writer. As they had no news of him for a couple of decades, they may have wondered. And when you wonder, you imagine the worst. In a certain line of work, it's only prudent. They might even have wanted to check.

XXVI

And they had the wherewithal. So they took it out of mothballs and put it in place. Still, they were in no hurry. Not until Nineteen Filthy Fine, that is. Then they suddenly felt pressed. And on Marchember Umpteenth, Willie Fischer gets himself arrested in Brooklyn, New York, by those FBI men and declares, *urbi et orbi:* I am Rudolph Abel. And the tabloids go ape, in the States and all over the place. And Orlov doesn't squeak. Evidently he doesn't want to see his old pal again.

XXVII

What was so special about Nineteen Filthy Fine, you may ask, and why was it imperative now to check the state of the beans in Orlov's hippothalamus? Even if they were still all there, hadn't

they gone stale and useless? And who says old pals must be seen?
Well, dear reader, brace yourself for loony assertions. For now
we are going to show you, in a big way, that we haven't forgotten
our subject. Now we are cooking literally with oil.

XXVIII

Contrary to popular demonology, the foreign policy of the Soviet Union was, from the beginning of its existence, always opportunistic. I am using this term in its literal, not its derogatory,
sense. Opportunism is the core of any foreign policy, regardless
of the degree of confidence a state may have in itself. It means
the use of opportunity: objectively present, imagined, or created.
For most of its sorry history, the Soviet Union remained a highly
insecure customer, traumatized by the circumstances of its birth,
its deportment vis-à-vis the rest of the world fluctuating between
caution and hostility. (Nobody fitted the width of that margin
better than Molotov, Stalin's foreign minister.) As a consequence, the Soviet Union could afford only objectively present
opportunities. Which it seized, notably in 1939, grabbing the
Baltic states and half of Poland, as offered to Stalin by Hitler,
and in the final stages of the war, when the Soviet Union found
itself in possession of Eastern Europe. As for the opportunities
imagined — the 1928 march on Warsaw, the 1936–39 adventure
in Spain, and the 1940 Finnish Campaign — the Soviet Union
paid dearly for these flights of fancy (though in the case of Spain
it was reimbursed with the country's gold reserve). The first to
pay, of course, was the General Staff, almost entirely beheaded
by 1941. Yet the worst consequence of all these fantasies, I suppose, was that the Red Army's performance against a handful of
Finnish troops made Hitler's temptation to attack Russia absolutely irresistible. The real price for the pleasure of playing with
imagined opportunities was the total number of divisions as-
signed to Operation Barbarossa.

XXIX

Victory in the war didn't change Soviet foreign policy much,
since the spoils of war hardly matched the gigantic human and

industrial losses the war inflicted. The scale of the devastation was extraordinary; the main postwar cry was reconstruction. This was carried out mainly by means of stripping the conquered territories of their technology and transplanting it into the USSR. Psychologically satisfactory, this however could not put the nation ahead industrially. The country remained a second- or third-rate power, its only claim to consequence being its sheer size and its military machine. Formidable and state of the art as the latter tried to be, the comfort the nation could derive from it was largely of the narcissistic sort, given the cumulative strength of its supposed adversaries and the emergence of nuclear weapons. What really fell under the onslaught of that machine, however, was the Soviet Union's foreign policy — its options defined, as it were, by its legions. To this reversal of Clausewitz one must add the growing rigidity of a state apparatus petrified by the fear of personal responsibility and imbued with the notion that the first word and the last word on all matters, above all on matters of foreign policy, belonged to Stalin. Under the circumstances, diplomatic initiatives, let alone attempts at creating opportunities, were unthinkable. What's more, the distinction between a created opportunity and an imagined one can be galling. It takes a mind accustomed to the dynamics of a well-heeled economy (to the accumulation of wealth, surplus production, and so on) to tell one from another. If you are short on that sort of expertise, you may confuse the one thing for the other. And well into the 1950s, the Soviet Union was short on it. It still is.

                                    xxx

And yet in the late 1950s the Soviet Union undertakes something rather spectacular, something that leaves you with the sense that, with the death of Stalin in 1953, Soviet foreign policy comes to life. After the Suez debacle in the autumn of 1956, the USSR undertakes an unusually well-coordinated and well-sustained push toward the eastern Mediterranean and North Africa. This departure is as sudden as it is successful. Its goal, as hindsight avails us, is control of the Middle East, or, more pointedly, of its oil fields. The logic behind this move is simple and fairly Marxist: whoever controls energy resources controls production. In other

words, the idea is to bring the Western industrial democracies to
their knees. Whether to do it directly, by sending troops into the
region, or by proxy, by supporting the local Arab regimes and
turning them pro-Soviet, is, for the moment, a matter of circumstance and logistics; the proxy option is obviously preferable.
And initially this works: a number of Arab states in the region
go pro-Soviet, and so fast that one may think that these societies
were ripe for Communist ideology, or at least accustomed to that
sort of discourse. They were not. The few existing CP cells in
King Farouk's Egypt, for instance, were wiped out under Nasser
entirely, their members turned into cellmates or dangled from
the rope. An even greater Marxist dearth marked — still does —
the rest of the Islamic world, east and west of Cairo: the culture
of the Book won't abide another one, especially one written by a
Jew. Still, the first Soviet steps in the region met with success, the
degree of which could be explained only by the newcomer's
recourse to some sort of network within those societies, and with
access to all its levels. Such a network couldn't be of German
origin (not even in Egypt), since Reinhard Gehlen, the postwar
head of West German intelligence, sold his entire file cabinet in
the late 1940s to the United States. Nor could it be French, who
were a marginal presence in the region to begin with, and then
fiercely loyal to France. That left the local pro-British element,
presumably taking its cue — in the vacuum left by the master
race's withdrawal — from some local resident (stationed, say, in
Beirut). Out of nostalgia, perhaps, out of the hope for the Empire's return. At any rate, it certainly wasn't the novelty of the
Russian version of the infidel that nearly delivered the region to
the Soviets in the late 1950s; it was a created opportunity.

XXXI

Imagine this blueprint on a drawing board somewhere in Moscow thirty-five or forty years ago. It says: there is a vacuum left
in the Middle East by the British. Fill it up. Support new Arab
leaders: one by one, or bundle them together into some sort of
confederation, say, into a United Arab Republic or League. Give
them arms, give them anything. Drive them into debt. Tell them
that they can pay you back if they hike their oil prices. Tell them

that they can be unreasonable about that, that you'll back them up all the way; and you've got nukes. In no time, the West cries uncle, the Arabs get rich, and you control the Arabs. You become top dog, as befits the first socialist country in the world. As for how to get your foot in the door, it's all taken care of. You'll get along with these guys just fine, they don't like Jews either.

XXXII

And imagine this blueprint being not of your own manufacture. For it simply could not have been. In order to conceive of it, you would have to be acquainted with the region, and intimately so. You ought to know who is who there, what this sheikh or that colonel is up to, his pedigree and hang-ups. In Moscow and its vicinity, there is nobody with that sort of data. Furthermore, you ought to know about oil revenues, the market, its fluctuations, stocks, this or that industrial democracy's annual intake of crude, tankers' fleets, refineries, stuff like that. There is nobody acquainted with this sort of thing on your staff, or moonlighting elsewhere either. And even if to imagine that such a fellow existed, a doctrinaire Marxist and a bookworm, with the clearance to read Western periodicals — even if such a fellow existed, and came up with such a blueprint, he would have to have a godfather in the Politburo to place this blueprint on the drawing board; and placing it there would give that member of the Politburo an edge that his colleagues wouldn't tolerate for a split second. Ultimately this plan could not have been conceived by a Russian, if only because Russia herself has oil; actually plenty of it. You don't regard as a source of energy something you waste. Had it been homemade, this blueprint would never have seen the light of day. Besides, it's too damn close to an imagined opportunity. The very reason that it is on your drawing board, though, is that it has nothing to do with the native imagination. That alone should be enough to qualify it as a created opportunity. For it comes from without, and its main attraction is that it is foreign-made. To members of the Soviet Politburo in the 1950s, this blueprint was what blue jeans are to their kids. They liked it very much. Still, they wanted to check the label. And they had the wherewithal.

XXXIII

And while they are checking the label, dear reader, let me give you something straight, without the author's interference. Harold Adrian Russell Philby, "Kim" to his chums in England and especially in Russia, where this nickname rang no Kipling bell, being instead a brand-new Soviet name, popular especially in the 1930s, since it was the acronym of Kommunisticzeskii Internatzional Molodezhi (Communist International of Youth), was born in Ambala, India, in — as the stamp rightly says — 1912. His daddy was Harry St. John Philby, a great English Arabist and explorer who subsequently converted to Islam and became an adviser to King Ibn Saud of guess which country. The boy was educated at Westminster and Trinity College, Cambridge, where he read history and economics and was a member of the Apostles. After Cambridge he free-lanced for various London publications, and in this capacity he went in 1937 to Spain to cover the Civil War and later on was taken up by the *Times,* for which he covered the initial stages of World War II. That's essentially what was known about the twenty-eight-year-old man by 1940, when he was employed by MI6, the counterintelligence branch of the fabled British SIS, and given the job of handling anti-Communist counterespionage matters. Presumably at his own request. During the war years he moves rapidly through the ranks, gets stationed in Istanbul, and becomes, in 1946, the head of Soviet counterintelligence. That's a big job, which he abandons only three years later, having been posted as first secretary of the British Embassy in Washington, that is, as chief liaison officer between the SIS and the CIA, where, among other things, he becomes a close friend of James Angleton, the CIA's head of counterintelligence. On the whole, it is a marvelous career. The man is awarded the OBE for his wartime services, he is greatly respected by the foreign office and the gentlemen of the press, and is groomed to become the head of the SIS. That, essentially, is what was known to his peers and his superiors about this thirty-nine-year-old man in 1951, when something rather untoward occurs. Two of his old pals, way back from Cambridge days, Guy Burgess and Donald Maclean, turn out to be Soviet spies, and flee to the Soviet Union. What's worse, a suspicion lurks in the

heads of people-in-the-know on both sides of the Atlantic that it
was Philby who warned them off. He is investigated, nothing is
proved, doubt persists, and he is asked to resign. Life is cruel,
the best of pals can bring you down. Such was the verdict of
many, including the Foreign Office. He resumes his journalistic
career — after all, he is still in his forties — but the inquiries
continue. Some people just don't give up. In 1955 Harold Macmillan, then the British foreign secretary, in a statement before
the Commons, fully exonerates Philby of any wrongdoing. His
slate wiped clean, Philby obtains, through the Foreign Office's
misty-eyed assistance, the job of foreign correspondent for the
Economist and the *Observer* in Beirut, whereto he sails in 1956,
never to see the chalk cliffs of Sussex again.

XXXIV

It's three years later that the fellows in Moscow click their
tongues admiring the blueprint. Still, they want to check the
label. For what is a clean slate to some is the writing on the wall
to others. They figure that the Brits couldn't get any goods on a
Brit because they were searching the Brits; they were doomed
because they were engaged in a tautology. For the job of a mole
is to outsmart the natives. As for the Russian end — should they
ever gain access to it, which is highly unlikely — it would reveal
nothing either. The identity of a mole, especially a mole so highly
placed, wouldn't be known even to the case officer running him,
it would be only a code name or a bunch of digits at best. That's
as much as even the most knowledgeable defector can tell you,
not to mention the fact that he would be defecting straight into
the arms of the SIS counterintelligence section, and guess who is
in charge of that. The only two people who might know his
identity would be the present Soviet head of counterintelligence,
and that far no Brit could ever go, or the counterintelligence
officer who recruited the man initially. A sergeant, by definition,
is older than his recruit, and since we are talking here about the
1950s, that sergeant should by now be either dead or indeed
running the whole Soviet counterintelligence show. Most likely
though he is dead, since the best way to protect the recruit's
identity is to kill the sergeant. Still, in 1933, when a twenty-one-
year-old Cambridge graduate was recruited, things were not as

watertight as they are now in the 1950s, when we are checking the label, and the good old — no, dead — sergeant might have said something to his superior (who was presumably dead, too: those purges of the state security apparatus in the late 1930s were not for nothing) or had a witness to the recruitment, or the poor young witless recruit himself might have rubbed shoulders with somebody who later went bad. After all, his choice of pals is what brought him down, though for a while they delivered all the comings and goings of the Anglo-American Atomic Energy Commission. (Good flies on the wall they were, but now look at them coming here to roost!) Let bygones be bygones, of course; but if we are to carry out this blueprint, we need something tighter than an exoneration by Harold Macmillan — bless his heart — in Commons, we need complete immunity for our man against any whistle-blowers. No surprises, no voices from the past, no skeletons in the closet. So who are those guys he might have rubbed shoulders with before they went bad? Where are their death certificates?

XXXV

And they can't find Orlov's. And Willie Fischer sings his world-famous Abel lyric. And Orlov doesn't want to see his old pal. And they conclude that he is either dead or not suicidal. And so they move into the Middle East, into Egypt, Syria, Yemen, Iraq, Libya; they seize the created opportunity. They shower new Arab leaders with planeloads and shiploads of military surplus, advisers, and whatnot; they drive those nations into debt. And the advisers advise the leaders to hike oil prices to pay them back. And the leaders do just that: by high margins and with impunity, backed by this new set of infidels with nukes. And the West starts to kowtow and cry "UN" — but that's just the first syllable of uncle. And now the faithful, the fidel and the infidel, hate the Jews together. It all works just like the man said it would.

XXXVI

But life is cruel, and one day the new oil-producing pals get greedy. They create a cartel, OPEC by name, and start filling up their own coffers. They put the squeeze on the West, but not for our sake! They also quarrel among themselves. Anyhow, they get richer than their old masters, not to mention us. That wasn't in the blueprint. The architect of our Middle East policy, the son of King Ibn Saud's adviser, an observer and economist to boot, our great and unexposed — well, technically speaking — secret agent, should have been able to foresee this turn of events! Thus far everything went according to the plan: he delivered, and now this. Well, he better tell us what to do next. Basically, we need him here now, on a day-to-day basis. Anyway, it's safer for him here in Moscow; fewer temptations as well. He can concentrate better. It ain't Beirut.

XXXVII

It certainly was much colder. At least for the spy who came in from the warmth. At long last. Actually, exactly thirty years after he was recruited. Whatever that means, except that he is fifty-one years old now and has to start a new life. Which, after all, isn't that hard, since the local lads go out of their privileged ways to assist you; and besides, at fifty-one no life is that new, no country is that foreign. Especially if you have spied for that country all your adult life. And especially if you did it not for money, but out of conviction. So the place should be familiar to you, at least mentally. For it's the conviction that is your home, your ultimate comfort: you blow all your life savings on furnishing it. If the world around you is poor and colorless, then you stuff this place with all manner of mental candelabra and Persian carpets. If that world used to be rich in texture, then you'll settle for mental monochrome, for a few abstract chairs.

XXXVIII

And, as we are on our last leg, dear suffering reader, let's get a bit anachronistic. There is a certain type of Englishman that appreciates frugality and inefficiency: the one who nods contentedly at a stalled elevator or at one boy being caned for another boy's prank. He recognizes botch and bungle the way one recognizes one's relatives. He recognizes himself in a peeling, wobbly railing, damp hotel sheets, slovenly trees in a soot-laden window, bad tobacco, the smelly carriage of a delayed train, bureaucratic obstacles, indecision and sloth, impotent shrugs; certainly in poorly cut serge clothes, in gray. So he loves Russia; mainly from a distance, as he cannot afford the trip, except perhaps later in life, in his fifties or sixties, when he retires. And he'd do a lot for Russia, for his inefficient yet dramatic, soulful, Doctor Zhivago–like (the movie, not the book) Russia, where the twentieth century hasn't yet set its Goodyear tire, where his childhood still continues. He doesn't want his Russia to go American. He wants her to stay intense and awkward, in brown woolen stockings with broad pink garters: no nylons, and please no pantyhose. It is his equivalent of rough trade, of the working-class lads for whom his old Cambridge pals will be prowling London pubs for the rest of their lives. He is straight, though; and it's Russia for him, if it's not Germany or Austria.

XXXIX

And if Russia is Communist, so much the better. Especially if it is 1933 and Germany is out of the question. And if somebody with a slight accent asks you to work for Russia, and you are just twenty-one, you say yes, because it's unlike anything else, and it sounds subversive. If school teaches you anything, it is to belong to a party, or at least to a club, and to form a cell. The CP is just another Apostles, a sort of frat, and it preaches brotherhood. At any rate, you go for what your pals do, and to them "the world proletariat" conjures up rough trade on a grand scale. And in a while you hear that slight accent again, and you are asked to do a job — nothing big, though faintly foul. And you do it; and now the slight accent has goods on you. If he is smart, the next time he asks you to do something, he doesn't mention the world proletariat, he mentions Russia. Because you won't do it, say, for India, though India, technically speaking, is part of the world, not to mention the proletariat. Fifty years ago social fiction was still ethnocentric, and so were spies. More Chekhov for you, then; more of Constance Garnett's Tolstoy on the train ride to Spain, for it's the time. It is also the place. A bright young thing can sample that brotherhood here: its blood, lice, hope, despair, defeat, apathy. Instead he hangs around in the lobby of the Nacional, sees some scum upstairs, and is told — to his secret relief, no doubt — to switch sides, for the sake of the greater good. That's how a bright young thing learns about the big picture, a.k.a. the future. The next time he hears the slight accent he knows it is a voice from the future. The accent will be different, since the first slightly accented throat has already been cut for the bright young thing's eventual safety; and if that throat had a beloved, she's already digging the permafrost of her twenty-five-year sentence in the Russian Far East, against the majestic snowy backdrop of a would-be Zhivago movie. Yet by the time the voice from the future enters your ear, there is WWII on your hands, Russia is an ally, and the SIS wants you to take part in the war effort. The big picture barges into view, and you ask for a Russian job. And since you are a gentleman, you are welcomed to it by senior gentlemen who can be identified as such, however, mainly by which door they push in a loo. Well, not even then.

XL

So you know the country where you end up thirty years later at the ripe age of fifty-one. Full of beans, no doubt, but past your prime. Ah, the chalk cliffs of Sussex! Ah, the accursed island! Ah, the whole Pax Britannica! They'll pay dearly for ruining such a brilliant career, for putting a clever man out to grass at the apogee of his ascent! A clever man knows how to get even with an empire: by using another empire. Never the twain shall meet. That's what makes a big picture grow bigger. Not a tooth for a tooth, but a mouthful for a tooth! Perhaps the greatest satisfaction of every spy is the thought that he is playing Fate, that it's he who pulls strings. Or else, cuts them. He fashions himself after Clotho, or perhaps after Arachne. A deus in machina that runs on petrol, he may not even catch the irony of being situated in Mazoutny Lane — well, not initially. At any rate, deus or deuce, controlling oil fields is a greater game than betraying the secrets of British intelligence to the Russians. There is not much left to betray in London anyway, whereas here the stakes are huge. The entire world order is at stake.

Whoever wins here, it will be *his* victory. He, an observer and economist to boot, didn't read *Das Kapital* and *The Seven Pillars of Wisdom* for nothing. Not to mention that the victory will be Russia's, since what can you expect of democracies: no resolve. Imagine Russia, his slovenly brown-woolen-stockings-cum-pink-garters-clad Russia, as the world's master, and not because of the nukes or the ballistic missiles only: imagine her, soulful and slothful, with all the Arabian peninsula's oil revenues under her pillow — uncertain, Chekhovian, anti-rationalist! A far better master (nay, mistress) of the world than his own Cartesian West, so easy to fool, himself being a good example. And should worse come to worst, should it be not Russia but some local, some sheikh or dictator, it's fine by him too. In fact, daddy would be proud of him if it should go all to the Saudis.

XLI

And there it went, practically all of it. So much of it, in any case, that it should be the Saudis issuing this stamp, not the Russians. Well, perhaps one day they will. Or the Iraqis, or the Iranians. Whoever is to master the oil monopoly should issue the stamp. Ah, Muslims, Muslims! Where would they be now, were it not for the Soviet foreign policy of the 1960s and 1970s, that is, were it not for the late Mr. Philby? Imagine them unable to purchase a Kalishnikov, let alone a rocket launcher. They'd be unfit for the front page, they wouldn't make even the backdrop for a pack of camels. . . . Ah, but life is cruel, and beneficiaries don't re-member their benefactors; nor, for that matter, do victims re-member the villain. And perhaps they shouldn't. Perhaps the origins of good and bad are better off remaining obscured — especially the latter. Does it really matter what clouds the god-head: the concept of dialectical materialism or the Prophet's turban? Can we tell one from another? In the final analysis, there is no hierarchy between the cherry orchard and the triviality of the sand; it is only a matter of preference. For men, as well as for their money. Money, evidently, lacks a conscience of its own, and the jackpot goes to the desert simply out of its kinship for multi-tudes. On the whole, like a certain kind of Englishman, money has an eastward longing, if only because that realm is extremely

populous. A secret agent, then, is but an early bird, a big bank's
harbinger. And if he settles there, in the East, and goes native,
helped along by local liquor or a willing maiden, well, so what?
Have Noah's pigeons returned? Ah, dear reader, imagine a letter sent today or in the near future from Moscow to Riyadh.
What do you think it will contain? A birthday greeting, vacation
plans, news of a loss in the family, complaints about the cold
climate? No, more likely a request for money. Say, for an investment in the well-being of Riyadh's fellow Muslims on Soviet
territory. And it will be written in English, this letter, and it won't
be worth perlustration. A postmaster, perhaps, having glanced
at its return address, may lift the crescent of the eyebrow obscured by his traditional headgear, but after a momentary hesitation he'll shove this envelope into an appropriate slot: an envelope with a Philby stamp on it.

XLII

A glum thought, nods the exhausted reader. But wouldn't things
have come to this juncture anyway, even without our English
friend's assistance? Sure they would have, given the so-called
dynamics of the modern world, which means the population
explosion and the industrial gluttony of the West. These two
would suffice; no need for a third party, let alone for an individual agency. At best, our English friend just articulated what was
in the air or, as it were, afoot. Other than that, he was utterly
insignificant. Sooner or later this was bound to happen, Kim or
no Kim, Russia or no Russia. Well, without Russia perhaps it
would have taken a touch longer, but so what. Individuals are
incidental, it's all economics, isn't it? In this sense, even if an
individual exists, he doesn't. Sounds a bit solipsistic, in a Marxist
way; but our English friend would be the first to appreciate that.
After all, historical necessity was his motto, his credo, his occasional rebuke to pangs of conscience. And after that, for all the
professional hazards of one's trade, a belief in the imminent
triumph of one's cause is safe betting, isn't it? (What if your cause
triumphs in your lifetime, eh?) At any rate, from the standpoint
of historical necessity, our man was of no use, at best he was
redundant. For the objective of history was to make the Arabs

rich, the West poor, and the Russians bob and bubble in limbo. This is what the bottom line says in that true bel canto of necessity, and who is the author to argue with it? A penny, then, for our friend's sense of mission; but not much more for the author's flight of fancy either. Anyway, what are his sources?

XLIII

"Sources?" shrugs the author contemptuously. Who needs them? Who can trust sources? And since when? And does the reader realize what he is getting into by suspecting his author of being wrong, not to mention by proving it? Aren't you afraid, dear reader, that your successful refutation of the author's little theory might boil down to an unescapable conclusion on your part that the dark brown substance in which you find yourself up to your nostrils in the world today is immanent, preordained on high, at the very least sponsored by Mother Nature? Do you really need that? Whereas the author aims to spare you this anguish by proving that the aforementioned substance is of human manufacture. In this respect, your author is a true humanist. No, dear reader, you don't need sources. Neither sources nor tributaries of defectors' evidence; not even electronic precipitation raining unto your lap from the satellite-studded heaven. With our sort of flow, all you need is an estuary, a mouth really; and beyond that a sea with the bottom line for a horizon. Well, that much you've already seen.

XLIV

Nobody, though, knows the future. Least of all those who believe in historical determinism; and next to them, spies and journalists. Perhaps that's why the former often disguise themselves as the latter. Of course, when it comes to the future, any occupation is good cover. Still, information-gathering beats them all, since any bit of information, including a secret one, is generated by the past: almost by definition, information deals with faits accomplis. Be it a new bomb, a planned invasion, or a shift in policy, you can learn only about what has already happened, what has already taken place. The paradox of espionage is that the more you know about your adversary, the more your own development is stunted, since this knowledge forces you into trying to catch up with him, to thwart his efforts. He keeps you occupied by altering your own priorities. The better your spies, therefore, the more you fall into dependence on what you learn. You are not acting any longer: you are reacting. This maroons you in the past, with little access to the present and none to the future. Well, not to a future of your own design, let alone your own making. Imagine the Soviets not stealing American atomic secrets and thus spending the last four decades with no nukes to brandish. It could have been a different country; not much more prosperous, perhaps, given the doctrine, but at least the fiasco that we have recently witnessed might have occurred much earlier. If worse came to worst, they might have built a viable version of their socialism. But when you steal something, the catch possesses you, or at least your faculties. Considering the industry of our English friend and his pals, it went far beyond faculties; both hands of their Russian fence were, for quite some time, too busy to build socialism, they were hoarding goods. It could be argued that by betraying the Empire in such volume, the boys in fact served the Empire in a far more substantial manner than its most ardent standard-bearers. For the wealth of secret intelligence passed to the Soviets by the Cambridge class of 1931 mesmerized its recipients to the point of making at least their foreign policy thoroughly contingent on the harvest yielded by their own plants. For the men in Moscow Center, it's been like reading the Sunday papers nonstop seven days a week instead of doing the dishes or taking the kids to the zoo.

XLV

So you can't say it was all in vain, dear reader, can you? Even though you may be as tired of the subject as the author himself. Let's claim fatigue, dear reader, and reach no conclusion, and spare ourselves the distrust, not to say the acrimony. On the whole, there is nothing wrong with intricacy of thought except that it's always achieved at the expense of thought's depth. Let's get into your Japanese Toyota, which doesn't consume a lot of the Arab oil-product, and go for a meal. Chinese? Vietnamese?

Thai? Indian? Mexican? Hungarian? Polish? The more we bungle abroad, the more varied our diet. Spanish? Greek? French?
Italian? Perhaps the only good thing about the dead spies was
that they had a choice. But as I write this, the news comes over
the wireless that the Soviet Union is no more. Armenian, then?
Uzbek? Kazakh? Estonian? For some reason, we don't feel like
eating at home tonight. We don't want to eat English.

XLVI

Why should one bother so much about dead spies? Why can't
one contain the repulsion that rises at the sight of a literary
magazine's cover? Isn't this an overreaction? What's so new
about someone's belief that a just society exists elsewhere, so
special about this old Rousseauist lunacy, enacted or not? Every
epoch and every generation is entitled to its own utopia, and so
was Philby's. Surely the ability to cling to that sort of garbage
beyond the age of down payment (not to mention the age of
retirement) is puzzling; but one can easily put this down to
temperament or to some organic disorder. A Catholic, a lapsed
Catholic especially, can appreciate the predicament and make a
meal out of it if he is a writer; and so can a heathen. Or did I feel
queasy simply because of the violation of scale, because of the
printing enlargement of something small, a stamp really, as a
result of which the perforation line takes on the dimension of a
cloth fringe: a hanky's, a pillowcase's, a bedspread's, a petti-
coat's? Maybe I have a problem with fringed linen — a childhood trauma again? The day was hot, and for a moment it felt
like the enlargement of the stamp on the magazine's cover would
go on and on, and envelop Belsize Park, Hampstead, and keep
growing, larger and larger. A vision, you know. Too much reading of surrealist poets. Or else too many placards with the Politburo members' faces on the old retina — and the man on the
stamp looks like one of them, for all his resemblances to Alec
Guinness and Trevor Howard. Plus, of course, the Cyrillic . . .
enough to get dizzy. But it wasn't like that. There was no vision.
There was just a face, of the kind you wouldn't pay attention to
were it not for the caption, which, apart from anything else, was
in Cyrillic. At that moment I regretted that I knew Russian. I

stood there groping for an English word to shield my wits from the familiarity that the Cyrillic letters exuded. As is often the case with mongrels, I couldn't come up with the right word instantly, and so I turned and left the store. I only remembered the word well outside, but because of what it was, I couldn't get myself back to the store to buy the issue. The word was "treachery."

XLVII

A wonderful word, that. It creaks like a board laid over a chasm. Onomatopoeically, it beats ethics. It has all the euphony of a taboo. For the ultimate boundary of a tribe is its language. If a word doesn't stop you, then a tribe isn't yours. Its vowels and its sibilants don't trigger your instincts, don't send your nerve cells into revulsion, don't make you wince. Which is to say, your command of this tribe's language is just a matter of mimicry. Which, in turn, points at your belonging to a different evolutionary order. Sublingual or supralingual, at least as regards the language that contains the word "treachery." Which is to prevent the sudden reversal of a bone to jelly. Which is to say, evolution never ends: it still continues. *The Origin of Species* ain't the end of the road; at best a milestone. Which is to say, not all people are people. Might as well add this stamp to the Shells and Mollusks series. It's still a seabed.

XLVIII

You can only enlarge a stamp, you can't reduce it. That is, you can but reduction will serve no purpose. That is the self-defense of small items, or, if you will, their raison d'être. They can only be enlarged. That is, if you are in the graphics department of a literary paper of humble strikebreaking origins. "Blow it up," says the editor, and you cheerfully trot off to the lab. Can't reduce it, can you? Simply wouldn't cross your mind. Nowadays just push a button, and it either grows or shrinks. To life-size, or to the size of a louse. Push it once more, and the louse is gone. Extinct. Not what the editor asked for, though. He wants it life-size: large. The size of his fantasy, if not his dilemma. "Would

you buy this man a drink or shake hands with him?" The old
English pickle, except now it's grown chic, with perhaps a touch
of retro to it. Ah, these days you push a button, and the whole
mental swamp gets heaving and gurgling, from Pas de Calais to
the Bering Strait, from the 1930s onward. For that's what history
is for the generation currently active: for lapsed Catholics, editors in chief, and the like. For nowadays everything is chic and
retro: this isn't the fin de siècle for nothing. There is little to look
forward to save your bank statement. Whom would you spy for
nowadays if you had access to secret information, if you still
ached to defy your class or your country? For the Arabs? For the
Japanese? Whose plant, let alone mole, could you be? The village
has gone truly global; there is a dearth of allegiance, a dearth of
affinity. Ay, you can't betray Europe to Asia any longer, nor, I'm
afraid, the other way around. It's goodbye to conviction, goodbye to the good old godless communism. From now on, it's all
nostalgia for you, old boy, all retro. From your baggy pants to
the matte black of your video, stereo, or dashboard echoing the
burnished steel of a gun barrel. That's about how radical, how
chic, it's going to be: in Europe, but in Asia too. So go ahead,
blow up that louse from the 1950s, for reducing it might rob you
of your emotional history: What would you be without that,
without a big-time traitor never caught and never recanting in
your past? Just a cipher in tax bracket hell, not dissimilar to that
of the old wretch when he still drew his salary in pounds. Go
ahead and blow it up; pity it can't be made three-dimensional.
Pity, too, that you have no idea, as you are pressing "enlarge,"
that in less than three weeks the whole thing on whose behalf
your man toiled all his life will go bust.

                               XLIX

In a dream. A cross between a meadow and a communal garden
somewhere in Kensington, with a fountain or a statue in the
middle of it. A sculpture, anyway. Modern, but not very modern.
Abstract, with a big hole in the center and a few strings across it:
like a guitar but less feminine. Gray. Sort of like by Barbara
Hepworth, but made of discarded thoughts and unfinished sen-

tences. Lacelike. On the plinth there is an inscription: "To Beloved Spider. Grateful Cobwebs."

L

Twangs of balalaika, the crackle of atmospherics. A hand fid-
dling with an eye-blinking wireless. It's Moscow, Russia, anytime
between 1963 and 1988. More atmospherics and balalaika. Then
the first bars of Lilliburlero and an upright female voice: "This
is the BBC World Service. The news. Read to you by . . ." In her
thirties, perhaps. Well-scrubbed face, almost no makeup. A chif-
fon blouse. White. And a cardigan. Most likely beige, the tea-
cum-milk color. A broadcloth skirt, knee-high. Black or dark
blue, like the evening sky outside. Or maybe it's gray; but knee-
high. Knee-high knee-high knee-high. And then there is a slip.
Oh my oh my oh my. Another Boeing is blown up in a desert.
Pol Pot, Phnom Penh. Mister — a split-second pause — Mugabe.
Knee-high. Main thing, the lace. Fragile and intricate like cir-
cumlocution. Minuscule dotty flowers. That never see the light
of day. And that's why they are so white. Oh blast! Sihanouk,
Pinochet, Rudi Deutchke. Chile, Chile, Chile, Chile. Dotty little
pansies smothered to death by light brown tights from a shop in
Islington. That's what the world came down to. From the step-
by-step approach, from the silks/flesh/garter/bingo system to the
either/or of pantyhose. Détente, sygint, ICBMs. New tricks but
the dog's too old. For these, and for the old ones too. Well, looks
like. And going to end up here after all. Pity. Can't win them all,
can you? Another whiskey then. "The main points again . . ." In
her thirties, if you ask me, and on the plump side. Dinnertime
anyway. Methuselah fancies dotty little pansies. Methuselah fancies . . . All that matters in this life is that cobwebs outlive the
spider. How does that thingummy — Tyutchev's! Tyutchev is
the name — lyric go?

> We are not given to appraise
> In whom or how our word may live on.
> And we are vouchsafed oblivion
> The way we once were given grace.

Dushen'ka! Dushen'ka! What's for dinner? "Ah, dahrleeng, I
thought we would eat English tonight. Boiled beef."

ANTHONY BURGESS

Mozart and the Wolf Gang

FROM THE WILSON QUARTERLY

WHAT CAN A MERE WRITER say about Mozart? Music is the art that takes over from words when words prove inadequate, and I've spent much of this bicentennial year trying to devise a verbal approach to Mozart which should not abet this inadequacy. A mere writer can deal only with the externals or superficialities of a musician's achievement. The Life of Mozart has been delineated far too often, sometimes with melodramatic falsehoods. The truth is mostly banal and has a great deal to do with money. I set up for myself a dialogue between Woferl and his father Leopold which portrays how shameful this banality is:

LEOPOLD:
A born musician should also be a born mathematician. The two faculties, for some reason that no doubt Pythagoras has explained somewhere, spring from an innate numeracy, notes themselves being vibrations that obey strict mathematical laws.

WOFERL:
But what has mathematics to do with money?

LEOPOLD:
Little perhaps except counting. You have still to get it into your thick skull that ten Viennese *gulden,* or *florins* as they should rightly be, are worth twelve Salzburg *gulden.* When you are offered sums of money for performances, you should know pre-

cisely what you are getting. A *thaler,* which the Americans call a dollar, is two *gulden.*

WOFERL:
That I knew.

LEOPOLD:
That you knew. But do not confuse a *speziesthaler* or common *thaler* with a *reichsthaler.* One *reichsthaler* is worth only one and a half *gulden.* Three *reichsthaler* are one *ducat* and amount to four and a half *gulden.* And, as you should have remembered from Paris, a *Louis d'Or* or *pistole* is worth seven and a half *gulden.* You have to know these things.

WOFERL:
And if I go to Venice?

LEOPOLD:
One Venetian *zecchino* will be what you will get for five *gulden.* But you will not be going to Venice. Nor, I think, to London, where they will give you two English shillings for a *gulden.*

WOFERL:
Money is complicated. Music is simple.

LEOPOLD:
Yes, music is the simple sauce to the gamy meat of a noble or royal or imperial court. And simple servants of the court must provide it. Break out on your own and you will be cheated. A regular salary, however modest, is to be preferred to the hazards of the itinerant musician's life. As you ought to know.

This is shameful. It answers no purpose. I wondered what purpose would be served by setting Mozart's life to his own music. I received, very belatedly, a commission from Salzburg itself, asking me to provide a libretto for such a setting. At least I could present Mozart caught in a net of musical rhythms, even if they were not his own. Let us imagine the setup. (Needless to say, nothing has come of the proposal.)

ACT I

*The scene is an indeterminate hall in the Vienna palace of the Prince
Archbishop Hieronymus Colloredo of Salzburg. Male and female servants scrub, polish, bring logs for the huge ornate fireplace. Mozart, as
court musician, warms himself gloomily. The servants sing in a minor
key.*

SERVANTS:
Humble humble humble humble
Servants of his princely grace,
Fashed and fagged we groan and grumble,
Outcasts of the human race.
Humble humble humble humble
Burdened boasts that know their place.
See us fumble, see us stumble,
See the bitter bread we crumble
And the skilly that we mumble.
Dare to look us in the face,
Helots of his high disgrace.
Hear our empty bellies rumble
Treble Alto Tenor Bass.

Mozart sings. He is a tenor.

MOZART:
Slavishly begot,
Slavery's your lot.
Luggers in of logs,
You are less than dogs.
Dogs at least are fed
Bones as well as bread.
Lowly born,
Accept my scorn.

SERVANTS:
Humbly humbly humbly humbly
May we ask if it's a crime
Dumbly dumbly dumbly dumbly

(Yes, we know that doesn't rhyme)
To be born beneath a star
Burning with malignant fire?
Humbly dumbly we enquire
Who the hell you think you are.

MOZART:
I was not born beneath a star. I
Am a star.
Leaning across the heavenly bar, I
Fell too far.
The crown of music on my head was
Knocked awry.
Fingering keys to earn my bread was
By and by
Ordained to be the life I led and
Still must lead.
So will it go till I am dead and
Dead indeed.

SERVANTS:
Humbly humbly humbly humbly
May we ask you what you mean?
All you said was soft and crumbly;
Words should cut as keen and clean
As the whip the gruff and grumbly
Major domo, rough and rumbly,
Lays on us to vent his spleen.

MOZART:
I played the harpsichord at four
And scribbled symphonies at five.
I played and played from shore to shore.
I labored — never bee in hive
Buzzed harder at its sticky store —
To keep the family alive.
For Leopold my father swore
I'd fiddle, tinkle, sweat, and strive
Until the name the family bore

Should gather honor and survive
Two centuries and even more.
But infant prodigies arrive
At puberty. Must we deplore
Our beards and balls, though noses dive
And patrons stay away or snore?
I serve his highness now, contrive
To play the postures of a whore.
Too meanly paid to woo or wive,
I sink and sink who used to soar.
Grant me your pity, friends, for I've
Heard slam that ever open door,
Been forced to kiss the nether floor,
Who once kissed queens —

SERVANTS:
Kissed queens?

MOZART:
Kissed queens. Not anymore, not anymore. My scullion companions, I've run out of hope. Also rhymes. To work. I hear steel
heels and the crack of a whip.

The major domo enters, also the Prince Archbishop's private secretary.

SERVANTS:
Humble humble humble humble
Servants of his princely grace,
Hear our empty bellies rumble
Treble Alto Tenor Bass.

MAJOR DOMO:
Scum. Go on. Hard at it.

SECRETARY:
Mozart, fifty new contredances were ordered for the next court
ball. Fifteen only have been delivered. The *Te Deum* for the
impending return to Salzburg of His Grace has still to be com-

posed. And the flute exercises for His Grace's nephew are
awaited with impatience.

MOZART:
Surely you mean His Grace's eldest bastard.

SECRETARY:
Insolence, insolence.

MOZART:
Perhaps, but I know that His Grace is an only child. His mother's
womb bore once and once only. To have produced siblings to
compete with His Holy Uniqueness would have been the true
insolence.

SECRETARY:
I let that float past me like flatulent air. If you seek dismissal
through my mediacy you will not get it. You have been paid for
work not yet done. Do it.

MOZART:
Music cannot be ordered like a pound of tripe. But it will be
done. It is being done now. In my head. But I hope the *Te Deum*
can be postponed a month or more. Why will he not stay in
Vienna?

SECRETARY:
His responsibility is in Salzburg.

MOZART:
There is no place like Vienna.

The dust of Vienna,
The lust of Vienna
Swirls round my brain.
Erotic phantasmas
And putrid miasmas
That rise from each drain.
Its filth is creative.

The stink of each native
Olfactory song.
So I wish to stay here
And I wish to play here.
It's where I belong.

    SECRETARY (who is a baritone):
But Salzburg is pretty
And it is no pity
There's little to do.
A munch at an apple,
A prayer in the chapel
Should satisfy you.
Erotic temptation
And free fornication
Pass everyone by,
And it is no wonder
For everyone's under
His Highness's eye.

And now, of course, they sing opposed words in a duet. This I
cannot present in written form. But I'm reminded of what the
writer most envies the musician. We're limited to the monodic,
while the composer has polyphony to play with. I think it was the
rage of this envy that drove James Joyce to compose *Finnegans
Wake*, where there is the illusion of several strands of dream-
melody proceeding at the same time. Perhaps the best tribute to
Mozart that a writer can make is, if not to achieve his harmony
and counterpoint, at least to learn something from his form.

This year I've been trying to write a novel entitled *K. 550*. If, like
myself, you have difficulty remembering what Köchel number
applies to which work, I'll decode this into the Symphony no. 40
in G Minor. Here is how the first movement started:

> The squarecut pattern of the carpet. Squarecut the carpet's pattern.
> Pattern the cut square carpet. Stretching from open doors to win-
> dows. Soon, if not burned, ripped, merely purloined, as was all too
> likely, other feet other feet other feet would. Tread. He himself he
> himself he himself trod in the glum morning. From shut casement to

open door and back, to and to and back. Wig fresh powdered, brocade unspotted, patch on cheek new pimple in decorum and decency hiding, stockings silk most lustrous, hands behind folded unfolded refolded as he trod on squarecut pattern's softness. Russet the hue, the hue russet. Past bust of Plato, of Aristotle's bust, Thucydides, Xenophon. Foreign voices trapped in print (he himself he himself he himself read) and print in leather, behind glass new polished, ranged, ranged, ranged, the silent army spoke in silence of certain truths, of above all the truth of the eternal stasis. Stasis stasis stasis. The squarecut pattern of the carpet. He trod.

Towards window, casement, treading back observed (he himself he himself he himself did) ranged gardens, stasis, walk with poplars, secular elms elms, under grim sky. But suddenly sun broke, squeezed out brief lemon juice, confirmed stasis, a future founded on past stasis, asphodels seen by Xenophon, rhododendra of Thucydides. The mobs would not come, the gates would rest not submitting to mob's fury. He himself he himself he himself smiled.

Triumph of unassailable order. Everything in its everybody in his place. Place. Place. Plate ranged catching sun's silver. That other triumph then possible? But no, what triumph in right assertion of right? Church rite, bed rite. This much delayed. He himself he himself he himself did. Not assert. Not assert. Not assert. Yet in moment when sun broke salutary to assert. Hurt, no. Assert, yes. Brief hurt ineluct ineluct ineluctable in assert, yes, in assert.

Out of door. Wide hall. Two powdered heads bow. Wide stairs. High stairs. And yet (magic of right, of rite, of lawful assert?) no passage noted, he himself he himself he himself stands by her door by her door by her door. Assert assert insert key. By foul magic wrong key. Not his key. Yes, his key. But lock blocked. Billet doux spittled pulped thrust (not trust lust, though right, rite) in lock, in lock? Anger hurled from sky? But no. Watery sun smiles still . . .

Let me now throw away these masks and speak in my own voice. Let me talk of Mozart and myself.

When we were young, a lot of us were rather sour about Mozart. We were jealous about his having so much talent and disclosing it at so early an age. Ordinary young people care little for infant prodigies. We were told that his ear was so sensitive that he fainted at the sound of a trumpet, and that his sense of pitch was so acute that he could distinguish a fifth from a sixth of a tone. He composed pretty little things at the age of four and played like an angel on the harpsichord. Complimented by the

Empress Maria Theresa, he leapt onto her lap and kissed her. So charming, with his little wig and his brocade and silk stockings. A milksop.

Even as a young man, I found it difficult to fit Mozart into my sonic universe. I was not alone in that. The reputation of Mozart is now at its highest and will presently suffer a reaction, but he was no demi-god in the 1930s. Musicians like Edward Dent and Sir Thomas Beecham had much to do with the promotion of a periwigged historical figure into the voice of a Western civilization that was under threat from the very race of which Mozart was a member. (Salzburg, his birthplace, was an independent city-state; he never saw himself as an Austrian national.) To appreciate him, it was necessary to hear a good deal of Mozart, and this was not easy. One could, of course, play the keyboard pieces, but, to a piano pupil or a self-taught pianist like myself, there was little that was attractive in the scale passages one fumbled over, or in the conventional tonic-dominant cadences. A boy born into the age of Schoenberg's *Pierrot Lunaire* (1912) and Stravinsky's *Le Sacre du Printemps* (1913) — I was born five years after the first, four years after the other — found it hard to be tolerant of the Mozartian blandness.

One great war and the threat of another justified barbaric dissonance and slate-pencil-screeching atonality. I needed the music of my own time — Hindemith, Honegger, Bartók. In the Soviet Union, Alexander Mosolov produced his *Factory* (1926–28) and *Dnieper Power Station,* and those banal chunks of onomatopoeia at least spoke of the modern world. The symphony orchestra had, following Richard Wagner and Richard Strauss, evolved into a virtuoso complex capable of anything. Mozart had been unlucky with his valveless horns and trumpets: He had been enclosed by the technically primitive. So, anyway, it seemed.

I wanted modernity, but where did modernity begin? Probably with Debussy's *L'Aprés-Midi d'un Faune* (1894), which had entranced my ear when, as a boy of thirteen, I had fiddled with the cat's whisker on my homemade crystal set, heard a silence punctuated by a cough or two, and then was overwhelmed by that opening flute descending a whole tritone. This was as much the new age as Mosolov's machine music: It denied the hegemony of tonic and dominant, exalted color, wallowed in sensuality. Debussy promised a full meal, well sauced. Mozart offered only bread and water.

The appetite for the modern did not exclude the ancient. I read Peter Warlock's study of Cecil Gray and Philip Heseltine's *Carlo Gesualdo, Prince of Venosa, Musician and Murderer* (1926), and was led to the perusal of madrigals I was not yet permitted to hear. The harmonic sequences looked hair-raising. The seventeenth century was closer to my own epoch than the ages in between. Henry Purcell broke the rules that the textbooks were eventually to make petrific. The baroque was acceptable if it meant Bach and Handel. Ezra Pound was yet to resurrect Vivaldi. Stravinsky had sounded the "Back to Bach" call, and the composer of *Le Sacre* could do no wrong. But this was, as Constant Lambert was to point out in *Music Ho* (1967), sheer evasion. Stravinsky was a "time traveler," prepared to go anywhere so long as it was not in the direction of neoromanticism. To Stravinsky there was something salutary in clockwork rhythms, the inexpressive deadpan, an eschewing of the dynamic. But true baroque was something different.

Its charm lay in its exaggeration, and Bach's counterpoint went too far. It imposed on the listener the task of hearing many voices at the same time. The effect was of intellectual rigor, and intellectual rigor was, in a curious way, analogous to physical shock. The approach to both the baroque and the modern was not by way of the emotions. Romantic music, reaching its apogee in Wagner's *Tristan and Isolde* (1865), depended on its capacity to rend the heart. Young people distrust emotion, indeed, are hardly capable of it unless it takes the form of self-pity. Sir Thomas Beecham promoted English composer Frederick Delius as much as Mozart, and the death-wish element in *The Walk to the Paradise Gardens* (1900–01) was acceptable to the misunderstood young.

But why this rejection of Mozart, the charming but unromantic, the restrained, the formal? He seemed too simple, too scared of the complex. He made neither an intellectual nor a physical impact. Bach, after a day's slaving at six-part counterpoint, would say: "Let's go and hear the pretty tunes." He meant plain sweet melody with a chordal accompaniment. He was not disparaging such art, but he recognized that it was diversion more than serious musical engagement. It was an art waiting to be turned into Mozart.

Looming behind modernism, but in a sense its father, was the personality of Ludwig van Beethoven. My benighted age group accepted the Beethoven symphony as a kind of musical ultimate, something that the composers of our own age could not aspire to because they had been forced into abandoning the key system on which it was based. The key system was worn out; it could linger in the dance or music hall, but modernity meant either a return to the Greek or folk modes, as with Bartók or Vaughan Williams, or the total explosion of tonality. Atonalism recognized no note of the chromatic scale as being more important than any other, but the diatonic scale that was good enough for Beethoven had a hierarchical basis: No. 1 of the scale, the tonic, was king; No. 5, the dominant, was queen; No. 4, the subdominant, was jack or knave. It spoke of a settled past, but Beethoven was not always easy in it. His sonatas and symphonies were dramas, storm-and-stress revelations of personal struggle and triumph. The Messiah from Bonn, of whom Joseph Haydn, not Mozart, was the prophet, belonged to a world striving to make itself modern. Beethoven moved forward; Mozart stayed where he was.

The term "rococo" got itself applied to Mozart's music, and the associations were of prettiness, sugary decorativeness, a dead end of diversion. We were not listening carefully enough to his Symphony no. 40 in G minor. We heard pleasing sounds, but we were not conscious of a language. If we talk of a musical language at all, it must be only in a metaphorical sense, but there was an assumption that Beethoven and his successors were sending messages while Mozart was merely spinning notes.

Music can properly have meaning only when language is imposed upon it, as in song, opera, oratorio, or other vocal genres, or when language is applied laterally — in the form of a literary program, as in Strauss's tone poems. And yet we assume that instrumental music has meaning: It is organized, as language can be, to an end that, if not semantic, is certainly aesthetic, and it produces mental effects as language does. It differs from the other arts, and spectacularly from literature, in being nonrepre-

sentational. Limited to metaphorical statements of a sort, it can
have only a semantic content through analogy.

As Ezra Pound pointed out, poetry decays when it moves too
far away from song, and music decays when it forgets the dance.
In the music of the eighteenth century, it may be said, the spirit
of the dance was raised to its highest level. That spirit progres-
sively deteriorated in the nineteenth century, and in the music
drama of Wagner it may be said to have yielded to the rhythms
of spoken discourse. Paradoxically, in a work specifically intended for ballet, the dance spirit seems to have been liquidated.
Le Sacre du Printemps reduces the dance to prehistoric gamboling,
unsure of its steps. But in Haydn, Mozart, and Beethoven, we
hear a fusion of dance and sonata form and, in the traditional
third-movement minuet, the invocation of a specific dance form.
But these dance movements are not intended for the physical
participation of dancers. The dance becomes an object of contemplation and, in so being, takes on a symbolic function.

The dance as a collective activity, whether in imperial courts
or on the village green, celebrates the union of man and woman
and that larger union known as the human collective. The
Haydn or Mozart symphony asks us to take in the dance in
archetypal *tempi* — moderately rapid, slow, furiously rapid, two
or three or four to the bar — and meditate on their communal
significance. The sonata or the string quartet or the concerto or
the symphony becomes symbolic of human order. With Mozart
it seems evident that the more or less static tranquillity of the
Austro-Hungarian Empire is being celebrated. Thus the music is
objective, lacks any personal content of a Mahlerian or Strauss-
ian kind, and, through that irony, which is a corrective to the
complacency of social order, works through the alternation of
stress and resolution. The heart is the organ that it imitates, but
it is the heart of the community. There may be a modicum of
personal inflection of the objective structure — comic in Haydn,
pathetic in Mozart — but any large incursion of idiosyncratic
symbols has to be resisted. In Mahler, banal barrel-organ tunes
may grind because of adventitious associations, but the Mozart
symphony remains aloof from such egotistical intrusion.

It seemed in my youth that the Austro-Hungarian Empire was
hopelessly remote. It had collapsed in World War I; before that

collapse Freud and Schoenberg recorded the turmoil of individual psyches, microcosms of a larger confusion. It was easy to
forget that, in respect to its art, that empire was still with us. A
failed Viennese architect was to tyrannize Europe; in the Adri-
atic port of the empire, James Joyce began to revolutionize world
literature; Rainer Maria Rilke affirmed poetic modernity in the
Duino Elegies (1923). And, of course, in music, atonality and
serialism portended a major revolution. Everything happened
in Vienna. If Mozart seemed to stand for a kind of imperial stasis, it ought to have been clear to the close listener that a chromatic restlessness was at work and that, within accepted frame-
works, the situation of an individual soul, not an abstract item in
the citizenry, was being delineated. Mozart was as Viennese as
Freud.

I must beware of overpersonalizing an art that manifests its
individuality in ways of managing pure sound. One aspect of
Mozart's greatness is a superiority in disposing of the sonic material that was the common stock of composers of his time. Sometimes he sleeps, nods, churns out what society requires or what
will pay an outstanding milliner's bill, but he is never less than
efficient. Clumsiness is sometimes associated with greatness: The
outstanding innovative composers, like Berlioz and Wagner, are
wrestling, not always successfully, with new techniques. Mozart
is never clumsy; his unvarying skill can repel romantic tempera-
ments. "Professionalism" can be a dirty word. He touched nothing that he did not adorn. If only, like Shakespeare, he had occasionally put a foot wrong — so some murmur. He never fails
to astonish with his suave or prickly elegance.

It is his excellence that prompts disparagement. The perfection of his work has perversely inspired denigration of his personality. There is a mostly fictitious Mozart whom it is convenient
to call Amadeus — a name he was never known to use. This is
the man whom an equally fictitious Salieri wished to kill from a
variety of motives — clear-headed recognition of his excellence
stoking jealousy, the horror of the disparity between his genius
and a scatomaniacal infantilism, a Christian conviction of the
diabolic provenance of his skill. This makes compelling drama
but bad biography. In personal letters the whole Mozart family
discloses a delight in the scatological, harmless, conventional, not

untypical of an Age of Reason that gained pleasurable shocks from the contrast between the muckheap of the body and the soaring cleanliness of the spirit. All the evidence shows a Mozart who obeyed most of the rules of Viennese propriety, accepting the God of the Church and the Great Architect of the Freemasons. An attempt to mythologize Mozart's end — the mysterious stranger with the commission to compose a Requiem, the pauper's grave, the desertion of the coffin in a sudden storm — collapses under scrutiny of the recorded fact. Meteorological records, the imperial decree to cut down on funeral expenses through the use of common graves, the not uncommon plagiarisms of amateur musicians with more money than talent, all melt the mythology into banality. The heresy of indecorous probing into an artist's life has been with us for a long time. Few can take their art straight.

I began my artistic career as a self-taught composer who, because of insufficient talent and a recognition that music could not say the things I wished to say, took, almost in middle age, to the practice of a more articulate craft. Yet the musical background will not be stilled, and the standards I set myself owe more to the great composers than to the great writers. It has always seemed to me that an artist's devotion to his art is primarily manifested in prolific production. Mozart, who produced a great deal of music in a short life, knew that mastery was to be attained only through steady application. His literary counterparts — Balzac in France, H. G. Wells and Arnold Bennett in England — have often been reviled for what is termed "overproduction." To discover virtue in costiveness was a mark of Bloomsbury gentility. Ladies and gentlemen should be above the exigencies of the tradesman's life. But art is a trade that ennobles itself, and the consumer, by giving more than is paid for. The market is served but also God. Mozart wrote for money, which E. M. Forster did not have to do: His scant production is as appropriate to a *rentier* as Mozart's fecundity is right both for a serious craftsman and a breadwinner. Ultimately artists must be judged not merely by excellence but by bulk and variety. The musician is, however, luckier than the writer: It is always possible to produce an acceptable minuet, rather more difficult to achieve a story or a poem.

The celebration of Mozart cannot be accomplished in words, except those of stringent technical analysis with ample music-type illustration. We can only celebrate by listening massively and then emitting some almost preverbal noise of approval, amazement, or exaltation. But, to the artist in whatever medium, Mozart presents an example to be followed, that of devotion to craft. Without craft there can be no art.

Those of us who practice, as I still inadequately do, the craft of music cannot easily stifle envy. It is not envy of individual genius so much as a bitterness that the cultural conditions which made Mozart possible have long passed away. The division between the music of the street and that of the salon and opera house was not so blatant as it now is. Bach could end his Goldberg Variations with a quodlibet based on the popular tunes of his day. Conversely, melodies from Mozart's operas could be whistled, and not solely by aristocrats dressing for dinner. Till quite recently the ghost of the sense of a musical community lingered. A Mozart sonata could be popularized, though condescendingly, as "In an Eighteenth-Century Drawing Room"; Frank Sinatra, in his earliest film, could sing *La ci darem la mano*. Simple tuneful melody was something of a constraint. Stravinsky tried to make money by converting a theme from *L'Oiseau de Feu* into a pop ballad. But what was popularized came from the classical or romantic past: no music by Schoenberg, Webern, or Bartók could hope to entrance the general ear. The gulf between the serious and the merely diverting is now firmly fixed.

A serious composer commissioned to write, say, an oboe concerto will feel dubious about using tonality with occasional concords; he is uneasy about critical sneers if he does not seem to be trying to outdo Pierre Boulez. There are various modes of musical expression available, perhaps too many, but none of them can have more than a tenuous link with the past. Atonality, polytonality, polymodalism, postmodality, Africanism, Indianism, minimalism, Cageism — the list is extensive. No composer can draw on the heritage that united Monteverdi and Mozart. Alban Berg, in his Violin Concerto (1935), could quote Bach's chorale *Es Ist Genug* only because its tritonal opening bar fitted, by accident, into his tone-row. Perhaps only the neurotic Mahler, last of the great tonal Viennese, provides the bridge between a dead and a living society. Mozart can be parodied or pastiched, as in Stravinsky's mannered *The Rake's Progress* (1951), but we cannot imagine his wearing a lounge suit, as we can imagine Beethoven coming back in stained sweater and baggy flannels.

We have to beware of approaching Mozart while polishing the spectacles of historical perspective. Nostalgia is behovely, but it is inert. The vision he purveys must not be that of a long-dead stability for which we hopelessly yearn. In a world which affronts us daily with war, starvation, pollution, the destruction of the rain forests, the breakdown of public and domestic morality, and the sheer bloody incompetence of government, we may put a Mozart string quartet on the compact disc apparatus in the expectation of a transient peace. But it is not Mozart's function to soothe: He is not a tranquilizer to be taken out of the bathroom cabinet. He purveys an image of a possible future rather than of an irrecoverable past.

As a literary practitioner I look for his analogue among great writers. He may not have the complex humanity of Shakespeare, but he has more than the gnomic neatness of an Augustan like Alexander Pope. It wouldn't be extravagant to find in him something like the serene skill of Dante Alighieri. If the paradisal is more characteristic of him than the infernal or even the purgatorial, that is because history itself has written the *Divine Comedy* backwards. He reminds us of human possibilities. Dead *nel mezzo del cammin di nostra vita* — in the middle of the road of our life — he nevertheless presents the whole compass of life and intimates that noble visions exist only because they can be realized.

I refuse to end on a grandiloquent note. Mozart himself wouldn't have liked it. So I come down to the ground level of the smell of ink, of greasepaint and stage lights. Works have to be written before they can excite ecstasy or vilification. The humus from which they arise can be accidental. Let's go to the cinema.

SCENE 20. INTERIOR. NIGHT. THE BURGTHEATER

There is an opera in progress. The auditorium candles remain lighted. The audience is not overattentive. There is chatter, flirtation. The opera is not by any composer we know. The composer presides at the harpsichord

*in the pit. On stage a soprano sings a cabaletta and falters on her high
notes. Rotten fruit and bad eggs are hurled. A member of the audience
stands to inveigh.*

MEMBER OF THE AUDIENCE:
Never mind about *her*. Throw something at *him*.

He points an accusatory finger at the cowering composer.

He's a thief. He stole that from Sacchini. Or it might be Paisiello.

The opera continues with difficulty.

21. INT. NIGHT. A VIENNESE COFFEE HOUSE

Vicente Martin Soler takes coffee with Giovanni Paisiello.

SOLER:
Outrageous behavior. Yet it may be taken as enthusiasm. For the
genre, that is. There is certainly no indifference.

PAISIELLO:
It's the rage for the ever-new that one finds oppressive. Operas
are like newspapers. You know how many I have written?

SOLER:
Twenty would be too much.

PAISIELLO:
Over a hundred. The maw of what you would call the aficiona-
dos is insatiable. You, me, Salieri, Cimarosa, Guglielmi, Sarti.
And there's Mozart pretending to be an Italian.

SOLER:
Touché.

PAISIELLO:
Oh, you're a Latin. Very nearly an Italian. These Viennese can't
tell the difference.

SOLER:

Your *Barbiere di Siviglia* exemplifies our internationalism. A Spanish setting, a French play, an Italian operatization.

PAISIELLO:

Your *Una cosa rara* is pure Italy. It's knocked out poor little Mozart's *Nozze di Figaro.* The insolence. Figaro's my property.

SOLER:

The man's an instrumentalist. His woodwind fights the voices. There's a certain talent there, but it's not operatic. Will he last?

PAISIELLO:

Will any of us? And does it matter? Come, we're going to be late for *La Grotta di Trofonio.* Salieri will never forgive us.

22. INT. NIGHT. THE BURGTHEATER

Salieri's insipid work is in progress. The camera pans over a moderately attentive audience. It reaches Mozart, who stands gloomily at the back. His inner voice speaks over the unmemorable music.

MOZART (voiceover):

And does it matter? Not to be understood? None of us shall see posterity. There's no advantage in working for the yet unborn. If my music dies with my death, I shall be in no position to complain. Am I serving the age I live in, live in very precariously, or am I serving God? Of God's existence I remain unsure, despite my choral praises. Does God manifest himself in the world in trickles of music? I don't know. The quest for perfection, even when perfection is unwanted. This is the crown of thorns. It cannot be rejected. God or no God, I must avoid blasphemy. I am only a little man whose health is not good and whose coffers are empty. Counting each *kreuzer.* Wondering whether I can afford the pulling of a tooth. The fingers of my right hand are deformed with the incessant penning of notes. And the true music remains unheard, taunting, demanding birth like a dream child. God help some of us. There are some who need no help.

He looks at the stage, where the opera is coming to an end.

23. INT. NIGHT. THE BURGTHEATER STAGE

The final ensemble comes to an end. Tonic and dominant. The audience bows. Salieri rises from the harpsichord and takes his bow. He smiles. Flowers are thrown.

I take my bow too. You will throw no flowers. I hope I've demonstrated adequately enough that there's nothing to say.

Oh — one last thing. My title — "Mozart and the Wolf Gang." It is we who are the wolves, ganging up to devour the *corpus verum* of the master. But he cannot be devoured. His musical flesh is eucharistic and bestows grace. And if that is blasphemy, God, whom Mozart, perhaps at this very moment, is busy teaching about music, will forgive it.

JACOB COHEN

Yes, Oswald Alone Killed Kennedy

FROM COMMENTARY

EVEN THE STRONGEST SUPPORTERS of *JFK*, Oliver Stone's notorious film on the assassination of President John F. Kennedy, concede that it is deceptive: fabricated footage gussied up as documentary fact; fictional characters and scenes offered as proof of perfidy; paranoid insinuations about the conscious involvement of the highest officials in the land; outright lies. Yet to an extraordinary number of often intelligent people, these characterizations seem utterly beside the point. "Don't trust anyone who says the movie is hogwash," writes a *Newsweek* critic, David Ansen, "and don't trust the movie either . . . [it] is a remarkable, a necessary, provocation." "One of the worst great movies ever made," declaims Norman Mailer. One wonders: how false, fanciful, and downright mendacious does a work purporting to portray and interpret historical events need to be before it is not just chided but discounted, disqualified, disgraced?

Those who defend the film's meta-purposes seem confident that if not all, then some and *certainly at least one* of its basal assertions of fact reflect what actually happened in Dallas: more than one person fired at the President. And if there was more than one gunman, there is *prima facie* evidence of a conspiracy of some sort or another.

Having spent a considerable part of my life over the last three decades studying and discussing the Kennedy assassination, I can testify to the tenacity of that basal assertion. Challenging the notion of multiple gunmen has become tantamount to suggesting that it was the United States which attacked Japan in 1941, Poland which attacked Germany in 1939. And yet, I will contend that for anyone who has seriously studied the original Warren Report on the assassination (and not just had it read to him by its critics); has gone over the materials produced in the reconsideration of that Report by the House of Representatives in 1977–78; and has familiarized himself with the many scientific studies over the years, including three separate reviews of the medical material, which have examined the testable bases of the single-assassin theory — to anyone who has done all this, the notion of multiple gunmen, on which nearly every conspiracy theory extant rests, is a demonstrable chimera. And if there was one and only one assassin, and if that assassin was Lee Harvey Oswald, then nearly every insinuation in *JFK*, and in the mountain of conspiracy literature which it summarizes, collapses.

II

The case for multiple assassins consists of four lines of argument: (1) there was not enough time for a single gunman to have done what the Warren Commission alleges Oswald did; (2) compelling eyewitness, photographic, and earwitness testimony place a second gunman on the fabled grassy knoll; (3) the evidence of Kennedy's wounds and the reaction of his body to the shots establishes the presence of assassins other than on the knoll; and (4) the so-called single-bullet theory, popularly known as the magic-bullet theory, the indispensable prerequisite of the notion that there was only one assassin, is a palpable absurdity.

These arguments are mutually reinforcing, but it is fair to say if any one of them holds water, the single-assassin theory would be untenable. However, as we shall see, all four are baseless.

Consider the issue of timing. Repeatedly, like a mantra, *JFK*, and the critics it mimics, declare that the famous Zapruder film (a home movie taken of the assassination by a Dallas manufacturer, Abraham Zapruder) "established three shots in 5.6 seconds" and that such a feat would stretch the capacity of the most expert rifleman, and undoubtedly was beyond Oswald and his

gun. In interviews and speeches Oliver Stone frequently refers
to "the 5.6-second Zapruder film," as if that were all there was to
it, 5.6 seconds, and many commentators on *JFK* dutifully repeat
these data, usually in the movie's own tone of outraged incre-
dulity.

Yet: (1) The Zapruder film, which is 30 seconds long in toto,
firmly establishes only the final and unmistakable shot to Kennedy's head. (2) Even assuming that two hits occurred 5.6 seconds apart, nothing in Zapruder indicates that a possible third
shot, which missed, had to have come *between* the two hits. The
Warren Commission concluded only that there were probably
three shots and that *the two hits,* not the three shots, came within
5.6 seconds of each other. The miss could have come first, or
last, though it probably came first. That means the gunman had
more than eight seconds to shoot, and more than five seconds —
ample time — between the two hits. (3) Even if the miss had
come between the two hits, there would still have been 2.8 seconds to fire and refire — enough time even for an amateur used
to handling guns, like Oswald. Stone and/or his advisers know
this, as does everyone who has studied the case.

Were there shots from the grassy knoll by another assassin?
Allegedly, eyewitness, photographic, and earwitness testimony
placed a second gunman there. The knoll, I would remind the
reader, was in front and to the right of the President's car when
he was first struck, and directly to his right when he was fatally
shot in the head. The Warren Commission placed the lone gunman above and behind the President in the Texas Book Depository building.

Surely, the most significant eye- and earwitnesses to the assassination were Abraham Zapruder himself and his secretary,
Marilyn Sitzman, who was standing next to him as he took his
famous home movie. The two of them were on the knoll, on a
three-foot-high concrete pedestal overlooking the scene and directly overlooking the entire area behind a five-foot wooden
fence at the top of the knoll from behind which, Stone and the
other conspiracists say, an assassin shot at and killed the President.

But here is a point omitted by Stone and the conspiracists:
Zapruder and Sitzman were within 50 feet, above, slightly *behind,*

and in clear line of sight of the alleged assassin and (in Stone's recreation) his alleged "spotter." Fifty feet is ten feet less than the distance between home plate and the mound. Understand: Zapruder and Sitzman were on the mound facing the batter, as it were, and Stone would have us believe that they did not happen to hear or see two assassins to their right front halfway down the third base line, firing two explosive shots. They simply failed to glance that way during the shooting or to notice the gunman while he waited for the President to arrive.

Zapruder is now dead, but Sitzman was interviewed for a sensational five-part documentary produced by the Arts and Entertainment (A&E) Network on cable TV. Somehow, the interviewer did not ask her whether she noticed a man shooting the President just to her right front.

Those who have seen the A&E documentary will recall the gripping analysis of a black-and-white Polaroid snapshot of the knoll which was taken by one Mary Moorman just before the fatal head shot. In that picture, we are told, one may now see the clear image of "the badge man," a man in uniform, who, allegedly, fired at the President from the knoll. Yet while that image may leap out at the consultants to the A&E documentary, it was not clear to the panel of photographic experts who, in 1977, perused it for the House Assassinations Committee.

Of course, those experts were not privy to the blown-up, "colorized" enhancement of the photo developed by the A&E consultants, who claim to see in the photo not only a man (nothing remarkable in that, it's a free country and people were allowed to roam about the knoll) but a hatless man in uniform. They even claim to be able to see the label on his shirt and, "perhaps," a gun. Well, if "badge man" is an assassin, he fired from a spot right next to, at most fifteen feet below and to the right of, Zapruder and Sitzman. Again, they did not notice.

There are other pictures of the knoll — twenty-two persons were taking pictures in Dealey Plaza, the assassination site, that afternoon — and several are of the knoll at the time of the shooting. Over the years conspiracists have discerned in these pictures riflemen and rifles, only to have photographic expertise reveal the illusions created by light and shadow.

For example, in one set of photos purporting to show a rifle-man in "the classic firing position," the rifleman, to be actual, would need to have been floating in the air nine feet above the ground. Another rifle, supposedly visible in Zapruder frame 413, turned out to be a small branch in a bush in front of the fence, and the head behind that bush, the one with a "tennis hat" on, would have to be the size of a lemon in order to have been where the critics say it is.

Notwithstanding Stone's insinuations, no one saw a gun on the knoll, though it would have been in the clear line of sight of hundreds of the 692 people who have been identified in Dealey Plaza. No one: not one of the eighteen people on the railroad bridge who, looking up Elm Street at the approaching President, could easily have spotted a gun about a hundred feet in front of them and slightly to their left; no one in the plaza, neither Zapruder nor Sitzman, who were on the knoll; none of the hundreds who, we presume, were following the presidential limousine with their eyes and need only have raised their gaze a few degrees to have seen the gun; not Lee Bowers, who surveyed the scene from a tower behind the alleged assassins; no one in the presidential caravan, including Secret Service men whom film and photos show scanning the surrounding scene. (Were they ordered not to see anything? Have they remained silent to this day about those criminal orders?) On the other hand, six people saw the rifle *inside* the sixth-floor, southeast corner window of the Book Depository: Oswald's rifle, the one that fired all the bullets that were recovered. Two people actually saw the rifle as it was fired, and two of them identified Oswald in a police lineup.

Those who have seen the Stone film, or the A&E documentary, or are familiar with the conspiracy literature, may now protest vehemently: what about Jean Hill, the woman in the Stone film who fervently claims she saw a "gunman" running? What about the others who swear passionately that the shots came from the knoll? What about the many, like A. J. Holland, who saw gunsmoke on the knoll, and the sheer weight of earwitness testimony that the shots came from the knoll? What about the deaf mute who for twenty-eight years has been trying to get someone to understand his signing message that, a few minutes before the assassination, from a distance of over a hundred yards, he saw men walking with rifles near the knoll?

And what about the lady who now claims to be the "babushka lady" visible in photos of the plaza, and who says she will go to her death believing there was a gunman on the knoll? And what of Gordon Arnold, who claims, after more than a quarter century of silence, that he filmed the assassination from in front of the fence on the knoll, that he sensed bullets whizzing past his ear, and that after the shooting a man with "dirty hands," in a uniform, came up to him, weeping, and threw him to the ground, physically forcing him to relinquish the incriminating film? Arnold's is one of several stories by people who claim they were roughed up and threatened because they had seen inadmissible things. Stone graphically depicts these alleged brutalities and the reign of terror which insiders to the assassination have been enduring.

Here are the answers. Jean Hill said she "saw a man running," not from the knoll but from the Depository. Stone has Hill say that the man was a "gunman." But a gunman, presumably, is a man holding a gun. Hill did not say that she saw a gun. Is it possible that, as many witnesses do, she has fused two disparate facts — the President is shot, a man is running — and created the saga she has made a career of telling?

Holland, who is the only one to say he saw a man with a submachine gun stand up in the back of the President's limousine, claims also to have seen smoke over the knoll. Others, too, saw smoke, and identified it with a shot. The Stone film shows a considerable puff of smoke wafting above the knoll, pretty much as Holland described it. But modern weapons do not make big puffs of smoke. Hot steam pipes do produce such cumulus effects, and there were hot steam pipes at the top of the knoll where the smoke was seen.

Beverly Oliver, the woman who claims to be the "babushka lady," not only swears "to her death" that the shots came from the knoll (although she saw no gun), but she also identifies herself as having been a nightclub singer in a club next to Jack Ruby's and has said that when Ruby, Oswald's eventual assassin, introduced her there to Oswald they casually identified themselves as "CIA agents." She says, too, that in 1968 she met for two hours with Richard Nixon, whom she ties to the killing. Stone knows all this detail, but omits much of it in order to create the character of a sympathetic nightclub singer terrified to tell the world about her certain knowledge of links between Oswald and Ruby. (No persuasive links between the two have ever been established.)

Was Gordon Arnold there? He does not appear in photos, though some find him in the Moorman photo right next to "badge man." (Apparently Arnold did not notice the "badge man" shooting the President.) As for the story that he was brutalized and his film removed — it is interesting that no one brutalized or even spoke to Zapruder and Sitzman, or removed them from the pivotal perch from which they filmed the assassination and, presumably, saw the assassins. And as for the deaf mute, whose twenty-eight years of silent frustration were ended when A&E finally found someone to read his signs and put him on television, is it indecorous to suggest that his story sounds like a routine on *Saturday Night Live?*

Stone and others would have us believe that on the knoll that day there was a platoon of conspirators, incognito, surveying every person's eyes, entering minds and cameras, knowing infallibly who had incriminating evidence and who did not. Like Santa Claus, they knew who had been bad or good, and they brutalized only those who saw or photographed the bad thing. And these people, in fear and trembling, agreed to be silent. Now, nearly three decades later, these same victims have agreed to take their ten minutes in the spotlight at the invitation of A&E and Oliver Stone.

And the earwitnesses? Undeniably, several people thought shots came from the knoll, said so freely to the Warren Commission, the FBI, the Secret Service, and the Dallas police, and were reported as having said so. Fourteen years later, in 1977, at the request of the House Assassinations Committee, a panel of acoustical scientists and psychologists examined all the earwitness evidence and then correlated it with observations they made at Dealey Plaza when rifles were test-fired from the knoll and the Book Depository. They discovered that of 178 earwitness accounts which they sampled, 132 thought there were three shots, 149 thought there were three or fewer. Six people thought there were four shots; one thought there were five, and one, Jean Hill, heard six. (Six is the number that Stone, and most conspiracists, say were fired.)

With regard to the source of the shots: 49 of the 178 thought it was the Depository, 21 thought it was the knoll, 30 gave other sources, 78 did not know. Crucially, however, only 4 of the 178 thought shots came from more than one direction. Since we know that at least some shots came from the Depository — the rifle, Oswald's, which fired all the recovered bullets and shells was found there, and six people saw a rifle in the window — shots would have needed to have come from two directions if there were also shots from the knoll. The panel concluded:

> It is hard to believe a rifle was fired from the knoll. . . . [D]espite the various sources of confusion in the locus of any single shot, a second shot from a different location should be distinctive and different enough to cause more than four witnesses to report multiple origins for the shots.[1]

According to *JFK*, there were ten to twelve assassins, firing six shots from three directions. No one heard it that way; no one. Nor do the conspiracists answer this question: if the idea (as Stone suggests) was to frame Oswald for having fired three shots, why fire six? Did the Conspiracy expect that no one would notice?

To take the full measure of what Stone and the others are suggesting, we must remember that this ingenious plot *intended* that the assassins on the knoll be invisible and escape unnoticed. But how could they have known where spectators would be, where cameras would be? Just behind the fence was a public parking lot, filled with cars. Anyone could have gone to retrieve his car at any time. And why does Stone not show us the (inevitably hilarious) planning session where it was decided that a

---

[1] One further comment on the matter of earwitness testimony. The House Assassinations Committee in 1979 concluded that a tape recording of police communications at the time of the assassination registered four, not three, shots, and specifically, three shots from the Depository and one from the knoll. Solely on the basis of that piece of evidence, the Committee decided that an unseen gunman shot an (unrecovered) bullet, and missed. In 1982 the National Academy of Science asked a blue ribbon panel of physicists and acoustical experts to review the recording and the accompanying studies which had persuaded the House Committee that there was a gunman on the knoll. The panel concluded unanimously and vigorously that the alleged sounds on the tape could not have been made at the time of the shooting, and also scoffed at the calculations and methodology of the House consultants.

feigned epileptic fit fifteen minutes before the shooting to distract attention from the gunmen on the knoll, a diversionary shot from the Depository, and an omniscient goon squad to rough up awkward witnesses would be enough to provide anonymity and safe passage to assassins standing in broad daylight, in clear view?

There is a further reason to scoff at speculations of a shot from the knoll: the alleged gunman, one of the world's finest (according to Stone) or one of the Mafia's finest (in other versions), firing at point-blank range, missed the car and everyone in it with a bullet which was never recovered. The now decisively authenticated X-rays and photographs which were taken of the President's body the night of the assassination establish that no shots struck the President or Governor John Connally (who was with him in the motorcade) except shots fired from above and behind. There were no hits from the knoll.

Again, viewers of Stone's film will protest: what of the doctors at Dallas's Parkland Hospital, who for years after the shooting insisted that the small neat wound in Kennedy's throat was a wound of entry, inflicted from the front (hence, by another gunman)? What of their insistence, for years, that there was a massive wound of exit in the back, occipital region of his head, where the autopsy doctors had purported to find only a small wound of entry? And most memorably, what of the dramatic thrust of the President's body, backward and "to the left" — Kevin Costner, playing Stone's heroic protagonist, New Orleans District Attorney Jim Garrison, repeats the phrase "to the left" five times, while the gory Zapruder frames show the President, indeed, thrust backward and leftward — a movement consistent only with a hit from the right front?

It is true that several Dallas doctors once thought the throat wound was an entry wound, and said so at the time. And a few of them later recalled massive damage to the back of his head, not on the right side where the autopsy doctors placed the damage. The Dallas doctors agreed that there was no time for a proper "medical examination" of the President; all of their efforts were aimed at saving his life, not examining his wounds. So frenzied were their ministrations that they did not even notice at the time a small wound of entry in his back and a small wound of

entry in the back of his head. Later, after the President was
peremptorily removed from Dallas to the autopsy in Washington, to the considerable professional chagrin of the Dallas doctors, several of them came to insist that the wound in the throat
"looked like" a wound of entry, and that there was a massive
default in the rear, occipital, portion of the President's head, a
glaring fact somehow missed by the official autopsy team.

Over and again, Stone and the conspiracists refer us to these
incongruous comments by the Dallas doctors. What they do not
tell us is that these doctors changed their minds when they
reviewed the X-rays and the photos taken at the autopsy for a
Nova documentary on public television. The evidence in the
X-rays and photos is of paramount importance. If the throat
wound was an entry wound, that bullet, fired from the right
front, would have torn into Kennedy's throat and probably out
of the back or side of his neck. Or it would have lodged in the
body, causing appropriate damage, all of which would be visible
in X-rays and photos. Unless the photos and X-rays are fake, the
throat wound is not a wound of entry. Every one of the by now
more than twenty forensic pathologists who have examined
those documents agrees there was no strike to the throat from
the front.

Similarly with regard to the alleged massive wound of exit in the
back of Kennedy's head — the result, according to Stone, of a
bullet administered from the front right. The X-rays and photos
clearly show that that massive wound of exit is on the right side
of the head, not in the back, and was caused by a bullet entering
in the rear of the skull where a small wound of entry was seen by
the autopsy doctors.

Again, this is the conclusion of every one of the prominent
forensic pathologists who have studied the photos and X-rays
which show the location and nature of the wounds and the
pattern of fracturing. Even Dr. Cyril Wecht, one of the stars of
the A&E documentary, a frenetic critic of the official version,
agreed on this point after examining the X-rays and photos over
a two-day period. The Dallas doctors, too, examining these documents for the *Nova* program, agreed that their memory of the
wound location had been erroneous.

Stone and the conspiracists, having spent hundreds of hours with the Zapruder film, examining it meticulously, frame by frame, must know all this. In frame 313, when Kennedy is struck in the head, and in subsequent frames, we see a large burst of pink — bone and brain matter — exploding out of the right side of his head, exactly where the X-rays and photos place it; the back of the head, clearly visible in these frames, is unruffled and completely intact. Where then is their theory of a massive rear exit? Robert Groden, one of Stone's technical advisers, has now taken to arguing that the Zapruder films too have been doctored, along with the X-rays and photos.

Well, are the X-rays and photos authentic? As to the photos, the analysis submitted to the House Assassinations Committee by a team of photographic experts found no evidence whatsoever of tampering. Far more important was the detailed report of the team of forensic anthropologists. Studying the photos of the President, fore and aft, the anthropologists meticulously measured the angle of his nasal septum, the lower third of the nose cavity, the nasal tip area, various features of his ear, the lip profile, facial creases, and the network of wrinkles across the back and side of his neck. All of them, when compared to previous, unquestionably valid photos, established that the wounded man in these photos was the dead President and no one else.

The authentication of the X-rays was equally decisive. X-rays are like fingerprints. Since every person has a unique bone structure, it is quite easy for forensic anthropologists to identify the mutilated remains of persons killed in combat or plane crashes. The only thing needed are previous X-rays for comparison; of course, many were available in this instance. Thus, the deviation in Kennedy's nasal septum was noted and compared with his other X-rays. The bony rims around his eyes, the honeycomb air cells of the mastoid bone, the saddle-shaped depressions at the base of his skull, the bony projections along the spine — all exactly matched the comparison X-rays, as did features in the X-rays of Kennedy's lower torso.

Furthermore, the damage in the photos matched the damage found in the X-rays. Let us be clear about what this means: these are X-rays and photos of the damaged President, taken the only time in his life that he was damaged in that way. If they are phony, whose body and face are in the fake X-rays and photos? The panel of experts did not argue that the government was incapable of contemplating forgery; they argued that such a forgery, even if contemplated, would be next to impossible: "There can be no doubt that they are the X-rays of John F. Kennedy, and no other person."

Why did President Kennedy lurch backward and to the left if he was struck from behind? Twice now, panels of experts examining the question — once for the Rockefeller Commission in 1972, yet again for the House Assassinations Committee — have concluded that no bullet, by itself, could have caused that physical reaction. Rather, the motion has been attributed to "a seizure-like neuromuscular reaction to major damage inflicted to nerve centers in the brain." The House panel even assassinated some live goats to demonstrate the effect.

Let us turn, finally, to the mother of all of Stone's and the other conspiracists' canards, their account of the so-called "magic bullet," a term so deeply entrenched in discussions of the assassination that routine newspaper accounts of the latest conspiracy allegations refer to it, without quotation marks, as if it were the God-given name of the bullet. I have seen Stone's film three times, and each time Kevin Costner's derisive account of the Warren Commission's supposed position on the subject has brought gasps of incredulous, mutinous laughter from the audience:

> The magic bullet enters the President's back headed downward at an angle of 17 degrees; it then moves upward in order to leave Kennedy's body from the front of his neck, wound number two, where it waits 1.6 seconds, presumably in midair, where it turns right then left [right then left, Costner repeats] and continues into Connally's body at the rear of his right armpit, wound number three. The bullet then heads downward at an angle of 27 degrees, shattering Connally's fifth rib, and exiting from the right side of his chest, wound number four. The bullet then turns right and reenters Connally's body at the right wrist, wound number five, shattering the radius bone. The bullet then exits Connally's wrist, wound number six, takes a dramatic U-turn and buries itself into Connally's left thigh, from which it later falls out

and is found in almost pristine condition in a corridor of Parkland Hospital.

The Warren Commission, it should be unnecessary to say, argued no such thing. It contended that Kennedy and Connally were struck by the same bullet, somewhere between frames 207 and 223 of the Zapruder film. During that one-second period, the two men disappear behind a road sign. Just before Connally disappears behind the sign, and again a little less than a second — fifteen frames — later when he reappears, his right wrist is close to his lap, directly over his left thigh. He is holding the lid of a big Texas hat, knuckles up. His head has turned to the right — Connally has remembered doing this after hearing a shot (probably the first shot, the one that missed) — and in turning, his shoulders rotate rightward slightly, bringing his body into perfect alignment to receive all five of his wounds. It is only then, when the Commission held the two men were hit, that Connally could have been struck in a way to cause the scars which he indubitably has, to this day.

On three separate occasions in the last twenty years, panels of photographic experts analyzing the Zapruder frames and all the photographs have confirmed this analysis. Using the same evidence, and with the added help of wound locations established by X-rays and photographs, the panel of experts assembled by the House Committee showed that a line drawn through Connally and Kennedy's wounds leads right back, straight as an arrow, to the window from which someone fired Oswald's gun: no turns, no pauses.

Now consider Connally's position when Stone and other conspiracists say he was struck. (Costner: "Connally's turning here now, frame 238, the fourth shot, it misses Kennedy and takes Connally.") As I pointed out in *Commentary* seventeen years ago, in that frame Connally

> has turned 90 degrees to the right and is facing out of the side of the car. A bullet striking Connally when the critics say he was hit would then have had to exit from the chest at a downward angle, to have taken two sharp turns upward, in midair — right and then left into the knuckle side of the wrist; and then, upon exiting on the palm side,

further up in the air than the wound of entry, would have had to
execute a very sharp U-turn into the thigh: plainly impossible.[2]

In other words, it is not the Warren Commission's account which
requires these absurd zigs and zags, it is Stone's.

And the "almost pristine" bullet found "in a corridor" at Parkland Hospital? That bullet, unquestionably fired from Oswald's
gun, was found next to Connally's stretcher in the basement of
the hospital, exactly where it would be to support the single-
bullet theory. It was not pristine; it lacked lead from its core in
the amount found in Connally. It was also flattened at one end,
and bent at its axis. In 1978, Professor Vincent Guinn, respond-
ing to a decade of demands by critics, employed recently improved neutron-activation techniques to compare the traces of
antimony, silver, and copper in the lead from the "magic bullet"
with the trace amounts of those metals in the lead recovered
from Connally's wrist. He concluded that the wrist lead almost
certainly came from lead missing from the "magic bullet."

Now, if the bullet found in the basement of Parkland Hospital
next to Connally's stretcher, fired from Oswald's gun and missing the very lead found in Connally's wrist, is not the one which
struck Connally, how did it get next to his stretcher? Stone
suggests that someone from Assassination Central was sent over
to drop a spare bullet somewhere in the hospital. Why the basement? Why Connally's stretcher and not Kennedy's? How could
the Conspiracy have known where Connally's stretcher would
be? How could it have known then that a bullet which had ended
in the soft flesh of Connally's thigh needed to be placed with his
stretcher in order to confirm a single-bullet theory which was not
developed for another two months? And if this was not the bullet
that hit Connally, what happened to the bullet that did?

In the film we see colonels and other gray eminences directing
the autopsy like puppeteers, ordering doctors to lie about the
damage to the President, to silence their curiosity about dangerous matters, and forever. But at that point the Conspiracy could
not have known what directions to give. The single-bullet theory,
to repeat, was not developed until months later, and only an
omniscient demon could have figured out so soon what precise

[2] "Conspiracy Fever," *Commentary*, October 1975.

changes would be necessary in the autopsy report. When and how did the Conspiracy brief its agents in the autopsy room, and who did the briefing, and who briefed the briefers? It is a shame that Stone did not invent scenes dramatizing all this; they too would have been hilarious.

Similar objections may be raised to the theory developed by David Lifton in a best-selling book and reiterated in the A&E documentary. Kennedy's body, we are told, was taken to a secret laboratory after its arrival in Washington while an elaborate ruse — empty coffins, diversionary caravans — convinced the public that his body was being taken directly to the Bethesda Naval Hospital. With about forty minutes to do their work, the agents of the Conspiracy completely altered the President's wounds to make it look as if he had been hit by one assassin, firing from behind, disguising even the signs of their intervention from the X-rays and photos, although not from Lifton and A&E.

In this version, then, the autopsy itself is honest, only the doctors are working on an altered body. But how could the Conspiracy have known what alterations to make? How could its agents be sure forty minutes would be enough? Scores of people would need to be involved: those who prepared the alternate route, those who switched the body, those who performed the forty-minute surgical miracle, those who carefully brought the body to Bethesda through the back door, those who sent advance news of the nature of the wounds from the Parkland Hospital or the President's plane. And all have remained silent about the matter to this day.

There was, in sum, nothing magic about the "magic bullet." And there was no need to alter the body, no need to fabricate an autopsy. The overwhelming burden of the evidence indicates that one assassin shot the President, just as the Warren Commission said.

III

Was Lee Harvey Oswald that single assassin? Chief Justice Earl Warren, who according to Stone was a perjurer and either a willing or a moronic accomplice to a massive cover-up, said that in a lifetime as a lawyer and judge he had never seen such a clear case of guilt. Here I can only sketch the outline of the case, but even a sketch is sufficient to demonstrate the absurdity of ubiquitous charges that Oswald did not shoot the President, that he was a "patsy" set up to deflect attention from other assassins.

First, there is this pivotal fact: Oswald worked in the building from which the President was shot and obtained the job there, unsuspiciously, three weeks before unsuspicious decisions were made (by Kenneth O'Donnell, Kennedy's friend) which occasioned the President's appearance in front of that building.

Stone tells us in the film that on the day of the assassination the Conspiracy "sent" Oswald to the building. But it did not have to; he reported for work as usual. What Stone does not tell us is that Oswald carried a gun to work that morning. A co-worker who drove him in (Oswald could not drive) reported that Oswald had a long object wrapped in paper which he held from below, cupped in his palm, military style. ("Curtain rods," was Oswald's answer to the obvious question.)

Paper that had been fashioned as a gun carrier was later found on the sixth floor, near the murder window. Oswald's fingerprints were on it, as was his palm print at the base where he would have cupped it in the manner described. Also on the bag were strands of wool from the blanket in which Oswald's rifle had been wrapped. There were no curtain rods. The murder rifle, Oswald's, which fired all the bullets and shells later recovered,[3] was also found on the sixth floor. On it were strands of wool from Oswald's shirt and Oswald's palm print.[4] Oswald's finger and palm prints were also on the card boxes used as a gun prop and on the brown bag. (Stone mentions none of this.) In addition, two eyewitnesses who saw the gunman in the window identified Oswald as that gunman.

According to Stone and the conspiracists, the plotters went to

[3] One wonders how the conspirators recovered and disposed of the embarrassing bullets from the other alleged guns. They could not have known where they would end up. Scores of collaborators would have been needed, at the ready, in the plaza, in the car, in the hospital, to snatch away the damning missiles without being noticed.
[4] Conspiracists make a good deal of the charge that there were no other prints on the gun. The charge is untrue. The FBI report did not say there were no other prints, it said there were no other "identifiable" prints, which is not unusual. As experts testified, the rough wood stock and poor-quality metal of the gun tended to absorb moisture from the skin, making a clear print unlikely.

extraordinary lengths to link Oswald to a rifle which they also claim was not used. But why not link him to the "real" gun? Viewers may remember very brief shots of a photograph of Oswald being altered. These shots are spliced into *JFK*, out of context and narrative sequence, in order to set the scene for Stone's later contention that a photograph of Oswald holding the murder rifle and pistol in his backyard was the crudest of forgeries. In that photo, the conspiracists say, two-thirds of Oswald's face has been pasted onto the chin and body of a stand-in. A distinct line across the chin shows the intervention clearly, and anyway the shadows cast by the nose are inconsistent with the shadows cast by the stand-in body.

What Stone does not tell us is that the photo was taken with Oswald's box camera, that his wife remembers taking it, that it is one of several taken of him with gun and pistol at that time, and that after exhaustive examination photographic experts employed by the House Assassinations Committee found even the challenged photo to be entirely unexceptionable, shadows and all. It also should be noted that this photo, found among Oswald's effects after the assassination, is superfluous to the proof that he possessed the gun: there are many other, superior, evidences of that.

Stone scoffs at the rifle, "the worst military weapon in the world." But the laugh is on him, for the neutron-activation analysis and ballistics findings prove that this supposedly defective rifle fired the bullet which deposited lead in Connally's wrist and also the bullet which hit Kennedy in the skull.[5] Someone used that rifle very effectively, and if it was not Oswald, Stone needs to explain why this brilliant Conspiracy, which used one world-class marksman, gave him the worst weapon in the world. He should also explain why, if the Conspiracy was framing Oswald, it would have wanted to link him to such a ridiculous weapon.

Oswald left the building immediately after the shooting, retrieved a light-colored jacket and pistol from his rooming house,

---

[5] The traces of silver and antimony in the lead removed from Kennedy's brain were compared to traces in the lead found in bullet fragments, fired from Oswald's gun, which were recovered from the presidential limousine. Again, as was the case with Connally's wrist, the match was perfect.

and about forty-five minutes after the assassination was seen shooting a Dallas policeman named Tippit. Twelve eyewitnesses identify Oswald as Tippit's assailant — although, to be sure, a few others, the ones presented by Stone and the A&E documentary, do not. The shells expended at the scene and the bullets in Tippit match the pistol found on Oswald when he was arrested. His jacket was found nearby. When the eyewitnesses reported the shooting to the police, using the radio in Tippit's car, police swarmed to the area. After a phoned report to them that a man had been seen ducking into a theater without paying, they rushed to the theater and arrested Oswald, who resisted, for the murder of Tippit. On him was the murder pistol; he had ordered it by mail, ten months earlier.

Astonishingly, Stone and many other conspiracists even question the contention that Oswald shot Tippit. Citing inconsistencies in eyewitness reports, which are to be expected in nearly all such reports, they imply that the bullets and shells were a plant, that the real ones were removed, that the jacket was a plant, and that the narrative by which the police traced Oswald to the theater was a contrived fiction.

What may have happened, according to Stone and the others, is that the Dallas police were expecting Oswald at the theater. They would murder someone in the neighborhood, a Dallas policeman murdered with the cooperation of Dallas policemen, and they would blame it on Oswald, presumably to prove that he was a murdering sort. The reader is invited to recapitulate the planning which would need to go into this part of the Conspiracy, involving now new bullet-snatchers and -replacers in the Dallas police, the elimination of anyone who could prove that Oswald was elsewhere than next to Tippit's car when the officer was shot, etc. Of course, all parties to this part of the Conspiracy have remained silent ever since.

It is often asked why Oswald denied having killed the President, as though guilty people do not deny things all the time. The fact is that Oswald denied everything. He himself was the first to insist that the backyard photo of him with the gun was a forgery. Shown it during his interrogation, he dismissed it at a glance. He denied having hunted in this country; he denied possessing the rifle, any rifle; he denied ever using the pseu-

donym Alec Hidell, which he had used to order the guns and on
several identification documents; he made up an easily contradicted story that the manager of the Depository brought a rifle
to the building; he denied the curtain rod tale, saying he carried
only his lunch to work that morning; he denied killing Tippit;
when asked his reason for visiting his estranged wife and children on Thursday, assassination eve, rather than his usual Friday, he made up a story about a birthday party; he denied using
an alias at his rooming house. He also refused to take a poly-
graph test. The law familiarly says that lies of this sort indicate a
"consciousness of guilt," especially if they are explicable only by
the hypothesis that the accused knows he is guilty.

To sum up: Oswald (1) worked in the building which was the
only source of shots; (2) owned and possessed the one and only
murder rifle; (3) brought it to work with him the morning of the
murder; (4) was at the murder window at the time the President
was shot; (5) left the scene immediately after the shooting; (6)
shot an officer who attempted to question him and then forcibly
resisted arrest; (7) lied about crucial matters of fact when inter-
rogated.

There is an eighth reason to believe he was the killer: this was
not his first assassination attempt. Among the photographs in
Oswald's effects were several of a house and adjoining driveway.
Weeks after the assassination, the FBI discovered that the house
in the photo was that of General Edwin Walker, a right-wing,
anti-Castro, anti–civil rights fanatic. The G-men irrefutably established the exact date the photo was taken, which turned out
to be just before someone unsuccessfully tried to assassinate
Walker on April 10, 1963. The photo was taken with Oswald's
camera; Oswald had a collection of news stories about the assassination attempt; bullets that had slammed into Walker's wall
were consistent with Oswald's gun; a note written to his wife at
the time, and her suspicions voiced then as well, indicate that he
was Walker's would-be assassin. In the Marines he had twice
been court-martialed, once for threatening a superior officer.
Needless to say, Oliver Stone tells us nothing of this.

Why would Oswald try to kill a right-wing general? An obvious
hypothesis, the one Stone and the critics feverishly try to silence,

is that the attempt had something to do with Oswald's intense left-wing sympathies. Stone's campaign to transform him into a long-term right-winger, in league with Castro-hating activists, involves biographical surgery even more radical than the surgery which allegedly transformed the President's wounds the night of the assassination.

Oswald was already a left-winger at the age of thirteen when he distributed pro-Rosenberg material in New York. He defected to the Soviet Union and attempted to commit suicide when, notwithstanding his offer of radar data, the land of his dreams refused him citizenship. Disillusioned with the Soviet Union, he returned to the United States and transferred his fantasies to a new hero, Castro, whose picture he kept by his bed. He monitored radio broadcasts from Havana on his shortwave radio.

Oswald subscribed to the Communist *Daily Worker* and the Trotskyist *Militant;* these are the newspapers he holds in the authentic photos of him with gun and pistol taken in his backyard. He formed a one-person chapter of the pro-Castro Fair Play for Cuba Committee (FPCC), handed out FPCC leaflets, which he himself printed, and spoke on the radio in its behalf. Imagining himself a Castro operative, and acting alone, as always, he briefly attempted to infiltrate an anti-Castro group in New Orleans but then immediately revealed his pro-Castro sympathies, to the group's considerable dismay. He composed a schmaltzy and horrifically spelled "historic diary," as he called it, and several paeans to Marxism. He visited the Cuban and Russian embassies in Mexico City in October 1963, seeking a visa to Cuba, and reacted in fury when denied his request.

This recital only scratches the surface of Oswald's left-wing record and his unstable, lone-wolf personality. But it is enough to sustain at least the possibility that the sole assassin of John F. Kennedy was a left-wing fantasist who found himself working in a building in front of which would come the President of the United States, the man whom Castro had publicly named as responsible for assassination attempts on his, Castro's, life. The same fantasist who went to the Soviet Union expecting to be accepted as a hero (and told his Russian wife that someday he would be "president of the world") now thought, incoherently, stupidly, that he would become a hero in Cuba as the assassin of Castro's enemies: General Walker and President Kennedy. Character, as the Greeks said, is fate.

IV

If there was only one assassin and he was Lee Harvey Oswald, if there was no massive frame-up or cover-up, then Stone's and every other conspiracy theory currently before the public are fatally wounded. The government's allegedly ubiquitous hand disappears. Absent that hand, what other grand conspirators — military industrialists, mafiosi — would use so unlikely a killer, stage so unlikely a killing?

For nearly thirty years, platoons of conspiracists have concertedly scavenged the record, floating their appalling and thrilling might-have-beens, unfazed by the contradictions and absurdities in their own wantonly selective accounts, often consciously, cunningly deceitful. They have refused to let go of any shred of their earliest suspicions, even when these have been demolished by decisive scientific findings. And the media have patronized them, for journalists love their thrilling insinuations and share many of their philosophical and political assumptions; and with regard to the assassination, they remain stone ignorant. Small wonder that 85 percent of the American public thinks there was a conspiracy of some sort.

Recently, thirteen thousand copies of a new study guide, sympathetic to *JFK*, were sent to American high school teachers. Our students know nothing about the case or the times; their teachers remember little, and many of them, especially the most "liberated," hold the view that to *question* any official version of anything is important in and of itself, even if the questions are based on palpable falsehoods. I do not think we should rejoice that our children ask questions in this manner. I think we should weep; and scold the scurrilous.

GERALD EARLY

Their Malcolm, My Problem

FROM HARPER'S MAGAZINE

LATE ONE AFTERNOON last spring I sat at home on my couch, disheartened, thumbing through an old copy of *The Autobiography of Malcolm X*. Earlier that afternoon I'd had a lengthy meeting with black students from my university, and although Malcolm X had been in the air on campus for some time — the proliferation of X caps and T-shirts, gossip about the Spike Lee movie, which would open at the end of the year — I suspect it was mostly the passionate and angry tone of the black voices at the meeting that prompted me to pull my copy of the book off the shelf.

I had reread *The Autobiography* many times, having taught it on several occasions. A considerable literary accomplishment, it borrows freely and innovatively from St. Augustine's *Confessions*, the slave narrative tradition, and the bildungsroman tradition of Fielding and Goethe. As a boy I felt it was the only book written expressly for me, a young black American male. But over the years my view changed: the book's rhetoric began to seem awkwardly out of date, and the energy of the man seemed contained in a vision that was as narrow as it was vivid; there was something about the nature of Malcolm's raillery that now left me unprovoked, something about his quest for humanity that left me unmoved.

But as I sat on the couch working my way through the narrative that afternoon, I found much of what I'd been moved by so long ago coming back to me with remarkable force. I read again with revived interest how Malcolm was born in Omaha in 1925, the seventh child of a father who was an itinerant preacher, a fierce follower of Marcus Garvey, and of a mother so light-skinned that she was frequently mistaken for white. When Malcolm was six years old his father was murdered, presumably by white terrorists, because of his black-nationalist beliefs. It is this death, as well as the institutionalization of his mother — who suffered a breakdown as the result of her husband's murder and her struggle to support her family on welfare — that establishes the pattern of both the book and the life as a critique of racism and liberalism. As Malcolm claims angrily, "I am a creation of the Northern white man and of his hypocritical attitude toward the Negro."

After growing up in a detention home in Mason, Michigan, and spending some time in Boston's Roxbury ghetto, living with his half-sister, Malcolm, at age seventeen, settled in Harlem and became a petty hustler and dope pusher. He participated in a string of burglaries of rich white suburban homes but was caught, convicted, and sentenced to ten years in prison. While in jail Malcolm converted to Elijah Muhammad's Nation of Islam, embracing a strict religious but militantly racialist outlook and dedicating himself to telling "the truth about the white man." Once out of prison, Malcolm became Muhammad's most effective minister and proselytizer, attracting adherents and also the attention of the white media. In 1964 Malcolm was excommunicated from the Nation, ostensibly for describing the assassination of John Kennedy as the "chickens coming home to roost." But a schism had been brewing for some time: Muhammad had become increasingly jealous over Malcolm's media attention, Malcolm's stardom, while Malcolm had become disillusioned by Muhammad's extramarital affairs and the older man's reluctance to become more politically active.

After leaving the Nation, Malcolm tried, unsuccessfully, to found two organizations, Muslim Mosque, Inc., and the Organization of Afro-American Unity, the latter patterned after the Organization of African Unity. During the last two years of his life, he traveled extensively in Africa and also made a pilgrimage to Mecca, during which he reconverted to a nonracialist Islam. He was assassinated in Harlem by members of the Nation of Islam in February 1965, just as he was about to give a speech. An angry end to an angry life.

Leafing through *The Autobiography*, I began to see that Malcolm X was the ideological standard of Africanness now being offered up by my students. His singular presence had been much in evidence at that afternoon's meeting. I had agreed to sit down with a coalition of black students — most of whom did not know me — soon after it was announced that I was to become the new director of African and Afro-American Studies at my university. In the weeks before we arranged to convene, I had been furiously denounced and publicly pilloried for not being sufficiently Afrocentric to head the department, a charge rather akin to being "not black enough" in the 1960s.

What I found particularly baffling about these attacks was that I do not possess any of the "social tokens" often associated with being "insufficiently black": I do not have a white wife; I have served on most of the university's affirmative action committees; I am intellectually engaged in the study of black subject matter; I have never publicly criticized any black person connected with the campus during my entire ten-year stay.

But in the eyes of these students, I had failed as a black man. I had never led a protest march or even proposed that one be held. I had never initiated or signed a petition. I had never attended any student meetings that focused on black issues. I had never, in short, done anything deemed heroic. And, for the young, a lack of demonstrable, outsized heroism is a lack of commitment and a lack of commitment is a sign of having sold out.

Some of this standard teacher-student strife is to be expected; I suppose it is generational. Still, I was deeply pained to have been seen by my black students as someone who compromised, who slouched, who shuffled, someone who had not stood up and been counted, someone who had never done anything heroic for the race.

When my ten-year-old daughter came home from school, she was surprised to find me home, and more surprised to find me visibly upset.

"What's wrong?" she asked.

"The American Negro," I began sarcastically, as she made herself a snack, "goes through periodic bouts of dementia when he romantically proclaims himself an African, lost from his brothers and sisters. These tides of benighted nationalism come and go, but this time it seems particularly acute." By now my voice had become strident, my rage nearly out of control.

"Never have I been subjected to more anti-intellectual, proto-fascistic nonsense than what I have had to endure in the name of Afrocentrism. And this man," I said, waving Malcolm's autobiography, "is the architect of it all, the father of Afrocentrism. This idiot, this fool." I slumped at the kitchen table, placing my forehead against the cool wood.

"But I thought you liked Malcolm X," she said.

Indeed, I was once keenly fond of Malcolm X. I first saw Malcolm on television in 1963, when I was a ten-year-old boy living in Philadelphia; three years later Malcolm, by now dead if not forgotten, left an indelible mark on my life. That year my oldest sister, then a college student, joined the local chapter of the Student Nonviolent Coordinating Committee (SNCC), which at the time was becoming an increasingly Marxist and militant group. Her conversation was now peppered with phrases like "the white power structure," "the man," "black power," and "self-determination for oppressed people." One day she brought home a recorded Malcolm X speech entitled "Message to the Grass Roots."

Hearing it for the first time was a shock and a revelation. I had heard men in barberships say many of the same things but never in public. I laughed and laughed at Malcolm's oratory, but I felt each word burn with the brightness of a truth that was both utterly new and profoundly familiar. Whenever I had the chance, I would play the record over and over. In a few days I had memorized the entire speech, every word, every turn of phrase, every vocal nuance. I could deliver the speech just as Malcolm had. I never looked at the world in quite the same way again.

During the days of segregation, which continued, de facto, into the sixties, belonging to an all-black institution — anything from a church to a social club to a Boy Scout troop — was like wearing a badge of inferiority. Participation in these groups was not a choice made by blacks but a fiat, decreed by whites, which clearly stated that blacks were not considered, in any way, part of the white world — for most blacks, a world where what happened, mattered. But Malcolm asserted blackness as a source of honor and accomplishment, not degradation and shame.

Within months of the time I first heard Malcolm's "Message to the Grass Roots," I not only had read his autobiography but had listened carefully to other of his speeches, such as "The Ballot or the Bullet" and "Malcolm X on Afro-American History." I had become knowledgeable about the Congo, Patrice Lumumba, the Bandung Conference, and the leadership of the American civil rights movement, topics that were hardly of interest to other boys my age.

Not everyone I knew responded enthusiastically to Malcolm X. I would often hear men in the barbershop making statements like "All that Malcolm X does is talk. In fact, that's what all them Muslims do is talk. Just another nigger hustle." And one day, when I was fourteen, my friend Gary became very angry with me when — with Malcolm X in mind — I called him black.

"Don't call me black, man. I don't like that. I ain't black," he said vehemently.

"We are all black people," I said. "You've been brainwashed by the white man to hate your color. But you're black, and you've got to accept that."

"I said don't call me black," he shouted. "What's wrong with you, anyway? You sound like you been hanging out with them Malcolm X guys. He was a phony just like all the rest of them Muslims. You sound like you snappin' out or something."

I was surprised at Gary's reaction. He was bigger and tougher than I was, and I assumed that he would view Malcolm as a hero, too. But when it became clear he didn't, I felt personally insulted.

"You're black, black, black," I said angrily. "Malcolm X was a great man who tried to free black people. What've you ever done to free black people? You're black and I'll call you black anytime I want to, you dumb nigger."

He hit me so hard in the chest that I fell down in the street, stunned and hurt by the blow.

"Don't call me that," he said, walking away.

It is unlikely that a young black person today would get swatted for defending Malcolm X. In fact, in many ways Malcolm's presence is more deeply felt in the black community now than at any time since his murder. The reasons for his enduring legacy are complex. Malcolm X does not remain an important figure in American cultural history simply because he was a charismatic black nationalist. Hubert H. Harrison, Henry McNeal Turner, Richard B. Moore, Martin Delany, David Walker, Elijah Muhammad, Alexander Crummell, Edward Wilmot Blyden, and Ron Karenga all were charismatic black nationalists of some sort in the nineteenth and twentieth centuries, and none is remembered as a distinct figure except by historians of African-American life and culture.

Malcolm was a fierce debater, a compelling public speaker, and a man of considerable intellectual agility. But, like Martin Luther King, he was hardly an original thinker: American blacks have been hearing some form of black nationalism — Ethiopianism, the back-to-Africa movement, Black Judaism, the Black Moors, Pan-Africanism, the Black Aesthetic, or Afrocentrism — for well over two hundred years. Malcolm's basic idea — a vision of millenarian race-based cultural nationalism culminating in a worldwide race war that would overturn European dominance forever — was, like the Puritanism of Jonathan Edwards, already hoary with age even when it seemed most current. But just as Edwards brilliantly disseminated Calvinist ideas, Malcolm, with valor and wit, popularized ideas about black nationalism, black self-determination, and a universal African identity.

More important, however, than Malcolm's ideas — that is, his popularizing of black nationalism — was, and is, Malcolm the man. His life unfolded like a myth, a heroic tale. He had the imprimatur of both prison (the mark of a revolutionary) and the street (the mark of the proletariat), which lent him authenticity. But, as a Muslim, he was also a firm believer in the bourgeois ideals of diligence, discipline, and entrepreneurship.

Then there was Malcolm's youth. Although generational conflict exists in many societies, it has a long and particularly intense history for blacks. Each new generation views its elders with suspicion, thinking them failures who compromised and accommodated themselves in order to survive among the whites. And each generation, in some way, wishes to free itself from the generation that produced it.

Malcolm's particular brand of youthfulness fed this desire. He embodied a daring and a recklessness that young blacks, especially young black men, have found compelling. At rallies I attended as a teenager in the early 1970s, men older than myself would describe the inspiring experience of having heard Malcolm live. They had, on several occasions a decade earlier, attended Savior's Day rallies, annual Muslim conventions during which Elijah Muhammad was scheduled to speak. But Malcolm would always appear on the dais first. He was supposed to serve, simply, as the warmup act, but for these young men he always stole the show. While black nationalist and separatist ideas coming from Elijah Muhammad seemed cranky, cultlike, backwaterish, and marginal, the same ideas coming from Malcolm seemed revolutionary, hip, and vibrant.

Malcolm arrived on the scene during the age of Kennedy and King, the blossoming of youth culture and the coming of rock and roll. Flaunting his youth as a symbol of masculinity and magnetic power, he exploited the generation gap among blacks. Because of Malcolm, the leaders of the civil rights movement were made, through their comparative conservatism, to seem even older than they were, more cowardly than they were, bigger sellouts than they were. He referred to them as "Uncle Toms" or as "Uncles," associating them with the conflated popular image of both Uncle Remus and Uncle Tom, fictional characters created by white writers, aged black men who "loved their white folks." Malcolm used this language even when talking about Martin Luther King, who was, in fact, younger than he was. And Malcolm remains forever young, having died at the age of thirty-nine. He — like the Kennedys and King — died the tragic death of a political martyr.

Malcolm, the dead hero, has grown in stature in our black consciousness even while other living former heroes are forgotten. It is telling to compare the current view of Malcolm with that of another important black figure of the 1960s, Muhammad Ali. Ali and Malcolm are often yoked together in the black mind: two militant Muslims, public troublemakers, disturbers of the peace. But today, those of us who lived through the 1960s return to thinking about Malcolm not simply because of his greater intellect but because we are unnerved by Ali now, by the brain damage he has suffered in the ring, by the way he has aged.

Malcolm remains frozen forever in his stern youthfulness, almost immortal, like a saint, while Ali is a mirror of our own aging and mortality, a busted-up, broken-down hero.

No doubt Malcolm's early death contributed to his enduring power for young people today. But it is the existence of *The Autobiography* that has mythologized him forever. If Malcolm — or Alex Haley (who assisted in writing *The Autobiography*) or Malcolm's wife, Betty Shabazz (who is said to have done extensive revisions on Haley's manuscript) — had not written his story, he would have died a negligible curiosity on the American political landscape in much the same way that, say, George Lincoln Rockwell or Father Divine did. Today it is rare to come upon a black student who has not read *The Autobiography of Malcolm X* or will not read it at some point during his or her college career. It has sold more than three million copies and is probably the most commonly taught and most frequently recommended book written by a black American male.

Malcolm, frozen in time, stands before us as the lonely outsider, a kind of bespectacled prince, estranged and embattled, holding a high-noon posture of startling and doomed confrontation. It is this man who has become for young blacks today the kind of figure that Thoreau, who espoused the overturning of generations and the uselessness of the elders in *Walden*, was for young whites in the late 1960s.

When I was growing up in the 1960s the goal for blacks was clear: equality and integration. The civil rights movement, which provided an arena for heroic political action aimed at destroying segregation, helped forge this consensus among blacks. Today blacks, confused and angered by the failure of "the dream," share little agreement about the future. There is a sense that integration has been halfhearted and has been achieved only at the expense of black identity.

To today's young, middle-class blacks in particular, Malcolm's espousal of all-blackness — the idea that everything black is inherently good and that blacks must purge themselves of white "contaminants" — may be especially crucial; it is certainly more important than it was to my generation. These young people have grown up, by and large, in an integrated world. Most of the

black students who attend the standard prestigious, private, re-
search-oriented university are the offspring of either black professional parents or a mixed marriage, have lived most of their
lives in mixed or largely white neighborhoods, and have attended white prep schools or predominantly white public
schools. When they arrive at a university that has an African or
Afro-American studies program, these students expect to find,
for the first time in their lives, an all-black community, one that
they have never experienced in the secular world, a sort of
intellectual "nation within a nation," to borrow W. E. B. Du Bois's
term. There they can be their "true" black selves. Yet in many
ways these black students share fundamentally the same values — a belief in upward mobility and the rewards of hard
work — as the whites who surround them. These students are
wholly neither inside nor outside of the American mainstream,
and they are unsure whether any ideal form of integration exists.
But, like Malcolm, they wish to rid themselves of their feelings
of ambiguity, their sense of the precariousness of their belonging. For many of them (and they are not entirely unjustified in
feeling this way) integration is the badge of degradation and
dishonor, of shame and inferiority, that segregation was for my
generation.

I also have felt great shame in the era of integration because,
as a student and as a professor, I have taken the money of whites,
been paid simply because I was black and was expected to make
"black statements" in order to be praised by whites for my Ne-
gro-ness. I have felt much as if I were doing what James Baldwin
described black domestics in white homes as doing: stealing
money and items from whites that the whites expected them to
take, wanted them to take, because it reinforced the whites'
superiority and our own degradation. Allowing the whites to
purchase my "specialness" through affirmative action has
seemed not like reparations but like a new form of enslavement.

And I worry about my daughters, wondering whether they
are getting too cozy with whites at school and whether they seem
too utterly middle class. So much are they protected from any
blatant form of racism that I fear they are likely never to understand that it existed and continues to exist today. At these times
I feel estranged from my children, knowing that I do not fully

understand their experience, nor do they understand mine. For instance, when we moved to an affluent white suburb they clamored for a golden retriever, no doubt because a neighbor down the street had a very attractive one. I adamantly refused to consent, thinking that purchasing a friendly, suburban, sit-com-type dog was another concession to white, middle-class taste. "I don't like dogs," I said childishly before I finally relented.

On occasions like this, when I have wanted to instill in my daughters a sense of "blackness," I tend to trot out a story about my boyhood. It is an anecdote that involves my friend Gary, and it took place about six months after our fight over Malcolm X. Think of my story as the black parent's jeremiad, a warning about the declension of the new generation. And once again Malcolm X seems central to it.

In order to get home from school each day, Gary and I had to walk through an Italian neighborhood. Often during these trips home, several older Italian boys and their Doberman pinschers would chase Gary and me, or a group of us, for several blocks. Once we hit the border of our black Philadelphia neighborhood, around Sixth Street, they would retreat. The Italian boys called this game "chasing the coons" or "spooking the spooks," and it sometimes resulted in a black kid being bitten by one of their dogs. The black kids never fought back; we just ran, later cursing the Italian boys, rhetorically wreaking all manner of vengeance upon them.

On this particular afternoon, both Gary and I had bought sodas and doughnuts, as we usually did, on our way home from school, and we were strolling along when we suddenly heard some voices cry out, "Get those niggers." We turned to see about five or six Italian boys and an unleashed Doberman coming after us. We started running like beings possessed. We were comfortably ahead and easily could have avoided getting caught when Gary abruptly pulled up and caught my arm.

"I'm tired of running from them guys. I ain't running anymore and neither are you."

"Hey, man," I said frantically. "Are you crazy or something? What are we gonna do? Fight 'em? You must be crazy. I'm getting out of here."

"You ain't going nowhere," he said angrily through his teeth.

"It's time we stood up for ourselves. I'm tired of having them white bastards chase me and laugh at me. If they beat us up, well, I guess that's one ass whipping we got to take. But I ain't running."

Gary turned his soda bottle over in his hand like a weapon and I reluctantly did the same. He picked up a brick from the street and I followed; we waited for the Italian boys to catch up. When they did they looked almost bewildered. They stood, perhaps twenty feet from us, slowly comprehending that we were standing our ground. For several moments, except for the growling dog, everyone was silent. Then one of them spoke.

"What you niggers doing walking through our neighborhood? We got a hunting season on jungle bunnies."

"We ain't causing no trouble," Gary said. "We just minding our own business. And if you come another step closer, I guarantee I'll put your ass in the hospital."

We all stood for what seemed the longest time, as if frozen in some sort of still life. I was gripping the brick and bottle so hard my hands ached. I felt ready, even eager, to fight, but I was also relieved when I realized we wouldn't have to.

One Italian boy mumbled something about watching ourselves "next time," and they all began to drift off.

As they were retreating, Gary shouted, "And we ain't no niggers. We're black. Don't ever call us niggers again."

At this I was more than slightly startled, but I was very proud, as if I had made a convert. I recalled at that instant something I had heard Malcolm X say on television, something like, "The so-called Negro has to stop the sit-in, the beg-in, the crawl-in, asking for something that is by rights already his. The so-called Negro has to approach the white man as a man himself." We felt like men, grown-up men, or what we thought grown-up men must feel like when they have been tested and found themselves adequate.

Never once have I told this story in any way that impresses my daughters. My youngest usually says, "Are you finished now, Daddy?"

They know the moral is something to the effect that it is good to be black and that it is something for which we must all stand up. "Yeah," my youngest says, "it's good to be black, but it's better

not to have to spend all your time thinking about how good it is
to be black."

So here I am, caught between my daughters, who find my race
lessons tiresome, and my students, who think me somehow insufficiently black. I need look no farther than Malcolm, old ally and
new nemesis, to find the source of this ambiguity. Malcolm embodied contradiction. He preached the importance of Africa, yet
he was the most American of men. His autobiography is the
quintessential Horatio Alger tale of the self-created individual. Even Malcolm's turn toward Islam, his attempt to embrace
something explicitly non-Western, is itself classically American.
Americans have long been attracted to the East — in the form
of nineteenth-century orientalism, twentieth-century Egyptol-
ogy, and the current-day popularity, among many middle-class
whites, of yoga and Zen Buddhism. Even Afrocentrism itself can
be seen as classically American in its urge to romanticize and
reinvent the past, much in the way that Jay Gatsby did.

And yet Fitzgerald's novel clearly warns against the temptation
to remake the past and the seduction of fraudulent identities. It
is in its defining of identity that Malcolm's thinking is uncomfortably rigid and finally false. He developed two distinct but related
beliefs about black identity: that blacks are not Americans and
that they are really Africans. "We are just as much African today
as we were in Africa four hundred years ago, only we are a
modern counterpart of it," Malcolm X said at Harvard in 1964.
"When you hear a black man playing music, whether it is jazz or
Bach, you still hear African music. In everything else we do we
still are African in color, feeling, everything. And we will always
be that whether we like it or not."

By preaching a romantic reunification with mythological Africa as a way of generating pride and racial unity, Malcolm
advocated a single identity for all black people, one that implic-
itly removed individual distinctions among blacks. In Malcolm's
view, individuality is a negligible European creation, while the
holy "community" — a creation of the African and other dark-
skinned peoples — is prized above everything else. The idea of
race as community, as invisible church, however, can demand a
stifling conformity; its popularity suggests that some aspects of

Afrocentrism, or all-blackness, as Malcolm popularized them and as they are preached in some quarters today, for from being imaginative or innovative, are utterly prosaic and philistine in their vision.

Despite the unrealistic romanticism of Malcolm's back-to-Africa preachings, he offers an important message for today's young blacks: that blacks are, indeed, as Du Bois argues, a people of "double-consciousness"; that both blackness and Americanness are real options, each having meaning only when measured against the other. Malcolm would not have argued with such passion and virulence against the validity of any kind of black *American* experience if he did not suspect that assimilation, that *being* American, was truly a rooted desire, if not a fulfilled reality, for most blacks. Yet he also knew that blacks in America cannot think about what their Americanness means without thinking about what it means to be of African descent: the two are inextricably bound together. As the historian Sterling Stuckey has argued, black people did not acquire a sense of what being African was until they came to America. They, like most people who came to this country, achieved their initial sense of identity through their clan — that is, slaves thought of themselves more as members of specific tribes or nations than as "Africans." Slavery compressed the diversity of African experience into one broad African identity, forcing blacks, in turn, to invent a collective sense of an African memory and an African self.

But Africanness is relevant to American blacks today only as a way of helping us understand what it means to be American. While it is necessary that we recognize our African ancestry, and remember that it was, in varying degrees, stripped away by slavery, we must acknowledge, finally, that our story is one of remaking ourselves as Americans. My world is shaped by two indelible ideas: first, that I was once an African, that I grew, generations ago, from that ancestral soil; and, second, that I will never be African again, that I will, like Joseph, not be buried in the soil of my long-ago ancestors.

Malcolm preached the necessity of being African at the complete expense of our American selves, a love of the misty past at the cost of our actual lives, our triumphs, our sufferings in the New World and as modern people. In this way, Malcolm merely increased our anxiety, further fueled our sense of inadequacy, and intensified our self-hatred and feelings of failure by providing us with a ready excuse: America is the white man's country, and the whites don't want you here and will never give you equal citizenship.

But it must always be remembered that our blood is here, our names are here, our fate is here, in a land we helped to invent. By that I have in mind much more than the fact that blacks gave America free labor; other groups have helped build this and other countries for no or for nominal wages. We have given America something far more valuable: we have given her her particular identity, an identity as a country dedicated to diversity, a nation of different peoples living together as one. And no black person should care what the whites want or don't want in the realm of integration. The whites simply must learn to live as committed equals with their former slaves.

Our profound past of being African, which we must never forget, must be balanced by the complex fate of being American, which we can never deny or, worse, evade. For we must accept who and what we are and the forces and conditions that have made us this, not as defeat or triumph, not in shame or with grandiose pride, but as the tangled, strange, yet poignant and immeasurable record of an imperishable human presence.

JEAN ERVIN

Afterthoughts

FROM IOWA WOMAN

I HAD BEEN HEARING about old maids and the dangers of becoming one all my life. It was said that once a woman reached thirty unmarried she was an old maid, which meant a domineering, fussy spoilsport who gossiped too much. But there were odd contradictions in my elders' composite pictures because I noticed that timid single women were often included with their too assertive sisters. Zona Gale's 1920s best-selling novel *Miss Lulu Bett,* though it seems overdrawn today, reflected many households where an unmarried sister or aunt became a virtual servant. But whatever her personality — domineering gossip or shrinking violet — if she remained unmarried, a woman was almost invariably referred to as a "girl" forever after. I got the impression that to be an old maid was akin to contracting an unmentionable disease. Certainly it was a family disgrace. A friend of mine whose older sister was living at home and working during the 1930s recalls that every morning at the breakfast table her mother would open up the paper and read off the announcements of engagements and weddings in their Boston suburb.

Single women were required to walk a tightrope, and though the very ones who eluded the epithet "spoilsport" might even be considered good sports, there was a catch there, too, for a good sport might be loose or easy, to use two of my parents' favorite terms. Some of the single women we knew came to Springfield and Northampton, Massachusetts, from little towns such as Turner's Falls and Chesterfield and Conway to find jobs and often stayed with relatives while they looked for work. Then they were expected to room in a boardinghouse. Others, who had parents in the area, lived on with their families until the older generation died. Married couples herded them like cattle into a pen marked "leftovers," and they were usually invited to someone's home only as an afterthought. More than once I had heard my mother say, "Oh, and bring Ginny" — or Ellie or Rose — "if you'd like; we haven't had her to the house in a long time." The "oh" told it all: it was a word you used when you added a postscript.

Although old maids were considered not quite up to code as females, I noticed that they had more freedom than married women and that they did not have to ask a husband for money to get a new pair of silk stockings or whether it was all right to skip making dinner in order to go to a meeting. Many of these unmarried women had become the financial mainstays of their families during the Great Depression. Because she had a good job even during the worst years, Mary's generosity to her sister's family meant that they had been able to keep their house when her brother-in-law was out of work and when many other people were losing their homes. She was domineering and often annoyed me with her rules and regulations that I, too, was expected to follow when I played with her niece and nephew. When we shared a cottage at the beach one summer, she got it into her head that we children should brush our teeth before eating a meal. Argue as I might, I wasn't able to shake her idea and for some reason my mother did not bother to interfere, so I found myself lined up with the other children dutifully brushing away before each meal. Momentarily, I could have killed her.

But Mary was as generous with her time as she was with her money, and she introduced us to complicated card games that were a godsend during some of New England's cold and rainy summer days. She was not prissy by any means and enjoyed a party as much as anyone. She was a great raconteur and told stories about growing up in a New England mill town during the early years of the century. Her daily adventures as a businesswoman in the small city of Springfield were as exciting to me as if they had taken place in Paris or New York. I can still see her as she sat in one of her good-looking skirts roaring with laughter after the punch line. Mary was a heavy smoker and one of the things that impressed me most was her ability to continue talking as smoke spilled from her nostrils. In today's sensible clean air world, it is hard to explain how impressive that was to a young girl in the 1930s, when few people worried about the dangers of smoking. Women who smoked then were considered not quite ladylike. What I detected in Mary's ability to wave her cigarette, tell a story, and snort smoke at the same time was a control over the world that too few of the women around me had achieved.

The ideal combination of nurturer and tyrant in the classroom, my favorite elementary school teacher, Miss Powers, was unmarried and probably over thirty, but I never thought of her as an old maid. She was extremely pretty and used a little more makeup than was considered respectable even during the 1930s, when lacquered faces were fashionable. She got me to grapple with fractions; no mean feat. She knew how to have fun, and I can still hear her marvelous laugh ringing through the classroom. I loved it when Mrs. Ryder from across the hall sent in one of her pupils with a picture of a spider or some other crawly creature because everyone knew it was the one thing that could make Miss Powers shriek. But if I sassed her or tried to put down another child, she had all the verbal equivalents of the ruler on the knuckle. I knew that she lived with her parents in a small town some distance away because they needed her support, financially and otherwise. This sort of arrangement was simply expected of single women at the time, and I don't recall anyone ever considering Hazel Powers a martyr or especially remarkable for her long drives to work and for living on with the old folks.

But there were Miss Lulu Betts hovering at the periphery of my family's social life, single women who laughed too readily at everyone else's jokes and asked polite questions of me as if they felt it was the price of being admitted to the magic circle of family life, if only for an afternoon or evening. My mother was forever trying to fix up Vi with any single male she and my father knew, and for a time she actually hoped that Vi would marry one of my father's colleagues, a man who was inclined to violence when he drank. Maybe Mother believed that by having stepped over the magic line into her thirties unwed, Vi couldn't be too particular.

My father's cousins, the Farrell "girls," in some ways came

closest to fitting the classic picture of old maids: they disapproved of alcohol and sometimes had narrow-minded attitudes toward people. For many years Marian and Clara had taught in the Springfield public school system and were financially comfortable. With their eighty-year-old mother, Ellen, they had developed a reverse parent-child relationship, teasing her about her tightfistedness, laughing that her black coat was turning green from age.

When I first knew her, Marian was about fifty and her hair was already snow white. Because she was more talkative than her sister and tended to blush and because her voice always suggested a little girl's, my mother and father decided that she was a lightweight. Clara, the elder of the two daughters, was the one they favored. I could see that she often put a damper on Marian's gushing, as though even at fifty Marian was still the little sister who rushed into things with a dangerous warmth and enthusiasm that might lead to trouble.

Ellen Farrell died in the late 1930s. A few years later, Clara had a stroke and Marian retired early from her teaching job to care for her. I don't suppose anyone ever suggested that she should do otherwise, although people in her school district told us that she was a successful and much-loved fifth-grade teacher; she often spoke affectionately of individual pupils, following their subsequent lives with genuine interest.

After her sister died, Marian was as lost as a widow who has devoted all her life to her family. Her teaching job and the two people she cared for most in the world were gone. She had friends and few of the financial problems that many women had in old age, particularly in those days, yet she seemed to be totally adrift, leaning on my parents for advice in any practical undertaking. All during the Second World War and in the austerity period afterward, Marian and Clara had sent a family of Scotch relations food packages, a thoughtfulness that must have made life much easier under Britain's grim living conditions. Not long after Clara's death, Marian wrote to them asking if she might visit for a week, but these small-minded people wrote back that it was quite inconvenient to have her stay with them.

Soon Marian decided that she could no longer drive her car — she was in her mid-sixties but seemed much older — and then with a rush came the broken hip, giving up her comfortable home, and moving in as a boarder with a rather chilly woman who took care of her physical needs but not much else.

My parents invited her to spend holidays and some weekends at their house, although she had to be fitted in around their time with friends and children. She was a leftover. One Christmas I had forgotten that she would be there for the family gathering. Hastily, I wrapped up an extra studio photograph of our eighteen-month-old son to give her, but it must have been obvious to her that it was an afterthought. The day was centered on our child, with both sets of grandparents making much of him; it could not have been easy for Marian to sit on the sidelines, but that is where life had placed her. At the end of the day, when my father and I drove her to the house where she boarded and helped her from the car — she was on crutches by then — Marian said to her landlady, "Shall I go upstairs or stay down here, Wanda?" clearly hoping that in the holiday spirit her landlady would invite her to sit downstairs for a while. But Wanda dismissed her. "You can go right up to your room," she said in a voice that told all. I was in my late twenties then, and with an icy shaft shooting down my spine, I envisioned the day when someone might send me upstairs.

Eight years earlier, in the summer of 1945, I was standing somewhere in the Chicago Loop waiting to meet a woman named Madge Clark. I was twenty and had gone from Massachusetts to stay in Winnetka with a classmate from Smith College while attending the summer session at Northwestern University. Madge was a retired governess, my great-uncle Ben's sister-in-law. She was not even a real relation but, because of my family's tendency to cling to any Scotch connection, my father had written to her telling her that I would be in the area.

Madge was wearing a small navy hat, white gloves, and a suitable blue print dress which I recognized as quality. Everything down to her navy purse and shoes spelled a proper lady. White-haired, blue-eyed Scotch men and women proliferated in our family, but I was surprised at how handsome she was, with fine bones and a trim figure. Her coloring made me think of snow and ice. Madge had come to Chicago from Scotland many years earlier to be near her sister Aggie, who was married to my great-uncle Ben, and there she had found a place as a governess. In another sense such women learned their place early in life and, short of marriage, expected nothing more than to keep a respectable job for as long as it lasted. And then, if their references were in order, they could hope to find another place. This usually meant living in. "Living in" is a peculiarly apt term, for it was not just a question of being given board and room for part of your salary. Live-in help lived in other people's lives as well as their homes.

As a governess, Madge was hired to "do" for the little girls and boys of men and women who did not want to be bothered with their own children. When I saw her in the summer of 1945 she had been retired for a time, but during the previous year one of her former charges, now grown and married, had called frantically. "Clarkie, you've got to help me out; I can't cope with these kids of mine."

"When I got thurr, I was shocked," she said in a soft Scots burr. "Mary Beth wants to do nothing but sit around her pool and drink cocktails instead of taking care of the gerruls." As the train bore us to our afternoon's destination, there was much clucking over Mary Beth's lapses as a mother, but I sensed that Madge's indignation was rhetorical, for her former charge's failings meant that she was needed once again. It was the eternal "I don't know what's happening to young people these days" response, and like so many grandmothers before and since her time, Madge had gone to the rescue of her surrogate child, now grown but forever a child in her eyes. She told me proudly that she had been teaching the little girls to write with a good hand, finish their homework, mind their manners, and get to bed on time.

"Now you can read their writing, they know to stand and curtsy whenever someone enters the room, and they're in bed at a decent hour, not hanging about where they've got no business downstairs."

When Madge had called to make this date with me, I expected nothing more than a dull but comforting chat about family news. But not at all. We were headed for the Washington Park racetrack. On the train she warned me, "Now watch out for your handbag, the place is overrun with the soldiers, and there're so many colored and foreigners and who-knows-what about. This town hasn't been the same since the war." I looked at the other passengers uneasily, yet she spoke so softly I hoped that no one around us could hear her.

I was a snob about racetracks because I associated gambling and racing with the disreputable side of my father's life. Certainly Madge's concerns with bringing up proper young ladies seemed at odds with a day at the races, and as for going to them without a man, it was at once unseemly and downright comical, like sex between people over the age of forty-five.

As we entered the racetrack grounds, I groaned inwardly; the noise and the crowds were worse than I had expected, and the place seemed to be populated chiefly with men in those clownlike but menacing outfits called zoot suits and women whose bright hair colors signified only one thing. The smells — a compound of horse dung, sweat, alcohol, and dimestore Lily of the Valley perfume — did nothing to reassure me. But it was clear that Madge was a habitué of the track, for she knew where the refreshment stand was located and soon was pressing into my hand a paper cup full of whisky. "This will help us pick the winners." Smelling the horrible stuff, I decided that only by faking sips would I ever be able to get through the afternoon without being sick, yet I did not have the nerve to refuse her. It was obvious that this was Madge's idea of a holiday.

Too many of my male relatives had taken to the bottle with a vengeance and some had died violent deaths as a result. My father was already a problem drinker and as a child I had grown to hate the very smell of alcohol, but when I entered college I found that I was made to feel like a kid hanging out with the grownups if I ordered a Coke while the rest of the group had something stronger. During several weekend trips to New York I had discovered the joys of sipping a Pink Lady or a Clover Club in the Biltmore Hotel cocktail lounge after meeting a date under the clock. This, I considered, was sophistication, worlds away from the shots of rye my father and his cronies would down standing at a bar. Young people often have very high standards for their elders, so I was uneasy at the sight of Madge drinking alcohol in the daytime and in public, too. It was all right for me to order a Pink Lady at the Biltmore, but not for a woman of my mother's age, and certainly not for Madge, who was nearly as old as my grandparents.

"Come now, dear, what do you think for the first race? Which horse appeals to you?" The afternoon's entertainment was serious business.

I hesitated since I had saved barely enough from farm work early in the summer to pay for my expenses. Even if I had had some loose cash, my distaste for betting would likely have prevented me. But good hostess that she was, Madge insisted that I take her money, urging this twenty-year-old snob from the East to loosen up, have a drink, place some money on the ponies. At this enormous track it was impossible to locate the horse I had bet on — Iwo Jima or Guadalcanal — and anyway I assumed the money had been thrown away. But Madge was visibly excited, although her voice never rose above the well-modulated tone suitable for the classroom. To my surprise, my horse came in first, and, embarrassed that I was feeling so ambivalent about the afternoon's entertainment, I tried to make her take my winnings. But she would not hear of it. "It's yours, lass, you picked the right one!"

Soon I got into the spirit and followed her lead. We lost on a few, but by the end of the day we were ahead by enough money so that Madge pronounced it "an afternoon well spent!" as though we had soaked up the cultural offerings of the Art Institute and the Museum of Science and Industry. Prig that I was, I doubt that I was fully able to take in the humorous scene: this blue-eyed, white-haired woman, the very picture of respectable grandmotherhood, studying her greensheet and placing her bets with the expertise of a Damon Runyon character while knocking back rotgut rye on a hot summer's day. What it certainly did take many more years for me to understand was that Madge's life may well have been so circumscribed by rules and regulations, those she had to impose on the children she cared for as well as the ones imposed on her, that a day at the races was a much-needed safety valve. She was having fun.

After the races, Madge announced that we were to dine at the Berghoff, a famous restaurant back in the city. As we entered, she pointed out the men's bar where women were not allowed and, like Madge, I accepted this, perfectly content to stand in line for twenty minutes before being shepherded to a table with a less than favorable location for two unescorted women.

Like many other things during the four years that America had been at war, cigarettes were in short supply, so we smoked a variety of peculiar weeds, some of them similar to the cornsilk I had been introduced to at the age of eight. When we were seated, resourceful Madge pulled out a package of little cigars called Puppies. I lit my Puppy expecting something slightly stronger than a Chesterfield or a Camel, but even a dedicated smoker like myself found it a challenge. The smell was somewhere between burning rubber and linseed oil, and I feared that each time I inhaled I'd have to bolt for the ladies' room, but I finally managed to puff away with Madge as we exchanged family news.

She told me that many years before, when her sister Aggie and my great-uncle Ben were to have a baby, she had come to Chicago to help out, but the baby died and there were to be no other children. Madge had stayed on and, over the years, they had formed a tight little island of family far from home. A few years before my visit, Ben and Aggie, both in poor health, had left Chicago for a warmer climate when Ben retired, and now, an old woman, Madge was on her own. I had seen Ben and Aggie a few times when I was younger, but to me they were simply an elderly couple who, for all I knew, had always been that age. During the late 1930s they had stayed with us in Massachusetts before sailing for a vacation in Scotland, and I had memories of Madge's sister Aggie as a rather grand lady with an impenetrable accent. Now for the first time it occurred to me that those staid old folks, with brown spots on their hands and faces, had once been young and in love; they had had a sex life and their own private tragedy.

I was just emerging from that stage in which it seems that the only friends worth having are those your own age, and as we talked I realized that Madge was confiding in me, not as an adult to a child, but as one adult to another. I was flattered that she would talk to me as if my opinion were worth something; it was the first time that I had become acquainted with an older family connection away from my parents and their tendency to pull the rug out from any naive admiration I might develop. So I was glad to sort out Madge for myself, with her odd combination of softspoken Old World gentility and her zest for some of the earthy pleasures in this city filled with New World push.

On another Saturday, we went after lunch to visit two more Scotch women. Staying in upper-class Winnetka, what I had not realized was that on some streets away from the glittering façade of apartment buildings and mansions on the Gold Coast of the Lake Shore Drive, most Chicagoans spent their lives in narrow little houses like the one the Campbells lived in. Unlike trim Madge, with her crown of white hair and her sapphire eyes, the Campbells were pedestrian in looks and manner, black-haired and fat and dull. One of them spent all of the time we were there ironing. Madge produced a pack of Puppies, and in the close quarters of the Campbells' home they smelled worse than ever. The talk dragged, and even peppy Madge seemed humdrum in the presence of the Campbells. I wondered why she had taken me there, but now I realize that, living in, she had no home of her own to take me to.

At the time, few of us could comprehend that those four years of war had created a deep ravine between the old America and the new. On one side stood women like Madge and the Campbells, who had learned to trim their lives to fit those of their employers. On the other side were many younger women, who might also have ended up caring for the children of the privileged or cleaning up after their parents had it not been for the opportunity provided by the world disaster. When the country geared up for war, defense plants met the labor shortage by hiring women and paying wages that far outstripped those of the average maid. These women discovered the pleasures of leading lives that were not in service to someone else, and in those four years America lost its servant class. Few returned to work as maids.

But Madge was not exactly a servant, for the governess has traditionally belonged neither downstairs nor upstairs. Just before I left home for Chicago, my mother had told me that Madge discovered a kickback scheme between the kitchen help and the family grocer at one place, and had brought the scam to the attention of her employer, an act which must have taken more than a little courage. And there was something else. Living in meant living with the quality, and perhaps Madge had learned to live *like* the quality in some ways.

I viewed her as a bit racy, but I was impressed by her independence because I was not accustomed to the women in my family being so self-confident. In getting about Chicago, Madge displayed none of the uncertainty that I so often discerned in my mother when she went to the smaller city of Boston for the day. Even more impressive was Madge's unapologetic enjoyment of Chicago, a far cry from the way Mother and her friends felt — they had to have a good story ready for their husbands when they got home. They were always saying, "He'd kill me if he knew how much I paid for . . ." or "I'd better get home by five or there'll be hell to pay." Madge was really part of my grandparents' generation, but she was a person in her own right.

In the 1940s, Madge's refusal to settle back into the prison of old ladydom took far more courage than it would today, when no one takes a second look if a white-haired woman gets on an overseas flight with running shoes and a backpack or decides to run for governor, but in 1945 older women were expected to "act their age," which meant drawing into a cocoon of dullness and conformity. And I see now that Madge was lonely and I was family, however tenuously. For a brief period that summer, perhaps she saw me as the niece she did not have in this country. With her good looks, her poise, and her commonsense intelligence, she would have been a much-valued addition to any family, and she must have commanded a good salary. But in recent years I have wondered if the children she raised repaid her in the most important way, with affection. If not, it did not show, for I never got a whiff of self-pity from her.

To many Easterners, Chicago was considered a joke in those days, a city that had burned to the ground only seventy-some years before, dubbed Hogtown and famous as the setting for lively gang warfare, notably the St. Valentine's Day Massacre of 1929. But to me, Chicago in 1945 was a cornucopia of urbanity, offering far more than I could gather up in the six weeks of the summer session at Northwestern. Through the friends I was staying with in Winnetka, I heard about the city's chic hangouts — or so they seemed to me — such as the Pump Room at the Ambassador East Hotel, where the waiters wore satin knee britches and coffee boys sported turbans and the dishes were flaming. I never made it to the Pump Room, but one evening after an outdoor concert at Ravinia Park, I drove with some friends to an elegant suburban cocktail lounge where the self-appointed sophisticate of our group ordered Ramos Fizzes all around. It was hard to swallow this frothy booze — it seemed like nothing more than a gin milkshake — but I considered that, like the Ravinia Festival concerts, a Ramos Fizz was part of the haut monde I had come West to find, unlike the Washington Park racetrack with its paper cups of rye.

The place I most longed to go was a nightclub of unimaginable glamour, and when Madge asked me what I hoped to see before I went back home, I mentioned the Edgewater Beach Hotel on Lake Michigan where they had dancing under the stars.

"Then we'll go, Saturday night."

Excited at the prospect of finally being at the Edgewater Beach, I wore my one good outfit, a black suit with a bolero jacket and bright yellow blouse. Madge had on one of her well-cut summer print dresses. In our prim little hats and white gloves, we must have looked exactly like mother and daughter at a proper tea party. At Madge's urging, I ordered a Planter's Punch and she insisted that I have the most expensive meal on the menu. As we ate dinner on the terrace, we watched a spotlit dancer execute what seemed to be Balinese–Latin American swirlings.

That night Madge talked more about the war than she had before, the experiences of her family still in Scotland, and the recent election in Great Britain, where Winston Churchill had been voted out of office.

"After all he's done for them, saving the country, such *ingratitude*." Several times she returned to those "incredible ingrates."

I was feeling increasingly uneasy about the evening. It was all too clear that we made a very odd couple in this Hollywoodish nightclub on the edge of a lake that was a virtual sea. Here I was at the start of my adulthood, with an old woman who was nearing the end of hers, a life of living in other people's lives. I was only half listening as Madge said, "I have a dear friend, Alf, a gardener who worked at one of my places here, but a great opportunity took him East."

Bored and let down by my foray into the elegant fleshpot, I wondered what had led me to an evening of drinking Planter's Punches and smoking the horrible Puppies with an elderly woman. The floor show at the Edgewater Beach alternated with a dance band that played the syrupy slow popular tunes of the day — "A Boy in Khaki, a Girl in Lace," and "When the Lights Go On Again All Over the World" — for couples doing the sedate fox trot. I felt that I should be here with some attractive Air Force pilot, and I could not imagine why Madge was going on about an old Scotch gardener whom she might marry when she finished her present job, for I couldn't imagine someone that age being in love.

Madge was subdued that night, perhaps realizing that this outing, which must have cost her a good deal of money, had fallen flat. She offered me an after-dinner brandy but, aware that we were both feeling out of place, I politely refused. After she had walked me to my train for Winnetka, we shook hands. "Goodbye, dear, my love to your folks." That evening, I was struck once again with the snow and ice of her coloring, but I saw too that there was fire underneath that northern ice; she had done her best to loosen up an old maid of twenty.

LAWRENCE OTIS GRAHAM

Invisible Man

FROM NEW YORK

I DRIVE UP the winding lane past a long stone wall and beneath
an archway of sixty-foot maples. At one bend of the drive, a
freshly clipped lawn and a trail of yellow daffodils slope gently
up to the four-pillared portico of a white Georgian colonial.
The building's six huge chimneys, the two wings with slate-gray
shutters, and the white brick façade loom over a luxuriant
golf course. Before me stands the hundred-year-old Greenwich
Country Club — *the* country club — in the affluent, patrician,
and very white town of Greenwich, Connecticut, where there are
eight clubs for 59,000 people.

I'm a thirty-year-old corporate lawyer at a midtown Manhattan firm, and I make $105,000 a year. I'm a graduate of Prince-
ton University (1983) and Harvard Law School (1988), and I've
written eleven nonfiction books. Although these might seem like
good credentials, they're not the ones that brought me here.
Quite frankly, I got into this country club the only way that a
black man like me could — as a $7-an-hour busboy.

After seeing dozens of news stories about Dan Quayle, Billy
Graham, Ross Perot, and others who either belonged to or frequented white country clubs, I decided to find out what things
were really like at a club where I saw no black members.

I remember stepping up to the pool at a country club when I
was ten and setting off a chain reaction: Several irate parents
dragged their children out of the water and fled. Back then, in
1972, I saw these clubs only as a place where families socialized.
I grew up in an affluent white neighborhood in Westchester, and

all my playmates and neighbors belonged somewhere. Across the street, my best friend introduced me to the Westchester Country Club before he left for Groton and Yale. My teenage tennis partner from Scarsdale introduced me to the Beach Point Club on weekends before he left for Harvard. The family next door belonged to the Scarsdale Golf Club. In my crowd, the question wasn't "Do you belong?" It was "Where?"

My grandparents owned a Memphis trucking firm, and as far back as I can remember, our family was well off and we had little trouble fitting in — even though I was the only black kid on the high school tennis team, the only one in the orchestra, the only one in my Roman Catholic confirmation class.

Today, I'm back where I started — on a street of five- and six-bedroom colonials with expensive cars, and neighbors who all belong somewhere. As a young lawyer, I realize that these clubs are where business people network, where lawyers and investment bankers meet potential clients and arrange deals. How many clients and deals am I going to line up on the asphalt parking lot of my local public tennis courts?

I am not ashamed to admit that I one day want to be a partner and a part of this network. When I talk to my black lawyer or investment-banker friends or my wife, a brilliant black woman who has degrees from Harvard College, law school, and business school, I learn that our white counterparts are being accepted by dozens of these elite institutions. So why shouldn't we — especially when we have the same ambitions, social graces, credentials, and salaries?

My black Ivy League friends and I talk about black company vice-presidents who have to beg white subordinates to invite them out for golf or tennis. We talk about the club in Westchester that rejected black Scarsdale resident and millionaire magazine publisher Earl Graves, who sits on *Fortune* 500 boards, owns a Pepsi distribution franchise, raised three bright Ivy League children, and holds prestigious honorary degrees. We talk about all the clubs that face a scandal and then run out to sign up one quiet, deferential black man who will remove the taint and deflect further scrutiny.

I wanted some answers. I knew I could never be treated as an equal at this Greenwich oasis — a place so insular that the word

"Negro" is still used in conversation. But I figured I could get close enough to understand what these people were thinking and why country clubs were so set on excluding people like me.

March 28 to April 7, 1992

I invented a completely new résumé for myself. I erased Harvard, Princeton, and my upper-middle-class suburban childhood from my life. So that I'd have to account for fewer years, I made myself seven years younger — an innocent twenty-three. I used my real name and made myself a graduate of the same high school. Since it was ludicrous to pretend I was from "the streets," I decided to become a sophomore-year dropout from Tufts University, a midsize college in suburban Boston. My years at nearby Harvard had given me enough knowledge about the school to pull it off. I contacted some older friends who owned large companies and restaurants in the Boston and New York areas and asked them to serve as references. I was already on a leave of absence from my law firm to work on a book.

I pieced together a wardrobe with a polyester blazer, ironed blue slacks, black loafers, and a horrendous pink, black, and silver tie, and I set up interviews at clubs. Over the telephone, five of the eight said that I sounded as if I would make a great waiter. But when I met them, the club managers told me I "would probably make a much better busboy."

"Busboy? Over the phone, you said you needed a waiter," I argued. "Yes, I know I said that, but you seem very alert, and I think you'd make an excellent busboy instead."

The maître d' at one of the clubs refused to accept my application. Only an hour earlier, she had enthusiastically urged me to come right over for an interview. Now, as two white kitchen workers looked on, she would only hold her hands tightly behind her back and shake her head emphatically.

April 8 to 11

After interviewing at five clubs and getting only two offers, I made my final selection in much the way I had decided on a college and a law school: I went for prestige. Not only was the Greenwich Country Club celebrating its hundredth anniversary but its roster boasted former president Gerald Ford (an honor-

ary member), baseball star Tom Seaver, former Securities and
Exchange Commission chairman and U.S. ambassador to the
Netherlands John Shad, as well as former Timex spokesman
John Cameron Swayze. Add to that a few dozen *Fortune* 500
executives, bankers, Wall Street lawyers, European entrepre-
neurs, a Presbyterian minister, and cartoonist Mort Walker, who
does "Beetle Bailey." [The Greenwich Country Club did not
respond to any questions from *New York* magazine about the club
and its members.]

For three days, I worked on my upper-arm muscles by walking
around the house with a sterling silver tray stacked high with
heavy dictionaries. I allowed a mustache to grow in, then added
a pair of arrestingly ugly Coke-bottle reading glasses.

April 12 (Sunday)

Today was my first day at work. My shift didn't start until 10:30
A.M., so I laid out my clothes at home: a white button-down shirt,
freshly ironed cotton khaki pants, white socks, and white leather
sneakers. I'd get my official club uniform in two days. Looking
in my wallet, I removed my American Express gold card, my
Harvard Club membership ID, and all of my business cards.

When I arrived at the club, I entered under the large portico,
stepping through the heavy doors and onto the black and white
checkerboard tiles of the entry hall.

A distracted receptionist pointed me toward Mr. Ryan's[1] office. I walked past glistening silver trophies and a guest book on
a pedestal to a windowless office with three desks. My new boss
waved me in and abruptly hung up the phone.

"Good morning, Larry," he said with a sufficiently warm smile.
The tight knot in his green tie made him look more fastidious
than I had remembered from the interview.

"Hi, Mr. Ryan. How's it going?"

Glancing at his watch to check my punctuality, he shook my
hand and handed me some papers. "Oh, and by the way, where'd
you park?"

"In front, near the tennis courts."

Already shaking his head, he tossed his pencil onto the desk.

---

[1] All names of club members and personnel have been changed.

"That's off limits to you. You should always park in the back, enter in the back, and leave from the back. No exceptions."

"I'll do the forms right now," I said. "And then I'll be an official busboy."

Mr. Ryan threw me an ominous nod. "And Larry, let me stop you now. We don't like that term 'busboy.' We find it demeaning. We prefer to call you busmen."

Leading me down the center stairwell to the basement, he added, "And in the future, you will always use the back stairway by the back entrance." He continued to talk as we trotted through a maze of hallways. "I think I'll have you trail with Carlos or Hector — no, Carlos. Unless you speak Spanish?"

"No." I ran to keep up with Mr. Ryan.

"That's the dishwasher room, where Juan works. And over here is where you'll be working." I looked at the brass sign. MEN'S GRILL.

It was a dark room with a mahogany finish, and it looked like a library in a large Victorian home. Dark walls, dark wood-beamed ceilings. Deep-green wool carpeting. Along one side of the room stood a long, highly polished mahogany bar with liquor bottles, wineglasses, and a two-and-a-half-foot-high silver trophy. Fifteen heavy round wooden tables, each encircled with four to six broad wooden armchairs padded with green leather on the backs and seats, broke up the room. A big-screen TV was set into the wall along with two shelves of books.

"This is the Men's Grill," Mr. Ryan said. "Ladies are not allowed except on Friday evenings."

Next was the brightly lit connecting kitchen. "Our kitchen serves hot and cold foods. You'll work six days a week here. The club is closed on Mondays. The kitchen serves the Men's Grill and an adjoining room called the Mixed Grill. That's where the ladies and kids can eat."

"And what about men? Can they eat in there, too?"

This elicited a laugh. "Of course they can. Time and place restrictions apply only to women and kids."

He showed me the Mixed Grill, a well-lit, pastel-blue room with glass French doors and white wood trim.

"Guys, say hello to Larry. He's a new busman at the club."

I waved.

"And this is Rick, Stephen, Drew, Buddy, and Lee." Five white waiters dressed in white polo shirts with blue "1892" club insignias nodded while busily slicing lemons.

"And this is Hector and Carlos, the other busmen." Hector, Carlos, and I were the only nonwhites on the serving staff. They greeted me in a mix of English and Spanish.

"Nice to meet all of you," I responded.

"Thank God," one of the taller waiters cried out. "Finally — somebody who can speak English."

Mr. Ryan took me and Carlos through a hall lined with old black-and-white portraits of former presidents of the club. "This is our one hundredth year, so you're joining the club at an important time," Mr. Ryan added before walking off. "Carlos, I'm going to leave Larry to trail with you — and no funny stuff."

Standing outside the ice room, Carlos and I talked about our pasts. He was twenty-five, originally from Colombia, and hadn't finished school. I said I had dropped out, too.

As I stood there talking, Carlos suddenly gestured for me to move out of the hallway. I looked behind me and noticed something staring down at us. "A video camera?"

"They're around," Carlos remarked quietly while scooping ice into large white tubs. "Now watch me scoop ice."

After we carried the heavy tubs back to the grill, I saw another video camera pointed down at us. I dropped my head.

"You gonna live in the Monkey House?" Carlos asked.

"What's that?"

We climbed the stairs to take our ten-minute lunch break before work began. "Monkey House is where workers live here," Carlos said.

I followed him through a rather filthy utility room and into a huge white kitchen. We got on line behind about twenty Hispanic men and women — all dressed in varying uniforms. At the head of the line were the white waiters I'd met earlier.

I was soon handed a hot plate with two red lumps of rice and some kind of sausage-shaped meat. There were two string beans, several pieces of zucchini, and a thin, broken slice of dried meat loaf that looked as if it had been cooked, burned, frozen, and then reheated.

I followed Carlos, plate in hand, out of the kitchen. To my

surprise, we walked back into the dank and dingy utility room, which turned out to be the workers' dining area.

The white waiters huddled together at one end of the tables, while the Hispanic workers ate quietly at the other end. Before I could decide which end to integrate, Carlos directed me to sit with him on the Hispanic end.

I was soon back downstairs working in the grill. At my first few tables, I tried to avoid making eye contact with members as I removed dirty plates and wiped down tables and chairs. I was sure I'd be recognized.

At around 1:15, four men who looked to be in their mid- to late fifties sat down at a six-chair table while pulling off their cotton windbreakers and golf sweaters.

"It's these damned newspeople that cause all the problems," said Golfer No. 1, shoving his hand deep into a popcorn bowl. "These Negroes wouldn't even be thinking about golf. They can't afford to join a club, anyway."

Golfer No. 2 squirmed out of his navy-blue sweater and nodded in agreement. "My big problem with this Clinton fellow is that he apologized." As I stood watching from the corner of the bar, I realized the men were talking about Governor Bill Clinton's recent apology for playing at an all-white golf club in Little Rock, Arkansas.

"Holt, I couldn't agree with you more," added Golfer No. 3, a hefty man who was biting off the end of a cigar.

"You got any iced tea?" Golfer No. 1 asked as I put the silverware and menus around the table. Popcorn flew out of his mouth as he attempted to speak and chew at the same time.

"Yes, we certainly do."

Golfer No. 3 removed a beat-up Rolex from his wrist. "It just sets a bad precedent. Instead of apologizing, he should try to discredit them — undercut them somehow. What's to apologize for?" I cleared my throat and backed away from the table.

Suddenly, Golfer No. 1 waved me back to his side. "Should we get four iced teas or just a pitcher and four glasses?"

"I'd be happy to bring whatever you'd like, sir."

Throughout the day, I carried "bus buckets" filled with dirty dishes from the grill to the dishwasher room. And each time I returned to the grill, I scanned the room for recognizable faces.

After almost four hours of running back and forth, clearing dishes, wiping down tables, and thanking departing members who left spilled coffee, dirty napkins, and unwanted business cards in their wake, I helped out in the coed Mixed Grill.

"Oh, busboy," a voice called out as I made the rounds with two pots of coffee. "Here, busboy. Here, busboy," the woman called out. "Busboy, my coffee is cold. Give me a refill."

"Certainly, I would be happy to." I reached over for her cup.

The fiftyish woman pushed her hand through her straw-blonde hair and turned to look me in the face. "Decaf, thank you."

"You are quite welcome."

Before I turned toward the kitchen, the woman leaned over to her companion. "My goodness. Did you hear that? That busboy has diction like an educated white person."

A curly-haired waiter walked up to me in the kitchen. "Larry, are you living in the Monkey House?"

"No, but why do they call it that?"

"Well, no offense against you, but it got that name since it's the house where the workers have lived at the club. And since the workers used to be Negroes — blacks — it was nicknamed the Monkey House. And the name just stuck — even though Negroes have been replaced by Hispanics."

April 13 (Monday)

I woke up and felt a pain shooting up my calves. As I turned to the clock, I realized I'd slept for eleven hours. I was thankful the club is closed on Mondays.

April 14 (Tuesday)

Rosa, the club seamstress, measured me for a uniform in the basement laundry room while her barking gray poodle jumped up on my feet and pants. "Down, Margarita, down," Rosa cried with pins in her mouth and marking chalk in her hand. But Margarita ignored her and continued to bark and do tiny pirouettes until I left with all of my new country club polo shirts and pants.

Today, I worked exclusively with the "veterans," including sixty-five-year-old Sam, the Polish bartender in the Men's Grill.

Hazel, an older waitress at the club, is quick, charming, and smart — the kind of waitress who makes any restaurant a success. She has worked for the club nearly twenty years and has become quite territorial with certain older male members.

Members in the Mixed Grill talked about hotel queen and Greenwich resident Leona Helmsley, who was on the clubhouse TV because of her upcoming prison term for tax evasion.

"I'd like to see them haul her off to jail," one irate woman said to the rest of her table. "She's nothing but a garish you-know-what."

"In every sense of the word," nodded her companion as she adjusted a pink headband in her blondish-white hair. "She makes the whole town look bad. The TV keeps showing those aerial shots of Greenwich and that dreadful house of hers."

A third woman shrugged her shoulders and looked into her bowl of salad. "Well, it is a beautiful piece of property."

"Yes, it is," said the first woman. "But why here? She should be in those other places like Beverly Hills or Scarsdale or Long Island, with the rest of them. What's she doing here?"

Woman No. 3 looked up. "Well, you know, he's not Jewish."

"Really?"

"So that explains it," said the first woman with an understanding expression on her tanned forehead. "Because, you know, the name didn't sound Jewish."

The second woman agreed: "I can usually tell."

April 15 (Wednesday)

Today, we introduced a new extended menu in the two grill rooms. We added shrimp quesadillas ($6) to the appetizer list — and neither the members nor Hazel could pronounce the name of the dish or fathom what it was. One man pounded on the table and demanded to know which country the dish had come from. He told Hazel how much he hated "changes like this. I like to know that some things are going to stay the same."

Another addition was the "New Dog in Town" ($3.50). It was billed as knackwurst, but one woman of German descent sent the dish back: "This is not knackwurst — this is just a big hot dog."

As I wiped down the length of the men's bar, I noticed a tall stack of postcards with color photos of nude busty women waving hello from sunny faraway beaches. I saw they had been sent from vacationing members with fond regards to Sam or Hazel. Several had come from married couples. One glossy photo boasted a detailed frontal shot of a red-haired beauty who was naked except for a shoestring around her waist. On the back, the message said, Dear Sam, Pull string in an emergency. Love always, The Atkinson Family.

April 16 (Thursday)
This afternoon, I realized I was doing okay. I was fairly comfortable with my few "serving" responsibilities and the rules that related to them:

• When a member is seated, bring out the silverware, cloth napkin, and a menu.
• Never take an order for food, but always bring water or iced tea if it is requested by a member or waiter.
• When a waiter takes a chili or salad order, bring out a basket of warm rolls and crackers, along with a scoop of butter.
• When getting iced tea, fill a tall glass with ice and serve it with a long spoon, a napkin on the bottom, and a lemon on the rim.
• When a member wants his alcoholic drink refilled, politely respond, "Certainly, I will have your waiter come right over."
• Remember that the member is always right.
• Never make offensive eye contact with a member or his guest.
• When serving a member fresh popcorn, serve to the left.
• When a member is finished with a dish or glass, clear it from the right.
• Never tell a member that the kitchen is out of something.

But there were also some "informal" rules that I discovered (but did not follow) while watching the more experienced waiters and kitchen staff in action:

• If you drop a hot roll on the floor in front of a member, apologize and throw it out. If you drop a hot roll on the floor in the kitchen, pick it up and put it back in the bread warmer.

- If you have cleared a table and are 75 percent sure that the member did not use the fork, put it back in the bin with the other clean forks.
- If, after pouring one glass of Coke and one of diet Coke, you get distracted and can't remember which is which, stick your finger in one of them to taste it.
- If a member asks for decaffeinated coffee and you have no time to make it, use regular and add water to cut the flavor.
- When members complain that the chili is too hot and spicy, instead of making a new batch, take the sting out by adding some chocolate syrup.
- If you're making a tuna on toasted wheat and you accidentally burn one side of the bread, don't throw it out. Instead, put the tuna on the burned side and lather on some extra mayo.

April 17 (Friday)

Today, I heard the word "nigger" four times. And it came from someone on the staff.

In the grill, several members were discussing Arthur Ashe, who had recently announced that he had contracted AIDS through a blood transfusion.

"It's a shame that poor man has to be humiliated like this," one woman golfer remarked to a friend over pasta and vegetable salad. "He's been such a good example for his people."

"Well, quite frankly," added a woman in a white sun visor, "I always knew he was gay. There was something about him that just seemed too perfect."

"No, Anne, he's not gay. It came from a blood transfusion."

"Umm," said the woman. "I suppose that's a good reason to stay out of all those big city hospitals. All that bad blood moving around."

Later that afternoon, one of the waiters, who had worked in the Mixed Grill for two years, told me that Tom Seaver and Gerald Ford were members. Of his brush with greatness, he added, "You know, Tom's real first name is George."

"That's something."

"And I've seen O. J. Simpson here, too."

"O. J. belongs here, too?" I asked.

"Oh, no, there aren't any black members here. No way. I

actually don't even think there are any Jews here, either."

"Really? Why is that?" I asked.

"I don't know. I guess it's just that the members probably want to have a place where they can go and not have to think about Jews, blacks, and other minorities. It's not really hurting anyone. It's really a WASP club. . . . But now that I think of it, there is a guy here who some people think is Jewish, but I can't really tell. Upstairs, there's a Jewish secretary too."

"And what about O. J.?"

"Oh, yeah, it was so funny to see him out there playing golf on the eighteenth hole." The waiter paused and pointed outside the window. "It never occurred to me before, but it seemed so odd to see a black man with a golf club here on this course."

April 18 (Saturday)

When I arrived, Stephen, one of the waiters, was hanging a poster and sign-up sheet for a soccer league whose main purpose was to "bridge the ethnic and language gap" between white and Hispanic workers at the country clubs in the Greenwich area. I congratulated Stephen on his idea.

Later, while I was wiping down a table, I heard a member snap his fingers in my direction. I turned to see a group of young men smoking cigars. They seemed to be my age or a couple of years younger. "Hey, do I know you?" the voice asked.

As I turned slowly toward the voice, I could hear my own heartbeat. I was sure it was someone I knew.

"No," I said, approaching the blond cigar smoker. He had on light green khaki pants and a light yellow V-neck cotton sweater adorned with a tiny green alligator. As I looked at the other men seated around the table, I noticed that all but one had alligators on their sweaters or shirts.

"I didn't think so. You must be new — what's your name?"

"My name is Larry. I just started a few days ago."

The cigar-smoking host grabbed me by the wrist while looking at his guests. "Well, Larry, welcome to the club. I'm Mr. Billings. And this is Mr. Dennis, a friend and new member."

"Hello, Mr. Dennis," I heard myself saying to a freckle-faced young man who puffed uncomfortably on his fat roll of tobacco.

The first cigar smoker gestured for me to bend over as if he were about to share some important confidence. "Now, Larry, here's what I want you to do. Go get us some of those peanuts and then give my guests and me a fresh ashtray. Can you manage that?"

It was Easter Sunday, and the Easter-egg hunt began with dozens of small children scampering around the tulips and daffodils while well-dressed parents watched wistfully from the rear patio of the club. A giant Easter bunny gave out little baskets filled with jelly beans to parents and then hopped over to the bushes, where he hugged the children. As we peered out from the closed blinds in the grill, we saw women in mink, husbands in gray suits, children in Ralph Lauren and Laura Ashley. Hazel let out a sigh. "Aren't they beautiful?" she said. For just a moment, I found myself agreeing.

As I raced around taking out orders of coffee and baskets of hot rolls, I got a chance to see groups of families. Fathers seemed to be uniformly taller than six feet. Most of them were wearing blue blazers, white shirts, and incredibly out-of-style silk ties — the kind with little blue whales or little green ducks floating downward. They were bespectacled and conspicuously clean-shaven.

The "ladies," as the club prefers to call them, almost invariably had straight blonde hair. Whether or not they had brown roots and whether they were twenty-five or forty-eight, ladies wore their hair blonde, straight, and off the face. No dangling earrings, five-carat diamonds, or designer handbags. Black velvet or pastel headbands were de rigueur.

There were also groups of high school kids who wore torn jeans, sneakers or unlaced L. L. Bean shoes and sweatshirts that said things like HOTCHKISS LACROSSE or ANDOVER CREW. At one table, two boys sat talking to two girls.

"No way, J.C.," one of the girls cried in disbelief while playing with the straw in her diet Coke.

The strawberry-blonde girl next to her flashed her unpainted nails in the air. "Way. She said that if she didn't get her grades up by this spring, they were going to take her out altogether."

"And where would they send her?" one of the guys asked.

The strawberry blonde's grin disappeared as she leaned in close. "Public school."

The group, in hysterics, shook the table. The guys stomped their feet.

"Oh, my God, J.C., oh, J.C., J.C.," the diet Coke girl cried.

Sitting in a tableless corner of the room, beneath the TV, was a young, dark-skinned black woman dressed in a white uniform and a thick wool coat. On her lap was a baby with silky white-blond hair. The woman sat patiently, shifting the baby in her lap while glancing over to where the baby's family ate, two tables away.

I ran to the kitchen, brought back a glass of tea, and offered it to her. The woman looked up at me, shook her head, and then turned back to the gurgling infant.

April 21 (Tuesday)

While Hector and I stood inside a deep walk in freezer, we scooped balls of butter into separate butter dishes and talked about our plans. "Will you go finish school sometime?" he asked as I dug deep into a vat of frozen butter.

"Maybe. In a couple years, when I save more money, but I'm not sure."

I felt lousy about having to lie.

Just as we were all leaving for the day, Mr. Ryan came down to hand out the new policies for those who were going to live in the Monkey House. Since it had recently been renovated, the club was requiring all new residents to sign the form. The policy included a rule that forbade employees to have overnight guests. Rule 14 stated that the club management had the right to enter an employee's locked bedroom at any time, without permission and without giving notice.

As I was making rounds with my coffeepots, I overheard a raspy-voiced woman talking to a mother and daughter who were thumbing through a catalogue of infants' clothing.

"The problem with au pairs is that they're usually only in the country for a year."

The mother and daughter nodded in agreement.

"But getting one that is a citizen has its own problems. For example, if you ever have to choose between a Negro and one of these Spanish people, always go for the Negro."

One of the women frowned, confused. "Really?"

"Yes," the raspy-voiced woman responded with cold logic.

"Even though you can't trust either one, at least Negroes speak English and can follow your directions."

Before I could refill the final cup, the raspy-voiced woman looked up at me and smiled. "Oh, thanks for the refill, Larry."

April 22 (Wednesday)

"This is our country, and don't you forget it. They came here and have to live by our rules!" Hazel pounded her fist into the palm of her pale white hand.

I had made the mistake of telling her I had learned a few Spanish phrases to help me communicate better with some of my co-workers. She wasn't impressed.

"I'll be damned if I'm going to learn or speak one word of Spanish. And I'd suggest you do the same," she said. She took a long drag on her cigarette while I loaded the empty shelves with clean glasses.

Today, the TV was tuned to testimony and closing arguments from the Rodney King police-beating trial in California.

"I am so sick of seeing that awful videotape," one woman said to friends at her table. "It shouldn't be on TV."

At around two, Lois, the club's official secretary, asked me to help her send out a mailing to six hundred members after my shift.

She took me up to her office on the main floor and introduced me to the two women who sat with her.

"Larry, this is Marge, whom you'll talk with in three months, because she's in charge of employee benefits."

I smiled at the brunette.

"And Larry, this is Sandy, whom you'll talk with after you become a member at the club, because she's in charge of members' accounts."

Both Sandy and I looked up at Lois with shocked expressions.

Lois winked, and at the same moment, the three jovial women burst out laughing.

Lois sat me down at a table in the middle of the club's cavernous ballroom and had me stamp ANNUAL MEMBER GUEST on the bottom of small postcards and stuff them into envelopes.

As I sat in the empty ballroom, I looked around at the mirrors and the silver and crystal chandeliers that dripped from the high ceiling. I thought about all the beautiful weddings and debutante balls that must have taken place in that room. I could imagine members asking themselves, "Why would anybody who is not like us want to join a club where they're not wanted?"

I stuffed my last envelope, forgot to clock out, and drove back to the Merritt Parkway and into New York.

April 23 (Thursday)

"Wow, that's great," I said to Mr. Ryan as he posted a memo entitled "Employee Relations Policy Statement: Employee Golf Privileges."

After quickly reading the memo, I realized this "policy" was a crock. The memo opened optimistically: "The club provides golf privileges for staff. . . . Current employees will be allowed golf privileges as outlined below." Unfortunately, the only employees that the memo listed "below" were department heads, golf-management personnel, teaching assistants, the general manager, and "key staff that appear on the club's organizational chart."

At the end of the day, Mr. Ryan handed me my first paycheck. The backbreaking work finally seemed worthwhile. When I opened the envelope and saw what I'd earned — $174.04 for five days — I laughed out loud.

Back in the security of a bathroom stall, where I had periodically been taking notes since my arrival, I studied the check and thought about how many hours — and how hard — I'd worked for so little money. It was less than one tenth of what I'd make in the same time at my law firm. I went upstairs and asked Mr. Ryan about my paycheck.

"Well, we decided to give you $7 an hour," he said in a tone overflowing with generosity. I had never actually been told my hourly rate. "But if the check looks especially big, that's because you got some extra pay in there for all of your terrific work on Good Friday. And by the way, Larry, don't tell the others what you're getting, because we're giving you a special deal and it's really nobody else's business."

I nodded and thanked him for his largess. I stuffed some more envelopes, emptied out my locker, and left.

The next morning, I was scheduled to work a double shift. Instead, I called and explained that I had a family emergency and would have to quit immediately. Mr. Ryan was very sympathetic and said I could return when things settled down. I told him, "No, thanks," but asked that he send my last paycheck to my home. I put my uniform and the key to my locker in a brown padded envelope, and I mailed it all to Mr. Ryan.

Somehow it took two months of phone calls for me to get my final paycheck ($123.74, after taxes and a $30 deduction).

I'm back at my law firm now, dressed in one of my dark gray Paul Stuart suits, sitting in a handsome office thirty floors above midtown. It's a long way from the Monkey House, but we have a long way to go.

DANIEL HARRIS

Cuteness

FROM SALMAGUNDI

SHE STANDS IN maroon bloomers and a pink dress that flares
tantalizingly above two acrylic legs that descend, unvaried in
diameter, all the way down to her gout-stricken ankles crammed
in her booties. Her feet, crippled and pigeon-toed, touch at their
tips. A sassy tuft of a synthetic topknot sprays out of a helmet of
auburn hair encircled by a polka-dot bow that sits atop her head
like a windmill, dwarfing the rest of her figure. Her nose is no
bigger than a button, and her astonishingly candid eyes are two
moist pools framed by eyebrows penciled like quizzical circum-
flexes on the vast dome of her forehead. Emptied of all internal
life, these mesmerizing orbs, composing at least 25 percent of a
face as wide as her shoulders, stare out directly at us with a
reticence exaggerated by the hectic flush of her complexion. Her
name is So Shy Sherri, and she is one of toy manufacturer
Galoob's nine new "Baby Faces" — a set of "superposin' " dolls
with names like So Sweet Sandi, So Sorry Sarah, and So Delightful Dee Dee, each with an "adorable" expression and personality
of her own.

Everywhere we turn we see cuteness, from cherubic figures
batting their peepers on Charmin toilet paper to teddy bears
frozen mid-embrace, the stubs of their pawless arms groping for
hugs. Within their natural setting of the consumeristic landscape, such sentimental products of the modern sensibility are so
commonplace that they have become the most invasive type of
image possible, a form of visual clutter we respond to without
really seeing. We tend to think of them not as inventions of the

eighteenth or nineteenth century but as something that tran-
scends history altogether and constitutes instead the timeless
and universal appearance of purity, instinct, and spontaneity. In
the eyes of most people, whose conditioned responses to this
most schematic of styles prevent them from recognizing its glaring artificiality, things like calendars with droopy-eyed puppies
pleading for attention or greeting cards with kitty cats in rain-
coats are the very embodiment of innocence and as such represent an absence of the designed and manipulated qualities characteristic of what is in fact a heavily mannered aesthetic.

For them, the foreshortened limbs and the deep wells of the
sad, saucer eyes of a doll like So Shy Sherri are part of a unique
and readily identifiable iconography whose distortions trigger
with Pavlovian predictability a nostalgia for a mythical condition
of endearing naiveté. The chilling paradox of the waxen fetishes
over which we croon so irrepressibly is that the gross hokum of
cuteness suggests the antithesis of what we would expect if we
were to judge it on the basis of its extreme stylization alone:
guilelessness, simplicity, and the refreshing lack of affectation.

Cuteness is not an aesthetic in the ordinary sense of the word
at all and must by no means be mistaken for the physically
appealing, the attractive. In fact, it is closely linked to the grotesque, the malformed. So Shy Sherri, for instance, is an anatomical disaster. Her legs are painfully swollen, her fingers are
useless pink stumps that seem to have been lopped off at the
knuckles, and her rosy cheeks are so bloated that her face is
actually wider than it is long. Medieval or Renaissance images of
the Christ child, those obese monstrosities whose Herculean
muscularity always strikes the modern viewer as bafflingly inaccurate, make an interesting comparison. For an era like our own
that prides itself on its ability to achieve effects of uncanny
realism, the disfigured putti of the Baby Face series mark a
decline rather than an advance in the representation of children,
an eerie throwback to the slant-eyed sphinxes of Sienese altar-
pieces — alien, carnivorous-looking creatures who are, in many
ways, as pictorially inexact as So Shy Sherri.

Far from being an accident of bad craftsmanship, the element
of the grotesque in cuteness is perfectly deliberate and must be
viewed as the explicit intention of manufacturers of objects

which elicit from us the complex emotions we feel when we encounter the fat faces and the squat, ruddy bodies of Galoob's dolls (or, to give another example, of the Trolls, a series of plastic figurines, extremely popular in the '60s, with potbellies, pug faces, and teased-up mops of brightly colored hair).

The grotesque is cute because the grotesque is pitiable, and pity is the primary emotion of this seductive and manipulative aesthetic which arouses our sympathies by creating anatomical pariahs, like the Cabbage Patch Dolls or even E.T., whose odd proportions and lack of symmetry diverge wildly from the relative balance and uniformity of ordinary bodies. The aesthetic of cuteness creates a class of outcasts and mutations, a ready-made race of lovable inferiors whom both children and adults collect, patronize, and enslave in the protective concubinage of their vast harems of homely dolls and snugglesome misfits. Something becomes cute not necessarily because of a quality it has but a quality it lacks, a certain neediness and inability to stand alone, as if it were an indigent starveling, lonely and rejected because of a hideousness we find more touching than unsightly.

The koalas, pandas, dalmatians, and lambs of the stuffed animal series "Lost 'n Founds" directly allude to this state of homeless destitution. With their "adorable 'so-sad' eyes" that shed real tears, these shameless examples of the waif or pauper syndrome seem to be begging to be rescued from their defenseless state, so tellingly emphasized by paws as cumbersome as boxing gloves — absurd appendages that lie uselessly in their laps, totally free of any of the prehensile functions hands usually serve. Because it generates enticing images like these of ugliness and dejection, cuteness has become essential in the marketplace in that advertisers have learned that consumers will "adopt" products that create, often in their packaging alone, an aura of motherlessness, ostracism, and melancholy, the silent desperation of the lost puppy dog clamoring to be befriended — namely, to be bought.

Cuteness, in short, is not something we find in our children but something we *do* to them. Because it aestheticizes unhappiness, helplessness, and deformity, it almost always involves an act of sadism on the part of its creator, who makes an unconscious attempt to maim, hobble, and embarrass the thing he seeks to idolize. The process of conveying cuteness to the viewer disempowers its objects, forcing them into ridiculous situations and making them appear more ignorant and vulnerable than they really are (as in William Wegman's hilarious photographs of his dog, the much-put-upon Man Ray, whose beseeching absurdity has made him the solemn mascot of cuteness at its most highbrow). Adorable things are often most adorable in the middle of a pratfall or a blunder: Winnie-the-Pooh with his snout stuck in the hive; the 101 dalmatians of Disney's classic collapsing in double splits and sprawling across the ice; Love-a-Lot Bear, in the movie *The Care Bears,* who stares disconsolately out at us with a paint bucket overturned on his head; or, the grimmest example of the cruelty of cuteness, the real live fainting goat which has acquired of late a perverse chic as a pet (bred with myatonia, a genetic heart defect, it coyly folds up and faints every time you scream at it). Although the gaze we turn on the cute thing seems maternal and solicitous, it is in actuality a transformative gaze that will stop at nothing to appease its hunger for expressing pity and bigheartedness, even at the expense of mutilating the object of its affections.

Turning its targets into statues and plush dolls, cuteness is ultimately dehumanizing, paralyzing its victims (who are often depicted asleep) into comatose or semiconscious things. In fact, the "thingness" of cute things is fixed firmly in our minds by means of the exaggerated textures and hues so characteristic of stuffed animals, with their shimmering satins and their luscious coats of fur, or dolls with their luxuriant profusion of hair, often of absurd length and body (as with the Cutie Kids of the Cutie Club series, a set of dolls whose psychedelic coiffures cascade down their sides in corkscrew curls that hang all of the way to their feet). "Anxiously awaiting power snuggles," F.A.O. Schwarz's huge grizzly bear is a slouching, seemingly invertebrate mammoth rippling with "serious spreads of soft spots" which are "just asking to be hauled and mauled," while their elephant, as large as a Saint Bernard, is described as "big, plump, and deliciously soft with soulful brown eyes that encourage bigtime hugging and smooching." Vacant and malleable, animals like these inhabit a world of soothing tactile immediacy in which there are no sharp corners or abrasive materials but in which everything has been conveniently soft-sculpturized to yield to our importunate squeezes and hugs. If such soulless insentience is any indication, cuteness is the most scrutable and externalized of aesthetics in that it creates a world of stationary objects and tempting exteriors that deliver themselves up to us, putting themselves at our disposal and allowing themselves to be apprehended entirely through the senses. In light of the intense physicality of our response to their helpless torpor, our compulsive gropings even constitute something one might call cute sex or, in point of fact, given that one of the partners lies there groggy and catatonic, a kind of necrophilia, a neutered coupling consummated in our smothering embrace of a serenely motionless object incapable of reciprocating. Far from being content with the helplessness of our young as we find them in their natural state, we take all kinds of artificial measures to dramatize this vulnerability even further by defacing them, embarrassing them, devitalizing them, depriving them of their selfhood, and converting them, with the help of all of the visual and sartorial tricks at our disposal, into disempowered objects, furry love balls quivering in soft fabrics as they lapse into convulsive withdrawal for their daily fix of TLC.

Exaggerating the vast discrepancies of power between the sturdy adult and the enfeebled and susceptible child, the narcissism of cuteness is also very evident in the way that the aesthetic ascribes human attributes to nonhuman things. Anthropomorphism is to a large extent the rhetorical strategy of children's books, which often generate their narratives from a kind of animal transvestism in which dogs, cats, bears, and pigs have the clothing and demeanor of human beings. Calendars, another rich source of cuteness, also employ animal transvestism as a major theme — mice as prima ballerinas in toe shoes and tutus, dogs in party hats and sunglasses, or swallow-tailed hamsters in tuxes and cummerbunds rearing up on their hind legs to give each other what appears to be an affectionate peck on the cheek. Even an artist as respected as William Wegman subtly refashions, in the appropriative style of postmodernism, the lowbrow aesthetic of cuteness by decking out his lugubrious mastiff, an irresistibly funereal pooch cheerlessly resigned to his fate, in everything from Christian Dior to Calvin Klein jeans.

Examples like these reveal that the cute worldview is one of massive human chauvinism, which rewrites the universe according to an iconographic agenda dominated by the pathetic fallacy. Multiplying our image a thousandfold and reverberating like an echo chamber with the familiar sounds of our own voices, the cute vision of the natural world is a world without nature, one that annihilates "otherness," ruthlessly suppresses the nonhuman, and allows nothing, including our own children, to be separate and distinct from us.

The imitative nature of cuteness can also be seen in the aesthetic's relation to precocity. One of the things we find cutest in the behavior of our children is their persistence in mimicking us, not only in such time-honored traditions as dress-up (the anthropomorphic version of which is played out obsessively in children's literature), but in that most basic form of child's play, mothering, whether it be of a doll or of a family pet. The spectacle of toddlers rocking their babies, changing the diapers of the many incontinent toys on the market, placating anxious dolls, or thrashing disobedient teddy bears elicits some of our most gloating and unrestrained responses to cuteness. Nothing delights us more than the strange sight of a one-year-old in a stroller meeting a barely ambulatory two-year-old, who, rather than seeking to establish a kind of spontaneous esprit de corps with his peer, breaks rank and jibbers baby talk at the bewildered object of his curiously perfunctory affections.

As co-conspirators in this game of make-believe maturity, we reward children who at once feign helplessness and assume adult authority in mothering others, reinforcing simultaneously both infantilism and precocity. The child is thus taught not only to be cute in himself but to recognize and enjoy cuteness, to play the dual roles of actor and audience, cootchy-cooing as much as he is cootchy-cooed. In this way, our culture actively inculcates the aesthetic doctrines of cuteness by giving our children what amounts to a thorough education in the subject involving extensive and rigorous training in role-playing. By encouraging them to imitate the way we ourselves fawn over their own preciousness, we give them the opportunity to know cuteness from both sides of the equation, not only from the standpoint of the object receiving the attention but from the standpoint of those giving it as well, from their appreciative audience-cum-artistic directors whom they impersonate for brief and touching intervals in their own highly informative charades of child-rearing. We teach our children the nature and value of cuteness almost from the dawn of consciousness and initiate them into the esoteric rituals of its art, passing on to them the tribal legacy of its iconographic traditions, its strange, self-mutilating ceremonies, as alien in their way, at least to a culture unindoctrinated in cuteness, as many of the scarification customs of Africa or New Guinea. Because imitation allows children to observe their own behavior with the analytic detachment with which they in turn are observed by their admirers, cuteness is unique among aesthetics because it lays the foundations for its own survival by building into itself a form of proselytizing.

The association of cuteness with a delusional state of artlessness prevents us from realizing that the qualities of primitivism and droll savagery around which we have woven this all-consuming folk religion are not naturally occurring elements of the universe but cheap alloys that embody something we would *like* to see in children rather than something we actually do see there. Its conventions are the residue of unfulfilled wishes that crystallize from the heated interaction of the daily realities of children with our quixotic and unobtainable notions of what they should ideally be like. Cuteness is every parent's portable utopia, the rose-colored lenses that color and blur the profound drudgery of child-rearing with soft-focused sentimentality. We use it to allay fears of our failures as parents and to numb us to the irritations of the vigilance we must maintain over creatures who are, in many instances, despite the anesthetizing ideology of cuteness, more in control of us than we are of them.

Although it is easy to sympathize with the disquieting frustrations that underlie this aesthetic, cuteness is in fact ultimately more a source of unhappiness among parents than comfort. To superimpose the vast edifice of fetishized images and intricate rituals onto the shallow foundations of a reality that cannot withstand its weight is to invite disappointment not only for us but for our children as well. Cuteness saturates the visual landscape of consumerism with images that cause feelings of inadequacy among parents, who inevitably measure the rowdy and selfish behavior of their own children by the exacting ideals of tractability, cuddliness, and quiescence promoted by an aesthetic at loggerheads with reality. Just as the inundation of our culture with the glitzy images of recent video pornography has elevated our aesthetic standards in regard to our partners (and consequently interfered with our sexual enjoyment of ordinary bodies in all of their imperfections), so cuteness elevates our expectations in regard to our children. It prevents us from enjoying them in their natural, unindoctrinated state, oppressed as we are by our apparent failures as care givers who strive unavailingly to discern in our headstrong offspring the lineaments of the model child, that ghoulish incubus summoned forth by an aesthetic that causes so much soul-searching and self-recrimination.

The result of this psychological malaise is an entirely new aesthetic, an invention of the last few decades: the anti-cute. In an effort to counteract the lethal toxicity of the images of children we are constantly ingesting, a culture like our own naturally produces as an antidote images of the exact opposite of cuteness: the perverse. Our belief that our children are harmless little cherubs collides with their intransigence and generates in the process so much hostility that we are inclined to view them as corrupt, possessed, even satanic.

Cuteness thus coexists in a dynamic relation with the perverse. The failure of the hyperboles of one aesthetic gives rise to the hyperboles of the other, of the child as the vehicle of diabolical powers from the Great Beyond which have appropriated the tiny, disobedient bodies of our elfish changelings as instruments for their assaults on the stability of family life. The spate of films about demonic possession shows just how assiduous we have become about building up the new iconography of the anti-cute. Catering to a deep need in the popular imagination, Hollywood has begun to manufacture images that function as outrageous travesties of cuteness, like those found in *Poltergeist,* in which a young girl becomes the conduit of tormented spirits of the damned who emerge from the throbbing blue light of the television set; or in *Child's Play,* in which the spirit of a dead serial killer inhabits the body of a doll named Chuckie, who, stalking down hallways with butcher knives tucked behind its back, murders Aunt Maggie, the babysitter, by giving her such a jolt that she staggers backwards out of the kitchen window and plummets ten floors to splatter on the hood of a parked car. Similarly, in David Kronenberg's *The Brood*, the dwarfish gnomes of the protagonist's children gestate in moldy embryonic sacs hanging outside of her belly where they begin spontaneously to respond to her volatile moods, ultimately bludgeoning her mother to death with kitchen utensils in a fit of rage.

Although it is still the dominant mode of representing children, cuteness is an aesthetic under siege, the object of contempt, laughter, and skepticism. Its commercialized aura of greeting-card naiveté makes it so fragile, so vulnerable to ridicule, that it cannot withstand the frank realism with which matters of parenting, divorce, and sexuality are now, for the first time, being addressed by the public at large. In the last few decades, cuteness has been subjected to remorseless satire as we attempt to loosen the grip of its iconography on an imagination hungry for images closer to the harsh realities of the era of the latchkey kid, the two-career family, the single-parent household, the crack baby, and the less than innocent drug-running sixth-grader with a beeper in one pocket and a .44 Magnum automatic pistol in the other. Loud and chaotic, *The Simpsons* is the new anti-cute show of the '90s, the "all-American dysfunctional family," as they have been nicknamed. Their household constitutes a direct subversion of the insipidity of cuteness, with its cartoon characters' harshly contoured shapes, gaping mouths, and enormous boiled-egg eyes goggling in such a way as to suggest the mindless somnambulism of compulsive TV viewers. The anti-cute launches a frontal assault on fuzzy-wuzziness with a blitz of images of the child as the monster, the petulant and demanding brat who disdains all of the sacrosanct laws of property ownership, gleefully annihilating Cuisinarts and microwaves as he mows a broad swathe of destruction through the very heart of the household's inner sanctum.

With the rise of the anti-cute, we are witnessing what amounts to civil war in the contemporary aesthetic of the family, a battle in which the image of the child as the unnatural spawn of Satan, an impish spirit of pure malevolent mischievousness, has locked horns with that of another sort of creature altogether. Generating their plots by pitting the cute against the anti-cute, Parts 1 and 2 of *Gremlins* provide a kind of allegory of this transformation. In Part 2, the adorable Gizmo (an appropriate name for this standard-bearer of cuteness, since it emphasizes the animal's status as an inert object) purrs with a contented coo, its droopy ears and sad eyes inviting the lubricious embraces of cute sex. After it is exposed to water, however, it begins to reproduce, laying eggs that enter a larval stage in repulsive cocoons covered in viscous membranes. Whereas Gizmo is soft, dry, and relatively well behaved, the ferocious aliens that quickly hatch from their water-induced hibernation in these protoplasmic pods are, as one character calls them, "ugly, slimy, mean-spirited, and gloppy." In them, both the behavior and appearance of cute objects are at once evoked and subverted.

Gizmo's strokable fur is transformed into a wet, scaly integument, while the vacant portholes of its eyes (the most important facial feature of the cute thing, giving us free access to its soul and ensuring its total scrutability, its incapacity to hold back anything in reserve) become diabolical slits hiding a lurking intelligence, just as its dainty paws metamorphose into talons and its pretty puckered lips into enormous Cheshire grimaces with full sets of sharp incisors. Whereas cute things have clean, sensuous surfaces that remain intact and unpenetrated (suggesting, in fact, that there is nothing at all inside, that what you see is what you get), the anti-cute Gremlins are constantly being squished and disemboweled, their entrails spilling out into the open, as they explode in microwaves and are run through paper shredders and blenders. With the help of food and water, they multiply exponentially and begin their devastating campaign — Hollywood's favorite plot device — against property ownership, destroying in Part 1 an entire town and, in Part 2, a skyscraper modeled on the Trump Tower. In this Manichean contrast between the precious Gizmo and its progeny, the hyperactive vandals who incarnate a new but equally stylized representation of youth and innocence, *Gremlins* neatly encapsulates the iconographic challenges to an aesthetic that is gradually relinquishing its hegemony over the popular imagination as the vapid artificialities of its conventions are burlesqued in our culture's recent attempts to purge itself of its antiquated religion of infantilism.

BARBARA GRIZZUTI HARRISON

P.C. on the Grill

FROM HARPER'S MAGAZINE

IN JUNIOR HIGH SCHOOL I knew a girl who, upon drinking her first pint of Southern Comfort, pressed her fingers to her pursed lips, applied them to her cheeks, and: *I Love (kiss, kiss) Myself,* she recited, *I Love (kiss, kiss) Myself.* Nowadays you don't have to get drunk to do that. If you're good enough at it — good (for example) as Gloria Steinem, or Marianne Course-in-Miracles Williamson — you stand to make a fortune (ask Oprah). If you're terribly, terribly sincere and muzzily user-friendly, and have intellectual pretensions and the gift of oversimplified gab, you get to go on PBS with your message of Self- and Universal Love, joining the ranks of Loving Leo Buscaglia, Sam-the-Man Keen, and dreadful John Bradshaw, tutor to those poor deprived stars (Barbra Streisand, for example) who need to talk to and (kiss, kiss) love their neglected Inner Child, also their Inner Toddler.

It helps to believe that happiness is a warm puppy, and to perform like one. It helps if you are anti-"Eurocentric." It is absolutely crucial that you be able to tell your audience (in all humility, of course, and extremely moistly) what and how to think, which is to say, feel; you gotta make them smile through their tears. And if you do — always provided that you eschew "elitism" and forbear making distinctions or (God forbid!) judgments — you might even get to talk to the Muppets! Imagine! The bliss of pitching speech and making nice to inanimate fuzzy things!

The Frugal Gourmet gets to talk to Muppets on public television.

I don't think Julia Child did. Julia cooked. Julia ate. Julia felt
no obligation to fill our minds with pure and lofty thoughts while
we were filling our stomachs with sauce velouté. Julia, bless her
soul, was old-fashioned.

The Frugal Gourmet clothes consumption in piety. Americans
are distancing themselves from the greedy eighties (as if life
could be carved neatly into decades); but, given a chance and the
sanction and the appropriate justification, Americans continue,
whenever possible, to consume the best of everything. The stakes
are higher, now, than money: vast amounts of self-love, other
people (also regional ethnic specialties). Our gurus tell us that
consumption is a useful social as well as personal occupation —
righteous, in a word.

You might think it takes a genius to drape the rags of piety
over conspicuous consumption. It doesn't. It takes the Frugal
Gourmet.

To be frugal, he is fond of declaiming, is not necessarily to be
" 'cheap.' It means that you use everything and are careful with
your time as well as with your food products," an unexceptional
culinary goal, except that he cooks so many dishes on any one
frenetic TV show — more loaves of bread than you might reasonably expect to have time to prepare in a month, pasta enough
to have fed the entire Italian resistance, if somewhat incoherently — you want to send out for a purgative.

You have to see him to believe him. So many do. His program
is the highest-rated cooking show ever. He electronically enters approximately 15 million households — that's more people
than, if things keep on as they are, will vote in this year's presidential election. His five companion cookbooks enjoyed first
printings of 300,000 copies or more. He was the first cook ever
to have two cookbooks on the *New York Times* best-seller list at the
same time. (Oh, dear Julia!)

His name is Jeff Smith (he refers to himself, with a fair dollop
of *amour-propre*, as "the Frug"). A Methodist minister whose
ministry and bully pulpit is the kitchen range, "If you have not
caught on to the fact . . . that I am trying to pump a little theology
into you, I've blown it," he says. Well, lo! (as God might say) and
behold: I've caught on. How could I not? The man is as subtle as
a jihad.

He wears a dangling talisman, a three-hundred-year-old jade fish, around his neck; he offends the serious cook, the inquiring mind. He has an awful lot of facial hair (a grizzly beard that joins forces with a full mustache, some of which must surely find its way into the cock-a-leekie) and a kind of halo of wiry Bride of Frankenstein hair on his underpopulated head. A toothy grin. Hard eyes behind thick glasses. He twitches his eyebrows at lobsters, slaps and tickles tongues (not his own, which would be a mercy), caresses lamb livers, fondles kidneys; he addresses internal organs with the anthropomorphic infatuation of a Jeffrey Dahmer. ("On Easter evening, when the priest says 'Behold the Lord is risen,' everyone runs home and eats innard soup.") Rolling his eyes upward in a simulation of ecstasy, he stands in front of the Spanish Steps eating pasta next to Bernini's fountain of a sinking boat, working up the orgasmic facial raptures one sees on the faces of the tone deaf when they are confronted with a Beethoven string quartet.

Everyone (I am sometimes taken aback to discover), no matter how aberrational his thinking processes, has a history; and this is the Frug's:

He graduated from the University of Puget Sound with a bachelor's degree in philosophy and sociology in 1962, and then, in 1965, from the Drew Theological School in Madison, New Jersey, which ordained him a minister of the United Methodist church. He was chaplain to the University of Puget Sound for seven years; he had an epiphany: "If we do not understand our ancestral table, I doubt that we can understand our history. If we do not understand our history, it is doubtful that we can understand our future." He taught his students to "eat history and memories." He opened a catering service, a cooking school, a restaurant, and a store called the Chaplain's Pantry, which led, in 1973, to a cooking show on Tacoma's public television station. In 1983 WTTW in Chicago began producing *The Frugal Gourmet,* for which turn of fortune Mr. Smith gives credit to onetime Windy Citizen Phil Donahue ("I adore him. I just adore him"). And to whom, on national television, he confided, in 1982, that he'd had open-heart surgery — "I have an artificial valve that is going clickety-clack. It's a *mar*velous thing." In 1989, he confided to Mr. Donahue and his television audience, he'd had "a minor stroke," owing to the fact that "the Holy Spirit's a practical joker."

(And remember: "Don't measure. There is no need for it.")

He loves factoids, which he conveys to his viewers with the kind of mock anger that is always a mask for real anger. His voice squeaking and escalating into thin exasperation and gratuitous contention, his reprimands are a failed attempt at folksiness. "Don't go squawking at me. . . . If you haven't eaten chicken livers you haven't lived. . . . I *know* it's a lotta work to make the sauce, I *know* it." The Romans, he instructs us, learned from the Greeks to dip their bread in wine — a skill, I should have thought, primates would have been capable of teaching Jane Goodall. "Now, you didn't know that, did you?" . . . "Now, don't start that on me! . . . Pay attention to this." Don't buy "little stinky bottles" of soy sauce. "No, no, I am not a part of that company — I can't *believe* you!" . . . "Oh, stop it! If you haven't tried [lamb brains] don't knock it. Remember the motto: 'Parts is parts.' " I don't remember it, actually, but it sounds vaguely sexual in a yucky (one of his favorite words) kind of way. *"You don't want to overcook brain!"* . . . *"No,* apples aren't American. *No,* chocolate is not European." Yassuh.

I cannot believe that at any given moment millions of people are making yogurt with a heating pad. (And I dare you to serve guests "Esau's Pottage — 2 cups lentils, 4 chicken bouillon cubes" — even as "a very important historical lesson and snack.") The Frug's fans are not purchasing recipes, they are buying comfy-cozy liberal pieties and beatitudes. He's a downscale Bill Moyers of the Insinkerator, an aproned P.C. guru of Ethnic Self-Esteem. And his message might be summarized (as he says) "thusly": *The Oppressed make better sausages.*

Give him Latvian dwarfs in funny hats cooking up a mess of tripe and snails in peanut butter and blueberry sauce, and he's in heaven:

"We should all taste the whole world. . . . That's an old biblical doctrine — to eat with someone is more intimate than making love," he says. He wrote *The Frugal Gourmet Cooks American* "as an effort," he says, "at digesting American history." ("Keep us mindful of those who starve.") Goodness. Although it is unlikely that I will do as instructed and "think of [my] own childhood" whilst sitting down to a repast of Northwest Indian oolichan grease (oil from little fermented fish "mixed . . . with raspberries to make a kind of ice cream"), it may be true that there are those for whom lamb-innard soup is "a bowl of memories." Pity.

The Frug wants us to "eat history rather than analyze it. . . . If I don't cook anything today," he tells his television audience, "it won't matter, particularly if you're a young person. . . . Understand how difficult it has been for the Japanese to maintain integrity in this country." Well, that's what he said; he was tying "an itty-bitty seaweed belt" around a piece of sushi and talking about the detention of Japanese in camps during World War II at the time. Please don't ask me to explain.

I will never "find [myself] using Serbian Pork Seasoning regularly," and do not expect on many occasions to buy "one large fresh octopus leg, about two to three pounds." But, oh! He makes me so happy, in an imbecilic kind of way; he gives me leave to hate wholeheartedly while roaring with laughter — an antiseptic kind of hatred for which I ought, I suppose, to be grateful to him: a noncorrosive hatred that is the opposite of toxic. In him I encounter viscerally the P.C. culture in all its ragged absurdity; and I find the encounter mind-scouring — although, I admit, it took me six months of concentrated watching (and reading) before I understood that I was engaged in more than just a random exercise in masochism. Generally speaking, I am not attracted to that by which I am repulsed; he is the exception that preposterously proves the rule.

He loves everyone. He does not love food: "I am primarily a people lover. . . . The events of the meal, the friends gathered, the family excited over the coming dishes are much more important to me than what is on the plate." It's no wonder, when what's on the plate are dishes made with frozen spinach and tinned artichokes; or a cheater's Bolognese sauce made with canned tomato paste, precooked shredded pot roast, and no provision at all for bathing ground beef in milk and wine so as to make it velvety; or Persian lamb tongues ("trim any cartilage and fat from the base"), Swedish pancakes with heated Hershey's chocolate syrup, or looed duck feet ("spit out the toes").

He is proof perfect of the axiom that to love everyone is to love no one. While he performs in a warm muddle of sentiment, he does allow himself to get angry at "Americans." But since he adores all our "immigrant ancestors" — even Native Americans, he says, must be thought of as immigrants, since they came here from Siberia — it is hard to know exactly who he means. He appears to mean "Puritans," who stalk, bloody-minded and invisible, in our midst. He reeks of bonhomie and smug vigor. He wishes most calculatedly not to give offense. The result is a romantic blur that has very little to do with food; the bipolarities of his affections betray him as they do a politician in an election year: one from column A, the industrialized world built on the shoulders of our immigrant ancestors; one from column B, the quaint, nonviolent, serene, offshore oppressed.

Never mind. His words are forever engraved in my heart (which is where he would like us to park our pork vindaloo: "Mix this up in your mouth and your heart with curry . . ."). Words such as "Hebrew was a desert language and as concrete as the desert." He doesn't always reach such inspired heights; but "hospitality is simply rampant" in Greece is pretty good; likewise "the German immigrants who came to this country were not all waiters. Not at all." And I immensely like being exhorted to eat pasta "el Dante." Almost as much as I rejoice to be told to "remember the prayer of thanksgiving to the Great One. It is a prayer in which you address the salmon and thank him for coming to your table." I have never before known what to say to a salmon, particularly one that has been cut into thin strips and placed on a rack in the oven in order to become "squaw candy."

> All the fine old frugal ways
> Of the early Pilgrim years
> Have the power to wake in me
> A deep sober ecstasy
> Close akin to tears.

He wrote that, don't you know. He wrote that in *The Frugal Gourmet Cooks American,* before it occurred to him that he despises Puritans:

"In American theology there is nothing about the history of the table. Why? Because Puritans were taught from the time they were little kids that they were not supposed to show their passions. Which means hunger is the biggest passion, so you're not supposed to really enjoy food. That is why we sit with one hand in our lap. Dumbest place in the world for one hand!"

He now speaks with multicultural missionary zeal; he embraces the virtues of tribalism: "The tribal mindset sees value in a person simply because he is a person. He is a member of the tribe and therefore everything is shared with that member. Puritan and European thinking stems from the belief that the only value a person has is connected with his ability to produce or manufacture. . . . For those of us who are white and decide to share, it is a matter of decision, not of custom or mores or ethical laws. No, the Native American gave us food and taught us how to use [it] because he felt he should. . . . And now he is so very sorry. He is tragically sorry."

Nothing compared to how sorry I am to be told that I am valued only according to my ability to produce — an error, if I may say so, that the Word became flesh and dwelt among us in order to refute. Although I am tempted to accuse the author of these slops of every kind of heresy, one might more temperately point out that every notion in the above sentimental lay to tribalism is, as sentiment so often is, contradicted by Scripture (the injunction to *love one another* is not widely regarded as a tribal imperative), common sense, received doctrine (which instructs us that we all have volition, tribes included), and the daily newspaper (is tribalism cutesy-wootsy when it acts, by slaughter, to exclude from communal love the tribe around the corner?).

Once, in a restaurant in Milan "on a May day . . . I kept closing my eyes and relishing the flavor" of risotto con funghi. "The waiter finally told me I would have to order lunch, as this dish was simply considered a pasta course." I see two possibilities in this story, which contradicts every eating experience I have ever had in Italy. One: the Milanese waiter thought he was dealing with an epileptic and quite wisely wanted to have done with him. And two: the Frug, his reiterated love of peasants notwithstanding, managed to convey to the waiter his contempt for the working class — "In Rome, the center of some of the most historically profound uses of food, assume that many taxi drivers are dishonest." I assume nothing of the sort. (But, on the other hand, I can't churn up any great enthusiasm for "vestral [sic] virgins" either.) There is a third possibility: this that he said happened on a day in May in Milan never happened, and is merely his way of conveying useless informationettes to us — "The primary use for beans in the Mediterranean has always been for food" — which are often, in any case, wrong ("Italians do not make lasagna much").

"The Japanese have a very long and involved name for everything. . . . You and I should all speak Japanese. Japanese and Spanish, kiddo, that's what it's gonna be, that's what we should do. *No No No No No.* I'm not asking us to give up anything . . ." That's how he adorabalizes and cutesifies the world and everything volatile in it.

How dare he call me kiddo.

"Don't let anybody talk you out of the knowledge that the tomato originated in North America." Why does this man turn purple asserting what I wouldn't dream of denying? "Blacks were Native Americans as much as any other culture. . . . Don't tell me that we're talking about something that is other than American, or foreign, that's just nonsense." I don't want to tell him *anything* . . .

I did want to interview him. Give the fella a break, I thought. Maybe he could in the flesh convince me of his good faith — the flesh often converts us to different points of view or allows us to see the point in what had seemed pointless or pernicious. And he does invite his readers and viewers to call him. All the time. Forget about it. I called and called. His business manager, James Paddleford, said the Frug thought it would be "neat" to be interviewed by *Harper's Magazine*. He said it the second time I called, and the third, and the fourth, and the fifth. But he never called me back. Maybe he thought I was a Puritan.

Why do people lap up his arts-and-craftsy pretentious approach to food, which owes nothing to art, science, or sensuality? The short answer is that we live in a debased intellectual climate. Why have they made him the guru cook of our troubled times? For an inspirational buzz that exacts no intellectual toll and obliges one to do nothing but be the passive recipient of factoids. For the same reason people take guided tours: to take home fortune cookies, packaged wisdom, not too stressful on the brain. And, loving everybody, he gives us all somebody to hate: the Puritan, a bogeyman we never meet at the grocery store, a specter who never tries to rent our apartment or take away our job. Why is he beloved? The short answer is that people are stupid.

He is not stupid. He writes, he says, to satisfy "a hunger for meaning." People are *not* stupid; they are needy. And he panders, the result being spiritual and political malnutrition . . . and sweet-and-sour pan-braised tongues with pine nuts. Why do people allow themselves to be patronized? Probably because, in spite of the fact that we are forever told that our trouble is lack of self-esteem, we are all indeed guilty of something; he's a minister — he knows this.

People like small, manageable worlds — hence our enduring fascination with dollhouses, our addiction to epigrammatic best-sellers, our attachment to slogans and buzzwords that address complexity without unraveling it. In a world of terrifying complexity, we keep the furniture of our minds tidy, light, disposable, ready for the next change of fashion, the season's trend.

He deals in capsule histories — thimble histories. To the history of the Vietnamese ("very family-oriented") he devotes one and a half pages and comes up with this conclusion: "Many nations suffered tremendous political and social upheaval, including the United States, Cambodia, and Laos." His factoids are the kinds of things that make you gnash your teeth when you hear them from lazy, ill-informed tourists who take pride in never having eaten in a tourist restaurant (*Stay out of those tourist restaurants, just stay out of them!* he says. Why?) or from the mouths of terminally dopey know-it-alls:

"The Japanese do everything in the most elegant manner possible. Everything is so aesthetic!"

"In Rome they love artichokes more than anything else."

"I consider the Chinese the greatest chefs in the world and the wise ones behind noodles; they do more with the noodle than anybody else."

"Venus de Milo's bellybutton was the pattern for tortellini."

"Have you ever thought of the influence Rome had on the Western world?"

George Washington ate one of Martha's hams every day at three o'clock. He also "treated his slaves quite well."

"There are more chickens in the world than there are human beings."

"It is rare that you meet a fireman who is not a very kind person."

He doesn't like flamingo brains. He's on reasonably sure ground there.

He likes something called advieh, a combination of spices the fragrance of which "is reminiscent of Persian nights, temples, and flying carpets." I would rather chew boiled erasers.

Actually, there is one recipe of his I quite like. It comes from Hong Kong ("where you will find the most profound and exciting Chinese food available"): Place in a pot of boiling water a three-pound chicken. When the water stops boiling, remove the chicken. Cover the pot and bring the water back to the boil. When it boils again, put the chicken back in the pot and the pot on the burner; but turn off the heat. After an hour the chicken will be poached. This is nice because you get firm flesh and the flavor remains in the chicken. You might want to give it a little more than an hour, though. Because otherwise the bird may still be bloody near the bone. . . . If you're scared of salmonella, that is. "Chickens are always kind to us. So treat him well."

Oh, do something with your noodle!

One does not wish to be patronized by the Frugal Gourmet.

He's good at it. Smarmy. Unctuous. Let me count the ways:

It's always "Mama" who buys the chicken. How does he know it's "Mama"? Maybe it's a slut.

Japan: "I think they are the most fascinating culture. . . . Brilliant and wonderful people. . . . They have the highest level of education you could possibly imagine — artists, musicians, scientists. Oh! Oh! Yo Yo Ma!" (He's Chinese.)

Morocco: "Very unusual people from a very unusual country with a fabulous cuisine . . . a major part of the world. . . . They were called the Berbers in the beginning." Well, the Berbers were, the Arabs weren't. "How involved and lovely this culture

is. First of all you wash your hands." And you eat with one hand
in your lap, which, as you may remember, is a "dumb" thing to
do if you happen to be descended from Puritans. "Terribly romantic. . . . This is the land of Casablanca, of fezzes and clinking
of glasses and dark taverns and cigar smoke and all the romantic
things we think of." Ah, romantic cigar smoke, fragrant as flying
carpets. And, being tribal and all, they share everything. Except,
of course — but we don't hear about this from him — when they
don't; except when they're carving up their enemies and grinding their bones to make mortar for triumphal gateways. The
point about the romantic Moroccans, of course, is that they are
just as bad — and, one supposes, just as good — as the rest of us.

Don't they teach Original Sin at Drew Theological?

India: "*Fascinating* people."

Puerto Rico: "Fascinating place."

Hungary: Budapest "is beautiful, the Hungarians charming,
and the food just outstanding. . . . If you want the real flavor of
Grandma's cooking you must render your own lard."

I visited Budapest — one of the most polluted cities in the
world, a city that has the air of a permanently deserted ballroom — in 1989. History had ended. The use of lard, however,
had not: I retched (although I'm not especially squeamish — I
was once required to eat sheep's eyes curry in Andhra Pradesh
for breakfast, and carried off my obligations to my hosts reasonably well, considering). I retched because lard seemed to be the
medium for national expression; my salvation lay in caviar and
in goocy desserts smothered in whipped cream, which disguised
the lard.

Jamaica: "Strikingly beautiful. . . . And the food from this island is just wonderful . . . delightful." Pickled pigs' tails. Go to
Kingston, where "you will find much lower prices, wonderful
food, charming people, and a great deal of poverty. . . . The real
Jamaica."

Russia: "Charming and creative." Mr. Smith visited Russian
nightclubs in Brighton Beach in Brooklyn. He tells us so. One
has no sense of his ever having been there, of this having happened in actual time and real space; this is a man, after all, who
is so insistent upon his own sensibilities — he cries a lot — that
he passes the Tartaruga Fountain in the Jewish ghetto (Rome's
loveliest fountain) without a glance or a word for it. It is in the

background. He is in the foreground . . . as he always is: "The Berlin Wall fell while I was cooking German dumplings. Then, Lithuania called for freedom while I was cooking Kugelis." Cause and effect, perhaps?

Greece — which taught the Romans "how to catch and appreciate fish": "So gracious that it is embarrassing." But "Watch the cabbie. He might try and take you for too much money."

Wales: "Absolutely charming. . . . This culture has produced some great intellectuals, among them the actor Richard Burton."

Armenia: "Fantastic!" and because the F. was "brought to tears with the stories of the tribulations of this wonderful people" — "the Turks caused wholesale massacre . . . like the Jewish Holocaust" — Turks are granted no space in *The Frugal Gourmet on Our Immigrant Ancestors*. What can you do with a man like that? And what, one wonders, is the cutoff point? I read in my paper this morning that Armenian militants killed a thousand people in one small town in Azerbaijan in one week: Do we stop eating Armenian stuffed meatballs now? Or what?

He is coy. He suggests using "beef caps" for sausages. Ask your sausage maker about beef caps, he says. So I do some research. I get, by means too tedious to detail, as far as "bung." Then I call the Jefferson Market in Manhattan and ask what beef caps are. They hang up on me. They think I am talking dirty. I call the Sausage Maker in Buffalo, New York. "It's a casing," a prim voice tells me. Yes, but made of what? "The *p* word," the voice says — "p-e-n-i-s."

"Please do not fill your kitchen with appliances that you will rarely use." For his recipes he uses: a noodle bird-nest fryer; a couscousier; a truffle cutter; a tostone press for the purpose of flattening out slices of plantains — "one of the great foods of Puerto Rico"; also a flavor injector — "a strange-looking plastic device that resembles a hypodermic needle and is used for injecting flavors and juices into meats." I was afraid of something like that.

I have it in mind to plumb the depths of his condescension — but first I want to get to his innards. According to the Frug: (1)

"Since prehistoric times" aristocratic Chinese and Italians ate innards — "the most prized part" of the animal. (2) In ancient Rome only peasants ate innards, and the aristocracy ate the rest of the animal. (3) "In America . . . we seem to feel that [innards] are symbols of poverty. In our three ancient cuisines, however, they were symbols of delight and joy at the table . . . offered at the most exclusive banquets." Well, you tell me; I can make no sense of it but to conclude that as long as he is putting down aristos and telling a story, accuracy can go and get stuffed.

Putting down aristos, a form of fake and Capraesque piety, is a sure way to purchase television success — Oprah Winfrey, for example (also a Windy Citizen), says she always speaks for and with her studio audiences, they are in perfect synch — and, the thing is, she's right. Achieving the lowest common denominator requires much honed intuition and skill; it is an art.

I reckon it is true that "certain foods are so fascinating" (and "Italians like salad"). I would like someone who has given it some serious consideration to tell me, for example, exactly what is meant by "peasant food" as opposed to "sophisticated food." The last time I was in Italy, for example, I ate, in the province of Molise, which has been called Italy's hillbilly country, a sublime dish of risotto cooked in wine with porcini and truffles. The people of Molise, rich and poor, eat seasonal foods. Truffles were in season. So is this peasant food? Or sophisticated food? Please tell. *He* never will. He thinks porcini are dried mushrooms; they are not; they are *boletus edulis,* big wild mushrooms, fresh or dried. Anyone who ventures into print makes blunders; it's the combination of error, pontification, and showmanship that vexes. *You didn't know that, did you?*

In his world boys are always "lads," chefs are always "charming and handsome," little old men are always beautiful and wise, and a black woman cooking in the South is "enormous and gorgeous . . . and she doesn't use MSG — she uses spices and love."

He condescends. "Taste your memories," he exhorts his black listeners; "barbecued ribs help you remember who you are." And if you can't get ribs, you can always eat watermelon.

What cook — what *ministerial* cook — would tell his listeners to eat real Jewish food in the ghetto, blithely urging upon them spaghetti carbonara, the ingredients for which are bacon (actually pancetta), eggs, cream, and cheese? Is he nuts?

Anyone with an irritable sensibility might conclude that his encomium to the Jews is indistinguishable from anti-Semitism: "Jews have been persecuted due to their commitment to their religious faith, which must come prior to any commitment to a particular country. . . . Jews have always valued education, good business, and the arts. . . . The most educated segment of our society, all have been the victims of prejudice since the Jews feel 'called' or chosen in terms of their place in world history." Besides, the Jews gave us Einstein, Harry Houdini, Jack Benny, Lenny Bruce, Bette Midler, and Barbra Streisand, to say nothing of Danny Kaye.

In the company of Julie Sahni, an Indian cookery writer (and "a true American"), he "learned in one short evening that Indian cuisine — one of the most profound cooking styles in the world — is not the complicated thing I thought." That is more than I learned in four years of living in India, which has many cuisines: northern, southern, Parsee, Goan, for example. (If he's going to be reductive, why doesn't he reduce veal stock? Ghee. I wouldn't trust him to clarify butter.) He asks Ms. Sahni, "Do you ever feel foreign in this culture? What about on the IRT subway?" Fortunately for him, she is well mannered. Telling us all to visit Twenty-ninth Street and Lexington in Manhattan, where there are lots of Indian restaurants and stores, he invites us to observe "all kinds of characters hanging around there. Wonderful people" — i.e., Indian people (or, as he prefers, peoples). "Hint on shopping in ethnic grocery stores: Do not be intimidated by the wonderful strangeness that you find around you" — i.e., Indian peoples.

"I feel" (by which he means he opines) "that Iranian-American immigrants will not be understood fairly if we use the more recent name. So, Persian immigrants it is." Sez who? Sez he. Patronizing poppycock.

He reaches the height of lyrical kitchi-kitchi-cooism writing about the "most profound users of food in the world," the Chinese, his knowledge deriving from Hong Kong, his quivering mysticism bouncing off the walls.

"The Chinese see themselves as a part of nature and its processes; the celebration of food is . . . not a *part* of living, it *is* living. . . . A culture cooks in a particular way because of the way it thinks." I doubt that a culture is an entity that can be said to think or to cook, in which it has a great deal in common with you-know-who.

In his epilogue to *The Frugal Gourmet Cooks Three Ancient Cuisines*, TFG tells us that "the earth is too small for private dinner parties": expand your table and invite the homeless for dinner. "Privatude, in the end, offers only one thing — and that is loneliness." I have observed that religious fanatics and zealots always fear solitude. In solitude — "privatude" — is born vice . . . and art.

TFG quotes "the author Gertrude Louise Cheney," who, at age nine, observed: "All people are made alike. They are made of bones, flesh, and dinners. Only the dinners are different." Children should be seen and not heard aside, I understand his affinity with the brat: in what is meant to be a "celebration" of "cultures" we are all smooshed together in a sticky soup of peoples; only our meatballs are different, and all of us are "neat." (No differences = no similarities. I read that in a fortune cookie. No, I didn't. But I can make things up, too. Anyway, G. L. Cheney, who she? I like better what a three-year-old friend of mine uttered: "A soufflé is something that isn't there and tastes very good.")

Mr. Smith has real trouble with two of his "cultures" — the Irish, who can lay claim to being oppressed but whose cuisine has not garnered much in the way of epicurean praise; and the Italians, who, whether or not they were the first to eat noodles, are undeniably dandy in the food department. They are — alas! — Roman Catholic. Mr. Smith is not particularly fond of the Roman church. What saves the Irish from his scorn is the fact that they managed to be oppressed by the English, whom he likes even less . . . and the fact that he married an Irish woman, Patty Smith ("a true American patriot"). "Irish immigrants came to this country wishing to maintain their love for the potato" is one of my favorite FG sentences, indeed one of my favorite all-time sentences. "One of the cardinals of the Church built [the

Villa Borghese] for himself so he'd have a place to talk to himself" is not.

I don't know why I should be surprised, all things considered, that he has an utterly tin ear when it comes to the conundrums, dilemmas, challenges, anxieties, and hopes of immigrants: in his stagy world, first-generation immigrants say to their children, "You are becoming too American. Don't you respect us anymore?" The truth is far more complicated, and far more poignant. (It has nothing to do with *The Peaceable Kingdom,* children sitting with animals, "nobody biting anyone, William Penn and the Indians in the background all getting along.") I am the child of one Italian immigrant parent, one native-born American parent, and four Italian immigrant grandparents. I know that for many children of immigrants, a great deal of life's tension resided in parents and grandparents wanting us to become American . . . and *not* wanting us to become American. The answer to the question What am I? was not waiting for us in the seven or eight or nine fish dishes the Frug variously claims we eat on Christmas Eve (in every Italian-American family I know, it's twelve fish dishes); I can assure you that baccala never solved anyone's identity problem.

What am I? is, in any case, the question we used to ask one another in grade school. (The answer — unless one was blonde Veronica, who was "American" — was Italian, or Jewish.) The grownup question is, Who am I? Who am I in relation to God and my fellow humans? And reading tea leaves or eating haggis and fish pudding is not likely to provide the answers.

"I'm trying to get rid of the secrecy, the gnosticism" is a sentence as opaque to me as "It is hard for Americans to understand the meaning of an appetizer." That's the kind of theologian he is. This is the kind of theologian he is: "Theology means that you admit you are dependent on something outside yourself." Of course it does not. A nonbeliever is perfectly capable of studying theology, which is a discipline (not an appetizer). I asked a couple of theology students, and one distinguished professor of theology, to parse these sentences for me: "The Gospel of St. John talks about creation just before being was. Remember? I think that is when I learned to cook." They could not. Maybe I should have asked Shirley MacLaine.

Only a man who tells us that Moroccan baked omelets, "called Kuku, are more flavorful than anything you have tasted in either France or Spain" would have the appallingly bad taste to entertain us with this anecdote: Following his ordination, a friend and mentor asked, " 'Well, can you do it? Can you change a perfectly good wine into, ugh, blood? . . . Jeff, listen to me. Always remember that no priest should ever raise the chalice and pronounce the presence of the healing blood of the lamb without being able to turn to the congregation and state the vintage, and state it proudly.' He was right, of course." He was wrong, of course.

How starved we are.

DIANE JOHNSON

Rolex

FROM THE MISSOURI REVIEW

J. HAD GONE to a meeting in Washington; I had begged off for once and was reveling in the quiet mornings at home, and the chance to work undisturbed on a novel I was writing. Then he telephoned to say he had forgotten to tell me that I would be getting a visit from someone named Yan Zhang, or Zhang Yan, who was coming to San Francisco, and could we put up this Yan Zhang for a couple of days? Yan was a young woman doctor we had met in Beijing — I would remember when I saw her. J. had had a letter from Dr. Li-Xing Wang in China about her, and then Yan Zhang herself had called him. She had been in the United States for several months, studying in Houston, and was planning a visit to San Francisco. She said she had something for me and wanted to deliver this item personally. J.'s voice expressed curiosity, but I could not guess what the item might be.

And naturally J. had proposed that she stay with us. I said of course. The reflex of traveling in foreign lands is that eventually people are likely to turn up in San Francisco. I, more than J., bore the brunt of entertaining them, for no one imagined that a doctor would interrupt his work; I would try to make them as comfortable as possible, and drive them to see the Golden Gate Bridge, Muir Woods, and the Palace of the Legion of Honor. While receiving kindnesses in foreign lands, I always vowed to make myself endlessly hospitable in return. At home, however, our visitors never failed to come at a bad moment, testing this resolution. I tried to behave as graciously as possible, but was never without a sense of shame, knowing myself to feel inconvenienced. Of course I understood that J. and I were just as inconvenient for them.

On the appointed Saturday, the doorbell rang at seven-thirty in the morning. The children were eating their cereal and I was idly reading the paper, and for a moment couldn't imagine who it could be. A young Chinese woman — small, newly permanented, wearing a maroon gabardine pant suit that had certainly come from China, styleless, vaguely military, reminding me of schoolteachers or certain orders of South American nuns. Her face was familiar — we had certainly met her in China. I thought maybe she had been the assistant of our host, Dr. Wang, the chief of the Department of Infectious Diseases in the hospital that J. was visiting. She had come to the many banquets, and had once, if I remembered, taken me to some of the stores along the Wangfujing Street. Now I smiled and welcomed her, but, though J. had told me, I could not remember the name until the woman said it.

"I'm Yan Zhang. Do you remember? Did you hear from Dr. Wang?" She held out a little manila envelope. "In it you will find your lost watch." She smiled, watching for my delighted reaction. Instead, I felt a moment of complete blankness. I did not believe I had lost a watch, could not remember one.

"Thank you so much," I said anyway. "It's so wonderful of you. Please come in." I laid the envelope on the table and helped Dr. Zhang with her small suitcase. "J. says you will be able to stay a day or two?"

"I can stay until Wednesday," said Dr. Zhang. "I am most eager to see your city, for I have heard it is very lovely. I am studying in Houston."

"How nice," I said. I made her some tea and toast, and asked her for news of Dr. Wang, and of Dr. Lo-wan Liu, the doctor from Canton, and Dr. Tong-jing Ng, the one who had taken us to the acrobats and the Chinese opera. This was the extent of the names I could remember. I felt, as we talked, a wave of nostalgia for Beijing, where I had spent a happy month living in the old Beijing Hotel, a rambling assemblage of several hotels near Tiananmen Square, venerable home of all journalists and business travelers and minor foreign diplomats waiting for quarters in the city.

I had spent an autumn month doing a little writing in the mornings, then in the afternoons wandering the Beijing streets, dodging bicycles, a scarf tied over my hair, leading the life of an anonymous observer of the doings of the capital. I stood in line to gaze at the corpse of Mao Tse-tung. I admired the fanciful temples, the faded cinnabar color of the buildings, the pounded grassless paths to the pagodas, and the little alleys where people persevered in their old-fashioned lives, with their piles of cabbages and little braziers puffing away among ugly new apartments on every side. The air of the mornings was damp with the tons of fresh washing hung out from all the windows. In the dingy department stores I could spend hours weighing a purchase of silk undershirts or feather coats, or embroidery turned out by numberless women in the provinces.

At first I had minded the infantalizing and powerless state of being unable to speak or read in which I passed my days, gesturing with signs and feeling frightened when I lost my way. I learned the simplest Chinese characters, for exit, entrance, woman, and I learned to say a word that sounded to me like neeehowma, hello, but I felt like an imposter saying it, hardly able to believe that such an odd sound could denote anything at all, or as if words were meaningless unless you understood them in your heart.

At other times, here as in other places where I could not speak or understand, I enjoyed this exclusion from language. In Persia I had learned to count, to thank, to greet, to write my name in the beautiful undulating script; but I was defeated by Chinese before I started, by the characters like inscrutable decoration, and the long nasal vowels and singing tones. Since it was meaningless to me, as devoid of signification as music, the words were as pure, as restful and lovely.

During the month, I lost my fear of the strangeness of a country where I couldn't read the signs; I philanthropically traded my hard currency for the local tattered yen and bought on the open market instead of in the Friendship Stores. It was the index of my adjustment that even Chinese art, which seemed so horrible in the beginning, began to look all right to me. At first I had been repelled by embroidered panda handkerchiefs and porcelain gnomes. Now, kimono dolls and rooms decorated in violent red and gold did not look peculiar to me. Dragons knitted onto pillow covers and ponds filled with strange, cement-colored rocks — it all seemed lovely. I came to understand calligraphy. I visited a needlework school. A hundred women embroidered kittens in microscopic stitches on transparent silk and sandwiched them in round frames set on little pedestals, and these looked natural and nice to me, though I knew I would lose this delusion when I got back, and didn't make the mistake of buying any panda handkerchiefs or kittens for my friends. For them I bought lacquer boxes and lapis necklaces. But what happened to the elegant aesthetic of Sung, of Tang? This puzzle remains intriguing to me. And I learned to eat whatever was served, without inquiring, depriving our hosts of the pleasure they seemed to feel in shocking Westerners with the revelation that they have just eaten bat or snake. Anyway, it seemed to me, once cut up in little pieces, all things, whether badger or toad, tasted remarkably alike.

In the evenings, J. and I would drink in the lobby bar in the hotel, where all the other foreigners did too. There you met people from countries you wouldn't expect — an oil salesman from Iran, suave in Western tailoring, who had defended the war with Iraq; and a violent German girl who denounced America's involvement in Vietnam with such persistence, though she surely had not been born then, that J. had been finally goaded into asking if she had heard of Nazis. Most of the foreigners were nice — jolly Dutch backpackers, people staying elsewhere in the city in youth hostels who came in here for the camaraderie of European voices. Westerners could walk in and out of the Beijing Hotel with impunity, and I had not at first realized that a Chinese person could not just come in and order a drink, the guards outside would prevent it.

All Chinese did not look alike to me, each one looked different. This happened all at once, in a moment, as with one of those puzzles with hidden shapes you cannot see until suddenly you see them and then cannot not see. I found the Chinese merry and stoic, and I concealed the number of my purchases from them, so that my extravagances would not offend. They were so poor, and wore their work clothes to dinners. Professor Wang, the greatest professor of medicine in all of China, lived in two rooms, and his dining table was made from boards set atop the television set. A bed was pushed into the corner. The Wangs had four books only — one a photo album, with cuttings of Western reviews of a novel written by Mrs. Wang's grandmother in the thirties. They had saved it by hiding it during the Cultural Revolution, when it could have been dangerous having a grandmother who wrote books.

While Dr. Zhang drank her tea, I opened the manila envelope containing the watch. With surprise I realized that it was my Rolex. Not a real Rolex of course, a fake one I had accidentally left behind in the Beijing Hotel; it hadn't even been worth writing to ask about it. I had hoped the porter or the maid had found it, and now, instead, here it was, more than a year later, returned to me still ticking, set on Chinese time. I thanked Yan Zhang over and over, my amazement passing, I hoped, for happiness to have my valuable treasure back again. Indeed, I was amazed, and tried to imagine the chain of events that could have brought it back to me. "How on earth did you find it? What a lot of trouble you've been to. How careless of me to have left it," I exclaimed.

Of course I had forgotten about it. I had bought it in Singapore, shopping with Huguette Cosset, who like all Frenchwomen had a carnet of good addresses collected from other Frenchwomen — where to get the good jewelry, and the name of the good tailor, the handmade shoes, the MontBlancs, and the watches. The best copy watches, almost indistinguishable from the *vrai*, guaranteed to work a year or two, made wonderful presents, everyone loved them. You could have Gucci, or Cartier, Rolex, whatever, for ten dollars. I hadn't planned to buy one, if only because they were illegal and you had to smuggle them into the United States. I had heard of people having them confiscated. The wives of customs officials wore them, I supposed.

Huguette and I had found the shopping mall with great difficulty. Singapore, which I had imagined as a steamy, palm-lined, vine-covered tropic, with louvered jalousies, verandas, planters' punches and sloe gin, had instead been entirely torn down, if it had ever existed outside of Maugham stories and old movies, and been replaced by shopping malls and giant hotels. One mall was much like another; the hotels outdid each other in vastness, in the chilly tomblike marble vaulting of their opulent lobbies, in the grandeur and authenticity of the European antiques carted across the Pacific to furnish the lobbies, and in the whimsy of their theme restaurants. J. and I clung to Raffles, the seedy survivor of more colorful days, but it looked like Raffles' time was about up too. Digging machines stood by in the garden, and there was no net on the tennis court.

In search of the New Horizon Shopping Center, Huguette and I wandered the boulevards, though it was quite obvious that you weren't meant to wander, were meant to have a car or go in a taxi. It could have been Los Angeles. "Singapore is the oogliest place I ever was," said Huguette. "I am so glad we went to Thailand first, or otherwise, this would be my sole idea of *l'Asie*, what a pity." We laughed when at last we found the New Horizon Shopping Center, and even more miraculously, the proper shop, from among the hundreds of little shops on endless floors, Mr. Woon — she had written it down. Inside it was even funnier because there were French people Huguette knew from Paris! Gilles and Marie-Anne Donon! And the Donons had seen Frédéric Barsac coming out as they came in. I watched irritation or mystification suffuse the features of the shopkeeper, Madame Woon, if it was she, at the French chatter she could not understand. Perhaps.

The French exchanged several anecdotes of local shopping, then "Au travaille," cried Huguette, returning to the business at hand, "May I see the watches?"

"Regardez les superbes Cartiers," cried Madame Donon, spreading out her Cartiers for Huguette to see. "Ils ont toutes les bonnes marques françaises."

In the end, I had been drawn in too. What better ten-dollar present could you take someone? The watches were perfect, absolutely indistinguishable from real. We turned them over and over, admiring them. It was hard to choose — Patek Philippe, Baume & Mercier, Gucci, Tiffany — in the end I bought two men's Cartiers for joke Christmas presents, a Rolex for myself, and a Gucci for my friend B. A few times during the afternoon, I had taken my Rolex out of my purse and looked closely at it.

How did I know it was not really real? It appeared to have tiny diamonds and little dots of luminescent paint to mark each number. ROLEX OYSTER PERPETUAL DATEJUST, it said, and in letters almost too tiny to read I had later with a magnifying glass read SUPERLATIVE CHRONOMETER OFFICIALLY CERTIFIED. There was a little window at three o'clock, through which you read the date. Perhaps this was the real Rolex, put into the batch by mistake? I had laughed at myself for even thinking the thought, but I had thought it. In fact I had a kind of interest in watches. I was once in Hong Kong for three weeks, and after the third day there is little else to do but marvel at the profusion of watches, the little glittering diamante ones, and big gold ones, onyx, steel, silver, water-resistant, waterproof, quartz, jeweled, bracelet, pendant, men's, women's, sport, dress, alarm . . .

At the dinner that evening, all the French women were wearing attractive, expensive-looking watches, their husbands too; all wrists were girded with imposing Rolexes and Tissots, and there was much merriment and comparing. J. had been disapproving, saying, "Isn't it a little — well — why would you want to pretend you had a Rolex?" very priggishly. "Why would you want to pretend you had a Rolex?" But he softened his attitude a little when he saw that it was some kind of French joke I had entered into.

While Huguette and I shopped, J.'s meeting, the quarterly meeting of the International Infectious Diseases Council, adjourned its deliberations for the afternoon at the request of the Thai, Dr. Sungsam Prangithornbupu. Although the council did not usually do field work, Dr. Prangithornbupu urged them to look at first hand into some of the conditions that might be contributing to the inexplicable deaths of young men from Thailand who had come to work in Singapore only to die mysteriously in their sleep. There were hundreds of these deaths now, young men who cried out in their sleep, and the other men in the bare bunkhouses who heard them and rushed to them to find them dead. Coming back to the hotel before dinner, J. had told me about the shacks of tin and straw, with water from the pump and a poor rice diet cooked on open fires in the mud streets behind the modern shopping centers, invisible.

"These boys do not live as well as my dogs in Thailand," Dr. Prangithornbupu had angrily said.

The local public health man, Lee, had brought a boy named Sridor to tell them about his friend Potha. Sridor, they could see, had told his story before; his voice had a certain narrative assurance. Yet his eyes had not lost an expression of dread as he remembered again, and perhaps his face would always wear the expression of terrified knowledge that death could come abruptly to a healthy young fellow like himself as it had to Potha. "He was well when he went to bed. I talked to him. There was nothing the matter. Then about midnight I heard him cry out."

"What kind of cry?" They had been over this in the reports and documents. "Not a loud cry, a sort of whimper, soft and surprised. His eyes like this." The eyes of Sridor became as round as the eyes of evil spirits portrayed on the temple doors. His friend had cried out, opened his eyes round, and died. The light had faded from his face as Sridor watched, as if a ghost had come for him. It seemed as if he had seen something in his sleep or upon waking. Other boys had died like this, and people said it was the widow ghost wanting to marry the boy. Sridor's fingernails were painted red to trick the widow ghost into thinking he was a woman so she would let him alone.

"These deaths have happened among Southeastern Asian immigrants in a number of places," J. told me. "It has a number of names — in Japan it's pokkuri, in the Philippines it's called bangungut, somewhere it's nonlaitai, something like that, but it always means the same thing, sudden death at night, usually affects only males. We're calling it SUDS, sudden unexpected death syndrome."

Since I did not approve of cheerful acronyms for grim events, I said nothing. I was setting out glasses, as the other members of the council were coming to the Raffles Hotel for drinks before the banquet.

They sat uncomfortably propped against the headboards of the beds or on the luggage bench, discussing the strange disease.

"In my view some curious electrical cardiac accident," Randy Deckhorne said. "The path reports show no real cardiac defects, except surprising heaviness. The hearts weigh more than you would expect in chaps with slight builds."

"Well, that's by definition a cardiac abnormality," Ben Harmon said. "Male hearts usually weigh less than four hundred grams of body weight, and these weigh considerably more."

"The symptoms are like shoshin beriberi," objected Dr. Kora. "I think a defect of the thiamine."

"Thymus," corrected Narcisse Cosset.

"A thiamine deficiency, he means," interpreted J.

"Yes," said Dr. Kora.

"Yes, I agree," said Dr. Cosset. "Leur nourriture is very bad, only a poor-quality rice."

"The issue of *Pseudomonas pseudomallei* hasn't been resolved," said J.

But it was clear to all the doctors that the young men had died of lonesome despair — thin-shouldered young men in ironed shirts huddled in foreign bars far from anyone who loved them, far from the happy jokes in their villages. Here in Singapore they were used to build the roads and the hideous shopping malls, and in the evenings sheltered in these shacks and maybe poisoned themselves by cooking their rice in plastic tubes. These deaths also happened among the Hmong from Laos when they went to Texas, among Kampucheans — always away from home, always young men, lonesome and sad, the victims of the builders of shopping malls. As I emptied ice cubes from the minibar into the plastic bucket I listened to the talk about the weight of the hearts of the young men. It seemed natural that their hearts would be heavy. The malls were made of glass and marble, as shining with brass as an English pub, as fountained as Versailles, fuller of Lacoste, Lanvin, Lauren, than department stores in Paris and New York, and wares from a thousand Asian basement factories, and gold, and silk, umbrellas, pens, crocodile bags, Rolexes.

It was not a watch you could wear in China. The gold, though fake, glittered too derisively in the blue-clad crowd, in the dun-colored dusty streets. The cheerful simplicity of the caps and sweaters, the battered bikes, the plastic shoes and absence of any finery pronounced such an object vulgar beyond vulgarity, ideologically disastrous, impure. Despising myself, I put it away in the little toilet kit the airline had passed out, out of sight, not wanting to tempt, or rather, not wanting to offend the serious young man who brought the thermos of hot water each morning, or the maid who set everything straight on the dresser. I grew fond of Chinese objects instead — the little plastic tube of

Peacock dentifrice, the tin box with chrysanthemums stenciled on, the plastic combs and heavy stockings.

Now here it was again. If in China I had come to feel rather ashamed of having wanted it, now I was glad to see it. Some people, I have heard, are free of the impulse to keep souvenirs. I am not. I like to have things which remind me of people and places — nothing vulgar as a pillow which said BEIJING, or swizzle sticks in the shapes of women, but some private symbol of a place or event, and something you can't get at home. This is getting harder and harder. The baskets in the market in Arusha can also be found in San Francisco Imports Emporium. The linens are the same in Chinatown here as in China itself. Although one hoped for a souvenir the amusing, the rare object or the bargain, perhaps the point was the hunt itself — tracking Woon's shop through the jungle of Singapore shopping centers, with the watch as a trophy testifying to valor and success, as stuffed heads did for the people who hunted animals.

I asked Yan if she would like to wash, and showed her to her room. When she came out again, she had some folded newspaper clippings, which she passed across to me.

"You will see that your watch had a good effect for one person at least."

"Yes, tell me how it happens to be here." I did want to hear. Obviously the porter or maid had found it, had turned it in — that in itself astonishing. Perhaps such honesty is only astonishing to an American?

"First the hotel delivered it to Dr. Wang." Dr. Wang was known to the hotel as the person responsible for our presence, had booked our room, exerting his influence to get us a good one. I could imagine the reproaches of the hotel manager: "Your people left something in their room. What a nuisance." I wondered if it was easy for the maid or porter to have handed it over. Had they despised the gaudy watch or wanted it? "They understood that Dr. Wang would know how to return it to you."

I unfolded the clipping, a news story from the pages of the *China Daily*, the English-language newspaper in Beijing. HOTEL REWARDS SMART THINKING read the headline.

> Wa Weng was recently commended by the management of the Beijing Hotel for many extra hours of service and for his brilliant thinking. When a valuable watch was found in the papers ready to be

emptied out from the rooms on his floor, it was not clear whose watch it could be. He tells the story:

"When I first saw the watch it was in an airlines bag, of plastic, such as they would give you on China Airlines, but this one said TWA. It is known that TWA is an American airplane, but the trouble was, the TWA does not fly into Beijing. So there was no clue there! Also in the airplane bag was a razor, a toothbrush and a little rag to polish shoes. Now here was a clue, for the little rag said Raffles Hotel, Singapore!

"Thus it is likely that our guest had come from Singapore. Some conversation with a friend who works at the airport confirmed my guess, that only three airlines come from Singapore: China Airlines, Qantas, and Singapore Airlines. Now we had something to go on! I was able to suggest to my manager that he get in touch with these three airlines, with the names of our guests who had been there not more than three months, and in time we would find the trail. The trail would lead to Raffles Hotel, and TWA, and it would give us a name! The name of the person who had flown to Singapore on TWA, and then stayed in Raffles Hotel and then come here. But in my heart I thought it was probably these certain Americans. From the timing of the discovery, it must be people who had just left, I reasoned, and two Americans had left that morning. Also, the bracelet of the watch is very small, and the American woman was smaller than most Americans. Also, Americans would be likely to be on TWA."

When commending Weng, the Manager Yetsu Yan noted that he will soon be given the job to be in charge of the entire 5th floor, a rapid step up for a dedicated worker.

"So, you see, it was an instrument of fate for Weng Wa," Yan said. I was touched, but could not help but be embarrassed that so much effort had been gone to. I was glad that at least the trouble I had put people to had produced a happy result for the hotel man, Weng. The lives of people in China, so many were there, hung on little accidents, chance preferments, anything to make you stand out from the others. I remembered the bureau in our room, covered with visiting cards given J. by dozens of young Chinese, each one hoping to be noticed by J., to be allowed to study abroad, or to travel, or even to be commended by J. to someone higher up in China. Thinking of this made me remember something rather malicious I had done to one of them, a Dr. Fang.

One day while out walking, I had become aware that someone

was following me. Looking back over my shoulder made me certain; one face in the approaching mass of faces halted and ducked when I looked around. I sensed as I faced ahead, walking quickly to keep pace with the quick walkers, the relevance of some certain footsteps behind me to my own pace, slowing when mine did. When I turned down a lane of low houses, someone else did too. I supposed it was someone from the hotel — a spy, a security agent, someone mistrusting me. This makes one feel curiously important. I stopped and whirled, to surprise him, but couldn't tell which it was among the people walking, dangling their plastic sacks or carrying briefcases or wheeling bicycles behind me. In China you cannot be alone, but no one would approach you either. Alone and not alone, among the billion, like a bean in a jar.

Once I had been asked to talk to a group of J.'s Beijing students about my work and life in America, and when I wrote my name on the blackboard, the group, usually so polite, had tittered. Why? Because I wrote with my left hand. Does no one in China write with their left hand? No, they said. And there is no Rh negative blood, J. told me. I am a compendium of recessive traits, but there were no recessives here. You had to be like everyone else right down to the genes.

Yet I was not, was conspicuously blue-eyed and Western, and someone was surely following me. As I turned again, this figure detached himself from the people in the lane and confidently advanced on me. Perhaps I had dropped something, or left something at the department store? He looked familiar, in his forties perhaps, a pale lemon-colored man, his eyes the tiniest slivers; his graying Fu Manchu beard, daintily stuck to the center of his chin, was several inches long, like a wisp of smoke trailing downward. Something frightening about him made me look down at myself, to see what I had lost or was missing, or what I had by me to ward him off with. Yet of course harm was unthinkable. There was no harm in China, unless you were a thief, and then they executed you in the football stadium, and were sometimes embarrassed when a tourist busload happened to spy the corpses. This had happened to a woman from Cincinnati, who had talked to me once in the bar of the Beijing Hotel.

As he approached, the man spoke. "Mrs. M.?" His voice had a

thin, artificial quality, as if produced mechanically, an imitation of a Western voice.

"Yes."

Still he advanced, drawing so close to me that I was obliged to step backward, and as he stepped still closer, another step backward until I had backed into the mud wall of the house behind me. When he leaned toward me, I smelled his strange vinegar smell. I shrank; he placed his face close to mine, and whispered in my ear, his words dispersed by the intimate sibilance of his whisper. "Pssssss," I heard, as in a playground game. Perhaps this was a Chinese form of menace, like the kiss of the Mafia don. Perhaps it was the dreaded Chinese whisper. It was the middle of the day now, with people trudging by in this normal little land, paying us no attention, so I did not scream. Instead I said loudly, "I'm afraid I didn't understand you."

"Psssssss." Now I did make something out of the tickling hiss. "I am Dr. Fang," he was whispering. "Can you speak to Dr. M. for me? I want to go to work with him in America. I have written to him. But if you will speak to him, all will be well."

Finally understanding, I squirmed away from the man's insistent breath in my ear.

"You must speak to my husband yourself," I said.

"Tell him I will work very hard. I will help him. I want to learn."

Relieved of my fright, I could now attend to what I was hearing in his music-box voice, its urgent despair, its desperation.

"I will tell him I saw you," I said. "I'm sorry, I have to go."

"I have brought you this," he said, stuffing a package into my shopping basket. "Oh, thank you, thank you, dear lady," and without warning, before I could give him back the package, he leapt into a wave of oncoming people and was swept away with them.

In the hotel room I opened the package, a green glass bird on a branch, meant to look like jade, I supposed, or was jade of some thick, dull, glasslike inferior kind. We had been taken to see the jade carvers, young women sitting at benches. Their blocks of jade had numbers and lines drawn on them in ink, like a paint-by-numbers canvas, and they had only to work away according to the numbers, with their little wheezing dentist's drills. Everywhere the whine of excavation and the gurgle of water gave the impression of being in a purgatory of dentists. J. had been upset at the thought of the lungs of the girls as they breathed the dangerous jade particles loosened in the air; he wrote, frowning, in his notebook. I minded the idea of the drudgery of these poor girls, not even allowed to make up their own designs.

"The master craftsmen make the designs," the factory manager had explained, proud of their industry.

"How sad. I find it sad that people should be confined like that," I said crisply to the factory manager, who paid no attention.

This was now my punishment, to own this ugly product of the sweat shop, symbol as well of the desperation of Dr. Fang, his sacrifice. As I put it on J.'s dresser, with Dr. Fang's card, my eye fell on the array of other cards stacked there. Drs. Liu, Ma, Ron, Ree, Li, Chang, Cui, Zhang, Hum — these indistinguishable monosyllables my stupid Western brain couldn't assimilate rendering indistinguishable also their hopes, personal histories, their brilliance or beauty, charm or lack of it, each one trying to stand out for me, or rather, for J. It was J. they wanted, they wanted jobs in his laboratory, they wanted training, wanted travel, wanted escape or some chance at small Western comforts, or whatever it was they did want, showering J. with cards, with presents he couldn't refuse and they couldn't afford, saving up to bring these ugly lacquer teacups, this embroidered kitten chasing a butterfly. This young man, whose card was on top, I remembered because of his Western first name — Roderick. They chose their Western names from a book, I had heard, or got them from some exchange student who mischievously called them Lionel or Marvin.

I wondered what Dr. Fang's first name might be. Wun Fang. Long Fang. Dam Fang. I felt sorry for him but I hated him because of the intimate way he had whispered into my ear, his breath making its way inside it, like someone blowing into a shell, a rape of my ear. I imagined him saying boastfully, "I had the ear of Dr. M.'s wife." I imagined palace eunuchs whispering in the ears of courtiers. Perhaps whispering was the normal medium of Chinese intrigue.

When I showed J. the jade bird, I didn't tell him about the insult to my ear.

"He must be desperate," I said.

"They're all desperate, for more training. It's the way to success here. They all want to come to America."

And later, when we were ready to leave, J. had turned over the cards on his bureau, trying to remember which one went with which face, which life, and asking me if I remembered this person or that, and when he said "Fang Won?" I had said nothing, had pretended not to remember him, when he was the one I remembered best.

Now I asked, continuing our conversation about China, if Yan had news of Dr. Fang?

"Oh, poor Dr. Fang," she said. "Not really. He did not succeed in coming to America as he had hoped, that I know. Instead he was sent to Shenyang, in the North. I think he was a little too old to profit from study in America. Some people have lost time during the Cultural Revolution. I think he had hoped to be the one to bring you your watch. I saw his letter to Dr. Wang." In her face I could just discern, now, the satisfaction of someone compliant and reliable who knows she is in good standing. She might even, from her sly little smile, have done something to hasten the exile of Dr. Fang.

"What would you like to do while you're here?" I asked. "I'll begin by showing you around the neighborhood." I was going to say "Chinatown," which is the name of our neighborhood, but suddenly wondered if that would be taken as racist. But why should it be? "This is a Chinese area, in fact, so you'll see many things to remind you of home."

I was not prepared, though, for Yan's reaction as she and I walked along Grant Avenue, looking at the Chinese grocery stores and souvenir shops, and stacks of soybean casks, and ducks hanging, and Chinese people in padded gray coats jostling and feeling the fruit at the vegetable stall. Her reaction was one of joy. Her face glowed, and she looked around her almost with hunger, her eyes shining. "How beautiful it is, it is like China!" she cried again and again.

Now I saw that tears were standing in Yan's eyes. Of course she must be homesick, she had been nine months in Houston

already, and would be away from China five years altogether —
the time it would take for a Ph.D. in biochemistry. Chinese stayed
away for even longer sometimes, lacking the money to go home
again or afraid to go back. Sometimes their child grew up without them. Even women left their children, had to leave them. I
remembered all this as I walked with Yan, in her permanent so
unsuitable for Chinese hair and the ugly clothes from the Wangfujing department store, finery she must have saved up for, and
the stout shoes so unsuitable for a girl her age — in her mid-
twenties, probably, with the little hands and rounded cheeks of a
doll.

We had lunch in the New Asia Dim Sum Parlor. I asked Yan to
order. "It's in Cantonese. I can't really speak Cantonese," she
apologized. "Though of course I can read the menu." I nodded
encouragingly at each selection and tried to suggest that we
needed another. She ordered five dishes, looking shyly at me.

Over her ginger chicken she said, "I did not know America
was like this. I thought it was all like Houston." I had never been
to Houston, but I could imagine it — freeways, skyscrapers, the
life of the automobile. How horrible it must seem to someone
used to footpaths and bicycles and trees in leaf overhead and the
pretty tiled roofs. "I am so relieved for America, that some of it
is nice," she said. Clearly her view of it had been as a horrible
place, violent, made of cement, its dark, overbearing buildings
with windows like mirrored sunglasses, eyes invisible, rendering
its soul indecipherable and menacing. America doesn't inevitably
strike people as wonderful. You often hear of people coming to
America with joyful hearts, to find only the chill of air-condition-
ing in high-rise buildings or the cockroaches of transient hotels.
In addition to physical discomforts, their hopeful dreams of
betterment are taken from them here.

Yan had a new American name, Iris, she said. She told me
about her life in Houston, at the Baylor University Medical
School. Her days consisted of working in the hospital laboratory
then going to the library to study. She studied medical textbooks,
English, biochemistry, microbiology. She ate in the hospital dining room, and at night made tea for herself in her dormitory
room. She studied until after midnight every night. There were

one or two other Chinese students, but it was a bleak and solitary
life, driven by something I knew I could never understand. It
was too late for people like us to feel those passions for study,
for excellence, for struggling to climb up to a safe spot.

When traveling, I had often thought of how it must be to be
stuck far from home, displaced, alone, lying in a room. In every
place I have visited I have seen some despised and lonesome
person from another place — usually a man, for it seems to be
the men who are extra, who are sent off, like the Chinese men
who built the California railroad, or the migrant Mexicans in
their tin barracks, lascars, solitary Turks in Munich, little Alge-
rians so proudly male in North Africa, so invisible and despised
in France. If you were a woman displaced you went on being a
woman, but men lose the advantage of being men, and become
dark personages glimpsed in restaurant kitchens or wearing fluorescent vests as they sweep the gutters, the bright colors seeming
to ask that people see them, and yet no one does. Surely it is
harder for men than for women — unless you are a boat person,
adrift, captured by pirates to be raped and drowned. Far from
home, men were reduced, resourceless and lonely. Sentiment
overcame them. They gathered in bars or squatted on dusty
curbings. Yugoslavs in chilly England, Israelis in New York, forlorn Ethiopians or Nigerians, selling ball-point pens in Paris or
Milan, alone in their blackness, away from their mothers, miserable with cold.

At the close of the meal, as I was mechanically opening my
fortune cookie, which said, "A happy surprise will reward you,"
Yan drew a long envelope from her purse.

"I wonder if I can ask you to talk about something to Dr. M.
for me," she said.

"Of course," I said, but vaguely, trying to read upside down
the papers which Yan unfolded and smoothed out. She put them
in front of me.

"These are some papers which an American must sign to
sponsor a Chinese student. I am sponsored by my adviser at
Baylor, but I am full of hope that my twin sister could come to
America too, and Dr. Hunter, my adviser, cannot sponsor two
people. It would be no trouble, and no expense. She will live in
my room with me, and I have a grant that will be enough for us

both. I know that the paper makes you promise to pay for us, but that would not be necessary. See, I have filled out all the details, all Dr. M. would have to do is sign." I saw the hope on Yan's face, the trustful expectation of a positive reply. She would make a sacred promise, she continued to explain, that her sister Ran would not do anything to make us ashamed, or cost us fear or inquietude. Dr. Hunter would have been happy to do it, but he could not, and since she knew she would be seeing Dr. and Mrs. M., in connection with the valuable watch, she had dared to hope . . .

I reassured her that I would speak to J., adding, however, that he had a fear of forms and papers and might not like it. I would do what I could. I had, in fact, to pick up J. at the airport that afternoon. Would Yan come? But Yan said she would stay to walk in Chinatown.

I was relieved, for I could imagine that J. would balk at the idea of becoming sponsor to an unknown Chinese twin. He would imagine debts, midnight phone calls, security deposits, complaints from landladies. But he agreed, even rose to the occasion, signing with great affability after dinner. Yan's face flushed with relief. She left the room to put the signed papers safely in her luggage. I knew that this had been her purpose in coming, explaining the unusual luxury of her spending money on a plane fare from Houston to San Francisco. Except for needing these papers signed, Yan would have gone on thinking that all America was like Houston, whatever Houston was like.

I found myself thinking of Dr. Fang's glass bird, so I had a look in the china cupboard and found it. I was relieved. It would have been like me to throw it out, and now it seemed important to have it, a little flame keeping alive the recollection of poor Dr. Fang, and to remind of the arbitrary operation of bad luck, that he should have whispered in my ear, and of my thoughtless cruelty. When Yan had gone to bed, I wrote the letter to Dr. Wang, thanking him for my watch and apologizing for the trouble I had put them all to. My words had the ring to me of the false contrition of self-criticism, yet they were sincere.

When It's Over Over There

FROM GQ

IN THE SPRING of 1986, a few months short of my fifty-first birthday, my wife and I decided to go abroad for a while. We said we were looking for excitement, but I think it was repose. We were living in a monotonous Boston suburb that had neither and were disaffected in the way that you sometimes get when everything feels familiar without being in any way comfortable or interesting. Reagan was not interesting. The economy was grotesque. The novels I was reading had lost their savor. The novel I was writing had lost its savor. I was tired of my own history and wanted someone else's.

Europe suddenly seemed more appealing than America. I had always been interested in expatriates, cosmopolitan people of double or sometimes triple nationality, people born in countries at war or under occupation, people who at some point in the past had "papers" that were not quite "in order" and were now living in a country not their own. These were people for whom World War II was still an open wound, and in a certain sense people for whom — to paraphrase Edith Wharton — scandal was worse than disease. They were people who did not call attention to themselves. American expatriates were not nearly so exotic, blessed (or burdened) as they were with vivid nationality and the freedom to travel wherever they damned pleased, more or less, and struggling always to avoid the Eleuthera Syndrome. That was when you sat on the beach at Eleuthera and read the weather reports from up north, chuckling while the barman fetched another rum punch — and you did this every day. I had lived

abroad before but always in the service of a newspaper or magazine that paid the bills in return for reportage. This would be
different altogether. This would be just us. The year wanted
some romance. So over the ocean we would go!

It couldn't be more expensive than Boston.

And it wouldn't *be* Boston.

So we spent some time examining maps and talking to friends.
London was not to our taste, so the choices boiled down to Paris
or Berlin. I had become obsessed by the Germans, convinced in
some undefined way that their long postwar slumber was over
and they were about to awake and move their shoulders. I
thought it more than likely that during the calisthenics some
serious crockery would be broken, and I was avid to make my
own on-site inspection. In Germany, questions of nationality
were inherently interesting, and memory was a daily fact of life.
Certainly in aroused Germany there would be much excitement,
though the word my wife used was "anxiety." But there was
unlikely to be much repose as the crockery shattered, and neither of us spoke German. Without it, we would be little better
than nosy tourists collecting half-understood anecdotes. I was
also uncertain I wanted to trade my history for German history.
Finally, we knew no Berliners, whereas in Paris we knew a number of foreign correspondents, always the merriest and most
knowledgeable of companions. Randal and Hoagland were
there for the *Washington Post,* and Blume and Bittermann and
Kramer and Reeves; and poor, sweet Jim Markham, who later
took his life. With comrades such as these, we wouldn't have to
struggle. It would be like knowing seven Baedekers, each with a
specialty.

So it would be Paris for six months, maybe a year. I would take
my typewriter, just in case; and of course we would bring the cat,
though she was very old and worn out from a life of unspeakable
indolence. As it happened, my wife spoke a little French. With
the help of the merry and knowledgeable foreign correspondents, we could embrace *la belle* France on her own terms. There
would be repose and excitement, and west of the Rhine the
crockery was intact. France had known defeat, and her history
was a tangled affair, but she slept easily at night. The point really
was to get away from the sullen suburb, just for a little while, and

try out a new attitude. Refreshed, we could return to Reagan's America.

That was six years ago, and Paris exceeded every expectation. I have never known a better place to work and play. We lived first in Montmartre, a few blocks from Picasso's old studio and down the street from the prismatic villa that Adolf Loos had designed for Stefan Zweig. Later, we moved to the Left Bank, to an apartment around the corner from the darkly named Quai Malaquais. Jean-Paul Belmondo lived next door, though I saw him only once, in the back seat of a gigantic bottle-green BMW — or was it a Jaguar? There was a café in Rue Jacob where my wife and I often took Saturday lunch, as had Hemingway and Joyce seven decades before. Richard Wagner had spent an unproductive few years at an apartment within sight of the café, and one street over, in Rue de Seine, a friend bought a low-ceilinged five-room flat that had been occupied by Molière. Our own building was not without romance. We were assured that Édouard Manet had lived there in his declining years. Not only that, the neighbor said, but he had committed suicide by hanging — perhaps in the very rooms we now occupied. I retailed that story often, and the later the hour, the more details I was able to add, until a scholarly friend observed that it could not possibly be true. If it were, there would be a plaque beside the entrance to the building. And that plaque would read:

DANS CETTE MAISON MOURUT
ÉDOUARD MANET, PEINTRE (1832–1883)

Ghosts in every doorway. For a time, I thought we would live in France forever, buying an apartment on the Left Bank, playing the horses at Longchamp, hanging out with Milan Kundera, discovering the true cassoulet and eventually arranging for a double plot in Père-Lachaise, either the east near Piaf or dead center near Hugo. As the francs poured in from the film sales of my many novels, perhaps there would be a small vineyard in Bordeaux, a hectare or two near Buzet. But we would never be far from Paris, where the natives were something much more appealing than merely friendly: They were indifferent. Paris did not care who you were or what you did, so long as you paid your bills and observed the local customs. I had no claim on Paris, nor

Paris on me. I published four books in five years and soon began
to think of the city as a kind of Utopian safe house where I could
exist without identity. Our life settled into an agreeable bourgeois routine — long lunches, even longer dinners, day trips,
weekend trips, bracing Sunday walks, afternoon visits to the
Impressionists in the Musée d'Orsay or the Marmottan — and I
became, in some sense, denationalized. Meanwhile, all the work
was getting done, and at a speed that astonished me, given the
charged political atmosphere in Europe.

There seemed to be a tremendous sense of possibility, the
tempo quickening in 1987 and 1988, and by 1989, it was revolutionary ragtime, as the Berlin Wall came down, the Ceaucescus
were executed, Václav Havel and his compatriots contrived a
bloodless revolution in Czechoslovakia, and Solidarity held the
balance of power in Poland. In France, the mood went from
fascination to exhilaration to caution to nervousness to alarm.
Where was this heading? And where did Germany fit in? The
United States was on the sidelines for the first time since 1945,
and if you were an American living in Europe, you were thrilled.
The United States was not uninvolved in the events, but it was
not controlling them either. Seen from Europe, this was a success
not of capitalism but of the idea of freedom. It was not an
American success but a success of the people in nations we used
to call "captive," and among these people were a great many
poets, novelists, playwrights, actors, musicians and artists. These
intellectuals actually *thought*, and acted.

We returned to New England every summer, arriving in July
and leaving in September — always happy to get there, always
eager to leave. On South Beach, no one cared about Europe
because the local economy was collapsing. Relations between the
races deteriorated further. In Washington, there was no political
will. We were interested, of course, and listened attentively to the
gossip and anecdotes, but, truth to tell, our hearts were elsewhere. The United States was modern music, peevish, dissonant
and flat; Europe was Brahms. I found I could not write in New
England. I had no desire to write, and didn't. Writing was what I
did in France, where the material seemed to be, and before long,
there arrived a certain pleasurable confusion of values, perhaps
even loyalties. I seemed to be a man not with two houses but with

two homes. I did not know where I belonged, and from this circumstance came a novel; but it was not a novel I could write in New England.

I never learned to speak French. In the beginning, it was stubbornness, and then I got to like it. I liked it more than you can imagine. I liked life at the margins, life in the balcony, loving the dance but ignorant of the dancer. I liked being deracinated from a society that was not mine and could never be mine, yet was one I admired deeply. I admired the everyday forms of French life, the louche cafés, riotous Sunday lunches in the country, the politeness of tradespeople in our neighborhood, the closeness of families, the ravishing fifty-year-old women swinging along Boulevard St.-Germain, the celebrity intellectuals waging conversation in Café de Flore, the great echoing electrical vastness of Gare St.-Lazare, the throat-closing monuments to the dead of World War I in the church square of every village I ever visited — the very long lists from World War I, the reproachful short lists from World War II — and so much more beyond description. Disclosure came reluctantly, when it came at all. It was easy for people to spend an entire evening and at the end of it not know what one another did, since that evening was spent discussing the wars. France is a society where much lies in shadows, and the thought is often not given voice. As the French say of the loss of Alsace and Lorraine in 1871, "Think of it always, speak of it never." And not only Alsace and Lorraine.

I struggled with the evening news, getting some of it on my own, most of it in translation from my wife. Shadows are rarely visible on television news, whether you are watching it in Paris or in Boston. When there was an embarrassment — political scandal or some dreadful reminder of World War II — a football match would often lead the hour. Coverage of the United States was erratic and often cockeyed. In 1986 and 1987, we would see Reagan often. Then, as events in Europe accelerated, Reagan began to disappear. Weeks would go by without a piece from Washington or anywhere else in the United States, except naturally for sexual misbehavior; fiercely protective of the private lives of their own leaders, the French have license to laugh or leer at the discomfort of those not so worldly and sensible.

In any case, French journalism is difficult to parse; a reader or viewer needs oceanic patience. My wife has a theory that the complexity of the news is a consequence of the language, which, like a perverse angler, hooks the most distant fact first. And the heavier the fact, the more slowly it is brought to the boat. The language is there to be savored, its structure reminiscent of the old *Time* style so wonderfully parodied by Woolcott Gibbs a generation ago. We heard this one night on television: In Alsace, an airbus was down. It had been en route from Lyon, the identical aircraft whose automated controls have been criticized by French pilots. This accident occurred on a mountain slope a few kilometers short of the airport at Strasbourg. Bad weather hampered rescue operations. The airbus contained almost a hundred people, and eighty-some of these were thought to be lost. But there were survivors.

Backward run facts until reels the news.

But there were many nights when I sat happily for thirty minutes, watching the pictures and not understanding a word of commentary.

We saw the president of the republic here and there on the streets of Paris. The first time was four or five years ago, near the Grand Palais, his appearance unmistakable. He has the granite shape and chilly climate of the state of New Hampshire, and he looks like a Florentine Henry James. He was with a friend, strolling in the spring sunshine, two companionable old parties on promenade, hands behind their back. It was instructive watching the bodyguards, spectacularly inconspicuous men in their thirties and forties, two in front, two behind, two at the corner, two across the street; probably there were others, unnoticed by us. This was a Sunday afternoon, and the streets were crowded. But hardly anyone noticed the president. Those who did muttered good day and passed on. What made the scene so memorable was the absence of cameramen and reporters, and I thought it a wonderful tribute to France's regard for privacy, and her sense of proportion. Passersby were as nonchalant as the wintry president, even though this was a time of great personal popularity for François Mitterrand.

The next time was provocative. It had political significance, for this was the late fall of 1990, in the weeks before the war with Iraq. My wife and I had walked up the Seine, again on a Sunday, pausing at a café across the street from the Institut du Monde Arabe, the museum and cultural center of Islam. And there he was again, this time solo, except for the usual pilot fish.

I said something to my wife, my voice louder than I'd intended.

What I said was "Jesus Christ, there's François Mitterrand."

Hearing me, he turned and offered a slow smile as he waited for the traffic light. Across the street, the Institut looked vacant and somehow forlorn. How could there not be political calculation to this visit? The thought of the president paying a call to the Institut du Monde Arabe while negotiations were under way was, as I said, provocative. But there was not a newspaper reporter in sight, not a television camera, not even an Élysée photographer. The president waited patiently for the light to change.

Around me, the blasé patrons of the café had returned to their drinks, indifferent to the solitary figure in the black greatcoat and red scarf and signature borsalino now crossing the street, nodding at a bus driver. He disappeared into the Institut, and I concluded that there could be no political calculation to this visit. Or if there was, it was entirely personal, because the deed was unwitnessed by the press. If François Mitterrand crashed in the forest and no one heard him, could he be said to have crashed at all? So the simplest explanation would have to do. He was going to the Institut to look at the ceramics.

In September of 1986, the terrorists arrived in Paris. I forget the specific grievance. There were numerous bomb scares, and in the Métro and on the streets, people were less voluble, though they went about their business with admirable sangfroid. If you were dark-skinned, you received suspicious stares. Air traffic from North America declined, and we thought this an unfortunate overreaction. But we did not think much about it. We had been in the country only a few weeks and were learning our way around the neighborhood. We were also planning our first journey.

On September 15, we left Gare Montparnasse for Brest, where

we would catch a taxi for Le Conquet, a fishing village on the western coast of Brittany. The hotel had been recommended. Oysters were in season. There were wonderful walks along the rocky shore, and the idea was to walk all day long and return to the hotel for a slow, large dinner of fresh seafood. We thought five days would be about right.

We came down for breakfast the third morning, noticing immediately a subdued and nervous atmosphere in the dining room. The maître d' handed my wife a newspaper. She took a look at page 1, turned away and handed the paper to me. It was the ghastly photograph of the bombing of Magasin Tati, the cut-rate department store in Rue de Rennes. Dead and wounded were everywhere, shards of glass littered the street. There seemed to be no idea who the bombers were (except they were assumed, correctly, to be Arab), no notion why Tati — which was not Cartier nor even Galeries Lafayette — was chosen. The paper said that a number of Arab customers were among the casualties. And it turned out that the terrorists had panicked; caught in traffic, they had thrown their bomb at the first available target. Thirteen people died.

We went in to breakfast. But it was not a cheerful breakfast, as the first and second had been. There was no discussion of where we would walk that day, and no replaying of the menu of the night before or speculation about the menu to come. We ate in silence, looking at the heaving sea, the sun brilliant on the water. Some fishermen were casting from the beach. Beyond the breakwater were small boats and a freighter, and if you could extend your eyesight you would see all the way to Cape Cod.

We had planned to take the morning boat to the Île d'Ouessant, perhaps walk around the island. It was a two-hour voyage. After breakfast, we went to the quay to check the times. We had difficulty making ourselves understood, and at last we turned away in frustration. The damned language. The day was gorgeous, but there didn't seem to be anything to do in it. My wife said, "Let's go home."

And so I went in and settled the bill and called a cab. There were trains all the time from Brest to Paris, no need to reserve; and we had Eurail passes. It was suddenly urgent that we return to our flat in Montmartre. This was no time to be in tranquil Le

Conquet. We had lived in Paris for only a few weeks, but it was home. And when there was trouble in the neighborhood, you went there, even if you knew no one but your concierge and the landlady and some foreign correspondents, who were now very busy and not so merry. I think it was at that moment, deciding to return at once to Paris, that we knew France was not a lark for six months or a year but a place to live in and call home and to go back to when there was trouble.

Last April, they sentenced the three terrorists responsible for Tati, found them guilty of complicity in assassination and sent them away. On the same day, an appeals court dismissed a charge of crimes against humanity against Paul Touvier, a French militia commander in Lyon who was responsible for the deaths of seven Jewish hostages during World War II. The court ruled that there was sufficient evidence to prosecute but that the killings were not part of a "methodical extermination plan" of the wartime Vichy government and hence not a crime against humanity. The ruling was 215 pages long, by all accounts a masterpiece of the fisherman's art. The three judges wrote as historians and exonerated Vichy from war crimes, even though there had been anti-Jewish laws on its books and its officials had delivered up to the Nazis 76,000 French Jews — French citizens — for deportation to Buchenwald and other Nazi camps. Touvier, who is seventy-seven, had been in hiding for many years, living mostly in monasteries in the South of France, protected by priests; he is said to have become devout.

On the general question of crimes against humanity committed on French soil during the war, the law now appears to hold that Germans can be guilty but the French cannot, even though the crimes are identical. The German Gestapo chief Klaus Barbie, who operated in Lyon as Touvier did, was imprisoned a few years ago for virtually the same crimes for which Touvier was allowed to go free. Barbie died in prison. The statute of limitations ruled out a trial on a lesser charge, such as murder; there is no statute of limitations on crimes against humanity.

The Touvier case brought embarrassment and protest, in the newspapers and elsewhere. A group of lawyers boycotted the appeals court and demanded an investigation into the "back-

ground" (meaning: wartime service) of the three judges. Simone
Veil, a former president of the European Parliament and a survivor of the Nazi camps, was so angry during a television interview that she was barely coherent; and Madame Veil is a formid-
ably articulate figure. "A terrible decision," she said. François
Mitterrand, admitting "surprise," indicated the case might still
go to trial, at a later date. But sotto voce, you could hear suggestions that France was merely invoking a higher law: France was
a Christian nation and therefore valued mercy, forgiveness and
redemption; Jews, as was well known, preferred vengeance. It
was a question of the spirit of the New Testament as opposed to
the Old. So Paul Touvier went free, and another spadeful of
earth fell on French memory. The poet George Bernanos wrote
after the war that France would not again be France — honorable France — until the last *résistant* buried the last *collabo*. They
are all so old now, it is really a question of who will outlive whom.
All over France, there are Touviers wrestling with the wartime
sorrows of their youth. Or else they aren't.

I was out walking, and thinking about European wars, invasion and occupation, and how people got on; this is a subject an
American is ill equipped to address. I was thinking about national shame and national atonement, national memory and its
importance in the civic scheme of things, and the wisdom of a
statute of limitations on wartime sorrows, and how a very old
and settled and worldly and self-conscious society cuts itself some
slack. Disgrace in World War II remains the central fact of
French political life today. What did you do in the war, Monsieur? It is an inquiry often pondered, seldom spoken. The war
won't go away, though distance helps some; history does move
right along. I think I can supply the exact date when France
turned from its visceral (and often preposterous) anti-American-
ism. It was April 30, 1975, the day the last helicopter lifted from
the roof of the American embassy in Saigon. The second Indo-
china war was over, and the Americans had been thrown out of
Saigon, as the French, twenty-one years before, had been thrown
out of Dien Bien Phu. They were able to say "All right. See? *You
are just like us now.*"

I was walking to the restaurant near the Invalides, thinking
that I had done a good job of trading my history for someone

else's. Now I knew neither very well, and this circumstance might produce a novel; but it was not a novel I wanted to write in France nor could write in France, so it seemed time to go home, to see if I could fit one with the other. I was neither happy nor sad with this circumstance, one with its upside and its down-, like most circumstances. And it wasn't solely my work or my wife's work or the wear and tear of expatriation, or even the high cost of living; it was all those things and a few more. We had looked at each other over dinner one night and said, "Let's go home. It's time. It's time to go home."

The restaurant is in sight, and I am hurrying. I've lunched there every three weeks for almost six years. Tom Johnston and I are never the first to arrive, but we are always the last to leave. We have the same menu each time, a *poule au pot* and a liter of Côtes-du-Rhône and a coffee. The bill is 218 francs (about $40 at today's wretched rate of exchange). This sum has not varied in six years. We are always greeted warmly and seated at the corner table and served by the same agile waiter, who follows form and hands us the *carte* even though he knows the order. We settle in for three hours. Probably this is a routine that only middle-aged men can love, but it gives a kind of boozy stability to the day.

There are a few other regulars, most of them diplomats from the French foreign office, which is located nearby, on the Quai d'Orsay. We eavesdrop on them as they eavesdrop on us. They talk politics and we talk politics, mostly French and European, occasionally American politics. Lately, it has all been American politics, a monotonous and dispiriting subject. So on this occasion, our last lunch together for some time, we say the hell with it. We talk about our children, all of them grown-up and leading grown-up lives. Two of mine are in the United States and one is here. What wonderful children they all are! The wineglasses are filled, emptied and filled again. The young couple next to us leaves. The diplomats leave. Soon we are alone in an empty restaurant. The waiter begins to clear the china and prepare the tables for the evening sitting. Tom Johnston and I talk on and on and on about our children, and then we decide, just this once, to have a Calvados — that one over there, Monsieur, the twenty-year-old Calvados in the stately bottle. We mean to cut ourselves some slack.

PAUL R. McHUGH

Psychiatric Misadventures

FROM THE AMERICAN SCHOLAR

PSYCHIATRY IS A RUDIMENTARY medical art. It lacks easy access to proof of its proposals even as it deals with disorders of
the most complex features of human life — mind and behavior.
Yet, probably because of the earlier examples of Freud and Jung,
a belief persists that psychiatrists are entitled to special privileges — that they know the secret of human nature — and thus
can venture beyond their clinic-based competencies to instruct
on nonmedical matters: interpreting literature, counseling the
electorate, prescribing for the millennium.

At the Johns Hopkins University, my better days are spent
teaching psychiatry to residents and medical students. As I attempt to make clear to them what psychiatrists actually do know
and how they know it, I am often aware that I am drawing them
back from trendy thought, redirecting them from salvationist
aspirations toward the traditional concerns of psychiatry, which
is about the differentiation, understanding, and treatment of the
mentally ill.

Part of my justification for curbing my students' expansive
impulses is that they have enough to learn, and several things to
unlearn, about patients. Such sciences as epidemiology, genetics,
and neuropharmacology, which support and surround psychiatry today, are bringing new power to our practice just as science
did for internal medicine and surgery earlier in this century.
Only those physicians with critical capacities — who see the con-
ceptual structure of this discipline and can distinguish valid from
invalid opinions — will be competent to make use of these new

scientific concepts and technologies in productive ways. I want my students to number among those who will transform psychiatry in the future.

But my other justification for corralling their enthusiasms is the sense that the intermingling of psychiatry with contemporary culture is excessive and injures both parties. During the thirty years of my professional experience, I have witnessed the power of cultural fashion to lead psychiatric thought and practice off in false, even disastrous, directions. I have become familiar with how these fashions and their consequences caused psychiatry to lose its moorings. Roughly every ten years, from the mid-1960s on, psychiatric practice has condoned some bizarre misdirection, proving how all too often the discipline has been the captive of the culture.

Each misdirection was the consequence of one of three common medical mistakes — oversimplification, misplaced emphasis, or pure invention. Psychiatry may be more vulnerable to such errors than other clinical endeavors, given its lack of checks and correctives, such as the autopsies and laboratory tests that protect other medical specialties. But for each error, cultural fashion provided the inclination and the impetus. When caught up by the social suppositions of their time, psychiatrists can do much harm.

II

The most conspicuous misdirection of psychiatric practice — the precipitate dismissal of patients with severe, chronic mental disorders such as schizophrenia from psychiatric hospitals — certainly required a vastly oversimplified view of mental illness. These actions were defended as efforts to bring "freedom" to these people, sounding a typical 1960s theme, as though it were not their illnesses but society that deprived them of freedom in the first place.

There were several collaborators in this sad enterprise — prominent among them the state governments looking for release from the traditional but heavy fiscal burden of housing the mentally ill. Crucial to the process were the fashionable opinions of the time about society's institutions and, specifically, the over-

simplified opinions about schizophrenia and other mental illnesses generated by the so-called anti-psychiatrists: Thomas
Szasz, R. D. Laing, Erving Goffman, Michel Foucault, and the
rest. These men provided an acid commentary on psychiatric
thought and practice, which in turn eroded confidence in the
spirit of psychiatric concern for the mentally ill that had previously generated, and regularly regenerated, advocacy on the
part of mainstream psychiatry for their welfare. This traditional
concern had lasted for more than 120 years in America, or ever
since the 1840s crusades led by Dorothea Dix to provide professional services and humane conditions for the mentally ill.

The "anti-psychiatry" school depicted mental institutions as
medically useless, self-serving institutions run for the management, and quite unnecessary for patients. These commentators
scorned social attitudes about the mentally ill and the contemporary psychiatric practice, but not one of them described the
impairments of mind in patients with schizophrenia, manic-de-
pressive illness, or mental retardation or senility. Data about
these impairments were what Dix and an enlightened public
came to emphasize when founding psychiatrically supervised,
state-supported hospitals. These hospitals rescued the mentally
ill from destitution, jails, and the mean streets of cities.

Description of the mental problems of psychiatric patients was
not the style of the popular 1960s commentators. They were
more interested in painting a picture of their own devising that
would provoke first suspicion and then disdain for contemporary psychiatric practices and did so, not by producing new
standards or reforming specific practices, but by ridiculing and
caricaturing efforts of the institutions and people at hand just as
fashion directed. The power of their scorn was surprising and
had amazing results, leading many to believe that it was the
institutions that provoked the patients' illnesses rather than the
illnesses that called out for shelter and treatment.

Here, from Szasz's book *Schizophrenia: The Sacred Symbol of Psychiatry,* is a typical comment:

> The sense in which I mean that Psychiatry creates schizophrenia is
> readily illustrated by the analogy between institutional psychiatry and
> involuntary servitude. If there is no slavery there can be no slaves. . . .
> Similarly if there is no psychiatry there can be no schizophrenics. In

other words, the identity of an individual as a schizophrenic depends on the existence of the social system of [institutional] psychiatry.

The only reply to such commentary is to know the patients for what they are — in schizophrenia, people disabled by delusions, hallucinations, and disruptions of thinking capacities — and to reject an approach that would trivialize their impairments and deny them their frequent need for hospital care.

On one occasion in the early 1970s, when I was working at Cornell University Medical Center in New York, a friend and senior member of the biochemistry faculty called me about a medical student who was balking over a term paper because his career plan was to become a champion of the "psychiatrically oppressed." Biochemistry term papers seemed "irrelevant." Could I offer him a project with psychiatric patients that might be developed into a term paper satisfying the requirements of her department? "He's a neat guy," she said, "but he is stubborn about this and full of views about contemporary psychiatry."

"Send him over," I said, but I awaited his arrival with some apprehension. I needn't have feared the encounter because, in contrast to many other students of those times, he was not look-ing for a fight. "It's just that I know what I want to do — under-stand the people who are isolated by the label schizophrenia — and help them achieve what they want in life. I've written enough irrelevant papers in my life," he said. He had graduated summa cum laude from Princeton, with a concentration in phi-losophy, so he certainly had placed a large number of words on paper.

"Have you ever seen anyone with schizophrenia?" I asked.

"Not in the flesh," he said, "but I think I know what you do with them."

"Well," I replied, "I will be glad to have you see one, and let you tell me how to appreciate his choice of an eccentric way of life that he could be released to express."

I had plenty of patients under my care at the time and chose one who was the same age as the student but who had a severe disruption in his thought processes. Even to talk with him was a distressing experience because few of his thoughts were con-nected, and all of them were vaguely tied to delusional beliefs

about the world, his family, and our society. He wasn't aggressive
or in any way threatening. He was just bewilderingly incoherent.
I left the student with the patient, promising to return in half an
hour to learn what he thought.

On my return, I found the student subdued. I started, in a
slightly teasing way, to ask where he suggested I might send the
patient to start his new life — but was quickly cut off by the
student who, finding his voice, said, "That was nothing like what
I expected and nothing like what I've read about. Obviously you
can't send this poor fellow out of the hospital. Please tell me how
you're treating him."

With this evidence confirming my colleague's judgment of the
student's basic good nature in what, after all, had been a heartfelt
if inexperienced opinion, we went on to talk about the impairments and disabilities of patients with serious mental illnesses,
their partial responses to combinations of medication and psychological management, and, finally, to the meretricious ideas
about their treatment that had been promulgated by contemporary fashion and the anti-psychiatry critics without making an
effort to examine patients.

The student wrote his biochemistry paper on emerging concepts of the neurochemistry of mental disorders. He buckled
down in medical school, and he came, after graduation, to join
me as a resident psychiatrist and eventually proved to be one of
the best doctors I ever taught. We had overcome something
together — all out of going to see a patient, recognizing his
burdens, and avoiding assumptions about what fashion said we
should find.

A saving grace for any medical theory or practice — the thing
that spares it *perpetual* thralldom to the gusty winds of fashion —
is the patients. They are real, they are around, and a knowledge
of their distressing symptoms guards against oversimplification.

III

The claim that schizophrenic patients are in any sense living an
alternative "life style" that our institutions were inhibiting was of
course fatuous. It is now obvious to every citizen of our cities that
these patients have impaired capacities to comprehend the world

and that they need protection and serious active treatment. Without such help, they drift back to precisely the place Dorothea Dix found them 150 years ago.

From the faddish idea of institutions as essentially oppressive emerged a nuance that became more dominant as the 1970s progressed. This was that social custom was itself oppressive. In fact, according to this view, all standards by which behaviors are judged are simply matters of opinion — and emotional opinions at that, likely to be enforced but never justified. In the 1970s, this antinomian idea fueled several psychiatric misdirections.

A challenge to standards can affect at least the discourse in a psychiatric clinic, if not the practice. These challenges are expressed in such slogans as "Do your own thing," "Whose life is it anyway?" "Be sure to get your own," or Joseph Campbell's "Follow your bliss." All of these slogans are familiar to psychiatrists trying to redirect confused, depressed, and often self-belittling patients. Such is their pervasiveness in the culture that they may even divert psychiatrists into misplaced emphases in their understanding of patients.

This interrelationship of cultural antinomianism and a psychiatric misplaced emphasis is seen at its grimmest in the practice known as sex reassignment surgery. I happen to know about this because Johns Hopkins was one of the places in the United States where this practice was given its start. It was part of my intention, when I arrived in Baltimore in 1975, to help end it.

Not uncommonly, a person comes to the clinic and says something like, "As long as I can remember, I've thought I was in the wrong body. True, I've married and had a couple of kids, and I've had a number of homosexual encounters, but always, in the back and now more often in the front of my mind, there's this idea that actually I'm more a woman than a man."

When we ask what he has done about this, the man often says, "I've tried dressing like a woman and feel quite comfortable. I've even made myself up and gone out in public. I can get away with it because it's all so natural to me. I'm here because all this male equipment is disgusting to me. I want medical help to change my body: hormone treatments, silicone implants, surgical amputation of my genitalia, and the construction of a vagina. Will you do it?"

The patient claims it is a torture for him to live as a man, especially now that he has read in the newspapers about the possibility of switching surgically to womanhood. Upon examination it is not difficult to identify other mental and personality difficulties in him, but he is primarily disquieted because of his intrusive thoughts that his sex is not a settled issue in his life.

Experts say that "gender identity," a sense of one's own maleness or femaleness, is complicated. They believe that it will emerge through the steplike features of most complex developmental processes in which nature and nurture combine. They venture that, although their research on those born with genital and hormonal abnormalities may not apply to a person with normal bodily structures, something must have gone wrong in this patient's early and formative life to cause him to feel as he does. Why not help him look more like what he says he feels? Our surgeons can do it. What the hell!

The skills of our plastic surgeons, particularly on the genitourinary system, are impressive. They were obtained, however, not to treat the gender identity problem but to repair congenital defects, injuries, and the effects of destructive diseases such as cancer in this region of the body.

That you can get something done doesn't always mean that you should do it. In sex reassignment cases, there are so many problems right at the start. The patient's claim that this has been a lifelong problem is seldom checked with others who have known him since childhood. It seems so intrusive and untrusting to discuss the problem with others, even though they might provide a better gauge of the seriousness of the problem, how it emerged, its fluctuations of intensity over time, and its connection with other experiences. When you discuss what the patient means by "feeling like a woman," you often get a sex stereotype in return — something that woman physicians note immediately is a male caricature of women's attitudes and interests. One of our patients, for example, said that, as a woman, he would be more "invested with being than with doing."

It is not obvious how this patient's feeling that he is a woman trapped in a man's body differs from the feeling of a patient with anorexia nervosa that she is obese despite her emaciated, cachectic state. We don't do liposuction on anorexics. Why amputate the genitals of these poor men? Surely, the fault is in the mind, not the member.

Yet, if you justify augmenting breasts for women who feel underendowed, why not do it and more for the man who wants to be a woman? A plastic surgeon at Johns Hopkins provided the voice of reality for me on this matter based on his practice and his natural awe at the mystery of the body. One day while we were talking about it, he said to me: "Imagine what it's like to get up at dawn and think about spending the day slashing with a knife at perfectly well-formed organs because you psychiatrists do not understand what is the problem here but hope surgery may do the poor wretch some good."

The zeal for this sex-change surgery — perhaps, with the exception of frontal lobotomy, the most radical therapy ever encouraged by twentieth-century psychiatrists — did not derive from critical reasoning or thoughtful assessments. These were so faulty that no one holds them up anymore as standards for launching any therapeutic exercise, let alone one so irretrievable as a sex-change operation. The energy came from the fashions of the seventies that invaded the clinic — if you can do it and he wants it, why not do it? It was all tied up with the spirit of doing your thing, following your bliss, an aesthetic that sees diversity as everything and can accept any idea, including that of permanent sex change, as interesting and that views resistance to such ideas as uptight if not oppressive.

Moral matters should have some salience here. These include the waste of human resources; the confusions imposed on society where these men/women insist on acceptance, even in athletic competition, with women; the encouragement of the "illusion of technique," which assumes that the body is like a suit of clothes to be hemmed and stitched to style; and, finally, the ghastliness of the mutilated anatomy.

But lay these strong moral objections aside and consider only that this surgical practice has distracted effort from genuine investigations attempting to find out just what has gone wrong for these people — what has, by their testimony, given them years of torment and psychological distress and prompted them to accept these grim and disfiguring surgical procedures.

We need to know how to prevent such sadness, indeed horror.

We have to learn how to manage this condition as a mental disorder when we fail to prevent it. If it depends on child rearing, then let's learn about its inner dynamics so that parents can be taught to guide their children properly. If it is an aspect of confusion tied to homosexuality, we need to understand its nature and exactly how to manage it as a manifestation of serious mental disorder among homosexual individuals.

But instead of attempting to learn enough to accomplish these worthy goals, psychiatrists collaborated in an exercise of folly with distressed people during a time when "do your own thing" had something akin to the force of a command. As physicians, psychiatrists, when they give in to this, abandon the role of protecting patients from their symptoms and become little more than technicians working on behalf of a cultural force.

IV

Medical errors of oversimplification and misplaced emphasis usually play themselves out for all to see. But the pure inventions bring out a darker, hateful potential when psychiatric thought goes awry. The invention of entities of mind and then their elaborate description, usually fueled by the energy from some social attitude they amplify, is a recurring event in the history of psychiatry.

Most psychiatric histories choose to describe such invention by detailing its most vivid example — witches. The experience in Salem, Massachusetts, of three hundred years ago is prototypical. Briefly, in 1692, several young women and girls who had for some weeks been secretly listening to tales of spells, voodoo, and illicit cultic practices from a Barbados slave suddenly displayed a set of mystifying mental and behavioral changes. They developed trancelike states, falling on the ground and flailing away, and screaming at night and at prayer, seemingly in great distress and in need of help. The local physician, who witnessed this, was as bewildered as anyone else and eventually made a diagnosis of "bewitchment." "The evil hand is on them," he said and turned them over to the local officials for care.

The clergy and magistrates, regarding the young people as victims and pampering them by showing much attention to their symptoms, assumed that local agents of Satan were at work and, using as grounds the answers to leading questions, indicted several citizens. The accepted proof of guilt was bizarre. The young women spoke of visions of the accused, of sensing their presence at night by pains and torments and of ghostly visitations to their homes, all occurring while the accused were known to be elsewhere. The victims even screeched out in court that they felt pinches and pains provoked by the accused, even while they were sitting quietly across the room. Judges believed this "spectral" evidence because it conformed to contemporary thought about the capacities of witches; they dismissed all denials of the accused and promptly executed them.

The whole exercise should have been discredited when, after the executions, there was no change in the distraught behavior of the young women. Instead more and more citizens were indicted. A prosecution depending on "spectral evidence" was at last seen as capricious — as irrefutable as it was undemonstrable. The trials ceased, and eventually several of the young women admitted that their beliefs had been "delusions" and their accusations false.

The modern diagnosis for these young women is, of course, hysteria, not bewitchment. Psychiatrists use the term "hysteria" to identify behavioral displays in which physical or mental disorders are imitated. The reasons for the behavior vary with the person displaying the disorder but are derived from that person's more or less unconscious effort to appear more significant to others and to be more entitled to their interest and support. The status of the putatively bewitched in Salem of 1692 brought both attentive concern and the license to indict to young women previously scarcely noticed by the community. The forms of hysterical behavior — whether they be physical activities, such as falling and shaking, or mental phenomena, such as pains, visions, or memories — are shaped by unintended suggestions from others and sustained by the attention of onlookers — especially such onlookers as doctors who are socially empowered to assign, by affixing a diagnosis, the status of "patient" to a person. Whenever these diagnosticians mistake hysteria for what it is attempting to imitate — misidentifying it either as a physical illness or inventing some psychological explanation such as bewitchment — then the behavioral display will continue, expand, and, in certain settings, spread to others. The usual result is trouble for everyone.

During the last seven or eight years, another example of misidentified hysterical behavior has surfaced and again has been bolstered by an invented view of its cause that fits a cultural fashion. This condition is "multiple personality disorder" (MPD, as it has come to be abbreviated). The majority of the patients who eventually receive this diagnosis come to therapists with standard psychiatric complaints, such as depression or difficulty in relationships. Some therapists see much more in these symptoms and suggest to the patient and to others that they represent the subtle actions of several alternative personalities, or "alters," coexisting in the patient's mental life. These suggestions encourage many patients to see their problems in a fresh and, to them, remarkably interesting way. Suddenly they are transformed into odd people with repeated shifts of demeanor and deportment that they display on command.

Sexual politics in the 1980s and 1990s, particularly those connected with sexual oppression and victimization, galvanize these inventions. Forgotten sexual mistreatment in childhood is the most frequently proffered explanation of MPD. Just as an epidemic of bewitchment served to prove the arrival of Satan in Salem, so in our day an epidemic of MPD is used to confirm that a vast number of adults were sexually abused by guardians during their childhood.

Now I don't for a moment deny that children are sometimes victims of sexual abuse, or that a behavioral problem originating from such abuse can be a hidden feature in any life. Such realities are not at issue. What I am concerned with here is what has been imagined from these realities and inventively applied to others.

Adults with MPD, so the theory goes, were assaulted as young children by a trusted and beloved person — usually a father, but grandfathers, uncles, brothers, or others, often abetted by women in their power, are also possibilities. This sexual assault, the theory holds, is blocked from memory (repressed and dissociated) because it was so shocking. This dissociating blockade itself — again according to the theory — destroys the integra-

tion of mind and evokes multiple personalities as separate, disconnected, sequestered, "alternative" collections of thought,
memory, and feeling. These resultant distinct "personalities"
produce a variety of what might seem standard psychiatric symptoms — depression, weight problems, panic states, demoralization, and so forth — that only careful review will reveal to be
expressions of MPD that is the outcome of sexual abuse.

These patients have not come to treatment reporting a sexual
assault in childhood. Only after therapy has promoted MPD
behavior is the possibility that they were sexually abused as children suggested to them. From recollections of the mists of childhood, a vague sense of vulnerability may slowly emerge, facili-
tated and encouraged by the treating group. This sense of
vulnerability is thought a harbinger of clearer memories of victimization that, although buried, have been active for decades,
producing the different "personalities." The long supposedly
forgotten abuse is finally "remembered" after months of "uncov-
ering" therapy, during which long conversations by the therapist with "alter" personalities take place. Any other actual proof
of the assault is thought unnecessary. Spectral evidence — developed through suggestions and just as irrefutable as that at
Salem — once again is sanctioned.

Like bewitchment from Satan's local agents, the idea of MPD
and its cause has caught on among large numbers of psychiatrists
and psychotherapists. Its partisans see the patients as victims,
cosset them in groups, encourage more expression of "alters"
(up to as many as eighty or ninety), and are ferocious toward any
defenders of those they believe are perpetrators of the abuse.
Just as the divines of Massachusetts were convinced that they
were fighting Satan by recognizing bewitchment, so the contemporary divines — these are therapists — are confident that they
are fighting perpetrators of a common expression of sexual oppression, child abuse, by recognizing MPD.

The incidence of MPD has of late indeed taken on epidemic
proportions, particularly in certain treatment centers. Whereas
its diagnosis was reported less than two hundred times from a
variety of supposed causes in the last century, it has been applied
to more than twenty thousand people in the last decade and
largely attributed to sexual abuse.

I have been involved in direct and indirect ways with five such cases in the past year alone. In every one, the very same story has been played out in a stereotyped scriptlike way. In each a young woman with a rather straightforward set of psychiatric symptoms — depression and demoralization — sought help and her case was stretched into a diagnosis of MPD. Eventually, in each example, an accusation of prior sexual abuse was leveled by her against her father. The accusation developed after months of therapy, first as vague feelings of a dreamlike kind — childhood reminiscences of danger and darkness eventually crystallizing, sometimes "in a flash," into a recollection of father forcing sex upon the patient as a child. No other evidence of these events was presented but the memory, and plenty of refuting testimony, coming from former nursemaids and the mother, was available, but dismissed.

On one occasion, the identity of the molester — forgotten for years and now first vaguely and then more surely remembered under the persuasive power of therapy — changed, but the change was as telling about the nature of evidence as was the emergence of the original charge. A woman called her mother to claim that she had come to realize that when she was young she was severely and repeatedly sexually molested by her uncle, the mother's brother. The mother questioned the daughter carefully about the dates and times of these incidents and then set about determining whether they were in fact possible. She soon discovered that her brother was on military service in Korea at the time of the alleged abuse. With this information, the mother went to her daughter with the hope of showing her that her therapist was misleading her in destructive ways. When she heard this new information, the daughter seemed momentarily taken aback, but then said, "I see, Mother. Yes. Well, let me think. If your dates are right, I suppose it must have been Dad." And with that, she began to claim that she had been a victim of her father's abusive attentions, and nothing could dissuade her.

The accused men whom I studied, denying the charges and amazed at their source, submitted to detailed reviews of their sexual lives and polygraphic testing to try to prove their innocence and thereby erase doubts about themselves. Professional requests by me to the daughters' therapists for better evidence of the abuse were dismissed as derived from the pleadings of the guilty and scorned as beneath contempt, given that the diagnosis of MPD and the testimony of the patients patently confirmed the assumptions.

In Salem, the conviction depended on how judges thought witches behaved. In our day, the conviction depends on how some therapists think a child's memory of trauma works. In fact, severe traumas are not blocked out by children but remembered all too well. They are amplified in consciousness, remaining like grief to be reborn and reemphasized on anniversaries and in settings that can simulate the environments where they occurred. Good evidence for this is found in the memories of children from concentration camps. More recently, the children of Chowchilla, California, who were kidnapped in their school bus and buried in sand for many hours, remembered every detail of their traumatic experience and need psychiatric assistance, not to bring out forgotten material that was repressed, but to help them move away from a constant ruminative preoccupation with the experience.

Many psychiatrists upon first hearing of these diagnostic formulations (MPD being the result of repressed memories of sexual abuse in childhood) have fallen back upon what they think is an evenhanded way of approaching it. "The mind is very mysterious in its ways," they say. "Anything is possible in a family." In fact, this credulous stance toward evidence and the failure to consider the alternative of hysterical behaviors and memories are what continue to support this crude psychiatric analysis.

The helpful clinical approach to the patient with putative MPD, as with any instance of hysterical display, is to direct attention away from the behavior — one simply never talks to an "alter." Within a few days of a consistent therapeutic emphasis away from the MPD behavior, it fades and generally useful psychotherapy on the presenting true problems begins. Real sexual traumas can be dealt with, if they are present, as can the ambivalent and confused feelings that many adults have about their parents.

Similarly, the proper approach to end epidemics of MPD and the assumptions of a vast prevalence of sexual abuse in ordinary families is for psychiatrists to be aware of the potential, whenever we are dealing with hysteria, to mistake it for something else. When it is so mistaken, this can lead to monstrous concepts defended by coincidence, the induction of memories, and a display of "spectral" evidence — all to justify a belief that the community is under siege. This belief, of course, is what releases the power of the witches' court and the lynch mob.

As a corrective, psychiatrists need only review with a patient how the MPD behavior was diagnosed and how the putative memories of sexual abuse were suggested. These practices will eventually be discredited, and this epidemic will end in the same way that the witch trials ended in Salem. But time is passing, many families are being hurt, and confidence in the competence and impartiality of psychiatry is eroding.

V

Major psychiatric misdirections often share this intimidating mixture of a medical mistake lashed to a trendy idea. Any challenge to such a misdirection must confront simultaneously the professional authority of the proponents and the political power of fashionable convictions. Such challenges are not for the fainthearted or inexperienced. They seldom quickly succeed because they are often misrepresented as ignorant or, in the cant word of our day, uncaring. Each of the three misdirections I have dealt with in this essay ran for a full decade, despite vigorous criticism. Eventually the mischief became obvious to nearly everyone and fashion moved on to attach itself to something else.

In ten years much damage can be done and much effort over a longer period of time is required to repair it. Thus with the mentally ill homeless, only a new crusade and social commitment will bring them adequate help again. Age accentuates the sad caricature of the sexual reassigned and saps their bravado. Some, pathetically, ask about re-reassignment. Groups of parents falsely accused of sexual mistreatment by their grown children are gathering together to fight back in ways that will produce dramatic but distressing spectacles. How good it would have been if in the first place all these misguided programs had been avoided or at least their span abbreviated.

Psychiatry, it needs always to be remembered, is a medical discipline — capable of glorious medical triumphs and hideous medical mistakes. We psychiatrists don't know the secret of human nature. We cannot build a New Jerusalem. But we can teach the lessons of our past. We can describe how our explanations for mental disorders are devised and develop — where they are strong and where they are vulnerable to misuse. We can clarify the presumptions about what we know and how we know it. We can strive within the traditional responsibilities of our profession to build a sound relationship with people who consult us — placing them on more equal terms with us and encouraging them to approach us as they would any other medical specialists, by asking questions and expecting answers, based on science, about our assumptions, practices, and plans. With effort and good sense, we can construct a clinical discipline that, while delivering less to fashion, will bring more to patients and their families.

SHAUN O'CONNELL

A Memory of Two Fathers

FROM THE MASSACHUSETTS REVIEW

I WAITED next to a huge boulder at the hollow of two hills, watching the two men who stood, tall and imposing, on the sixth tee. The late-afternoon sun burned behind them as they contemplated their tee shots on this down-and-up-hill par-five and they cast long shadows towards me. I squinted and concentrated, as I knew a good caddie should, so I would be able to follow the flight of their shots, which should land in the fairway, to my left, beyond the boulder. On the boulder was painted MCC in huge letters, for Marlborough Country Club, and the fairway was burned brown, for this was August.

It was 1946, the summer after the war. I was eleven. Vin, my father, then in his early forties, a wandering man, was back from four years of wartime service as a Navy sailor in the Seabees. Cliff, my uncle, then in his mid-fifties, a dependable man, had been too old for wartime service, so he stayed at his job, working for the United Shoe Machinery Company. Vin built landing strips under Japanese fire on South Pacific islands, while Cliff oversaw the repairs of shoe machinery in shops scattered throughout towns in central Massachusetts.

Vin was a dreamy, boozy Celt, seldom there when you needed him, but often charming. When he wasn't squeezed by the vice of depression, Vin laughed frequently and cried occasionally, but mainly he talked his way through life, telling wonderful stories — many of them true. Cliff was a practical, abstemious, New England Yankee, always there for you, but not much fun. Though Cliff was frugal with words and emotions, he was a man who meant what he said. Cliff gave an honest day's work for his

day's pay and he never questioned the right of an employer to
set the wage rate, but Vin jumped from job to job, avoided heavy
lifting and complained about exploitation. Vin was prodigal,
unreliable, and winning: "Let a smile be your umbrella," he told
me, "and you'll have a wet face." Cliff, suspicious of joy, was
circumspect and austere: "there's a right way and a wrong way
to do everything," he told me repeatedly. Cliff was morning, a
glaring sun, and Vin was night, a blue moon. Their alternating
presences filled my sky. Now they stood together, upon a hill, in
late-summer twilight, playing the same game, while I carried
their golf bags.

After my mother died when I was a baby, Vin had entrusted the
care of his only son to his older sister, Jane, and her husband,
Cliff. So, as I thought of it, I had two "fathers" to show me the
way. But which way? Now, at long last, I might find out, for we
were all together, just as I had so often dreamed during the war.
The lights had gone on again, all over the world, just as Vaughn
Monroe, with his foggy voice, sang in the song that ran through
my mind as I watched Vin take his long, graceful, Bobby Jones–
style swing, which he had learned from a Florida golf pro in the
1920s. "That's *it*," I thought, as his clubhead silently came down
upon the ball.

  Vin's hair had gone gray and he now carried more weight, but
his smooth swing still ended in a classic, hands-high body turn.
At the same time I heard the belated *crack* of his hit, I was
amazed to see his drive soar high over the boulder, dead on line
with the distant pin; then his ball hit on the up-slope of the
fairway and bounced into a trap, some 250 yards from the tee.
Though I had been caddying all that summer, I had never seen
a drive so long, so risky, so doomed — for the trap was gouged
into the hill like a bomb crater. When his ball stopped, half-
embedded in sand, I looked back, up the hill to the tee, and saw
Vin, annoyed, toss away his driver, then turn his back, cup his
hands and light a Lucky, as though that — a great drive, hit
long, low and straight at the hole, but ending up stuck, deep in a
trap — was about all he might expect from a life of bad fortune.
Vin wasn't even watching when Cliff hit, though I was.
  Cliff had a different style of swing. Stiffened by years of desk-
work and commuting, Cliff had learned the game on his own, in

his fifties, so he developed a short stab at the ball, a jerky whip which looked like the swing a right-handed batter uses when he chokes up on his bat and punches a hit to right field. Cliff's drives were chopped out 150 yards, while Vin's drives soared and, like Ted Williams' home runs, hung suspended, then dropped at impossible distances. I didn't have to worry about spotting Cliff's golf balls, which always fell near mid-fairway, but Vin's shots could come down anywhere — left or right side rough, woods, water. Or, rarely, they reached long and straight, far past Cliff's humpy shots.

Sure enough, Cliff's shot, accompanied by a grunt, as though he were pushing open a stuck door, dropped into the fairway — safe, sure and short. Two more like it and he would have a chip and a putt for a possible par. But Vin's score could be anything from an eagle to a triple bogey.

Vin, born in 1903, was the petted, youngest son in a family of six children; his father, an Irish immigrant from Cork, worked for the railroad. Before Vin left home, his sainted mother sprinkled him with holy water, to protect him on his journeys. She must have sensed how difficult his voyages would become.

Cliff, born in 1890, was the steady, eldest son in a family of three children; his father was a solid Yankee farmer. A lapsed Episcopalian, Cliff needed no holy water for his journeys. He never left the home in which he was born; nor did he stray from the straight and narrow path he set for himself. At age thirteen Cliff quit school to labor in a shoe factory; then he became a whiz at machine repair and so he made that his life's work. Cliff, in his only rash act, crossed the region's ethnic line to marry a pretty Irish American, a young woman from nearby Framingham, Jane O'Connell. By doing so, Cliff allowed into his life an astonishing range of Celtic intemperance, wit and eruptions of powerful feelings.

Cliff hunched over, wagged his three-wood, and whacked his ball up the fairway, not far above the trap in which Vin's shot had landed. Vin walked up to the deep trap and studied his shot, shaking his head in dismay. A huge lip of grass hung over the top of the trap and a clump of trees stood, ominously, between his ball and the green.

"You gonna chip it out to the side of the trap?" I asked.

"That what you think I should do?"

"Well, uh, yuh, I guess," I said, with my characteristic conviction and eloquence.

He tossed away his inevitable Lucky, flashed his wry smile and said, "That's not what I'm going to do, Sonny Boy. Stand back and keep your eye on the ball."

He took a seven-iron, a club which would give his ball both loft and distance; then he set himself and swung, down and through, blasting the sand. Wondrously, his ball cleared the lip of the trap and lifted off in flight toward the green, but I winced when, just before flying free of the trees, it clipped a branch of an elm and caromed off to the side, onto the fairway, seventy-five yards behind Cliff's second shot.

"Almost cleared the trees," I said.

" 'Almost' doesn't count for much, does it?"

I didn't know, so I walked over to Vin's ball and waited for him to pick a club for his third shot.

During the 1920s, Vin worked as a chauffeur for the family of a Framingham railroad owner; Vin drove them in their Packard to Florida, where they wintered. To them he was more than an employee, but he was less than the adopted son he imagined himself; he learned the manners and tastes of those of the manor to which he was not born while he romanced one of the Irish maids. With his slicked-back, Valentino-style hair and his dapper duds, Vin made himself into a small-time Gatsby, for Vin too had a "heightened sensitivity to the promises of life." In a yellowing picture — which I have propped before me as I write — Vin still poses on a Florida golf course, beneath a palm tree, decked out in a dazzling white shirt and slacks, leaning on a putter, one ankle jauntily crossing the other, free hand on hip, flashing a no-flies-on-me smile.

Then, in his most reckless act, Vin gave up all that borrowed glamour. Like Cliff, Vin too married a pretty, young woman from Framingham. Vin took a job that required no travel and he made a home for their new baby — me. For a while Vin was happy, but soon his life fell apart.

When I was little more than a year old, in 1936, my mother

had a miscarriage; infection set in and she died. So I lost a
mother, a sibling and a home, but my father lost more. Never
again would his world make sense. Grieving, drinking and restless, he was in no shape to care for me, then or later. After I was
passed around among relatives, I finally stuck at my Aunt Jane's,
in Marlborough. She and Cliff had tried but failed to have children, so, though they were then in their mid-forties, they welcomed me. There I stayed, throughout my school years, rooted
in one perpetual place.

Late in the 1930s, by then a confirmed wanderer, Vin worked
in Northern Ireland, on construction projects. On his way home,
a German sub torpedoed his boat, so he became a fierce patriot.
After Pearl Harbor, Vin was the first man from Framingham to
enlist in the Navy, though at age thirty-eight he could have
avoided the draft. Indeed, he managed to join up only by volun-
teering for the Seabees. Nothing would keep him home. Vin was
always seeking a new life, beyond the blue horizon. Though he
never forgot me. His censored mail arrived regularly during the
war. No force, however, could tear Cliff away from his primary
responsibilities: his home, his family and his work. Cliff was
always *there*, a steady beacon, but Vin came and went, a sweeping
arc of light.

Vin pulled a two-wood out of the golf bag, again flicked his
Lucky into the grass, set himself, unwound his lovely swing and
sent a shot buzzing, long and low, over the fairway rise. We all
watched it hit, jump and roll onto the front edge of the green. I
felt my heart lift and my eyes blur, for I had never before been
so close to anything so marvelous as that shot, still vivid after all
these years. Then Vin casually tossed me his club, as though he
did this every day, and lit a fresh Lucky. Cliff, unspectacularly
but predictably, jerked a three-wood shot into the air and
watched it plop down, fifty yards short of the green.

Vin winked at me and yelled across to Cliff, lifting an imaginary glass. "I'll drink to that!" But Cliff looked down, looking
for a divot to replace, pretending he did not hear.

Vin drank — crazily, self-destructively, seeking perfect oblivion — but Cliff was as sober and as just as a judge. Vin went off

on bats — on wild, shore-leave drunks — and woke up in surprising places, finding himself without money, shaking and guilty, but briefly purged. (What a *dramatic* life Vin had, shot full of passionate intensities.) After he had been missing for days, he would turn up, reeling, while his sister cringed at the sight of him. Or she would get a call from one of his buddies, a solicitous bartender or even the police. She would then drive to Boston or Providence or Worcester, wherever Vin ended up, and bring him back to Marlborough to sleep it off. She would be furious at her wayward, younger brother, but Cliff would say nothing. (What a *quiet* life Cliff had, apart from all those Mick, in-law dramatics.)

When Vin came to, groggily, on his many mornings-after, he would make his way to the kitchen, where he boiled coffee, scrambled piles of eggs, fried stacks of bacon, toasted bread and ate it all with a focused passion. Then he would lean back from the kitchen table and silently smoke his Luckys — he held his cigarettes tip-down, so the smoke curled up through his fingers, leaving them sickly yellow. Eventually he would talk, at first to me, dutifully checking up on how I was doing in school, but edgy with this attentive lad whose presence reminded him of too many painful things; then, more familiarly, Vin would toss words, like flowers, at his sister's back as she moved about the kitchen, tense with disapproval. Vin would recall old times, before World War I, when he and Jane were children — when the O'Connell kids played together in the horse barn or when she was supposed to keep him from giggling in church but often joined him. Soon my Aunt Jane, enticed from her sulk, would also settle down at the kitchen table — drinking coffee, smoking and "batting the breeze," as she called it, with her incorrigible but beloved brother. Cliff, of course, was off putting in another honest day's work, but I was there in the kitchen, with Jiggs, my dog, both of us alert, watching the pieces of my scattered world come together.

Sometimes Vin took me to Boston, on the Boston & Worcester bus, to a Red Sox game — Cliff preferred the less flashy Boston Braves — or to movies along Washington Street. (During ball games Vin spent many innings lining up to buy beers; during movies he would slip out for nips at nearby pubs.) Then, just like that, Vin's shore leave would be over. I would ride into Boston, sitting in the back of the Plymouth sedan with Jiggs, while Aunt Jane drove and Vin gabbed; at crowded South Station, he would wave and then disappear into a crowd of sailors and soldiers, off again to the war.

When Vin returned, he was often unable to make it past one of several barrooms — particularly the West End Café, at the bottom of the hill on which Cliff's house stood. When he did make it home, sometimes Vin woke me in the middle of the night, gripped me, breathed boozy fumes, cried and told me *never, never* to forget my mother — a woman I could not remember. On other days, when I got up to let Jiggs out, I would find Vin asleep on our lawn, under a pear tree, unable or unwilling to enter Cliff's house. His sister would blush with shame at what the neighbors might think.

Cliff took a drink only once in my presence. One blistering, August day, when I was nine or ten and he was on his two-week vacation, he was uncharacteristically idle, between home improvement projects — how I used to dread the labors of his vacations — and sweltering in the summer heat. "I want a glass of beer," he declared. I was amazed. Surrounded by Irish blatherers and drinkers, Cliff was a strong, silent man who distrusted the lifts of language or liquor.

"Well, are you going to stand there with your mouth open, catching flies, or are you coming with me?"

I closed my mouth and went with him. Cliff set his summer straw hat on his head. He bought a new hat every summer; he donned it every Memorial Day and, every Labor Day, he punched a hole in the hat and threw it away; he wore it straight and flat, the way Buster Keaton wore his porkpie hat, and Cliff had Keaton's deadpan, though no one ever laughed at my uncle and got away with it. That's the kind of man he was.

The West End Café was full of louts and layabouts, card players and bull throwers, the usual crowd — many of them Vin's drinking buddies. "So how's your old man?" one barfly asked me, until he was silenced by my uncle's glare. Cliff ordered his dime beer and a nickel Coke for me. I stood by, breathing in the acid odor of cigarettes and the stink of beer, trying to figure all this out. Cliff drank down his beer as if it were a glass of lemon-

ade. Then he ordered another and drank *half* a glass. He then
smoked a Camel, holding it between his lips, straight out, never
inhaling, talking to no one. After his one and a half beers and
his cigarette, he did a stunning thing: he tipped his straw hat
back an inch, revealing a red line across his brow — a shocking
violation of his self-imposed dress code.

"Are you going to drink that or hold it all afternoon?" he
asked me.

"I'm not thirsty," I said.

"Then don't drink it," he said.

So that was it. Cliff only drank beer because he was *thirsty* on
this hot summer day. After a beer and a half, his thirst was slaked
and he was ready to leave. Why else would a man stay? We
trudged back up the hill to our home, to take up a man's proper
tasks (wallpapering, roof-tarring, drainage-ditch digging, floor-
sanding). I wondered why Vin, my "real" father, drank so much.
Maybe he was gripped by a thirst so fierce that no amount of
booze could drown it, a thirst so deep that Cliff could never
understand. Cliff had brought me to that tavern, Vin's tavern, to
show me just how much beer an honorable man needs. But I
knew from Vin's example that there was more mystery to it than
that. Between the lessons of my two fathers, I was simultaneously
intrigued and repelled by alcohol.

On a Christmas Eve, late in World War II, Vin, home on leave,
grew restless. I was picking my way through a piano performance of "White Christmas" while the elders in my odd family
sat in attendance. We were all in the "front room," where all of
my aunt's "nice things" and the decorated Christmas tree were
on display. Impatient, annoyed at hearing again that moving
tune, which Tokyo Rose had played repeatedly to American
troops who listened to her from the Solomon Islands, Vin began
idly to examine his sister's knickknacks that cluttered every table.
He was, by then, drunk, awash in his own private griefs. He
discovered a figurine of a cat with Made in Japan painted on the
bottom, brooded over it and then hurled it against a wall. Then
he lurched around the room, cursing and searching for more
ceramics to shatter, while I hurriedly concluded my concert.
"May all your Christmases be bright!" Soon all the offending
knickknacks were smashed, and so was Vin, who was helped off

to bed by his furious sister. Cliff, a cigarette clenched in his lips, watched all this, never saying a word, but I could see the ire in his narrowed eyes as Vin staggered past.

So I was not surprised, that afternoon after the war on the golf course, when Cliff was again silent after Vin joked about drinking.

Cliff was off the green in three shots and Vin was on the green, two putts away from a par. I did not know which man to root for. I couldn't help but be impressed by Vin's grace, dash and willingness to take risks, but I knew he was here today and gone tomorrow. I knew too that Cliff's slow and steady ways made my world safe, if a bit dull. Indeed, I never have been sure which way to go, so I have been, at various times, each of my fathers — cautious here, rash there, pulled this way and that by the voices and images of these men in my head.

That day they played out that hole in silence. Cliff took a long time with his fourth shot — clearly it mattered. His chip, gently scooped rather than poked, was an occasion of rare beauty in the life of a man who set more value in efficiency than grace. It hit and held, two feet from the cup. Vin, clearly impressed, nodded respectfully at Cliff, then took his putter from me and, without hesitation, knocked his putt toward the cup. Its speed and distance were perfect. The ball curved up over a rise and dropped slowly, right on line — but, at the last moment, it rimmed the cup and stayed out, hanging on the edge. Vin smiled sardonically — of course! — and tapped in his ball. Then Cliff took his putter from me. For some reason, my stomach ached. Again pausing, always considering, Cliff deliberately rolled in his two-foot putt. I felt a sudden release. Each of my fathers, each in his own characteristic way, had parred the hole. There was, after all, as my Aunt Jane liked to say, more than one way to skin a cat.

Vin never made it to age fifty. He died in the spring of 1950, in his forty-seventh year, of carbon monoxide poisoning, in his father's house. The Certificate of Death said it was "accidental," but I know it was not. The doors to the kitchen, where Vin died, were closed. I know he had had enough disappointments and losses — he had raved enough, smashed enough and finally had enough to drink — so he slipped away while no one was watching. No farewell note, just a half-empty bottle of rye on the table to be remembered by. I was angry at him then, but I am getting over it.

Six years later, Cliff died of lung cancer, at age sixty-six. Though he did not inhale, all those cigarettes clenched between his lips leaked enough poison into his lungs to do him in. During his last months, I drove Cliff into Boston for radiation treatments at Massachusetts General Hospital and saw the startling deterioration of this once tall and stiff man into a bent, withered being, a man who needed to be helped to walk. However, during his final hours my impressive uncle rose from his death bed and, in withering pain, led me down to the basement of his house to show me where the water level had to be set to keep the oil burner from exploding. Cliff was determined to show me the right way to take care of things when he was gone.

Neither Vin, for all his blarney, nor Cliff, for all his honesty, spoke with me about important things, but their lives sent cryptic messages which I am still trying to decode, more than three decades later. Each man has shaped my days and ways. Like Vin, I left my hometown in search of something. But, like Cliff, I never went far. The "important places" for me have been local. From Boston's western suburbs, I too have accompanied my children on trips to Boston to see the Red Sox — the Braves, surprisingly, skipped town — or to movies. However, I made sure that I stayed with my children for the full nine innings or the whole movies. Which is not to say that I am not my fathers' son. For years I drank like Vin, but then I took up sobriety, like Cliff. For years I smoked but, in memory of both my fathers, I finally quit. As Hamlet's father pursued him, so do the ghosts of these men haunt my imagination, like the faint, sweet odors of whiskey and cigarettes. I will not look on their likes again.

At age fifty-six I have now outlived Vin by ten years; when Cliff died, he was a decade older than I am now. So I hang suspended between my two fathers, between two different styles of swinging at the world — between rashness and rigidity, elegance and caution, excess and understatement — indeed, between two different kinds of love. Now, with both Cliff and Vin long gone, I seek the proper words to bring them back so that they might be with me again, as they were more than forty years ago, when I walked between them on the long fairways of Marlborough Country Club. I need both fathers beside me as I play the back nine. As they showed me, I try to keep my eye on the ball and my swing smooth. I try to know what does and does not count in the final score.

CYNTHIA OZICK

Alfred Chester's Wig

FROM THE NEW YORKER

THE OTHER DAY, I received in the mail a card announcing the retirement of an old friend — not an intimate but an editor with whom, over the years, I have occasionally been entangled, sometimes in rapport, sometimes in antagonism. The news that a man almost exactly my contemporary could be considered ready to retire struck me as one more disconcerting symptom of a progressive unreality. I say "one more" because there have been so many others. Passing my reflection in a shop window, for instance, I am taken by surprise at the sight of a striding woman with white hair: she is still wearing the bangs of her late youth, but there are shocking pockets and trenches in her face; she has a preposterous dewlap; she is no one I can recognize. Or I am struck by a generational pang: the discovery that the most able and arresting intellects currently engaging my attention were little children when I was first possessed by the passions of mind they have brilliantly mastered.

All the same, whatever assertively supplanting waves may lap around me — signals of redundancy, or of superannuation — I know I am held fast. Or, rather, it is not so much a fixity of self as it is of certain exactnesses, neither lost nor forgotten: a phrase, a scene, a voice, a moment. These exactnesses do not count as memory, and even more surely escape the net of nostalgia or memoir. They are platonic enclosures, or islands, independent of time, though not of place; in short, they irrevocably *are*. Nothing can snuff them. They are not like candle flames, liable to waver or sputter, and not like windows or looking glasses, which streak or cloud. They have the quality of clear photographs, or of stone friezes, or of the living eyes in ancient portraits. They are not subject to erasure or dimming.

Upon one of these impermeable platonic islands, the image of Alfred Chester stands firm. It is likely that this name — Alfred Chester — is no longer resonant in literary circles. As it happens, the editor who is now retiring was an early publisher of Chester. And Chester had his heyday. He knew Truman Capote, or said he did, and Susan Sontag and Paul Bowles and Princess Marguerite Caetani, the legendary aristocrat who sponsored a magazine called *Botteghe Oscure*. He wrote energetically snotty reviews that swaggered and intimidated — the kind of reviews that many young men (and very few young women) in the fifties and sixties wrote, in order to found a reputation. But his real calling was for fiction, and anyhow it was a time when reputations were sought mainly through the writing of stories and novels.

There is, by the way, another reason these reflections cannot be shrugged off as simply a "memoir," that souvenir elevation of trifles. A memoir, even at its best, is a recollection of what once was; distance and old-fashionedness are taken for granted. But who and what Chester was, long ago, and who and what I was have neither vanished nor grown quaint. Every new half decade sprouts a fresh harvesting of literary writers, equally soaked in the lust of ambition, equally sickened (or galvanized) by envy. There is something natural in all this — something of nature, that is. The snows of yesteryear may be the nostalgic confetti of memoir, but last year's writers are routinely replaced by this year's; the baby carriages are brimming over with poets and novelists. Chester, though, has the sorrowful advantage of being irreplaceable, not so much because of his portion of genius (he may not, when all is said and done, deserve this term) as because he was cut down in the middle of the trajectory of his literary growth, so there is no suitable measure, really, by which to judge what he might have been in full maturity. He never came to fruition. He died young.

Or relatively young. He was forty-two. Well, Keats was twenty-five, Kafka forty, and, in truth, we are satisfied: no one feels a need for more Keats or more Kafka. What is there is prodigy enough. It might be argued that Chester had plenty of time to

achieve his masterpieces, if he was going to achieve them at all —
and yet, with Chester, it is difficult to agree. He rarely sat still.
Time ran away with him — hauled him from America to Europe
to North Africa, and muddled him, and got in his way. His
dogs — repulsive wild things he kept as pets — got in his way.
His impatient and exotic loves got in his way. His fears and
imaginings got in his way. Finally — the most dangerous condition for any writer — it was the desolation of life itself that got in
his way: moral anguish, illness, aimless and helpless wanting,
relentless loneliness, decline.

All this I know from the hearsay of a small accumulation of
letters and essays and other testimony by witnesses to his latter-
day bitterness, and the suffering it led to. By then, Chester and I
had long been estranged — or merely, on my part, out of touch.
I am as certain as I can be of anything that I was never in
Chester's mind in the last decade of his life; but he was always in
mine. He was a figure, a presence, a regret, a light, an ache. And
no matter how remote he became, geographically or psychologically, he always retained the power to wound. He wounded me
when he was in Paris. He wounded me when, in 1970, we were
both in Jerusalem. And once — much, much earlier — in an
epistolary discussion of what we both termed "the nature of
love," I wounded him terribly: so terribly that after those letters
were irretrievably written, and read, and answered, our friendship deteriorated. Paris, Tangier, Jerusalem: he lived in all these
fabled cities, but I knew him only in New York. I knew him only
at — so to speak — the beginning. "In my beginning is my end"
was not true for Chester; and, having been there at the beginning, I am convinced that he was intended for an end utterly
unlike the one he had. I have always believed this — that his life
as he was driven to conduct it was a distortion, not a destiny. At
one time, I even believed that if Chester and I had not been so
severely separated I might have persuaded him (how he would
have scoffed at such arrogance) away from what was never, in
my view, inevitable.

Unless you count the wig. Chester was the wig's guardian. He
was fanatically careful of it in the rain: he wore a rain hat if rain
was expected, or, if it was not, covered his head with his coat. He
was also the wig's prisoner and puppet; it gave him the life he
had, and perhaps the life he eventually chose.

So it is possible, even likely, that I am wrong in my belief — a conviction four decades old — that Chester was not meant to die drugged, drunken, desolate, in the company of a pair of famished wild dogs. It may be — if you count the wig as the beginning — that his end *was* in his beginning. It may be that that curly orange-yellow wig he so meticulously kept from being rained on determined Chester's solitary death.

Most people called him Al and, later, Alfred. As far as I can tell, except for Mr. Emerson I am the only one who ever called him Chester, and, of course, I still call him that. Chester has a casual and natural sound to it, and not merely because it can pass as a given name. I go on saying Chester because that is how I first heard him referred to. Mr. Emerson regularly said Chester. Me he called, according to the manners of the time, Miss. Yet it was not quite the manners of the time; it was a parody of the time before our time. Sarcasm and parody and a kind of thrillingly sardonic spite were what Mr. Emerson specialized in. Mr. Emerson's own first name was not accessible to us; if it was, I cannot recollect it. Like Chester in Jerusalem a quarter of a century on, Mr. Emerson either was or was not a suicide. In the summer following our semester with him, the story went, Mr. Emerson stepped into a wood and shot himself. The wood, the shotgun, the acid torque of Mr. Emerson's mouth at the moment of extinction — they all scattered into chill drops of conjecture, drowned in the roil of the thousands of ex-soldiers who were flooding New York University that year. The only thing verifiable in the rumor of Mr. Emerson's suicide was the certainty of his absence: in the fall, he was gone.

Mr. Emerson's class was Freshman Composition, and it was in this class, in 1946, that Chester and I first met. We were starting college immediately after the war — the Second World War, which my generation, despite Korea and Vietnam, will always call, plainly and unqualifiedly, "the war." The G.I. Bill was in full steam, and Washington Square College — the downtown, liberal arts branch of N.Y.U., and rumored to be a former factory building — had reverted to assembly-line procedures for the returning swarms of serious men still in Army jackets and boots, many of them New Yorkers but many of them not: diffident Midwesterners with names like Vernon and Wendell, wretchedly quartered in Quonset huts on Long Island together with old-fashioned wives and quantities of babies. To the local teenagers just out of high school they seemed unimpassioned and literal-minded — grave, patient, humorless old men. Some of them actually *were* old: twenty-seven, thirty-two, even thirty-five. The government, in a historic act of public gratitude, was footing the bill for the higher education of veterans; the veterans, for their part, were intent on getting through. They were nothing if not pragmatic. They wanted to know what poetry and history were *for*.

The truth is, I despised these anxious grownups, in their seasoned khaki, with their sticky domestic worries and ugly practical needs. I felt them to be intruders, or obstacles, or something worse: contaminants. Their massive presence was an affront to literature, to the classical vision, to the purity of awe and reverence, to *mind*. They had an indolent contempt for philosophy, for beauty, for contemplation. There were so many of them that the thronged, unventilated lecture halls smelled of old shoes, stale flatulence, boredom. The younger students sprawled or squatted in the aisles while the veterans took mechanical notes in childishly slanted handwriting. Their gaze was thickened; dense, as if in trance; exhausted. When, in the first session of the term, a professor of Government (a required course), quoting Aristotle, startled the air with "Man is by nature a political animal," they never looked up — as if "animal" used like that were not the most amazing word in the world. Nothing struck them as new, nothing enchanted them, nothing could astonish them. They were too old, too enervated, too indifferent. In the commons, I would hear them comparing used cars. They were despoiling my youth.

And youth was what I was jealous of: youth in combination with literary passion. Nowadays, one can hardly set down this phrase — "literary passion" — without the teasing irony of quotation marks, representing abashed self-mockery: the silly laughter of old shame. Of course, the veterans were right: they had survived the battlegrounds of catastrophic Asia and Europe, had seen mortal fragility and burned human flesh up close, and were preparing for the restoration of their lives — whereas I, lately besotted by the Aeneid, by "Christabel," by Shelley's cloud and Keats' nightingale, was an adolescent of seventeen. Chester, though, claimed to be sixteen still — the other side of the divide. He had the face of a very young child. His skin was as pure and unmarked as a three-year-old's, and he had a little rosy mouth, with small rosy lips. His lips were as beautifully formed as a doll's. His pretty nose was the least noticeable element of his pretty face; the most noticeable was the eyelids, which seemed oddly fat. It took some time — weeks, or perhaps months — to fathom that what distinguished these eyelids, what gave them their strangeness, was that they were altogether bald. Chester had neither eyebrows nor eyelashes. He was a completely hair-less boy.

He was, besides, short and ovoid, with short, active fingers like working pencil erasers. His pale eyes were small and shy; but they had a hidden look — a kind of skip, a quickstep of momen-tary caution. We stood at the blackboard in a mostly empty classroom, doodling with the chalk. The veterans, those wearily cynical old men, began straggling in, swallowing up the rows of chairs, while Chester and I made tentative tugs at each other's credentials. He identified himself as a writer. Ordinarily, I was skeptical about such claims; high school had already proved the limitations of the so-called flair. He told me the name of his high school. I told him the name of mine. I knew without his mention-ing it that he had arrived by subway from Brooklyn. I knew it because he had one of the two varieties of Brooklyn speech I could recognize: the first was exceedingly quick; the other was exceedingly slow, dragging out the vowels. Chester's talk sped, the toe of the next sentence stumbling over the heel of the last. He was an engine of eagerness. I was, in those days, priggishly speech-conscious, having been subdued by the Shavian Pygma-lions of my high school Speech Department, under whose fierce eyes, only a couple of weeks earlier, I had delivered the gradu-ating address. These zealous teachers, missionaries of the glottis and the diaphragm, had effectively suppressed the miscreant northeast Bronx dentalizations of Pelham Bay: a fragrant nook of meadows and vacant lots overgrown with cattails and wild-flowers, archeologically pocked with the ruins of old founda-tions — contractors' start-ups halted by the Depression, and rot-ting now into mossy caverns. I lived at the subway's farthest vertebra — the end of the Pelham Bay line — but the ladies of the Speech Department (all three of whom had nineteenth-century literary names: Ruby, Olive, Evangeline) had turned *me* into a lady, and severed me forever from the hot notes of New York. Chester, rapid-fire, slid up and down those notes — not brashly but minstrel-like, ardent, pizzicato. I saw into him then — a tender, sheltered, eager child. And also: an envious, hungry writing beast, and not in embryo. In short, he was what I knew myself to be, though mine was the heavier envy, the envy that stung all the more, because Chester was sixteen and I was not.

The veterans were invisible. We dismissed them as not pertinent. What was pertinent was this room and what would happen in it. Here were the veterans, who were invisible; here was a resentful young woman, who was to vanish within the week; here was Chester; and Mr. Emerson; and myself, the only surviving female. The young woman who deserted complained that Mr. Emerson never acknowledged her, never called on her to speak, even when her hand was conspicuously up. "Woman hater!" she spat out, and ran off to another course section. What it came to, then, when you subtracted the veterans, was three. But since Mr. Emerson was what he was — a force of nature, a geological fault, a gorge, a thunderstorm — what it came to, in reality, was two. For Chester and for me, whatever it might have been for the veterans, in their colorless hordes, there was no "freshman composition." A cauldron, perhaps; a cockpit. Chester and I were roped-off roosters, or a pair of dogs set against each other — pit bulls — or gladiators, obliged to fight to the death. All this was Mr. Emerson's scheme — or call it his vise or toy — arbitrarily settled on after the first assignment: a character study, in five hundred words.

On the day the papers were returned, Mr. Emerson ordered me to stand in front of the class — in front of Chester, in effect — and read aloud what I had written. There was an explicit format for these essays: an official tablet had to be bought at the university bookstore, with blanks to be filled in. Then the sheets had to be folded in half. The outer surface was for the instructor's grade and comment.

"Read that first sentence!" Mr. Emerson bawled.

I looked down at my paper. There was no grade and no comment.

" 'Gifford was a taciturn man,' " I read.

"Louder! Wake up those sleeping soldiers back there! And keep in mind that I'm a man who's deaf in one ear. What's that goddam adjective?"

" 'Taciturn.' "

"Where'd you swipe it from?"

"I guess I just thought of it," I said.

"Picked it up someplace, hah? Well, what in hell's it mean?"

It was true that I had only recently learned this word, and was putting it to use for the first time.

"Does it mean quiet?" I choked out.

"Don't ask *me*, Miss. I'm the one that's supposed to do the goddam asking."

"I think it means quiet."

"You think! *I* think you got it out of some trash heap. Read on," he commanded.

He let me continue, quavering, for another paragraph or so. Then his arm shot out like a Mussolini salute.

"All right, Miss. Sit! Now you! Chester!"

Chester stood. The somnolent veterans were surprised into alertness: they stared across at the ringmaster and his livestock. Now the rapid Brooklyn voice began — a boy's voice, a boy's throat. The little pink lips — that rosy bouquet — stretched and pursed, looped and flattened. Chester read almost to the end; Mr. Emerson never interrupted. Humiliated, concentrating, I knew what I was hearing. Behind that fragile mouth, dangerous fires curled: a furnace, a burning bush. The coarse cap of false orange-yellow hair shook — it narrowed Chester's forehead, lifted itself off his nape, wobbled along the tops of his ears. He was bold, he was rousing, he was loud enough for a man deaf in one ear. It was ambition. It was my secret self.

"That's enough. Sit, Chester!" Mr. Emerson yelled. "Gentlemen, you'll never find a woman who can write. The ladies can't do it. They don't have what it takes, that's well known. It's universal wisdom, and I believe it. All the same," he said, "these two, Chester and the lady, I'm not the fool that's going to let them drop back into the pond with the catfish."

After that, Chester and I had separate writing assignments — separate, that is, from the rest of the class. Mr. Emerson may have been a woman hater, but it was the veterans he declined to notice and looked to snub. His teaching (if that is what it was) was exclusively for the two of us. It was for our sakes that he disparaged Walt Whitman — "that plumber," he sneered. It was for our sakes that he devoted minutes every day — irascible still, yet reverential — to praising *Brideshead Revisited,* the Evelyn Waugh best-seller he was reading between classes. And sometimes *in* class. While the veterans slid down in their seats, Mr. Emerson opened to where he had left off and fell into a dry recital:

> I was always given the room I had on my first visit; it was next to Sebastian's, and we shared what had once been a dressing-room and had been changed to a bathroom twenty years back by the substitution for the bed of a deep, copper, mahogany-framed bath, that was filled by pulling a brass lever heavy as a piece of marine engineering; the rest of the room remained unchanged; a coal fire always burned there in winter. I often think of that bathroom — the water colours dimmed by steam and the huge towel warming on the back of the chintz armchair — and contrast it with the uniform, clinical little chambers, glittering with chromium plate and looking-glass, which pass for luxury in the modern world.

Dry, but there was a suppressed rapture in it — rapture for the brass lever, for the water colours (in their transporting British spelling) dimmed by steam. It was clear that Mr. Emerson himself, an unhappy man with tired eyes — they often teared — did not like the modern world; perhaps he would not have liked any world, even one with picturesque coal fires. In the grip of some defenseless fatigue, he gave way to fits of yawning. His snarl was inexhaustible; also comically unpredictable. He took a sardonic pleasure in shock. Certainly he shocked me, newly hatched out of the decorous claims of Hunter High (finishing school cum Latin prep), where civilization hung on the position of a consonant struck upon the palate (never against the teeth), and mastery of the ablative absolute marked one out for higher things. Mr. Emerson said "God damn," he said "hell," he even alluded, now and then, to what I took to be sexual heat.

It was not that I was ignorant of sexual heat; I had already come upon it in the Aeneid. There it was, in Dido and Aeneas — Dido on her pyre, burning for love! And here it was again, between Agnes and Gerald in the dell, in *The Longest Journey*, the early E. M. Forster novel, which was included in our Freshman Composition curriculum. The first paragraphs alone — well before sexual heat made its appearance — were undiluted pleasure:

> "The cow is there," said Ansell, lighting a match and holding it out over the carpet. No one spoke. He waited till the end of the match fell off. Then he said again, "She is there, the cow. There, now."
> "You have not proved it," said a voice.
> "I have proved it to myself."
> "I have proved to myself that she isn't," said the voice. "The cow is *not* there." Ansell frowned and lit another match.
> "She's there for me," he declared. "I don't care whether she's there for you or not. Whether I'm in Cambridge or Iceland or dead, the cow will be there."
> It was philosophy. They were discussing the existence of objects. Do they exist only when there is some one to look at them? or have they a real existence of their own? It is all very interesting, but at the same time it is difficult. Hence the cow. She seemed to make things easier. She was so familiar, so solid.

None of this was familiar in the spring of 1946: E. M. Forster was an unknown name, at least to me; philosophy lay ahead. Nothing was solid. Rickie and Ansell were lost in Mr. Emerson's mercurial derisions. For years afterward, I remembered only Rickie's limp. Much later, I began to read *The Longest Journey* over and over again until, ultimately, I had certain passages by heart. In class, it was hardly discussed at all. It appeared to hold no interest for Mr. Emerson, and Chester and I never spoke of it. It was not what we read that counted for Mr. Emerson anyhow; it was what we wrote. Chester and I wrote — were intended to write — as rivals, as yoked competitors under the whip. "Got you that time, didn't she? Made you look small, didn't she?" he chortled at Chester. And, the following week, to me: "Males beat females, it's in the nature of things. He's got the stuff, the genuine shout. He's wiped you out to an echo, Miss, believe me." Sometimes he made no comment at all, and returned our papers, along with the weekly work of the rest of the class, giving us no more than a cocky glare. That left us stymied; there was no way to find out which of us had won. Since Mr. Emerson never graded what Chester and I turned in (he routinely graded the others' papers), the only possible conclusion was that we were both unworthy. And the next week he would be at it again: "She knocked you off your high horse, hah, Chester?" Or "You'd better quit, Miss, you'll never be in the running." All that term, we were — Chester and I — a pair of cymbals, striking and ringing in midair; or two panting hares, flanks heaving, in a mad marathon; or a couple of legs-entangled wrestlers in a fevered embrace. It was as if — for whatever obscure reason — Mr. Emerson had flung himself into the role of some sly, languid, and vainglorious Roman emperor presiding over the bloody goings on in the Colosseum of his classroom, with the little green buds of Washington Square Park just beginning to unfold below the college windows.

What came out of it, besides a conflagration of jealousy, was fraternity. I loved Chester: he was my brother; he was the first real writer of my generation I had ever met — a thing I knew immediately. It was evident in the increasingly rococo noise of his language and in Mr. Emerson's retributive glee. If, conceivably, promoting envy was Mr. Emerson's hidden object in encouraging the savagery of Chester's competitiveness with me, and mine with him, it was his own envy that Mr. Emerson suffered from, and was picking at. It is not unheard of for older would-be writers to be enraged by younger would-be writers. The economy of writing always operates according to a feudal logic: the aristocracy blots out all the rest. There is no middle class. The heights belong to, at most, four or five writers, a princely crew; the remainder are invisible, or else have the partial, now-and-then visibility that attaches to minor status. Every young writer imagines only the heights; no one aspires to be minor or invisible, and when, finally, the recognition of where one stands arrives, as it must, in maturity, one accepts the limitations of fate or talent, or else surrenders to sour cynicism. Whether Mr. Emerson was embittered by chances lost or hope denied or by some sorrowful secret narrowing of his private life, it was impossible to tell. Whatever it was, it threw Chester and me, red in tooth and claw, into each other's arms. It also made us proud: we had been set apart and declared to be of noble blood. (All this, of course, may be retrospective hubris. Perhaps Mr. Emerson saw us as no more than what we were: a couple of literary-minded freshmen whose strenuousness an attentive teacher was generously serving and cultivating.)

We took to walking up and down Fourth Avenue in the afternoons, the two of us, darting into one after another of those rows of secondhand bookstores the long, straight street was famous for. The cheapest books were crammed into sidewalk racks under awnings, to protect them from the rain. It seemed to be always raining that spring — a tenderly fickle drizzle and fizz, which first speckled and then darkened the pavement, and made Chester hood the crown of his head with his jacket. We drilled into back rooms and creaked down wooden basement steps; everywhere, those thousands of books had the sewery smell of cellar — repellent, earthen, heart-catching. In these dank crypts, with their dim electric bulbs hanging low on wires over tables heaped with comatose and forgotten volumes, and an infinity of collapsing shelves lining broken-plastered walls and labeled THEOSOPHY, HISTORY, POETRY (signs nailed up decades back, faded and curled by dampness), one could loiter uninterrupted forever. The proprietor was somewhere above, most likely on a folding chair in the doorway, hunched over a book of his own, cozily insulated from the intrusions of customers, bothering nobody and hoping not to be bothered himself. Gradually, the cellar smells would be converted, or consecrated, into a sort of blissful incense; nostrils that flinched in retreat opened to the tremulous savor of books waiting to be aroused, and to arouse. Meandering in the skinny aisles of these seductive cellars, Chester and I talked of our childhoods, and of our noses. I admired Chester's nose and deplored my own. "Yours isn't so bad, just a little wide," he said kindly. He told me of his long-ago childhood disease; he did not name it, though he explained that because of it he had lost all his hair. He did not say that he wore a wig.

There was something Hansel-and-Gretelish about our excursions, so brotherly and sisterly, so childlike and intimate, yet prickly in their newness. Fresh from an all-girls' high school, I had never before conversed with a boy about books and life. I had never before gone anywhere with a boy. Boys were strangers, and also — in my experience, if not in principle — as biologically unfathomable as extraterrestrials. Though I had a brother, there was a divide between us: he had ascended to college when I was in grade school and at this hour was in the Army. At home, with my parents at work in their pharmacy, I had the house to myself: I sat at my little wooden Sears, Roebuck desk (a hand-me-down from my brother, the very desk I am using right now) and fearfully grappled with my five hundred words for Mr. Emerson, jealous of what I imagined Chester might be contriving on the same subject, and burning against him with a wild will. I wanted more than anything to beat him; I was afraid he would beat me. When I listened to him read his paper aloud, as Mr. Emerson occasionally had us do even well into the semester, a shrewdly hooked narrative turn or an ingenious figure of speech or some turbulently reckless flash of power would afflict me like a wound. Chester was startling, he was robust, he was lyrical, he was wry, he was psychological, he was playful, he was scandalous. He was better than I was! In one respect, though, I began to think I was stronger. We were equally attracted to the usual adolescent literary moonings: to loneliness, morbidity, a certain freakishness of personality. But I felt in myself stirrings of history, of idea, of something beyond the senses: I was infatuated with German and Latin, I exulted over the Reformation. I supposed that this enthusiasm meant I was more *serious* than Chester — more serious, I presumed, about the courses we were enrolled in. Chester was indifferent to all that. Except for English classes, he was careless, unexcited. He was already on his way to bohemianism (a term then still in its flower). I, more naively, more conventionally, valued getting an A; I pressed to excel, and to be seen to excel. I thought of myself as a neophyte, a beginner, an apprentice; it would be years and years (decades, eons) before I could accomplish anything worth noticing. I regarded my teachers not as gods but as those who wore the garments of the gods. I was as conscious of my youth as if it were a sealed envelope and I myself a coded message inside it, indefinitely encased, arrested, waiting. But Chester was poking through that envelope with an impatient fist. He was becoming gregarious. He was putting his noisiness to use.

And still he was soft, susceptible. He was easily emotional. I saw him as sentimental, too quickly inflamed. He fell soppily in

love at a moment's glance. And, because we were brother and
sister, I was his confidante; he would tell me his loves, and
afterward leave me feeling resentful and deserted. I was not one
of the pretty girls. Boys ignored me; their habitual reconnoi-
tring wheeled right over me and ran to the beauties. And here
was Chester, no different from the others, with an eye out
for looks — flirting, teasing, chasing. Nearly all young women
seemed extraordinary that spring: archaic, Edwardian. The
postwar fashion revolution, appropriately called the New Look,
had descended — literally descended — in the form of long
skirts whipping around ankles. All at once, half the population
appeared to be in costume. Only a few months earlier, there had
been a rigid measure for the length of a skirt: hems were obliged
to reach precisely, uncompromisingly, to the lower part of the
knee. What else had that meant but an irreversible modernity?
Now the girls were trailing yards of bright or sober stuff, trip-
ping over themselves, delightedly conspicuous, enchanted with
their own clear absurdity. Chester chased after them; more
often, they chased after Chester. When I came to meet him in
the commons nowadays, he had a retinue. The girls moved in on
him, and so did the incipient bohemians; he was more and more
in the center of a raucous crowd. He was beginning to display
himself — to accept or define himself — as a wit, and his wit,
kamikaze assaults of paradox or shock, caught on. In no time at
all, he had made himself famous in the commons — a businesslike place, where the resolute veterans, grinding away, ate their
sandwiches with their elbows in their accounting texts. Chester's
success was mine. He was my conduit and guide. Without him, I
would have been buried alive in Washington Square, consumed
by timidity.

He journeyed out to visit me twice — a tediously endless subway trip from the bowels of Brooklyn to Pelham Bay. We walked
in the barren park, along untenanted crisscross paths, down the
hill through the big meadow to the beach. I was proud of this
cattailed scene — it was mine, it was my childhood, it was my
Brontëan heath. Untrammeled grasses, the gray, keen water
knocking against mossy stones: here I was master. Now that
Chester was celebrated at school, I warmed to the privilege of
having him to myself, steering him from prospect to prospect,

until we were light-headed with the drizzly air. At the end of the
day, at the foot of the high stair that led to the train, we said
goodbye. He bent toward me — he was taller than I, though not
by much — and kissed me. The pale, perfect lips and their cold
spittle rested on my mouth; it was all new. It had never happened before — not with any other boy. I was bewildered, wildly
uncertain; I shrank back, and told him I could not think of him
like that — he was my brother. (Ah, to retrieve that instant, that
Movietone remark learned from the silver screen of the Pilgrim
Theatre, half a mile down the tracks! To retrieve it, to undo it, to
wipe it out!) He wormed his blunt white fingers into his jacket
pockets and stood for a while. The El's stanchions shook. Overhead, the train growled and headed downtown. Two puddles lay
against his lower eyelids, unstanched by the missing lashes. It
was the same, he said, with Diana; it was just the same, though
Diana wasn't a brute, she hadn't said it outright. He didn't want
to be anyone's brother — mine, maybe, but not Diana's. I knew
Diana, a brilliant streak in the commons excitements: in those
new-fangled long skirts, she had a fleet, flashing step, and she
wore postwar nylons and neat formal pumps. (Unrenovated, I
was still in my high school Sloppy Joes and saddle shoes.) Diana
was one of the beauties, among the loveliest of all, with a last
name that sounded as if it had fallen out of a Trollope novel but
was actually Lebanese. In after years, I happened on a replica of
her face on the salvaged wall of an ancient Roman villa, with its
crimson tones preserved indelibly: black-rimmed Mediterranean
eyes fixed in intelligence, blackly lit; round cheeks and chin, all
creamy pink. An exquisite ur-Madonna. Diana had a generous
heart, she was vastly kind and a little shy, with a penetrating
attentiveness untypical of the young. Like many in Chester's
crew, she was singlemindedly literary. (She is a poet of reputation now.) Chester yearned, and, more than anyone, Diana was
the object and representation of his yearning.

But I yearned, too. The word itself — soaked in dream and
Poesy — pretty well embodies what we were, Chester and I, in a
time when there was no ostensible sex, only romance, and the
erotic habits of the urban bookish young were confined to daring
cafeteria discussions of the orgone box (a contrivance touted by
Wilhelm Reich) and to severely limited gropings at parties in the
parental domicile. One of these parties drew me to Brooklyn —

it was my first look at this fabled place. The suburban atmosphere of Flatbush took me by surprise — wide streets and tall
brick Tudor-style houses flawed only by being set too close together. The party, though it was given by a girl I will call Carla
Baumblatt, was altogether Chester's: he had chosen the guests.
Carla would not allow us to enter through the front door. Instead, she herded us toward the back yard and into the kitchen.
She had managed to persuade her parents to leave the house,
but her mother's admonishments were in the air. Carla worried
about cigarette ashes, about food spilling, about muddy shoes —
she especially worried about the condition of the living room
rug. Someone whispered to me that she was terribly afraid of
her mother. And soon enough her mother came home: a tough,
thin, tight little woman, with black hair tightly curled. Carla was
big and matronly, twice her mother's size. She had capacious
breasts that rode before her, and a homely mouth like a twist of
wax, and springy brown hair, which she hated and attempted to
squash down. She was dissatisfied with herself and with her life;
there was no movie rhapsody in it. An argument began in the
kitchen, and there was Carla, cowed by her tiny mother. Curiously, a kitchen scene turns up in Chester's first novel, *Jamie Is
My Heart's Desire*, which was published in England in 1956, a
decade after Carla's party — the last time she ever tried to give a
party at home. The narrator describes a young woman's "largeness": "I have always felt that her body was the wrong one, that
it was an exaggerated contrast with her personality, and that one
must disregard it in order to know Emily at all. It is her fault I
have believed this so long, for in all her ways she has negated the
strength and bigness her figure shows, and substituted weakness
and dependency and fright, so that one imagines Emily within
as a small powerless girl." When Carla reappeared in the living
room after quarreling with her mother, she seemed, despite her
largeness, a small powerless girl; she was as pale as if she had
been beaten, and she again warned us about dirtying the carpet.

   In the middle of that carpet, a young woman lay in a mustard
glow. Her head was on a fat cushion. Her mustard-colored hair
flowed out over the floor. Her mustard-colored New Look skirt
was flung into folds around her. She was sprawled there like an
indolent cat. Now and again, she sat up and perched her chin on
her knee; then the dark trough between her breasts filled with

lamplight. She had tigers' eyes, greenly chiaroscuro, dappled
with unexpected tinsel flecks. Her name was Tatyana; she gave
out the urgency of theater, of Dostoyevski, of seagulls. A circle
of chairs had somehow grouped in front of her; she had us as
audience, or as a body of travelers stung by a spell into fixity.

Carla, stumbling in from the kitchen, seemed devoured by the
sight: it was the majesty of pure sexuality. It was animal beauty.
Carla's plump stooped shoulders and plump homely nose fell
into humility. She called to Chester — they were old neighborhood friends, affectionate old school friends. The familial currents that passed between them had the unearned rhythms of
priority. I resented Carla: she had earlier claims than I, almost
the earliest of all. I thought of her as a leftover from Chester's
former life — the life before Mr. Emerson. It was only sentimentality that continued to bind him to her. She was a blot on his
escutcheon. She had no talents other than easy sociability.

Chester had inherited her along with other remnants of his
younger experience. He rested in Carla's sympathy. I imagined
she knew the secret of the yellow wig. Away from home, in the
commons, she was freely companionable and hospitable: she
would catch hold of me in the incoming lunch crowd and wave
me over to her table. But we did not like each other. On Chester's
account we pretended congeniality. Worse yet, Carla simulated
bookishness; it was an attempt to keep up. In April, on my
eighteenth birthday, she astonished me with a present: it was
Proust, *Cities of the Plain,* in the Modern Library edition. Carla
was so far from actual good will that her gift struck me as an
intrusion, or an act of hollow flattery, or an appeasement. I
owned few books (like everyone else, I frequented the public
library), and wanted to love with a body-love the volumes that
came permanently into my hands. I could not love a book from
Carla. When I eventually undertook to read *Cities of the Plain,* it
was not the copy she had given me. I have Carla's copy in front
of me now, still unfondled, and inscribed as follows: *"Ma chère —
c'est domage que ce livre n'est pas dans l'originale — mais vous devriez
être une si marveilleuse linguiste comme moi pour lire cela — Amour
toujours —"* Carla's English was equally breezy and misspelled.
Her handwriting was a superlegible series of girlish loops.

Because of Tatyana — the mustard glow on Carla's mother's
carpet — Chester was undistractible. When Carla tried to get his

attention, he grunted some mockery, but it was directed at Tatyana. He was a man in a trance of adoration; he was illuminated.
Tatyana stretched her catlike flanks and laughed her mermaid's
laughter. She was woman, cat, fish — silvery, slithery, mustard-
colored. She spread her hair and whirled it. She teased, turned,
played, parried, flirted. The room swam with jealousy — not
simply Carla's, or mine, or the other girls'. Call it the jealousy of
the gods: Tatyana, a mortal young woman, was in the seizure of
an unearthly instant. With the holy power of their femaleness,
her eyes traversed our faces.

The second, and last, time Chester came to Pelham Bay, it was
in the company of Ben Solomons. Ben had become Chester's
unlikely sidekick. Together, they were Mutt and Jeff, tall
broom and squat pepper pot, Arthur's handsomest knight and
Humpty-Dumpty. Ben was nicely dressed and not very talkative — taciturn! He was a little older than I (even weeks
counted), and had the well-polished shoes of a serious pre-med
student. (When I heard, decades later, that he was Dr. Solomons,
the psychiatrist, I was surprised. Not urology? Not gastroenter-
ology?) Since he did not say much, it was hard to assess his
intelligence. What mattered to me, though, was his tallness, his
nearness, his breath. I had been sickened, that afternoon, by
infatuation: out of the blue, I was in love with Ben. The lunch
my mother had left us was mysteriously unsatisfactory; it lacked
some bourgeois quality I was growing aware of — the plates, the
tablecloth, the dining room chairs. It was only food. All my tries
at entertainment were a nervous failure. At three o'clock, we
walked, in the eternal rain (Chester's jacket up over his head), to
see a movie at the Pilgrim — called, in the neighborhood, the
Pillbox, because it was so cramped. In the middle of the day, the
theater was desolate. I was self-conscious, guilty, embarrassed. It
was as if I had dragged us to a pointless moonscape. We settled
into the center of the house — I, Ben, and Chester, in that order,
along a row of vacant seats. The movie came on; I suffered. Next
to me, Ben was bored. Chester tossed out cracks about the dialogue; I laughed, miserably; Ben was silent. Then I shut my eyes,
and kept them shut. It was a wall against tears. It was to fabricate
boredom and flatter Ben's judgment. It was to get Ben to notice.
His big hand on his left knee, with his gold high school grad-

uation ring pressed against the knuckle, drew me into teary desire. I unsealed an eye to be sure that they were still there —
the hand, the ring, the knuckle. Ben was sedate, waiting out the
hours.

At the time, it seemed a long friendship — Chester's with
Ben — and except for that single, aching afternoon in Pelham
Bay, which came like a fever and passed like a fever, I was as
wary of Ben as I was of Carla, as I was of Chester's ascent into
Tatyana's apotheosis. Jealous like Byron's sister, I wanted Chester for myself. I understood that it was useless: he was a public
magnet. Everyone was his straight man and acolyte. To be with
Chester was to join his gang at the edge of bohemia — or what
was imagined to be bohemia, since all the would-be bohemians
went home every night, by subway, to their fathers and mothers
in their Bronx and Brooklyn apartments. In our little house in
Pelham Bay, I had my own tiny room, flowery with the do-it-
yourself yellow wallpaper my mother had put up as a surprise.
Onto this surface I pasted, with Scotch tape, a disjointed Picasso
woman, cut out from *Life*. She was all bright whorls and stripes
and misplaced eyes and ears. She had whirligig breasts. She gave
me pride but no pleasure. She stood for eccentricity, for the
Unconventional — she was an inkling of what Chester was deliberately heading for. There was nothing of any of this in Ben —
no scrambled testing grounds, no pugnacity, no recklessness, no
longing for the inchoate, no unconventionality. No intimations
of unknown realms. He was a solid student, with inconspicuous
notions. He was conspicuously good-looking, in the style of the
familiar hero of a 1940s B-movie: broad-shouldered, square-
chinned, long-lashed. His chief attraction was the velvety pleni-
tude of his deeply black hair; one wavy lock dropped in a scallop
on his forehead, like Superman's. Ben was rarely seen in the
commons. He was not one of Chester's cosmopolitan hangers-
on; he was too businesslike, too intent on propriety. But he
represented for Chester what my Picasso woman represented
for me: the thing closed off, the thing one could not become. I
could not become one of the bohemians: I was diffident and too
earnest, too "inhibited"; I was considered "naive"; I was not
daring enough. When Chester's gang began to meet in Village
bars after classes, I envied but could not follow.

Yellowing on the yellow walls, my cutout Picasso lingered for years. Chester's attachment to Ben was, by contrast, brief, though while it lasted it was a stretched-out, slow-motion sequence — the stages of a laboratory experiment requiring watchful patience. Ben had the glamorous long torso Chester would have liked to have. He had, especially, the hair. Ben was a surrogate body, a surrogate head of hair. Girls were smitten by him. He was an ambassador from the nation of the normal and the ordinary. When Chester cast off Ben, it was his farewell to the normal and the ordinary. It was the beginning of the voyage out. In the commons one day not long after Ben was jettisoned, I came on Chester surrounded by his gang and dangling, between third finger and thumb, a single hair. I asked (the innocent candor of an assistant clown) what it was. "A pubic hair," he retorted.

He was never again not outrageous; he was never again soft. He had determined to shut down the dreamy boy who mooned over girls. Either they rebuffed him or, worse, they embraced him as a friendly pet, good for banter or hilarity. He was nobody's serious boyfriend. Tatyana, after Carla's party, had gone on cosseting him as a plaything to tantalize. Diana, always empathic, withheld the recesses of her heart. I was a literary rival — a puritan and a bluestocking. Carla was an old shoe. What was left for Chester's moist sensibility, having been so crushed? It dried into celebrity. It dried into insolence and caprice. Chester's college fame depended — was founded — on the acid riposte, the quick sting; on anything implausible. He flung out the unexpected, the grotesque, the abnormal. Truman Capote's short stories were in vogue then — miniature gothic concoctions specializing in weird little girls, in clairvoyance, in the uncanny. Chester began modeling his own stories on them. He committed to memory long passages from an eerie narrative called "Miriam"; he was bewitched by Truman Capote's lushness, mystery, baroque style. In his own writing he was gradually melting into Truman Capote. He opened his wallet and pulled out an address book: that number there, he bragged, was Truman Capote's unlisted telephone, set down by the polished little Master himself.

All this while, Chester was wearing the yellow wig. He wore it more and more carelessly. It was as crinkled as a sheep's belly, and now took on a grimy, ragged, neglected look. It hardly mattered to him if it went askew, lifting from his ears or pressing too far down over where the eyebrows should have been.

In 1966, he completed *The Foot,* a novel that is more diary and memoir than fiction. By then, his style was entering its last phase: disjointed, arbitrary, surreal; deliberately beautiful for a phrase or two, then deliberately unbeautiful, then dissolved into sloth. The characters are mercurial fragments or shadowless ghosts, wrested from exhaustion by a drugged and disintegrating will: Mary Monday and her double, also named Mary Monday, a play on Susan Sontag; Peter Plate, representing Paul Bowles, the novelist and composer, whom Chester knew in Morocco; Larbi ("the Arab"), a stand-in for Chester's cook, servant, and sexual companion. All changing themes and short takes, *The Foot* is part travelogue (portraits of Morocco and of New York), part writhing confession ("my long idle life, always occupied with my suffering," "I am afraid of who I am behind my own impersonations"), and part portentous, pointless fantasy. The effect is of a home slide show in a blackened room: the slides click by, mainly of gargoyles, and then, without warning, a series of recognizable family shots flashes out — but even these responsible, ordinary people are engaging in gargoylish activity. In this way, one impressionistic sketch after another jumps into the light, interrupted by satiric riffs — satiric even when mildly pornographic — until four heartbreaking pages of suffering recollected without tranquillity all at once break out of their frames of dread, cry their child's cry, and fall back into the blackness. "Do you let a book like this, this book, go back into the world just as it is — with its wounds and blemishes, its bald head and lashless eyes, exposed to the light?" the section starts off, and darkens into a melancholy unburdening:

> I was fourteen when I put on my first wig. It was, I believe, my sister's idea. So she and my mother and I went — I forget where . . . Simmons & Co.? — some elegantish salon with gold lamé drapes where they did not do such splendid work.
>
> I sat and accepted the wig. It was like having an ax driven straight down the middle of my body. Beginning at the head. Whack! Hacked in two with one blow like a dry little tree. Like a sad little New York tree.

I wore it to school only. Every morning my mother put it on for me in front of the mirror in the kitchen and carefully combed it and puffed it and fluffed it and pasted it down. Then, before going out of the house, I would jam a hat on top of it, a brown fedora, and flatten the wig into a kind of matting. I hated it and was ashamed of it, and it made me feel guilty.

And so to school. The Abraham Lincoln High School.

Up until then I'd gone to a Yeshiva where all the boys wore hats, little black yarmulkas. I too wore a hat, though not a yarmulka, which only covered the tip of the head. I wore a variety of caps. I'd wear a cap to shreds before getting a new one, since I felt any change at all focused more attention on my head. . . .

Coming home from school was a problem. As once the world had been divided for me into Jews and Italians, it was now divided between those who could see me with the wig and those who could see me with a hat. Only my most immediate family — mother, father, sister, brother — could see me with both, and only they could see me bald.

Hat people and wig people. Wig people at school. Hat people at home. The wig people could see me with both wig *and* hat (hat-on-top-of-wig, that is). But the hat people must never see me with wig, or even with wig and hat.

This went on for years, decades.

The terror of encountering one side in the camp of the other. Of the wig people catching me without the wig. Of the hat people catching me with it. Terror . . .

And then, there from the corner where the trolley stopped, if it was a fair day, I would see my mother and maybe an aunt or two or a neighbor sitting on our porch in the sun.

Hat people.

Horrible, unbearable, the thought of walking past those ladies to get into the house. . . .

Sometimes I would go around corners, down alleys, through other people's gardens to reach our back fence. I'd climb over the back fence so I could get into the house via the back door which was usually open.

A thief! Just like a thief I'd have to sneak through the side lanes, unseen across back yards. . . .

I could bear no references to the wig. If I had to wear one, all right. But I wasn't going to talk about it. It was like some obscenity, some desperate crime on my head. It was hot coals in my mouth, steel claws gripping my heart, etc. I didn't want to recognize the wig . . . or even my baldness. It just wasn't there. Nothing was there. It was just something that didn't exist, like a third arm, so how could you talk about it? But it hurt, it hurt. . . .

My second wig was a much fancier job than the first. An old Alsatian couple made it; I think they were anti-Semitic, she out of tradition, he out of fidelity to her.

When the wig was ready, my father and mother and I went to collect it. Evening. I wish I could remember my father's reaction. Mama probably fussed and complained. I imagine Papa, though, like me, simply pretending that the whole thing didn't exist, wasn't even happening. . . .

Anyway, most likely, he said something polite like — how nice it looks! . . .

But the evening of the new wig we went to a restaurant, me wearing the wig. A white-tiled Jewish restaurant. Vegetarian . . . With fluorescent lights . . .

I just want you to see the three of us — even at home we never ate together — at that white-linened, white-tiled, blue-white-lighted restaurant. . . .

I wonder what we ate that night or why the evening took place at all. It is such a strange thing for Papa to have done. Gone to the wigmakers at all. Met me and Mama in the city. Taken us out to supper.

Perhaps there were a lot of mirrors in that restaurant. Catching a glimpse of myself, wig or no, is dreadful for me. I have to approach a mirror fully prepared, with all my armor on.

But I have a turn-off mechanism for mirrors as well. The glimpse-mirrors, I mean. I simply go blind.

When Chester set down these afflicted paragraphs, he was thirty-seven years old. He had long ago discarded the wig. He had long ago discarded our friendship. He had ascended into the hanging gardens of literary celebrity: *Esquire* included him in its "Red Hot Center" of American writing, and he was a prolific and provocative reviewer in periodicals such as *Partisan Review* and *Commentary*. He had lived in Paris, close to the founding circle of *Paris Review;* at parties, he drank with Jimmy Baldwin and George Plimpton. He had been drawn to Morocco by Paul Bowles, who, according to legend, ruled in Tangier like a foreign mandarin, ringed by respectful disciples and vaguely literary satellites devoted to smoking kif. In Morocco, Chester finally took off the wig for good; I, who knew him only when he

was still at home with his family in Brooklyn, never saw him
without it. His anguish was an undisclosable secret. The wig
could not be mentioned — neither by wig wearer nor by wig
watcher. No one dared any kind of comment or gesture. Yet
there were hints that Ben Solomons had somehow passed
through this taboo: on the rainy day Chester brought him to
Pelham Bay, it was Ben who, with a sheltering sweep around
Chester's shoulders, made the first move to raise Chester's jacket
up over his matted crown.

Gore Vidal, in his introduction to a posthumous collection —
including *The Foot* — of Chester's fiction (*Head of a Sad Angel:
Stories 1953–1966*, edited by Edward Field; Black Sparrow;
1990), speaks of Chester's life as "a fascinating black comedy"
and concludes, "Drink and drugs, paranoia and sinister pieces
of trade did him in early." I suppose he is not wrong. Yet "sinister pieces of trade" is an odious locution and a hard judgment,
even if one lacks, as I confess I do, the wherewithal — the plain
data — to see into its unreachable recesses. Vidal calls Chester
"Genet with a brain." But if Vidal is alluding to the bleaker side
of homosexual mores Chester himself can be neither his source
nor his guide; Chester's breezy erotic spirit has more in common
with the goat-god Pan at play than with Genet in prison scratch-
ing a recording pencil across brown paper bags. (Genet's portraits of homosexuals were anyhow tantamount to heartbreak
for Chester. "The naked truth of Genet's writing continues to be
unbearable," he remarked in a 1964 review of *Our Lady of the
Flowers*. And he noted that even "the ecstatic whole of [a] masterpiece" is "cold comfort to a man in agony.")

Though in *The Foot* Chester had fleetingly touched on home
and family, almost nothing in his mind was not literary. His life,
nearly all of it, was a lyrical, satirical, and theatrical mirage. In
the end, the mirage hardened into a looking glass. But what was
not strained through literary affectation or imitation or dream-
scape, what it would be crueler than cruel to think of as black
comedy, is the child's shame, the child's naked truth, that hits
out like a blast of lightning at the close of *The Foot*. The child is
set apart as a freak. And then the bald boy grows into a bold
man; but inside the unfinished man — unfinished because the
boy has still not been exorcised — the hairless child goes on

suffering, the harried boy runs. "I did have the great good luck
never to have so much as glimpsed Alfred Chester," Vidal ac-
knowledges. Nevertheless, he does not hesitate to name him "a
genuine monster." It may require a worldly imagination of a
certain toughened particularity — a temperament familiar with
kinkiness and hospitable to it — to follow Vidal into his conjec-
tures concerning Chester's sexual practices ("sinister pieces of
trade"), but one must leave all heartlessness behind in order to
enter the terrors of the man, or the child, who believes he is a
monster.

And it was only baldness. Or it was not so much baldness as
wig. From any common-sense point of view, baldness is not a
significant abnormality, and in the adult male is no anomaly at
all. But the child felt himself to be abnormal, monstrous. The
child was stricken. The child saw himself a frenzied freak tearing
down lane after lane in search of a path of escape.

That path of escape (I was sure of it four decades ago, and am
partly persuaded of it even now) was homosexuality — implying
an alternative community, an alternative ethos, an alternative
system of getting and receiving attention. Chester loved women;
women would not love him back; Q.E.D. They would not love
him back because, by his own reckoning, he was abnormal,
monstrous, freakish. He was too horrifically ugly. With this
gruesome impetus, he turned his hairless, beardless, lashless
countenance to the alternative world, a world without women,
where no woman could wound him, because no woman belonged.

All this — folded invisibly, or not so invisibly, into notions of
"the nature of love" — I wrote to Chester, in a letter sent to
Paris. I had heard that he had "become homosexual." (I had
learned the phrase at Washington Square College — not from
Mr. Emerson — at eighteen. "Gay" had not yet come into general use.) We had been corresponding, not without acrimony,
about Thomas Mann. Chester was contemptuous. "Middlebrow!
Somerset Maugham in German," he growled from across the
sea, though he had so far not approached a word of anything by
Mann. I urged him to read *Death in Venice*. He wrote back,
exalted. It was, he said, among the great works of literature; he
declared himself converted. By then, we had been separated for

two or three years. He had gone off to be one of the expatriates in the second Parisian wave — modeled on Hemingway and Gertrude Stein in the first — and I, returning from graduate school in the Midwest, had settled back into my tiny yellow bedroom in Pelham Bay to become a writer. My idea was to produce a long philosophical novel that would combine the attributes of André Gide, Henry James, George Eliot, Graham Greene, and Santayana's *The Last Puritan;* it was an awkward and juvenile sort of thing, and kept me in the dark for years. Chester, meanwhile, was actually publishing short stories in newly established postwar periodicals — *Merlin, Botteghe Oscure, Paris Review, Proefschrift.* It was the era of the little magazines. These, springing up in Europe, had a luster beyond the merely contemporary: they smacked of old literary capitals, of Americans abroad (Scott and Zelda), of bistros, of Sartre and de Beauvoir, of existentialist ennui; they were as intellectually distant from my meager desk in Pelham Bay as it was possible to be. The Scotch tape that held my Picasso woman on the wall turned brittle; superannuated, she fell to pieces and was put in the trash. Chester in Paris was well into the beginnings of an international reputation — he was brilliantly in the world — while I, stuck in the same room where I had fussed over Mr. Emerson's assignments, was only another tormented inky cipher. I had nothing of the literary life but my trips on the bus to the Westchester Square Public Library and the changing heaps of books these occasioned.

The letters from Paris crowed. Chester made it plain that he had arrived, and that I had been left behind. He condescended, I smarted. *Death in Venice* brought him up short. Literature — its beauty and humanity — had nothing to do with the literary barometer, with ambition and rivalry and the Red Hot Center. Only the comely sentence mattered. The sentence!

> Aschenbach noted with astonishment the lad's perfect beauty. His face recalled the noblest moment of Greek sculpture — pale, with a sweet reserve, with clustering honey-colored ringlets, the brow and nose descending in one line, the winning mouth, the expression of pure and godlike serenity. Yet with all this chaste perfection of form it was of such unique personal charm that the observer thought he had never seen, either in nature or art, anything so utterly happy and consummate.

We began to talk, as we never had before, of the varieties of human attraction. He was not "naturally" homosexual, I insisted: I *knew* he was not; he knew it himself. I reminded him of his old stirrings and infatuations. I made no mention of the old rebuffs. I felt a large, earnest, and intimate freedom to say what I thought; we had between us, after all, a history of undisguised tenderness. And had he not yearned after Diana? He was not obliged, or destined, to be homosexual; he had chosen dramatic adaptation over honest appetite.

His reply was a savage bellow. The French stamps running helter-skelter on the envelope had been licked into displacement by a wild tongue and pounded down by a furious fist. He roared back at me, in capital letters, "YOU KNOW NOTHING ABOUT LOVE!"

He broke with me then, and I saw how I had transgressed. Privately, I took virulence to be confirmation. He was protesting too much. His rage was an admission that he had followed the path of escape rather than the promptings of his own nature. He was not what he seemed; he was an injured boy absurdly compelled to wear a yellow wig. Shame gave him the power of sham — an outrageously idiosyncratic, if illusional, negation of his heart's truth. He could, as it were, hallucinate in life as vividly as on a page of fiction; he had license now for anything.

Chester is long dead, and though I speak retrospectively about the letter that exasperated him and put an end to our friendship, there are living voices much like his own, and probably just as exasperated. They will claim I am simpleminded in theorizing that Chester's self-revulsion was the true engine of his turning from women. Gay men will know better than I, bisexual men will know better, psychologists and psychoanalysts will know better. And, yes, I know nothing about it. Or, rather, I know that no one knows anything about it: about the real sources of homosexuality. Besides, not every boy who supposes himself unattractive to girls will become a man who courts men. No doubt thousands of young men unhappy with their looks and their lives have moved on to conventionally heterosexual arrangements, including marriage. A wig is superficial: its site is on top of the head, not inside it. Proclivities are likely innate, not pasted on to accommodate circumstance. The homoerotic matrix may inhabit the neural system.

These are fair objections. But how can I surrender what I genuinely saw? I saw that Chester had once loved, and had wanted to be loved by, women. Believing himself radically unfit, he sought an anodyne. Homosexuality was, at least initially, a kind of literary elixir. It brought him apparitions. Who does not recall, on the dust jacket of *Other Voices, Other Rooms*, the photograph of the beautiful young Truman Capote in a tattersall vest, reclining on a sofa, indolent as an odalisque, with lucent, galactic eyes? And what of those luring draughts of Paris and Morocco — brilliant Proustian scenes, North African sweeps of albino light? Anodyne; elixir; apparition. Beyond this, my understanding dims. I cannot pursue Chester into his future; I was not witness to it.

After our last exchange, I never expected to hear from him again. I recognized that I had inflicted a violent hurt — though I had no accurate measure of that violence, or violation, until long afterward, when I came on *The Foot* and the "ax driven straight down the middle of my body."

But Chester had his revenge; he repaid me wound for wound. If I had intruded on his erotic turf, he, it developed, would tread on ground equally unnamable — our rivalry, or what was left of it. Nothing, in fact, was left of it. Chester was publishing, and being talked of, in Paris and New York. I was still futilely mired in my "ambitious first novel," which reached three hundred thousand words before I had the sense to give up on it. Mr. Emerson had pushed us into a race, and Chester had indisputably won.

About two years after I lectured him on love, I took the bus to the post office and mailed a short story to Italy — to *Botteghe Oscure*, at an address in Rome. It had already been submitted to *The New Yorker*, for which I had hungrily but mistakenly designed it, relying on some imitative notion of what "a *New Yorker* story" was in those days reputed to be. The story was a failure: the characters were artificial, the theme absurd. When *The New Yorker* rejected it, instead of disposing of my folly I thought, with the recklessness of envy, of Chester's dazzlements in *Botteghe Oscure*. He had matured quickly. Whereas I was still writing what I would eventually classify as juvenilia, Chester's Paris stories were exquisite; focused and given over to high diction, they seemed the work of an old hand. They had the tone and weight of translations from this or that renowned classical European author whose name you could not quite put your finger on: Colette, or Gide, or the author of *Death in Venice*. Their worked and burnished openings were redolent of delectable old library books: "Once, in autumn, I sat all night beside the immense stone wall that surrounds the ancient cemetery of Père Lachaise." Or "Our appointment was for after lunch, down the street from my house in a little formal park full of trees and flowers called the Garden of the Frog." When I reread these early stories now, they sometimes have, here and there, a poison drop of archaism — as if the 1950s had all collapsed into the very, very long ago. And I am startled to notice that we were writing then — both of us — in what from this distance begins to look like the same style: possessed, in the manner of the young, by the ravishments of other voices.

Several months went by. A letter from Paris! But Chester and I had stopped corresponding. He had cut me off and thrown me out. It was a period, I discovered later, when he was writing hundreds of letters, a number of them to new friends made at Columbia University, where, after college, he was briefly enrolled as a graduate student. When his father died and left him a little money, he escaped courses and schedules and headed for Mexico, and then on to Paris. With no constraints now, he was fashioning a nonconformist life for himself — partly out of books, but mainly inspired by the self-proclaimed expatriate nonconformists who were doing exactly the same. He had made it plain that there was no place in that life for me. Impossible, after our rupture, that I would hear from him; yet I knew no one else in Paris. I looked again at the letter. In the upper-left-hand corner, in faint green rubber-stamped print, were two intoxicating words: *Botteghe Oscure*. The big manila envelope with my story in it, containing another big manila envelope for its return, had been addressed to Rome. This was not a big manila envelope; no manuscript was being returned. It was a thin, small letter. Why from Paris, and not from Rome? *Botteghe Oscure* had its headquarters, whatever they might be (a row of dark shops?), in Rome. Princess Marguerite Caetani, the founder, sponsor, and deep pockets of *Botteghe Oscure*, was a princess of Italy. But, ah, nobility travels glitteringly from capital to capital. Princess Caetani — it must be she — was writing not from Rome, where the season had ended, but from a grand apartment in Paris, in the grandest arrondissement of all, not far from a little formal park full of trees and flowers. She had put aside her gold-embossed lorgnette to pick up a silver-nibbed pen. A thin green sheet peeped from the thin, small envelope. I drew the paper out in a strange kind of jubilation, half regretful. It was late, nearly too late, for this glimmer of good fortune. It was years after Chester's success, though we had set out together. I had been writing seriously since the age of twenty-two, and had never yet been published; all my literary eggs, so far, were in that dubious basket of an unfinished, unfinishable novel.

I recognized the handwriting in an instant. The letter was not from the Princess. Chester was reading for the Princess, he explained: winnowing, going through the pile of awful things the mail habitually brought — the Princess sent everything over from Rome. You wouldn't believe what awful things he was obliged to slog through. Well, here was my story. It wasn't all that good, he liked a few things in it, they weren't completely awful — he would make sure the Princess got his recommendation anyhow.

Chester on Mount Olympus, tossing crumbs. Humiliation: my story was published in *Botteghe Oscure*. He had won, he had won.

What happened afterward I gathered from rumor and report. Chester left Paris in 1959. Between 1959 and 1963, he lived in New York, and so did I. We never met, spoke, or wrote. As always, he was noisily surrounded, prodding to get a rise out of people, on the lookout for adventures, upheavals, darkening mischiefs. His reviews, of books and theater, were ubiquitous, like skywriting: you looked up, and there he was. For a while he abandoned the wig; then he put it on again. Edmund Wilson, notorious for crusty reclusiveness, sent him a fan letter. But he was restless, and ambitious for more, especially for fame of the right sort. He wanted to be writing stories and novels. In 1960, he went off to the perilously companionable isolation of the MacDowell Colony and stumbled into a private loneliness so

profound that he was beginning to populate it with phantom
voices. Unable to sustain his own company, he took on the more
engaging job of busybody and troublemaker, begging for attention by riling everyone in sight. In letters that have since been
published (how this would have delighted him: he did nothing
not for dissemination) he complained to a pair of friends back in
New York:

> They all have cars and seem rich. Except some of the painters. They
> see me walking into town and wave to me as they fly by in their con-
> vertibles on their way to lakes and cookouts. They are mainly dumb.
> They are very square. Nobody's queer, not even me anymore. Besides
> I hate myself too. I can't stand it anymore not having any stable I. It
> is too much. Thrust into a totally new situation, here, I don't know
> who I am. My neighbor Hortense Powdermaker walks by and I feel
> some creature in me rise. I just want to scream fuck I am alfred
> chester who? But no one will believe me, not even me, who is writing
> this now? . . . And the voices in my head go on and on. As there is no
> me except situationally, I have to have mental conversations in order
> to be. . . . Ugh. It's to die. . . . WRITE TO ME WRITE TO ME WRITE TO ME
> WRITE TO ME WRITE TO ME AS I FADE AWAY WITH LONELINESS.
>
> I have had a blowout with Mme. Powdermaker at breakfast this
> morning and am still quivering. I come to the table, at which she,
> Ernst Bacon, Leon Hartl (a French painter I adore), and Panos, a
> Greek, sit. Morning, Powdie, say I, for I have been shaking since last
> night, aching to give it to her. Aching to give it to most of them in
> fact, this rude, ungenerous, terrified, ungiving teaparty group who
> preserve nothing but the surface, so illmannered and illbred, so lack-
> ing in spirit. . . . Last night I decided I was no longer going to submit,
> but to rebel against every act of unkindness. The colony is in an
> uproar. . . . First of all I have been persona non grata since last
> Saturday night when I danced with Gus the cook at the MacDowell
> version of wild party in Savidge Library. . . . Gus wanted to fuck me
> but I wouldn't let him because of his wife. There has been a party
> every day since, sometimes twice a day, to which I have been cordially
> uninvited by the wild young set. I don't mind. It is all like a tea party
> with the people made of china. But what I do mind is their hypocrisy,
> the extreme courtesy toward someone they can't bear: me. I also mind
> their bad manners, like leaving me to put away the pieces in the
> scrabble board, or Powdie saying yes, very snidely, yes she'd guessed
> I was a Russian Jew.

There followed a dustup over Chester's having asked Hor-
tense Powdermaker for a lift in her car, which, according to

Chester's account, she refused, deliberately allowing him to stand futilely in the road in the dark of a summer's night.

It got pretty hysterical after this and the other tables as well as the kitchen staff were hysterical.

She: (to Ernst Bacon) As head of the house committee, I wish you would take this matter up with this young man. I'm not obliged to be anyone's chauffeur. It is customary to wait to be offered something. Not to ask for it. You're a brash young man. You don't know anything about communal living. You have no place in this colony.

After an official dressing-down, he was asked to leave Mac-Dowell. He was, as he put it in a telegram, "flung out." He announced that Gus, the cook, and Gus's wife were departing with him, along with Chester's two rambunctious dogs, Columbine and Skoura, who had sunk their teeth into assorted mattresses and the body parts of other residents. (He had been given special permission to bring the dogs with him to MacDowell. He had also been supplied with a new typewriter and "a full-length mirror for my yoga.") "And he is lovely," he said of himself. "I love him. He is sweet and cute. . . . O I'm so much gladder to be me than all these pathetic silly other people."

Half a decade later, he was similarly flung out of Morocco, where he had been living since 1963, invited there by Paul Bowles. A young Arab fisherman named Dris, who practiced sympathetic witchcraft and genial conning — the Larbi of *The Fool* — became his lover, factotum, and dependent. "It is traditional in Morocco," Chester remarks in a story ("Glory Hole," subtitled "Nickel Views of the Infidel in Tangier"), "to pay for sex. There are nicer, but not truer, ways of putting it. The lover gives a gift to the beloved: food, clothing, cash. The older pays the younger." It was not because of his sexual conduct that Chester was expelled from Morocco. Tangier was, one might say, a mecca for "Nazarene" homosexuals from the States, who were as officially welcome as any other dollar-bearing visitors. As far as anyone can make out, Chester's landlord complained to the authorities about the savagery of Chester's dogs, and of Chester's own furies, his fits of quarreling with the neighbors over the racket their numerous children made. At MacDowell, he had brought in booze to supplement the bland fare in the dining room. In Tangier, he turned to pills and kif, and fell into spells of madness. Bounced out of Morocco, he fled to New York and then to London, where he was deranged enough to be tended by a psychiatric social worker. He repeatedly attempted to be allowed back into Morocco, enlisting Paul Bowles to intervene for him. Morocco remained obdurate.

In 1970, I was in Jerusalem for the first time, to read a literary paper at a conference. I had published, four years earlier, a very long "first" novel, which was really a third novel. It was sparsely reviewed, and it dropped, as first novels are wont to do, into a ready oblivion. In Jerusalem, though, I was surprised by a fleeting celebrity: my essay — many thousands of words, which had taken nearly two hours to deliver — was reprinted almost in its entirety, along with my picture, in the weekend book section of the English-language Jerusalem *Post*. All this I saw as fortuitous and happy bait.

Chester was now living in Jerusalem. The moment I arrived in Israel, I tried to find him. I had been given the address of a poet who might know how to reach him, but the poet was himself inaccessible — he was sick and in the hospital. I waited for Chester to come to me. I felt hugely *there;* you couldn't miss me. The *Post* had published, gratuitously, the biggest "personals" ad imaginable. Every day, I expected Chester's telephone call. It was now fourteen years since he had winnowed on behalf of the Princess, and more than two decades since I had last looked into his bleached and lashless eyes. I longed for a reunion; I thought of him with all the old baby tenderness. I wanted to be forgiven, and to forgive. As I contemplated the journey to Israel, my secret, nearly singleminded hope was to track him down. In New York, his reputation had dwindled; his name was no longer scrawled across the sky. An episodic "experimental" novel, *The Exquisite Corpse* (horrific phantasmagoria bathed in picture-book prose that Chester himself, in a letter, called "delicious"), appearing three years before, had left no mark. Even rumors of Chester's travels had eluded me: I had heard nothing about the life in Morocco, or about his meanderings in Spain and Greece and Sicily; I had no idea of any of it. Jealousy, of Chester or anyone, had long ago burned itself out. It was an emotion I could not recognize in myself. I was clear of it — cured. The ember deposited on the cold hearth of Mr. Emerson's ancient conflagration was of a different nature altogether: call it love's cinder. It lay there, black and gray, of a certain remembered configuration, not yet disintegrated. Chester did not turn up to collect it.

He did not turn up at all. He was already dead, or dying, or close to dying — perhaps even while I was walking the curved and flowering streets of Jerusalem, searching for the ailing poet's house, the poet who was to supply the clue to Chester's whereabouts.

Why had Chester come to Jerusalem? In 1967, back in Paris, he put on a new English fedora over his now exposed and glossy scalp, and plunged into the byways of the Marais to seek out a synagogue. Not since his boyhood in the yeshiva had he approached the Hebrew liturgy. Despite this singular visit, his habits continued unrestrained and impenitent. He drank vodka and bourbon and cognac by the bottle, smoked kif and hashish, took barbiturates and tranquilizers, and was unrelentingly, profoundly, mercilessly unhappy.

In Jerusalem, he set to work on a travel report, never published, called "Letter from the Wandering Jew" — a record, really, of personal affronts, most of them provoked by loneliness in quest of sensationalism. In it he purports to explain why he left Europe for Israel. "No roads lead to Israel," the manuscript begins. A parenthesis about the opening of a "sex aids" shop in Tel Aviv follows. And then:

> Why I came is a very long story, a couple of thousand years long, I suppose. I'd been living unhappily in France since May, I and my two dogs Momzer [Hebrew for "bastard"] and Towzer who are Arabs, having been born in Morocco. The idea of Israel had been with me for some time, a kind of latent half-hearted hope that there was a place on this planet where people who had suffered had come together to shelter each other from pain and persecution: a place of lovingkindness. Besides, does a Jew ever stop being a Jew? Especially one like me whose parents had fled the Russian pogroms for the subtler barbarisms of New York? Yiddish was as much my first language as English, and Hebrew came soon after, for [since I was his] youngest and belated child, my father was determined that at least one of his sons would be a good Jew.

This faintly sentimental opening (not counting the sex-shop parenthesis) misrepresents. The rest is bitter stuff, bitter against father and mother, against going to school, against childhood and children, against teachers and rabbis and restaurants and waiters, against God ("that pig called Jehovah"), against France and the French, against Arab hotels and Jewish hotels, against Arabs, against Jews, against traffic noise, even against the scenery. Once again, there are the rows over the dogs, flocks of urchins teasing, exasperated neighbors, bewildered policemen. There are forays after eccentric houses to rent; unreasonable landlords; opportunistic taxi drivers. There are rages and aggression and digression and jokes in the mode of sarcasm and jokes in the mode of nihilism. Satire wears out and reverts to snideness, and snideness to open fury. Eventually, vodka and Nembutal and little blue Israeli tranquilizers take charge of the language: now gripping, now banal; now thrilling, now deteriorated; now manic, now shocking. At moments, it is no more than pretty, a make-do remnant of what was once a literary style:

> The neighborhood was quiet, the house pleasant and sunny; the dogs had a great garden to run around in and there was a pack of ferocious Airedales next door to bark at all the time. Flowers grew all through the winter — roses, narcissi, pansies, and lots of others whose names I don't know — and when spring came, virtually on the heels of [winter], the roof of the house went absolutely crazy with those gorgeous Mediterranean lilacs that have hardly any smell but almost make up for it by the tidal madness of their bloom.

"Letter from the Wandering Jew" was Chester's last performance. A paranoid document, it is not without self-understanding. The Promised Land is always over the crest of the hill, and then, when you have surmounted the hill and stepped into the lovely garden on the other side, you look around and in ten minutes discover that everything has been corrupted. The truth is that the traveler himself, arriving, is the corrupter. Chester, in his last words, fathomed all this to the lees:

> Aren't you tired of listening to me? I am. If I had any tears left, I would cry myself to sleep each night. But I haven't, so I don't. Besides, it is morning that comes twisting and torturing my spirit, not nights of dreamless sleep. Morning, another day. I open the shutters and am assailed by the long day unstretching itself like a hideous snake. Does hope spring eternal? Is there still within me the inane dream that somewhere, sometime, will be better?

A few wild poppies are blooming in my littered weedy garden. When I walk out with the dogs I see the poppies opening here and there among the weeds, and here and there a few sickly wilting narcissi. Surely death is no dream . . . and that being the case, there is then in truth a homeland, a nowhere, a notime, noiseless and peaceful, the ultimate utopia, the eternal freedom, the end to all hunting for goodness and home.

Chester wrote these sad cadences, I learned afterward, less than a block from my Jerusalem hotel. He never looked for me; I never found him. I never saw him alive again. (His dogs, I heard, were discovered locked in a closet, ravenous.)

He lives in my mind, a brilliant boy in a wig.

Very few are familiar with Chester's work or name nowadays — not even bookish people of his own generation. He counts, I suppose, as a "neglected" writer — or perhaps, more to the point, as a minor one. To be able to say what a minor writer is — if it could be done at all — would bring us a little nearer to defining a culture. The tone of a culture cannot depend only on the occasional genius, or the illusion of one; the prevailing temper of a society and a time is situated in its minor voices, in their variegated chorus, but, above all, in the certainty of their collective presence. There can be no major work, in fact, without the screen, or ground, of lesser artists against whom the major figure is illuminated. Or put it that minor writers are the armature onto which the clay of greatness is thrown, pressed, prodded. If we looked to see who headed the best-seller list the year *The Golden Bowl* came out, the likelihood is that not a single name or title would be recognizable. Minor writers are mainly dead writers who do not rise again, who depend on research projects — often on behalf of this ideology or that movement — to dig up their forgotten influence. Minor writers are the objects of literary scholarship: who if not the scholars will creep through archives in search of the most popular novelists of 1904?

Quantity is not irrelevant. A minor writer may own an electrifying gift, but a trickle of work generally reduces power. In the absence of a surrounding forest of similar evidences, one book, no matter how striking, will tend to diminish even an extraordinary pen to minor status. There are, to be sure, certain blazing exceptions — think, for example, of *Wuthering Heights,* a solo masterwork that descends to us unaccompanied but consummate. By and large, though, abundance counts. Balzac is Balzac because of the vast, thick row of novel after novel, shelf upon shelf. Imagine Balzac as the author only of *Lost Illusions,* say, a remarkable work in itself. Or imagine James as having written *The Golden Bowl* and nothing else. If *Lost Illusions* were to stand alone, if *The Golden Bowl* were to stand alone, if there were no others, would Balzac be Balzac and James James?

Sectarianism also touches on minorness. There is, of course, nothing in the human predicament which is truly sectarian, parochial, narrow, foreign, of "special" or "limited" or "minority" interest; all subjects are universal. That is the convenience — for writers, anyhow — of monotheism, which, envisioning one Creator, posits the unity of humankind. Trollope, writing about nineteenth-century small-town parish politics, exactly describes my local synagogue and, no doubt, an ashram along the Ganges. All "parochialisms" are inclusive. Sholem Aleichem's, Jane Austen's, Faulkner's, Garcia Márquez's villages have a census of millions. By sectarianism, for want of a better term, I intend something like monomania — which is different from obsessiveness. Geniuses are obsessive: Kafka is obsessive, Melville is obsessive. Obsessiveness belongs to ultimate meaning; it is a category of metaphysics. But a minor writer will show you a barroom, or a murder victim, or a sexual occasion, relentlessly, monomaniacally. Nothing displays minorness so much as the "genre" novel, however brilliantly turned out, whether it is a Western or a detective story or *Story of O,* even when it is being deliberately parodied as a postmodernist conceit.

Yet minor status is not always the same as oblivion. A delectable preciousness (not inevitably a pejorative, if you consider Max Beerbohm), or a calculated smallness, or an unstoppable scheme of idiosyncrasy, comic or other — or simply the persnickety insistence on *being* minor — can claim permanence as easily as the more capacious qualities of a Proust or a Joyce. The names of such self-circumscribed indelibles rush in: Christina Rossetti, Edward Lear, and W. S. Gilbert out of the past, and, near our own period, Ronald Firbank, Ivy Compton-Burnett, Edward

Dahlberg, S. J. Perelman, James Thurber. Perhaps Beerbohm above all. (There are a handful more among the living.) Minor art is incontrovertibly art, and minor artists, like major ones, can live on and on. Who can tell if Alfred Chester — whose fiction and essays are currently tunneling out into the world again via new editions — will carry on among the minor who are designed to survive or among those others who will be lost because, beyond their given moment, they speak to no one?

The question leads once more to sectarianism and its dooms. It may be that Chester is a sectarian writer in a mode far subtler than genre writing (he once published a pornographic novel under a pseudonym, but let that pass) or monomania. Homosexual life, insofar as he made it his subject, was never a one-note monody for Chester: what moved him was the loneliness and the longing, not the mechanics. His sectarianism, if I am on the right track, took the form of what is sometimes called, unkindly and imprecisely, ventriloquism. It is a romantic, even a sentimental, vice that only unusually talented writers can excel at: the vice, to say it quickly, of excessive love of literature — of the *sound* of certain literatures. Ventriloquist writers reject what they have in common with their time and place, including ordinary talk, and are so permeated with the redolence of Elsewhere that their work, even if it is naturally robust, is plagued by wistfulness. I am not speaking of nostalgia alone, the desire to revisit old scenes and old moods. Nor am I speaking of the concerns of "mandarin" writers — those who are pointedly out of tune with the vernacular, who heighten and burnish language in order to pry out of it judgments and ironies beyond the imagination of the colloquial. Ventriloquist writers may or may not be nostalgic, they may or may not be drawn to the mandarin voice. What ventriloquist writers want is to live inside *other literatures*.

Chester, I believe, was one of these. It made him seem a poseur to some, a madman to others; and he was probably a little of both. He drove himself from continent to continent, trying out the Moroccan sunlight as he had read of it. Malcolm Cowley's Paris as the garden of liberating "exile," the isles of Greece for the poetry of the words, Jerusalem for the eternal dream. Literature was a costume — or, at any rate, a garment. He hardly ever went naked. He saw landscapes and cities through a veil of bookish imaginings. Inexorably, they failed him. His Greek island had unworkable plumbing. Jerusalem had traffic noise. Paris turned out to be exile in earnest. The Moroccan sunlight came through as promised, but so did human nature. Wherever he ran, the nimbus grew tattered, there were quotidian holes in the literary gauze.

This is not to say that Chester was not an original, or that he had a secondhand imagination. Who is more original than a man who fears he is not there? "And I would watch myself, mistrustful of my presence ... *I want to be real,*" he wrote in an early story. (Its title, "As I Was Going Up the Stair," echoes the nursery chant "I met a man who wasn't there.") For the tormented who blind themselves before mirrors, a wash of hallucination will fill the screen of sight. Woody Allen's Zelig falls into old newsreels, his Kugelmass into a chapter of *Madame Bovary.* Chester allowed himself to become, or to struggle to become, if not a character in fiction, then someone who tilted at life in order to transmogrify it into fiction. He is remembered now less as the vividly endowed writer he was born to be than as an eccentric ruin in the comical or sorrowing anecdotes of a tiny circle of aging scribblers.

Most of the writers who on occasion reminisce about Chester have by now lived long enough to confirm their own minor status. If he was in a gladiatorial contest, and not only from the perspective of Mr. Emerson's adolescent amphitheater but with all his literary generation, then it is clear that Chester has lost. In 1962, commenting on an early collection of short stories by John Updike, he was caustic and flashy: "A God who has allowed a writer to lavish such craft upon these worthless tales is capable of anything." A reviewer's callow mistake, yes. Updike has gone from augmentation to augmentation, and nobody can so much as recognize Chester's name. It is common enough that immediately after writers die their reputations plummet into ferocious eclipse: all at once, and unaccountably, a formerly zealous constituency will stop reading and teaching and talking about the books that only a short while before were objects of excitement and gossip. It is as if for writers vengeful mortality erases not only the woman or the man but the page, the paragraph, the sentence — pages, paragraphs, and sentences honed and furbished precisely in order to spite mortality. Writers, major or

minor, may covet fame, but what they really *work* for is that
transient little daily illusion — phrase by phrase, comma after
comma — of the stay against erasure.

I sometimes try to imagine Chester alive, my own age (well, a
few months younger), still ambitiously turning out novels, stories, essays. No white hair for Chester: he would be perfectly
bald, and, given his seniority, perfectly undistinguished by his
baldness. I see him as tamed, though not restrained; a practiced
intellectual by now; industrious; all craziness spent. Instead of
those barbaric dogs, he owns a pair of civilized cats. If I cannot
untangle the sex life of his later years, I also know that it is none
of my business. (In *The Foot* he speaks glancingly of having first
had sexual relations with a woman at thirty-seven.) His ambition,
industry, and cantankerous wit have brought him a quizzical new
celebrity; he is often on television. In degree of attention-getting
he is somewhere between Norman Mailer and Allen Ginsberg,
though less political than either. He avoids old friends, or, if not,
he anyhow avoids me; my visits with him take place in front of
the television set. There he is, talking speedy Brooklynese, on a
literary panel with Joyce Carol Oates and E. L. Doctorow.

I look into the bright tube at those small, suffering, dangerous
eyes under the shining scalp and think: *You've won, Chester, you've
won.*

THOMAS PALMER

The Case for Human Beings

FROM THE ATLANTIC MONTHLY

AN ARGUMENT, a human argument, maintains that we ought to be concerned about the disappearance of individual animal species. If it could be directed at the objects of its solicitude, it would go approximately as follows: "You lesser beasts had better watch your step — *we'll* decide when you can leave." It recognizes that once chromosome patterns combine at the species level, they become unique and irreplaceable — one cannot make a rattlesnake, for instance, out of anything but more rattlesnakes. It looks at the speed at which such patterns are disappearing and shudders to think how empty our grandchildren's world might become, patternwise.

In the past twenty years this argument has conquered much of the world; it may soon become part of the thinking of nearly every schoolchild.

Perhaps because we ourselves are a species, we regard the species level as that at which deaths become truly irreversible. Populations, for instance, can and do fade in and out; when a species dies, however, we call it extinct and retire its name forever, being reasonably certain that it will not reappear in its old form.

Students of evolution have shown that species death, or extinction, is going on all the time, and that it is an essential feature of life history. Species are adapted to their environments; as environments change, some species find themselves in the position of islanders whose islands are washing away, and they go under. Similarly, new islands (or environments) are appearing all the time, and they almost invariably produce new species.

What alarms so many life historians is not that extinctions are occurring but that they appear to be occurring at a greater rate than they have at all but a few times in the past, raising the specter of the sort of wholesale die-offs that ended the reign of the dinosaurs. Do we want, they ask, to exile most of our neighbors to posterity? Exactly how much of our planet's resources do we mean to funnel into people-making? Such questions are serious; they involve choosing among futures, and some of these futures are already with us, in the form of collapsing international fisheries, rich grasslands gnawed and trampled into deserts, forests skeletonized by windborne acids, and so forth. Thus high rates of extinction are seen as a symptom of major problems in the way our species operates — problems that may, if we're not careful, be solved for us. A new word has been coined to define the value most threatened by these overheated rates: "biodiversity." As species disappear, biodiversity declines, and our planet's not-quite-limitless fund of native complexities — so some argue — declines with it.

The process described above is indeed occurring. Human beings tend to change environments; when they do, species vanish. The Puritans, for example, though famous for their efforts to discipline sexuality, imposed upon Massachusetts an orgy of ecological licentiousness: they introduced dozens of microbes, weeds, and pests foreign to the region, some of which played havoc with the natives. Human beings tend to travel everywhere, and to bring their cats, rats, and fleas with them, so that hardly any environment is truly isolated today, and creatures that evolved in isolated environments have paid a high price. Of the 171 species and subspecies of birds that have become extinct in the past three hundred years, for example, 155 were island forms.

Since extinction is a particularly final and comprehensive form of death, species preservation and its corollary, habitat protection, are now seen as the most important means available to stem the erosion of biodiversity. So far, so good — but I wonder if these ideas, which emphasize diversity at the species level, fail to give an adequate picture of recent biological history. If, for instance, biodiversity is regarded as the chief measure of a landscape's richness, then the American continents reached their peak of splendor on the day after the first Siberian spearmen arrived, and have been deteriorating ever since. More recent developments — such as the domestication of maize, the rise of civilizations in Mexico and Peru, and the passage of the U.S. Bill of Rights — are neutral at best, and are essentially invisible, since they are the work of a single species, a species no more or less weighty than any other, and already present at the start of the interval. But what kind of yardstick measures a handful of skin-clad hunters against Chicago, Los Angeles, and Caracas, and finds one group no more "diverse" than the other?

A considerable amount of pessimism is built into this species-based notion of diversity. Nearly all change on such a scale is change for the worse — especially human-mediated change. Change involves stress, and stress causes extinctions; each extinction is another pock in the skin of an edenic original. This original is frozen in time; more often than not, it is defined as the blissful instant just prior to the arrival of the first human being. In fact, the only way to recreate this instant, and restore biodiversity to its greatest possible richness, would be to arrange for every human being on earth to drop dead tomorrow.

This is not to say that cities are better than coral reefs, or that binary codes are an improvement on genetic ones, but only that "biodiversity" cannot adequately account for the phenomenon of *Homo sapiens*.

Maybe it's time to give up the notion of human beings as intruders, tramplers, and destroyers. We are all of these, there's no doubt about it, but they are not all we are. And yet the same mind-set that interprets human history as little more than a string of increasingly lurid ecological crimes also insists that our species represents the last, best hope of "saving" the planet. Is it any wonder that the future looks bleak?

Here we have the essential Puritan outlook disguised as science — human beings, the sinners, occupy center stage, and cannot move a muscle without risking the direst consequences in a cosmic drama. At stake is the fate of the world; thousands of innocents (other species) rely on the shaky powers of human foresight. One false step — and our ancestors, as we know, have taken almost nothing but false steps — and our dwelling place may be mutilated beyond redemption.

This outlook is realistic in its recognition that our species is different in kind from all others, as any visitor from outer space would admit; it is obnoxious in the limits it places on the organic experiment. Human consciousness — whether in the form of Bach chorales, three-masted schooners, or microwave communications — cannot, in this view, contribute to biodiversity, except by staying as far out of the picture as possible, so as to avoid tainting still-intact landscapes with unnatural influences. The possibility that chorales and schooners might represent positive contributions to biotic richness — that they might, just as much as any rain forest orchid, embody the special genius of this planet — is never admitted. Somehow an agreement has been reached to exclude whatever is human from the sum of biodiversity — as if the Apollo landings, for example, do not represent an astonishing breakthrough *in strictly biological terms*.

This view has a certain legitimacy as long as its definition of diversity is narrowly chromosomal, or species-based. Those environments richest in species — the tropical forests and the warmwater seas — are, from its perspective, the most diverse and complex. But I would argue that this definition, though accurate enough for most of the history of life, became obsolete about a half million years ago, when *Homo sapiens* came on the scene. This creature released organic change from its age-old dependence on genetic recombination and harnessed it to new energies — culture, symbolic language, and imagination. As is becoming more and more evident, nothing has been the same since.

Being reluctant to acknowledge this fact, ecologists, biologists, and environmentalists have had fits trying to introduce our species into their models of the natural world. These models are based on the idea of balance, or equilibrium, wherein each variety of plant or animal plays a limited, genetically prescribed role in the cycling of materials and energy. The roles are not absolutely fixed — natural selection, by sorting and resorting chromosomes, can adapt lines of descent to new ones — but change, by and large, is assumed to be gradual, and millions of years can pass without any notable restructuring of communities.

Human beings cannot be worked into such models. One cannot look at human beings and predict what they will eat, or where they will live, or how many of their children a given landscape will support. If they inhabit a forest, they may burn it down and raise vegetables, or flood it and plant rice, or sell it to a pulp and paper manufacturer. They may think of anything; the life their parents led is not a reliable blueprint, but merely a box with a thousand exits. Moralists in search of instructive contrasts will sometimes idealize primitive societies, claiming that they deliberately live "in balance" with their environments, but these examples don't stand up to scrutiny. The Massachuset Indians, for instance, though sometimes presented as sterling conservationists, were the descendants of aboriginal American hunters who appear to have pursued a whole constellation of Ice Age mammals to extinction (including several species of horses). When, in historical times, they were offered metal fishhooks, knives, and firearms, they didn't say, "Thanks, but we prefer rock-chipping."

The revelation that we are not like other creatures in certain crucial respects is an ancient one, and may be nearly as old as humanity; it probably contributed to the idea, central to several major religions, that we inhabit a sort of permanent exile. Until recently, however, we could still imagine ourselves encompassed by, if not entirely contained in, landscapes dominated by non-human forces — weather, infectious illness, growing seasons, light and darkness, and so forth. This is no longer so; today most human beings live in artificial wildernesses called cities, and don't raise the food they eat, or know where the water they drink fell as rain. A sort of vertigo has set in — a feeling that a rhythm has been upset, and that soon nothing will be left of the worlds that made us. This feeling is substantiated by population curves, ocean pollution, chemical changes in the earth's atmosphere, vanishing wildlife, mountains of garbage, and numerous other signs that anyone can read. The nineteenth-century conservation movement, which sought to preserve landscapes for largely aesthetic reasons, has become absorbed in the twentieth-century environmental movement, which insists that more is at stake than postcard views. We are, it argues, near to exceeding the carrying capacity of our planet's natural systems, systems whose importance to us will become very obvious when they begin to wobble and fail.

These are not empty warnings. Human communities can and occasionally do self-destruct by overstraining their resource bases. Historical examples include the Easter Islanders, the lowland Maya, and some of the classical-era city-dwellers of the Middle East and North Africa. But if we set aside the equilibrium-based models of the ecologists and do not limit ourselves to species-bound notions of diversity — in other words, if we seek to include human beings in the landscape of nature, rather than make them outcasts — what sort of picture do we get of the phenomenon of life?

The difference between life and nonlife, according to the biologists, is a matter of degree. A glass of seawater, for instance, contains many of the same materials as a condor (or a green turtle). What makes one alive and the other not are the varying chemical pathways those materials follow. The glass of water contains few internal boundaries, and gases diffuse freely across its surface. In the condor, in contrast, a much more complex array of reactions is in progress, reactions that maintain certain molecular-energy potentials in an oddly elevated state, even though the bird as a whole shows a net energy loss. In other words, both the condor and the glass of water cycle energy, but in the condor the energy goes to support a level of complexity not present in the water.

Perhaps the condor is more like a candle flame — both burn energy, and that burning keeps certain patterns intact. The condor, like the candle, can burn out. But although one can relight the candle, one cannot relight the condor — it is too delicately tuned, too dependent on various internal continuities.

As useful as these distinctions are, they tend to blur under increased magnification. A virus, for instance, is more condorlike than flamelike, because the energy and materials it draws from its surroundings reappear not primarily as heat, light, and simple oxides but as viral protein and nucleic acids — complex substances that the flame cannot construct but only disassemble. And yet most students agree that viruses are not alive, because they cannot build these substances without the aid of the machineries inside a living cell. A certain level of independence is necessary — living things, according to this definition, not only must transform simple compounds into more varied and characteristic ones but also must be able to do so in an atmosphere of non-life.

Life, for the biologists, is an uphill or retrograde process — it adds order and complexity to environments whose overall tendency is toward diffusion and disorder. It captures energies released by decay and exploits them for growth and rebirth. It is startlingly anomalous in this respect: so far as we know, it occurs nowhere but on the surface of this planet, and even here its appearance seems to have been a one-time-only event; though many lifelike substances have been produced inside sterile glassware, none has ever quickened into veritable beasthood.

The evidence suggests that life continued to fructify and elaborate itself for several billion years after its appearance. The milestones along the way — the nucleated cell, photosynthesis, sexual reproduction, multicellularity, the internal skeleton, the invasion of the land and sky, and so forth — are usually interpreted as advances, because they added additional layers of complexity, interconnection, and ordered interaction to existing systems. This drama did not proceed without crises — photosynthesis, for instance, probably wiped out entire ecosystems by loading the atmosphere with a deadly poison, free oxygen — but life as a whole laughed at such insults, and continued on its protean way.

If we believe that all life — in contrast to rocks and gases — shares a certain quality of sensitivity, or self-awareness, then *Homo sapiens* was an astonishing and wholly unpredictable leap forward in this respect, because human beings manifested an idea of personhood never before achieved. The exact moment of this discovery is of course problematic, as are most events in evolution, but I would date it from early summer about sixty thousand years ago, when a group of Neanderthals living in present-day Iraq lost one of their members, dug a grave for him in the Shanidar Cave of the Zagros Mountain highlands, placed his body inside, and covered it with yarrow blossoms, cornflowers, hyacinths, and mallows. Here, in a gesture of remarkable grace, a group of living creatures betrayed an awareness that creatureliness is a pose, a pose that can't be held forever.

The poignancy of this moment is profound. Though the idea

is startling to consider, all the evidence suggests that most of life's history has unfolded unobserved, so to speak. I would bet that the dinosaurs, for instance, did not know that they were reptiles, or that they had faces like their neighbors, or that they once hatched from eggs like their offspring.

Consciousness. Mind. Insight. Here are qualities that, if not exclusively human, seem appallingly rudimentary elsewhere. Primitive peoples distributed them throughout their worlds; we moderns hold to stricter standards of evidence. Does a cloud yearn, for instance, to drop rain? Is a seed eager to sprout?

The irruption of thoughtfulness that our species represents is not inexplicable in Darwinian terms. Once our apelike and erect ancestors began using weapons, hunting large animals, and sharing the spoils, the ability to develop plans and communicate them acquired considerable survival value, and was genetically enhanced. This ability, and the tripling in brain weight that accompanied it, turned out to be one of the most revolutionary experiments in the history of gene-sorting. It was as if Nature, after wearing out several billion years tossing off new creatures like nutshells, looked up to see that one had come back, and was eyeing her strangely.

The distance between that moment and today is barely a hiccup, geologically speaking. We are genetically almost indistinguishable from those bear-roasters and mammoth-stickers. But the world is a different place now. Grad students in ecology, for instance, are expected to do a certain amount of "fieldwork," and many of them have to travel hundreds and even thousands of miles before they consider themselves far enough from classrooms to be in the field.

Plainly, our planet contained vast opportunities for creatures willing to shape it consciously toward their ends. The way was clear; we know of no other species that has divined what we've been up to or has a mind to object. What seems simple to us is far beyond them; it's almost as if we move so fast that we are invisible, and they are still trying to pretend — without much success — that the world is the same as it was before we arrived.

This speed on the uptake appears to be the chief advantage that cultural adaptation has over genetic. When human beings encounter new circumstances, adaptation rarely depends on which individuals are genetically best suited to adjust, passing on their abilities more successfully than others and producing subsequent generations better adapted to the new order. No, human beings tend to cut the loop short by noticing the new, puzzling over it, telling their friends, and attempting to find out immediately whether it is edible, combustible, domesticable, or whatever. In this way we develop traditions that are immaterial, so to speak, in that they evolve on a track largely disengaged from the double helix.

This talent for endless jabber and experiment, and the pooling of useful knowledge it makes possible, means that human beings, unlike orangutans or condors, operate not primarily as individuals scattered over a landscape but as shareholders in a common fund of acquired skills, many of them the work of previous generations. This fund is extraordinarily deep and sophisticated, even among the most isolated bands of hunter-gatherers; when, as in recent times, it has included experience accumulated by thousands or even millions of forebears, it has enabled our species to become the quickest-acting agent of change in life's history. In fact, we might sensibly think of the human species not as five billion distinct selves but as five billion nodes in a single matrix, just as the human body is more commonly considered a unit than an accumulation of cells.

If life, as before noted, is a paradoxical chemical process by which order arises from disorder, and a movement toward uniformity produces more complex local conditions, then human enterprise, though full of disasters for other species, is clearly not outside the main line of development. Equatorial rain forests, for instance, are probably the most diverse and multifaceted communities of species on earth. But are they more densely stuffed with highly refined codes and labels than, say, the Library of Congress? Long ago certain moths learned to communicate over as much as two miles of thick woods by releasing subtle chemicals that prospective mates could detect at levels measured in parts per million; today a currency broker in Tokyo can pick up a phone and hear accurate copies of sounds vocalized a split second earlier by a counterpart on the other side of the world. Which system of signals is more sensitive and flexible?

*

I am concerned, as is obvious, with an image — the image of our species as a vast, featureless mob of yahoos mindlessly trampling this planet's most ancient and delicate harmonies. This image, which is on its way to becoming an article of faith, is not a completely inaccurate description of present conditions in some parts of the world, but it portrays the human presence as a sort of monolithic disaster, when in fact *Homo sapiens* is the crown of creation, if by creation we mean the explosion of earthly vitality and particularity long ago ignited by a weak solution of amino acids mixing in sunlit waters. Change — dramatic, wholesale change — is one of the most reliable constants of this story. To say that the changes we have brought, and will continue to bring, are somehow alien to the world, and are within a half inch of making its "natural" continuance impossible, displays some contempt, I think, for the forces at work, along with a large dose of inverted pride. Who are we, for instance, to say what's possible and what isn't? Have we already glimpsed the end? Where exactly did things go awry? It's useful to remember that just yesterday our main concern was finding something to eat.

I prefer to suppose that we will be here awhile, and that such abilities as we have, though unprecedented in certain respects, are not regrettable. The human mind, for instance, could never have set itself the task of preserving rare species if earlier minds had not learned how to distinguish light from darkness, or coordinate limbs, or identify mates. Now that we think we know something about our immediate neighborhood, we are beginning to realize what a rare quality life is, and if we think of its multibillion-year history on earth as a sort of gradual awakening of matter, we must conclude that the dawning of human consciousness represents one of the most extraordinary sunrises on record. Is it any wonder, then, that the world is changing?

Perhaps because we have become so expert at interrogating our surroundings, we tremble a little at our own shadows. God, for instance, has become almost a fugitive. We have disassembled the atom; we have paced off the galaxies; He doesn't figure in our equations.

Maybe it would be useful at this point to compare our common birthplace to a fertile hen's egg. Nearly everyone has seen the delicate tracery of blood vessels that begins to spread across the yolk of such an egg within a few hours of laying. Before long a tiny pump starts to twitch rhythmically, and it drives a bright scarlet fluid through these vessels. The egg doesn't know that it is on its way to becoming a chicken. Chickens, for the egg, lie somewhere on the far side of the beginning of time. And yet the egg couldn't be better equipped to make a chicken out of itself.

I would argue that our planet, like the egg, is on a mission of sorts. We don't know what that mission is any more than the nascent nerve cells in the egg know why they are forming a network. All we know is that things are changing rapidly and dramatically.

Today many believe that these changes are often for the worse, and represent a fever or virus from which the body of life will emerge crippled and scarred. We look back with longing on a time, only a moment ago, when the human presence barely dimpled the landscape — when the yolk, so to speak, was at its creamiest, and no angry little eye spots signaled an intent to devour everything.

I'm not persuaded by this picture — I think it arises from a mistaken belief that the outlines of earthly perfection are already evident. It has inspired a small army of doomsayers — if we burn the forests of the Amazon, we are told, our planet's lungs will give out, and we will slowly asphyxiate. Surely we have better, more practical reasons for not burning them than to stave off universal catastrophe. I can easily imagine similar arguments that would have required the interior of North America to remain empty of cities — and yet I don't think this continent is a poorer place now than it was twenty thousand years ago. The more convinced we are that our species is a plague, the more we are obliged to yearn for disasters.

Students of historical psychology have noticed that the end of the world is always at hand. For the Puritan preachers it was to take the form of divine wrath, and they warned that the Wampanoag war was only a foretaste. The Yankees saw it coming in the flood of nineteenth-century immigrants, who meant to drown true Americanism. Today we are more likely to glimpse it in canned aerosols, poisoned winds, and melting ice caps.

Curiously enough, the end of the world always *is* at hand — the world dies and is reborn on a daily basis. A fertile hen's egg is never today what it was yesterday, or will be tomorrow. Few would deny that the effort to preserve and protect as many as possible of the millions of species now existing represents a fresh and heartening expansion of human ambitions. But to suppose that earthly diversity is past its prime, and that a strenuous program of self-effacement is the best contribution our species has left to offer, is neither good biology nor good history.

JAMES SALTER

You Must

FROM ESQUIRE

MY FATHER, hair parted in the middle, confident and proud, was first in his class. A brilliant unknown with a talent for mathematics and a prodigious memory, he graduated just ahead of a rival whose own father was first in 1886.

The school was West Point and he had also been first captain, though that was harder for me to imagine. In any case, the glory had slipped away by the time I was a boy. He had resigned his commission after only a few years and not much evidence of those days remained. There were a pair of riding boots, some yearbooks, and in a scabbard in the closet, an officer's saber with his name and rank engraved on the blade.

Once a year on the dresser in the morning there was a beautiful medal on a ribbon of black, gray, and gold. It was a name tag from the alumni dinner at the Waldorf the night before. He liked going to them; they were held toward the end of the winter and he was a persona there, more or less admired, though as it turned out there was a flaw in his makeup not visible at the time that brought him, like Raleigh, to the block. It was not his head he lost but his kidneys, from high blood pressure, the result of mortal anguish, of having failed at life.

When I was older he took me to football games, which we left during the fourth quarter. Army was a weak but gritty team that came to Yankee Stadium to play Notre Dame. Behind us, the stands were a mass of gray, hoarse from cheering, and a roar went up as a third-string halfback, thin-legged and quick, somehow got through the line and ran a delirious, slanting eighty

yards or so until he was at last pulled down. If he had scored,
Army would have won.

In the end I went to the same school my father did, though I
never intended to. He had arranged a second alternate's appointment and asked me as a favor to study for the entrance
exam. I had already been accepted at Stanford and was dream-
ing of life on the coast, working for the summer on a farm in
Connecticut and sleeping on a bare mattress in the stifling attic,
when suddenly a telegram came. Improbably, both the principal
and first alternate had failed, one the physical and the other the
written, and I was notified that I had been admitted. Seventeen,
vain, and spoiled by poems, I prepared to enter a remote West
Point. I would succeed there, it was hoped, as my father had.

In mid-July up the steep road from the station we walked as a
group. I knew no one. Like the others, I carried a small suitcase
in which would be put clothes I would not see again for years.
We passed large, silent buildings and crossed a road beneath
some trees. A few minutes later, having signed a consent paper,
we stood in the hall in a harried line, trying to memorize a
sentence to be used in reporting to the cadet first sergeant. It
had to be spoken loudly and exactly. Failure meant going out
and getting in line to do it again. There was constant shouting
and beyond the door of the barracks an ominous noise, alive,
that flared when the door was opened like the roar of a furnace.
It was the din of the Area, upperclassmen, some bellowing, some
whispering, some hissing like snakes. They were giving the same
commands over and over as they stalked the nervous ranks that
stood stiffly at attention, still in civilian clothes, already forbidden to look anywhere but straight ahead. The air was rabid. The
heat poured down.

I had come to a place like Joyce's Clongowes Wood College,
which had caused such a long shiver of fear to flow over him.
There were the same dark entrances, the Gothic facades, the
rounded bastion corners with crenellated tops, the prisonlike
windows. In front was a great expanse, which was the parade
ground, the Plain.

It was the hard school, the forge. To enter you passed, that
first day, into an inferno. Demands, many of them incompre-

hensible, rained down. Always at rigid attention, hair freshly
cropped, chin withdrawn and trembling, barked at by unseen
voices, we stood or ran like insects from one place to another,
two or three times to the Cadet Store returning with piles of
clothing and equipment. Some had the courage to quit immediately, others slowly failed. Someone's roommate, on the third
trip to the store, hadn't come back but had simply gone on and
out the gate a mile away. That afternoon we were formed up in
new uniforms and marched to Trophy Point to be sworn in.

It is the sounds I remember, the iron orchestra, the feet on the
stairways, the clanging bells, the shouting, cries of Yes, No, I do
not know, sir!, the clatter of sixty or seventy rifle butts as they
came down on the pavement at nearly the same time. Life was
anxious minutes, running everywhere, scrambling to formations. Among the things I knew nothing of were drill and the
manual of arms. Many of the other new cadets, from tin schools,
as they called them, or the National Guard, knew all that and
even the doggerel that had to be memorized, answers to trivial
questions, dictums dating to the Mexican War. How many gallons of water, how many names, what had Schofield said, what
was the definition of leather? These had to be rattled off word
for word.

All was tradition, the language, the gray woolen cloth, the high
black collars of the dress coats, the stiffly starched white pants
that you got into standing on a chair. Always in summer the
Corps had lived in tents out on the Plain, under canvas, with
duckboard streets — summer camp with its fraternal snapshots
and first classmen lounging against tent poles; this was among
the few things that had disappeared. There was the honor system about which we heard from the very beginning, which belonged to the cadets rather than to the authorities and had as its
most severe punishment "silencing." Someone who was guilty of
a violation and refused to resign could be silenced, never spoken
to by his classmates except officially for the rest of his life. He
was made to room by himself and one of the few acknowledg-
ments of his existence was at a dance — if he appeared everyone
walked from the floor, leaving him, the girl, and the band all
alone. Even his pleasures were quarantined.

West Point was a keep of tradition and its name was a hall-

mark. It drew honest, Protestant, often rural, and largely un-
complicated men — although there were figures like Poe, Whis-
tler, and even Robert E. Lee, who later said that getting a military
education had been the greatest mistake of his life.

I remember the sweating, the heat and thirst, the banned
ecstasy of long gulping from the spigot. At parades, three or
four a week, above the drone of hazing floated the music of the
band. It seemed part of another, far-off world. There was the
feeling of being on a hopeless journey, an exile that would last
for years. In the distance, women in light frocks strolled with
officers and the fine house of the Superintendent gleamed toy-
like and white. In the terrific sun someone in the next rank or
beside you begins to sway, takes an involuntary step, and like a
beaten fighter falls forward. Rifles litter the ground. Afterward
a tactical officer walks among them as among bodies on a battle-
field, noting down the serial numbers.

Bang! the door flies open. We leap to our feet. Haughty, sway-
backed, wearing white gloves, a cadet sergeant named Melton
saunters into the room. He glances at us. "Who are you, misters?
Sound off!" he commands. He turns to the wall lockers on which
we have worked for hours preparing for inspection. Everything
has its shelf and place, the folds are clean and sharp, the undershirts like pads of paper, the neat linen cuffs, the black socks.

"Whose locker is this?" he asks with disdain. Not waiting for
an answer, he sweeps its contents to the floor. "It's a mess. Are
these supposed to be folded? Do it over." Shelf after shelf, one
locker after another, everything is tumbled out. "Do it right this
time, understand?"

Implacable hatred floods upward: "Yes, sir!"

One of my first roommates was the son of a congressman. He
was twenty. In Chicago, he said offhandedly, he'd been living in
an apartment with two prostitutes. As a sort of proof, he smoked,
walked around in his underwear, and marveled at nothing. We
were, for the most part, fingerlings, boys in our teens, and his
swagger seemed the mark of an enviable thing with which he was
already familiar: dissipation. We ran up and down the stairs
together but in formation stood far apart. There I was next to a
tall, skinny boy who had a cackling laugh and astonishing irrev-

erence. He was a colonel's son and had come from Hawaii, crossing the continent in a Pullman and spending the night in some woman's lower berth as she moaned over and over, "My son, my son." His name was Horner; in time he introduced me to rum, seduction, cards, and as a last flourish, poison ivy.

The most urgent thing was to somehow fit in, to become unnoticed, the same. My father had managed to do it although, seeing what it was like, I did not understand how. I remembered him only strolling in a princely way; I had never seen him run, I could not imagine him in the exhausting routine of each day.

But it was also hard to be nothing and no one, to be faceless in ranks and unpraised. In still another line, this one in the Cadet Store, where we were being measured for winter uniforms, one of the tailors, a Mr. Walsh, frail and yellowish-haired, noticed my name and asked if I was the son of the honor man in the class of 1919. It was the first feeling I had of belonging, of having a creditable past.

What you had been before meant something — athletic ability mattered, of course, but it was not always enough to see you through. The most important quality was more elusive; I suppose it could be called dignity, but it was not really that. It was closer to endurance.

You were never alone. Above all, it was this that marked the life. As a boy I had had my own room, and though familiar enough with teeming hallways and schoolboy games, these existed only temporarily. Afterward there was home with its solitude, lights in the evening, the rich smell of dinner. There was nothing of that at West Point. We brushed shoulders everywhere, as if it were a troopship, and waited a turn to wash and shave. In the earliest morning, in the great summer kiln of the Hudson Valley, we stood for long periods at strict attention, dangerous upperclassmen drifting behind us sullenly, the whole of the day ahead. Over and over to make the minutes pass I recited lines to myself, sometimes to the bullet-hard beat of drums, buried and lost, but for the moment wrapped in words.

I was an unpromising cadet, not the worst but a laggard. Among the youngest, and more immature than my years, I had neither the wisdom of country boys who knew beasts and the axioms of hardware stores, nor the toughness of the city. I had

been forced to learn a new vocabulary and new meanings, what
was meant by "polished," for instance, or "neatly folded." For
parade and inspections we wore eighteenth-century accessories,
crossed white belts and dummy cartridge box, with breastplate
and belt buckle shined to a mirrorlike finish. In the doorway of
the room at night, before taps, we sat feverishly polishing them.
Pencil erasers and jeweler's rouge were used to painstakingly rub
away small imperfections, and the rest was done with a constantly refolded polishing cloth. It took hours. The terrible ring
of metal on the floor — a breastplate that had slipped from
someone's hand — was like the dropping of an heirloom.

At the end of the summer, assignment to regular companies was
made. There were sixteen companies, each made up of men who
were approximately the same height. Drawn up in a long front
before parade, the tallest companies were at each end grading
down to the shortest in the middle. The laws of perspective made
the entire Corps seem of uniform size, and as it passed in review,
bayonets at the same angle, legs flashing as one, it looked as if
every particle of the whole must be well formed and bright. The
tall companies were known to be easygoing and unmilitary in
barracks, but among the runts it was the opposite. To even pass
by their barracks was hazardous. This was not only fable but fact.
   The stone barracks were arranged around large quadrangles
called areas. Central Area was the oldest, and on opposite sides
of it were South Area and North Area and a small appendix
near the gym called New North. They were distinct, like provinces, though you walked through several of them every day.
Beyond and unseen were the leafy arrondissements where West
Point seemed like a serene river town. In mild September, with
classes about to begin, it settled into routine. There was autumn
sun on the playing fields but the real tone was Wagnerian. We
passed by the large houses, all in a long row, of the colonels,
heads of academic departments, some of them classmates or
friends of my father, old brick houses to which I would one day
be invited for Sunday lunch.
   We had clean slates. All demerits from the summer had been
removed and we were as men paroled. Demerits were a black
mark and a kind of indebtedness. The allowance was fifteen a

month. Beyond that, there were punishment tours, one hour for
each demerit, an inflexible rate of exchange. The hours were
spent on the Area walking back and forth, rifle on shoulder, and
with this came a further lesson: At the inspection, which took
place before the tours began, demerits were frequently given
out. For shoes with a scuff mark accidentally made or brass with
the least breath of tarnish you could receive more tours than you
were able to walk off.

We had learned the skills of a butler, which were meant to be
those of gentry. We wore pajamas and bathrobes, garters for our
socks. Fingernails were scrubbed pink and hair cut weekly. We
learned to take off a hat without touching the bill, to sleep on
trousers carefully folded beneath the mattress to press them,
to announce menus, birthdays, and weekend films with their
cast. Like butlers we had Sunday off, but only after mandatory
chapel.

Three times a day through three separate doors the entire
Corps, like a great religious order, entered the mess hall and
stood in whispery silence — there was always muted talk and
menace — until the command "Take seats!" With the scrape of
chairs the roar of dining began. Meals were a constant terror,
and as if to enhance it, near their end the orders of the day were
announced, often including grave punishments awarded by the
regimental or brigade board. At the ten-man tables upperclassmen sat at one end, plebes at the other. We ate at attention, eyes
fixed on plates, sometimes made part of the conversation like an
amusing servant but mostly silent or bawling information. At any
moment, after being banged on the table, a cup or glass might
come flying. The plebe in charge of pouring looked up quickly,
hands ready, crying, "Cup, please!" It was a forbidden practice
but a favorite. A missed catch was serious since the result might
be broken china and possible demerits for an upperclassman. It
was better to be hit with a cup in the chest or even the head.

"Sit up!" was a frequent command. It meant "stop eating," the
consequence of having failed to know something — passing the
wrong dish or putting cream in someone's coffee who never took
it that way — and might result in no meal at all, though usually
at the end permission was given to wolf a few bites. Somewhere,
in what was called the Corps Squad area, the athletes, plebes
among them, were eating at ease.

Like a hereditary lord's, the table commandant's whim was absolute. Some were kindly figures fond of teasing and school-boy skits. Others were more serpentlike, and most companies had a table that was Siberia ruled by a stern disciplinarian, in our case an ugly Greek first classman, dark and humorless. In the table assignments you made your way downward to it, and there, among the incorrigibles, even felt a kind of pride.

The hour before dawn, everything silent, the air chill with the first bite of fall. The Area was empty, the hallway still. The room was on the second floor at the head of the stairs, the white name cards pale on the door. I waited for a moment, listening, and cautiously turned the knob. Within it was dark, the windows barely distinguishable. At right angles, separated by desks, were the beds. Waters, a blue-jawed captain, the battalion command-er, slept in one. Mills, a sergeant and squad leader, was in the other. I could not hear them breathing; I could hear nothing, the silence was complete. I was afraid to make a sound.

"Sir!" I cried, and shouting my name went on, "reporting as ordered, ten minutes before reveille!" A muffled voice said, "Don't make so much noise." It was Mills. His quilt moved higher against the cold and as an afterthought he muttered, "Move your chin in."

I stood in the blackness. Nothing, not the tick of a clock or the creaking of a radiator. The minutes had come to a stop. I might stand there forever, invisible and ignored, while they dreamed.

It was Mills who had ordered me to come, for some misde-meanor or other, every morning for a week. He was my squad leader but more than that was famous, known to everyone as king of the goats.

The first man in the class was celebrated; the second was not, nor any of the rest. It was only when you got to the end that a name became imperishable again, the last man, the goat, and it was with well-founded pride that a goat regarded himself. Cus-ter had been last in his class, Grant, nearly. The goat was the Achilles of the unstudious. He was champion of the rear. In front of him went all the main body with its outstanding and also mediocre figures; behind him was nothing, oblivion.

It was a triumph like any other, if you were not meant for the classroom, to end up at the very bottom. Those with worse

274 *You Must*

grades had gone under, those with only slightly better were lost in the crowd. Mills had a bathrobe covered with stars. Each one represented the passing of a turn-out examination, the last, all-or-nothing chance in a failed subject — his robe blazed with them. He had come to this naturally; his father had made a good run at it and been fifth from last in 1915. Mills knew the responsibilities of heritage. He had fended off the attacks of men of lesser distinction who nevertheless wanted to vault to renown. Blond and good-looking, he was easy to admire and far from ungifted. A well-executed retreat was said to be among the most difficult of all military operations, at which some commanders were adept. It meant passing close to the abyss, skirting disaster, and surviving by a hair. It was a special realm with its tension and desperate acts, with men who would purposely spill ink over their drawing in engineering on the final day when nothing else, no possibility, was left.

Mills was also a good athlete. He had come from South Carolina and gone to the Citadel for a year. There was a joy of life in him and a kind of tenderness untainted by the merely gentle.

Nothing more had been said to me. I stood in silence. There was neither present nor future. They were unaware of me but I was somehow important, proof of their power. I began to feel dizzy, as if the floor were tilting, as if I might fall. I had lost track of how long I had been there; time seemed to have stopped when from the distance came a single, clear report: the cannon.

Immediately, like a demonic machine, the sounds begin. Outside in the void, drums explode. Someone is shouting in the hallway, "Sir, there are five minutes until assembly for reveille! Uniform, dress gray with overcoats! Five minutes, sir!" Music is playing. Feet can be heard overhead and on the stairs. The hives of sleeping men are spilling out. The drums begin again.

In the room, not a movement. It is still as a vault. Four minutes until assembly. They have not stirred. The plebes are already standing in place with spaces between them that will be filled by unhurrying upperclassmen. The drums start once more. Three minutes.

Something is wrong. For some reason they are not going to the formation, but if I am late or, unthinkable, miss it entirely . . . The clamor continues, bugles, drums, slamming doors. Two minutes now. Should I say something, dare I? At the last moment a bored voice murmurs, "Post, dumbjohn."

I hurry down the steps and into the cold. Less than a minute remains. Hastily making square corners, I reach my place in ranks just as two figures slip past, overcoats flapping, naked chests beneath: Waters and Mills. Fastening the last buttons, Waters arrives in front of the battalion as the noise dies and final bells ring. He appears instantly resolute and calm, as if he had been waiting patiently all along. In a clear, deep voice he orders, "Report!"

I did not exist for Waters, and for Mills, barely. We marched early one Saturday, down to the river where the Corps boarded a many-decked white dayliner to sail to New York. At the football game that afternoon, jammed in the halftime crowd, Mills was coming the other way, by chance behind a very beautiful girl, just behind her with an expression of pure innocence on his face. As he passed me, he winked.

His class graduated early, that January of 1943, hastened by the war. There was a tremendous cheer as he walked up to receive his diploma, and for some reason I felt as they did, that he was mine. I thought of him for a long time afterward, the ease and godlike face of the last man in his class.

In the safety of that autumn, I foundered. The demerits began again — unpolished shoes, dirty rifle, late for athletics, Blue Book misplaced — there were fifty the first month. One night in the mess hall a spontaneous roar went up when it was announced that at the request of a British field marshal — I think it was Field Marshal Dill — all punishments were revoked. According to custom, a distinguished visitor could do that. The cheers passed over my head, so to speak, but the amnesty did not; I had thirty-five tours erased, seven weeks of walking.

Still I was swept along as if by a current. I felt lost. There were faces you did not recognize, formations being held no one knew where, the pressure of crammed schedules, the formality of the classrooms, the impersonality of everyone in authority from the distant Superintendent to the company tactical officers. . . . It was plain to see why they called it the Factory. It was a male world. In the gym we fought one another, wrestled one another, slammed into one another on darkened fields battling for regimental championships. There were no women except for nurses in the hospital and hardened secretaries, but there was the existence of women always, outside. An upperclassman had his laundry come back with a note pinned to the pajama bottoms, which had gone out with a stiffened area on them. A girl who worked in the laundry had written, "The next time you feel like this, call me."

We were inmates. The world was fading. There were cadets who wet the bed and others who wept. There was one who hanged himself. In the gloom of the sally ports were lighted boards where grades from classes were posted at the end of the week. My roommate was failing in mathematics and I was in difficulty in languages. "Don't worry," the professor, a major, had said, "it'll get tougher." We stayed up after taps studying with a flashlight, exhausted and trying to comprehend italicized phrases in the red algebra book. "Let's rest for a few minutes," we said, and kneeling side by side on the wooden floor dozed briefly with only our upper bodies on the bed. Often we studied past midnight in the lavatory.

The field marshal's gift was soon squandered. My name appeared on the gig sheet three or four times a week; I was walking tours and coming back to the room at dusk, dry from the cold and wary, putting my rifle in the rack, taking off my crossbelts and breastplate, and sitting down for a few minutes before washing for supper. Punishment had a moral, which was to avoid it, but I could not. There was something alien and rebellious in me. The ease with which others got along was mysterious. I was losing courage, the thing I always feared having too little of. I was losing hope.

In the first captain's room in the oldest division of barracks there were the names of all those who had once had the honor. I wanted to see it, to linger for a moment and find my bearing as had happened long ago in the Cadet Store line. Late one Sunday afternoon, telling no one, I went there — nothing forbade it — and stood before the door. I nearly turned away but then, impulsively, knocked.

The first captain was in his undershirt. He was sitting at his desk writing letters and his roommate was folding laundry. He looked up, "Yes, mister, what is it?" he said.

Somehow I explained what I had come for. There was a fireplace and on the wall beside it was a long, varnished board with the names. I was told to have a look at it. The list was by year. "Which one is your father?" they asked. I searched for his name and for some reason missed it. My eye went down the column again. "Well?" It was inexplicable. I couldn't find it; it wasn't there. I didn't know what to say. There had been some mistake, I managed to utter. I felt absolutely empty and ashamed.

My father, in a letter, was able to explain. His class, in wartime, had graduated early and had come back to West Point after the armistice as student officers. As highest-ranking lieutenant, the result of his academic standing, my father had been student commander. He called this being first captain and I realized later that I should never have brought it up.

He had been recalled and was now a colonel stationed in Washington. When he came up to visit we walked on the lawn near the Thayer Hotel in winter sunshine. Bits of the wide river glittered like light. I wanted him to counsel me and looking moodily at the ground recited from "Dover Beach." What was I struggling for and what should I believe? It would be more clear later, he finally said. He had never forsaken West Point. He believed in it and would in fact one day be buried near the old chapel. He was counting on the school to steady me, fix me as the quivering needle in a compass firms on the pole, a process he did not describe but that in his case had been more or less successful.

There was the idea that you could be changed, that West Point could make you an aristocrat. In a way it did; it relied on the stoic, outdoor life that is the domain of the aristocrat: sport, hunting, hardship. Ultimately, however, it was a school of less privileged classes with no true connection to the upper world. You were an aristocrat to sergeants and reserve officers, men who believed the myth.

It was a place of bleak emotions, a great orphanage, cold in its appearance, rigid in its demands. There was occasional kindness but little love. The teachers did not love their pupils or the coach the mud-flecked fullback — the word was never spoken al-

though I often heard its opposite. In its place were comradeship
and a standard that seemed as high as anyone could know. It
included self-reliance and death if need be. West Point did not
make character, it extolled it. It taught you to believe in difficulty, the hard way, and to sleep, as it were, on bare ground.
Duty, honor, country. The great virtues were cut into stone
above the archways and inscribed in the gold of class rings, not
the classic virtues — not virtues at all, in fact, but commands. In
life you might know defeat and see things you revered fall into
darkness and disgrace, but never these.

Honor was second but in many ways it was the most important.
Duty might be shirked, country one took for granted, but honor
was indivisible. The word of an officer or cadet could not be
doubted. One did not cheat, one never lied. At night a question
was asked through the closed door, "All right, sir?" and the
answer was the same, "All right." It meant that whoever was
supposed to be in the room was there and no one besides — one
voice answered for all. Absences, attendance, all humdrum was
on the same basis and anything written or signed was absolutely
true. Even the most minor violation was grave. There was an
honor committee; its proceedings were solemn; from its judgment there was no appeal. The committee had no actual disci-
plinary power. It was so august that anyone convicted — and
there were no degrees of guilt, only thumbs up or down — was
expected to resign. Almost always they did. Inadvertence could
sometimes excuse an honor violation, but not much else. Word
traveled swiftly — someone had been brought up on honor. A
few days later there was an empty bed.

In the winter there were parades within the barracks area
rather than on the Plain: the band, the slap of hands on rifles,
the glint of steel, the first companies sailing past. One of the
earliest, in the rain, was for the graduation of the January class.
They were walking along the stoops afterward in the brilliance
of their army uniforms, Roberts, Jarrell, Mills, all of them. The
wooden packing boxes stenciled with their names and new rank
were waiting to be shipped off, the sinks strewn with things
they had no use for, that in the space of a single day had lost
their value, cadet things they had not given away or sold, textbooks, papers. The next morning they, the boxes, everything

was gone — it was like a divorced household, with them somehow went a sense of legitimacy and order. The new first class
seemed unfledged — it would always exist in the shadow of the
one gone on.

One afternoon near the end of winter we ordered class rings.
The ring was a potent object, an insignia and reward. Heavy and
gold, it was worn on the third finger of the left hand, the wedding finger, with the class crest inward until graduation. After, it
was turned around so the academy crest would be closest to the
heart. Engraved within was one's name and "United States
Army." I had decided I wanted something more, perhaps not
the *non serviam* of Lucifer, but a coda. Someone, I knew, somewhere, would take this ring from my lifeless finger and within
find the words that would sanctify me. The line moved steadily
forward, the salesman filling out order blanks and explaining
the merits of various stones. Could I have something else engraved in my ring? I asked. What did I mean, something else? I
wasn't sure; I hadn't decided, and I had the feeling I was taking
up too much time. Finally he wrote "To follow" in the space for
what was to be engraved.

Unknown to me, all this was overheard. That evening in the
mess hall before "Take seats," a cadet captain was ferreting his
way between the tables, here and there whispering a question. I
had never seen him before. He was looking for me. I saw him
come around the table and the next moment he was beside me.
Was I the one who didn't want "United States Army" in his ring?
he asked in a low voice. I didn't have the chance to reply before
he continued icily, "If you don't think the U.S. Army is good
enough for you, did you ever stop to think that you might not be
good enough for the U.S. Army?" On the other side of me
another face had appeared. They were converging from far off.
"Did you ever make a statement that you would resign just
before graduation?" someone said. It was true that I had. "Only
facetiously, sir." I could feel the sweat on my forehead. "Did you
ever say you came here only for the education?" "No, sir!"

Their voices were scornful. They wanted to get a look at me,
they said, they wanted to remember my face. "Mister, the Corps
will see to it that you earn your ring." It was useless to try to

explain. Who informed them, I never knew. Later I realized it
had been a classmate, of course. The worst part was that it all
took place in front of my own company. I was confirmed as a
rebel, a misfit.

Incidents form you, events that are unexpected, unseen trials.
I defied this school. I took its punishment and its hatred. I
dreamed of telling the story, of making that my triumph. There
was a legendary book in the library said to have been written by
a cadet, to contain damning description and to have been suppressed and all copies except one destroyed. It was called *The
Tin Soldier* and was not in the card file nor did anyone I asked
admit having heard of it. It was a kind of literary mirage, though
the title seemed real. If there were no such book, then I would
write it. I thought of its power all that spring during endless
hours of walking back and forth on the Area at shoulder arms.
Pitiless and spare, it would be published in secret and read by all.
Apart from that I was indifferent and tried to get by doing as
little as possible since whatever I did would not be enough.

At the same time, kindled in me somehow was another urge,
the urge to manhood. I did not recognize it as such because I
had rejected its form. "Try to be one of us," they had said, and
I had not been able to. It was this that was haunting me,
though I would not admit it. I struggled against everything, it
now seems clear, because I wanted to belong.

Then in sunlight the music floated over us and when it
ended — the unachievable last parade as plebes — we turned
and in a delirious moment, having forgotten everything, shook
hands with our tormentors. They came along the ranks at ease
seeking us out, and with self-loathing I found myself shaking
hands with men I had sworn not to.

So the year ended. I have returned to it many times in dreams.
The river is smooth and ice clings to its banks. The trees are
bare. Through the open window from the far shore comes the
sound of a train, the faint, distant clicking of wheels on the rail
joints, the Albany or Montreal train with its lighted cars and
white tablecloths, the blur of luxury from which we are ever
barred.

At night the barracks, seen from the Plain, look like a city. All
of us are within, unseen, studying determinants, general orders,

law. I had walked the pavement of the interior quadrangles interminably, burning with anger against what I was required to be. In the darkness the uniform flags hung limply. In a few minutes it would be taps, then quickly the next day. Ten minutes to formation. What are we wearing? I ask. Where are we going? Bells begin to ring. People are vanishing. The room, the hallways, are empty. Dressing, I run down the stairs.

That summer, after leave, we went into the field and to a camp by a lake, wooden barracks, firing ranges, and maneuver grounds of all kinds. Yearling summer. In the new and sunny freedom, weedy friendships grew. We fired machine guns and learned to roll cigarettes by hand. In off-hours I lay on my bed, reading. I knew lines of Powys's *Love and Death* by heart and reserved them for a slim, witty girl who came up from New York on several weekends. She was the daughter of a famous newspaperman. We danced, swam, and went for walks in permitted areas, where the sensuous phrases fell to the ground, useless against her. I was disappointed. The words had been written by someone else but I had assumed them, they were my own. I was posing as part of a doomed generation, *They shall not grow old, as we who are left grow old. . . .* She did not take it seriously. "Kiss the back of your letters, will you?" I asked her. Such things were noticed by the mail orderly.

There is a final week of maneuvers before we return to the post, of digging when exhausted and then being told abruptly that we are moving to different positions; and deeper, they say, dig deeper. There is the new, energetic company commander with wens on his face who seems to like me and for whom, exhilarated, I would do anything. His affection for me was probably imagined, but mine for him was not. He was someone for whom I had waited impatiently, intelligent, patrician, and governed by a sense of duty — this became a significant word, something valuable, like a dense metal buried in the earth that could guide one's actions. There were things that must be done; there were faces that would be turned toward yours and rely on you.

That year we studied Napoleon and obscure campaigns around Lake Garda. There were arrows of red and blue printed on the map but little in the way of thrilling detail, the distant ranks at Eylau, the fires, the snow, the wan-faced emperor wearing sable, the obscure horizon and arms reaching out. We studied movement and numbers. We studied leadership, in part from German texts, given to us not so much to know the enemy but because of their quality, with nothing in them of politics or race.

There was one with the title *Der Kompaniechef*, the company commander. This youthful but experienced figure was nothing less than a living example to each of his men. Alone, half obscured by those he commanded, similar to them but without their faults, self-disciplined, modest, cheerful, he was at the same time both master and servant, each of admirable character. His real authority was not based on shoulder straps or rank but on a model life that granted the right to demand anything from others.

"An officer," wrote Dumas, "is like a father with greater responsibilities than an ordinary father." The food his men ate, he ate, and only when the last of them slept exhausted did he go to sleep himself. His privilege lay in being given these obligations and a harder duty than any of the rest.

The company commander was someone whom difficulties could not dishearten, privation could not crush. It was not his strength that was unbreakable but something deeper, his spirit. He must not only have his men obey, they must do it when they are absolutely worn out and quarreling among themselves, when they are at the end of their ropes and another senseless order comes down from above.

He could be severe but only when it was needed and then briefly. It had to be just, it had to wash things clean like a sudden, fierce storm. When he looked over his men he was conscious that 150 families had placed a son in his care. Sometimes, unannounced, he went among these sons in the evening to talk or just sit and drink a beer, not in the role of superior but of an older, sympathetic comrade. He went among them as kings once went unknown among their subjects, to hear their real thoughts and to know them. Among his most important traits were decency and compassion. He was not unfeeling, not made of wood. Especially in time of grief, as a death in a soldier's family at home, he brought this news himself — no one else should be expected to — and granted leave, if possible, even before it was asked for, in his own words expressing sympathy. Ties like this would never be broken.

This was not the parade ground captain, the mannequin promoted for a spotless record. It was not someone behind the lines, some careerist with ambitions. It was another breed, someone whose life was joined with that of his men, someone hardened and uncomplaining, upon whom the entire struggle somehow depended, someone almost fated to fall.

I knew this hypothetical figure. I had seen him as a schoolboy, latent among the sixth-formers, and at times had caught a glimpse of him at West Point. Stroke by stroke, the description of him was like seeing a portrait emerging. I was almost afraid to recognize the face. In it was no self-importance; that had been thrown away, we are beyond that, stripped of it. When I read that among the desired traits of the leader was a sense of humor that marked a balanced and indomitable outlook, when I realized that every quality was one in which I instinctively believed, I felt an overwhelming happiness, like seeing a card you cannot believe you are lucky enough to have drawn, at this moment, in this game.

I did not dare to believe it but I imagined, I thought, I somehow dreamed the face was my own.

I began to change, not what I was truly but what I seemed to be. Dissatisfied, eager to become better, I shed as if they were old clothes the laziness and rebellion of the first year and began anew.

I was undergoing a conversion, from a self divided and consciously inferior, as William James described it, to one that was unified and, to use his word, right. I saw myself as the heir of many strangers, the faces of those who had gone before, my new roommate's brother, for one, John Eckert, who had graduated two years earlier and was now a medium bomber pilot in England. I had a photograph of him and his wife that I kept in my desk, the pilot with his rakish hat, the young wife, the clarity of their features, the distinction. Perhaps it was in part because of this snapshot that I thought of becoming a pilot. At least it was one more branch thrown onto the pyre. When he was killed on a mission not long after, I felt a secret thrill and envy. His life, the scraps I knew of it, seemed worthy, complete. He had left something behind, a woman who could never forget him, I had her picture. Death seemed the purest act. Comfortably distant from it I had no fear.

There were images of the struggle in the air on every side, the worn fighter pilots back from missions far into Europe, rendezvous times still written in ink on the backs of their hands, gunners with shawls of bullets over their shoulders, grinning and risky, I saw them, I saw myself, in the rattle and thunder of takeoff, the world of warm cots, cigarettes, stand-downs, everything that had mattered falling away. Then the long hours of nervousness as the formation went deeper and deeper into enemy skies and suddenly, called out by jittery voices, high above, the first of them appear, floating harmlessly, then turning, falling, firing, plummeting past, untouchable in their speed. The guns are going everywhere; the sky is filled with smoke and dark explosions and then it happens, something great and crucial tearing from the ship, a vast flat of wing, and we begin to roll over, slowly at first and then faster, screaming to one another, going down.

That was death: to leave behind a photograph, a twenty-year-old wife, the story of how it happened. What more is there to wish than to be remembered? To go on living in the narrative of others? More than anything I felt the desire to be rid of the undistinguished past, to belong to nothing and to no one beyond the war. At the same time I longed for the opposite, country, family, God, perhaps not in that order. In death I would have them or be done with the need; I would be at last the other I yearned to be.

"That person in the army, that wasn't me," Cheever wrote after the war. In my case, it was. I did not know the army meant bad teeth, drab quarters, men with small minds, and colonels wearing sunglasses. Anyone from the life below can be a soldier. I imagined campaigns like Caesar's, the sun going down in wooded country, encampments on hilltops, cool dawns. The army was that; it was like a beautifully dressed woman, I saw her smile at me and stood erect.

The army. They are playing the last songs at the hop, the sentimental favorites. I am dancing with a girl named Pat Potter, blond and elegant, whom I somehow knew. There are moments when one is part of the real beauty, the pageant. They are playing "Army Blue," the matrimonial and farewell song. A hundred, two hundred couples are on the floor. The army. Familiar faces. This immense brotherhood in which they bend you slowly to their ways. This great family in which one is always advancing, even while asleep.

There was a special physical examination that winter that included the eyes, aligning two pegs in a sort of lighted shoe box by pulling strings, "Am I good enough for the Air Corps, sir?" and identifying colors by picking up various balls of yarn. In April 1944, those who had passed, hundreds of us, including my two roommates and me, left for flight training in the South and Southwest. Hardly believing our good fortune, we went as if it were a holiday, by train. Left behind were classes, inspections, and many full-dress parades. Ahead was freedom and the joy of months away.

We were gone all spring and summer and returned much changed. We marched less perfectly, dressed with less care. West Point, its officers' sashes and cock feathers fluttering from shakos, its stewardship, somehow passed over to those who had stayed.

In the fall of 1944, amid the battles on the Continent, came word of the death of Benny Mills. He was killed in action in Belgium, a company commander. Beneath a shroud his body had lain in the square of a small town; people had placed flowers around it and his men, one by one, saluted as they passed through and left him, like Sir John Moore at Corunna, alone with his glory. He had fallen and in that act been preserved, made untarnishable. He had not married. He had left no one.

His death was one of many and sped away quickly, like an oar swirl. I could never imitate him, I knew, or be like him. He was part of a great dynamic of which I, in a useless way, was also part, and classmates, women, his men, all had more reason to remember him than I, but it may have been for some of them as it was for me: He represented the flawless and was the first of that category to disappear.

We bought officers' uniforms from military clothiers who came on weekends in the spring and set up tables and racks in the gymnasium. The pleasure of examining and choosing clothes and various pieces of decoration — should pilot's wings be embroidered in handsome silver thread or merely be a metal version, was it worthwhile to order one or two handmade "green" shirts, was the hat to be Bancroft or Luxemburg — all this was savored. Luxemburg, thought to be the very finest, was in fact two tailor brothers surrounded by walls of signed photographs in their New York offices. The pair of them were to the army as Babel was to the Cossacks.

Like young priests or brides, immaculately dressed, filled with vision, pride, and barely any knowledge, we would go forth. The army would care for us. We had little idea of how careers were fashioned or generals made. Napoleon, I remembered, when he no longer knew personally all those recommended for promotion, would jot next to a strange name on the list three words: Is he lucky? And of course I would be.

At Stewart Field that final spring, nearly pilots, we had the last segment of training. This was near Newburgh, about forty minutes from West Point. We wore flying suits most of the day and lived in long, open-bay barracks. That photograph of oneself, unfading, that no one ever sees, in my case was taken in the morning by the doorway of what must be the dayroom and I am drinking a Coke from an icy, greenish bottle, a delicious prelude to all the breakfastless mornings of flying that were to come. During all the training there had been few fatalities. We were that good. At least I knew I was.

On a May evening after supper we took off, one by one, on a navigation flight. It was still daylight and the planes, as they departed, were thrilling in their solitude. On the maps the course was drawn, miles marked off in ticks of ten. The route lay to the west, over the wedged-up Allegheny ridges to Port Jervis and Scranton, then down to Reading, and the last long leg of the triangle back home. It was all mechanical with one exception: The winds aloft had been incorrectly forecast. Unknown to us, they were from a different direction and stronger. Alone and confident we headed west.

The air at altitude has a different smell, metallic and faintly tinged with gasoline or exhaust. The ground floats by with tidal slowness, roads desolate, the rivers unmoving. It is exactly like the map with certain insignificant differences that one ponders over but leaves unresolved. The sun has turned red and sunk lower. The airspeed reads 160. The fifteen or twenty airplanes, invisible to one another, are in a long, phantom string. Behind, the sky has become a deeper shade. We were flying not only in the idleness of spring but in a kind of idyll that was the end of the war. The color of the earth was muted and the towns seemed empty shadows. There was no one to see or talk to. The wind, unsuspected, was shifting us slowly, like sand.

Of what was I thinking? The inexactness of navigation, I suppose, New York nights, the lure of the city, various achievements that a year or two before I had only dreamed of. The first dim star appeared and then, somewhat to the left of where it should be, the drab scrawl of Scranton.

Flying, like most things of consequence, is method. Though I did not know it then, I was behaving offhandedly. There were light lines between cities in those days, like lights on an unseen highway but much further apart. By reading their flashed codes you could tell where you were, but I was not bothering with that. I turned south toward Reading. The sky was dark now. Far below, the earth was cooling, giving up the heat of the day. A mist had begun to form. In it, the light lines would fade away and also, almost shyly, the towns. I flew on.

It is a different world at night. The instruments become harder to read, details disappear from the map. After a while I tuned to the Reading frequency and managed to pick up its signal. I had no radio compass but there was a way of determining, by flying a certain sequence of headings, where you were. If the signal slowly increased in strength you were inbound toward the station. If not and you had to turn up the volume to continue hearing it, you were going away. It was primitive but it worked. When the time came I waited to see if I had passed or was still approaching Reading. The minutes went by. At first I couldn't detect a change but then the signal seemed to grow weaker. I turned north and flew watching the clock. Something was wrong, something serious: The signal didn't change. I was lost, not only literally but in relation to reality. Meanwhile the wind, unseen, fateful, was forcing me further north.

Among the stars, one was moving. It was the lights of another plane, perhaps from the squadron. In any case, wherever it was headed there would be a field. I pushed up the throttle. As I drew closer, I began to make out what it was, an airliner, a DC-3. It might be going to St. Louis or Chicago. I had already been flying for what seemed like hours and had begun, weakhearted, a repeated checking of fuel. The gauges were on the floor. I tried not to think of them but they were like a wound; I could not keep myself from glancing down.

Slowly the airliner and its lights became more distant. I turned northeast, the general direction of home. I had been scribbling illegibly on the page of memory which way I had gone and for how long. I now had no idea where I was. The occasional lights on the ground of unknown towns, lights blurred and yellowish, meant nothing. Allentown, which should have been somewhere, never appeared. There was a terrible temptation to abandon everything, to give up, as with a hopeless puzzle. I had the greatest difficulty not praying and finally I did, flying in the noisy darkness, desperate for the sight of a city or anything that would give me my position.

In the map case of the airplane was a booklet, *What to Do If Lost,* and suddenly remembering it, I got it out and with my flashlight began to read. There was a list of half a dozen steps to take in order. My eye skidded down it. The first ones I had already tried. Others, like tuning in any radio range and orienting yourself on it, I had given up on. I managed to get the signal from Stewart Field but didn't take up the prescribed heading. I could tell from its faintness — it was indistinct in a thicket of other sounds — that I was far away, and I had lost faith in the procedure. The final advice seemed more practical. If you think you are to the west of Stewart, it said, head east until you come to the Hudson River and then fly north or south, you will eventually come to New York or Albany.

It was past eleven, the sky dense with stars, the earth a void. I had turned east. The dimly lit fuel gauges read twenty-five gallons or so in each wing. The idea slowly growing, of opening the canopy and struggling into the wind, over the side into blackness, parachuting down, was not as unthinkable as that of giving the airplane itself up to destruction. I would be washed out, I knew. The anguish was unbearable. I had been flying east for

ten minutes but it seemed hours. Occasionally I made out the
paltry lights of some small town or group of houses, but otherwise nothing. The cities had vanished, sunken to darkness. I
looked down again. Twenty gallons.

Suddenly off to the left there was a glimmer that became — I
was just able to make it out — a faint string of lights and then
slowly, magically, two parallel lines. It was the bridge at Pough-
keepsie! Dazed with relief, I tried to pick out its dark lines and
those of the river, turning to keep it in sight, going lower and
lower. Then in the way that all things certain had changed that
night, the bridge changed, too. At about a thousand feet above
them, stricken, I saw I was looking at the streetlights of some
town.

The gauges read fifteen gallons. One thing that should never
be done — it had been repeated to us often — was to attempt a
forced landing at night. But I had no choice. I began to circle,
able in the mist to see clearly only what was just beneath. The
town was at the edge of some hills; I banked away from them in
the blackness. If I went too far from the brightly lit, abandoned
main street, I lost my bearings. Dropping even lower I saw dark
roofs everywhere and amid them, unexpectedly, a blank area
like a lake or small park. I had passed it quickly, turned, and lost
it. Finally, lower still, I saw it again. It was not big but there was
nothing else. I ducked my head for a moment to look down —
the number beneath each index line was wavering slightly; ten
gallons, perhaps twelve.

The rule for any strange field was to first fly across at minimum altitude to examine the surface. I was not even sure it was
a field; it might be water or a patch of woods. If a park, it might
have buildings or fences. I turned onto a downwind leg or what
I judged to be one, then a base leg, letting down over swiftly
enlarging roofs. I had the canopy open to cut reflection, the
ghostly duplication of instruments and warning lights. I stared
ahead through the wind and noise. I was at a hundred feet or so,
flaps down, still descending. In front, coming fast, was my field.
On a panel near my knee were the landing light switches with
balled tips to make them identifiable by feel. I reached for them
blindly. The instant they came on I knew I'd made a mistake.
They blazed like searchlights in the mist; I could see more with-

out them but the ground was twenty feet beneath me, I was at minimum speed and dared not bend to turn them off. Something went by on the left. Trees, in the middle of the park. I had barely missed them. No landing here. A moment later, at the far end, more trees. They were higher than I was, and without speed to climb I banked to get through them. I heard foliage slap the wings as just ahead, shielded, a second rank of trees appeared. There was no time to do anything. Something great struck a wing. It tore away. The plane careened up. It stood poised for an endless moment, one landing light flooding a house into which an instant later it crashed.

Nothing has vanished, not even the stunned first seconds of silence, the torn leaves drifting down. Reflexively, as a slain man might bewilderedly shut a door, I reached to turn off the ignition. I was badly injured, though in what way I did not know. There was no pain. My legs, I realized. I tried to move them. Nothing seemed wrong. My front teeth were loose; I could feel them move as I breathed. In absolute quiet I sat for a few moments at a loss, then unbuckled the harness and stepped over the cockpit onto what had been the front porch. The nose of the plane was in the wreckage of a room. The severed wing lay back in the street.

The house, as it turned out, belonged to a family that was welcoming home a son who had been a prisoner of war in Germany. They were having a party and had taken the startling noise of the plane as it passed low over town many times to be some sort of military salute and, though it was nearly midnight, had all gone into the street to have a look. I had come in like a meteorite over their heads. The town was Great Barrington. I had to be shown where it was on a map, in Massachusetts, miles to the north and east.

That night I slept in the mayor's house, in a feather bed. I say slept but in fact I hung endlessly in the tilted darkness, the landing light pouring down at the large frame house. The wing came off countless times. I turned over in bed and began again.

They came for me the next day in a wrecking truck and I rode back with the remains of the plane. In the barracks, which were empty when I arrived, my bed was littered with messages, all mock congratulations. I found myself, unexpectedly, a popular figure. It was as if I had somehow defied the authorities. On the blackboard in the briefing room was a drawing of a house with the tail of an airplane sticking from the roof and written beneath, GEISLER'S STUDENT. I survived the obligatory check rides and the proceedings of the accident board, which were unexpectedly brief. Gradually transformed into a comedy, the story was told by me many times as I felt, for one shameless instant, it would be that night when the boughs of the first trees hit the wings before I saw the second. There was a bent, enameled Pratt and Whitney emblem from the engine that I kept for a long time until it was lost somewhere, and years later a single unsigned postcard reached me, addressed care of the adjutant general. It was from Great Barrington. "We are still praying for you here," it said.

Confident and indestructible now, I put a dummy of dirty clothes in my bed and one night after taps met Horner near the barracks door. We were going off limits, over the fence, the punishment for which was severe. Graduation was only days away; if we were caught there would be no time for confinement to quarters or walking the Area; the sentence would be more lasting: late graduation and loss of class standing. The risk, though, was not great. "Anita is coming up," he told me. "She's bringing a girlfriend." They would be waiting in a convertible at the bottom of a hill.

Anita was new. I admired her. She was the kind of girl I would never have, who bored me, in fact, and was made intriguing only by the mischievous behavior of Horner. In some ways I was in that position myself, his Pinocchio, willing and enthralled.

Anita was the daughter of a carpet manufacturer. She wore silk stockings and print dresses. She had red fingernails and was tall. Her efforts to discipline Horner were ineffective and charming. "Well, you know Jack . . ." she would explain helplessly. I did know him and liked him, I think, at least as much as she did and probably for longer.

Staying close to the buildings we made it in the darkness to the open space near the fence and climbed over quickly. The road was not too long a walk away. We came over a slight crest and halfway down the hill, delirious in our goatlike freedom, saw the faint lights of the dashboard. One of the doors was open, the radio was softly playing. Two faces turned to us. Anita was smiling. "Where the hell have you been?" she said, and we drove off toward Newburgh to find a liquor store. Jack was in front with her; their laughter streamed back like smoke.

The Anitas. I had more or less forgotten them. Ages later, decades literally, in the deepest part of the night the telephone rings in the darkness and I reach for it. It's 2:00 in the morning, the house is asleep. There is a cackle that I recognize immediately. "Who is this?" I say. To someone else, aside, gleefully he says, "He wants to know who it is." Then to me, "Did I wake you up?"

"What could possibly give you that idea?"

Another cackle. "Jim, this is Jack Horner," he says in a businessman's voice. He was divorced and traveling around. Doing what? I ask. "Inspecting post offices," he says. Bobbing around his voice are others, careless, soft as feathers. One of them comes on the phone. "Where are you?" I ask. My wife is sleeping beside me. A low voice replies, "In a motel. About three blocks from you." In the background I can hear him telling them I am a writer, he has known me since we were cadets. He tries to take the phone again. I can hear them struggling, the laughter of the women and his own, high and almost as feminine, infectious.

That May night, however, we parked near an orchard and went up beneath the trees. We got back to the barracks very late. A day or two afterward I came up to him while he was shaving before breakfast. "Have you noticed anything strange?" I asked. "Yes. What is it? Have you got it, too?" It was a rash. It turned out to be poison ivy covering our arms and legs, a first mock rendering to Venus.

We went without neckties, excused from formation. Skin blistered and unable to wear a full dress coat, I stood at the window of my room and heard the band playing in the distance and the long pauses that were part of the ceremony of the last parade. There came the sound of the music played just once a year, when the graduating class, some of them openly weeping, removed their hats as the first of the companies, in salute, came abreast, officers' sabers coming up, glinting, then whipping downward.

Far off, the long years were passing in review, the seasons and settings, the cold walls and sally ports, the endless routine. Through high windows the sun fell on the choir as it came with majestic slowness, singing, up the aisle. The uniforms, the rifles, the books. The winter mornings, dark outside, smoking and listening to the radio as we cleaned the room. The gym, dank and forbidding. The class sections forming in haste along the road.

The Area was filled with footlockers and boxes. Everyone would be leaving, scattered, dismissed for the last time, to the chapel for weddings, to restaurants with their families, to the coast, the Midwest, to the smallest of towns. We were comparing orders, destinations. I felt both happiness and the pain of farewell. We were entering the army, which was like a huge, deep lake, slower and deeper than one dreamed. At the bottom it was fed by springs, fresh and everlastingly pure. On the surface, near the spillway, the water was older and less clear, but this water was soon to leave. We were the new and untainted.

On my finger I had a gold ring with the year of my class on it, a ring that would be recognizable to everyone I would meet. I wore it always; I flew with it on my finger; it lay in my shoe while I slept. It signified everything, and I had given everything to have it. I also had a silver identification bracelet all flyers wore, with a welt of metal that rang when it touched the table or bar. I was arrogant, perhaps, different from the boy who had come here and different even from the others, not quite knowing how, or the danger.

As we packed to leave, a pair of my roommate's shoe trees got mixed up with mine. I did not notice it until after we had gone. In a hand distinctly his, ECKERT, R. P. in ink was neatly printed on the wooden toe block. He was killed later in a crash, like his brother. His life disappeared but not his name, which I saw over the years as I dressed and then saw him, cool blue eyes as if faded, pale skin, a way of smoking that was oddly abrupt, a way of walking with his feet turned out. I also kept a shako, some pants, and a gray shirt, but slowly, like paint flaking away, they were left behind or lost, though in memory very clear.

One thing I saw again, long afterward. I was driving on a lonely road in the West about twenty miles out of Cheyenne. It was winter and the snow had drifted. I tried to push through but in the end got stuck. It was late in the afternoon. The wind was blowing. There was not a house to be seen in any direction, only fences and flat, buried fields.

I got out and started back along the road. It was very cold; my tire tracks were already being erased. Gloved hands over my ears, I was alternately walking and running, thinking of the outcome of Jack London stories. After a mile or two I heard dogs barking. Off to the right, half-hidden in the snow, was a plain, unpainted house and some sheds. I struggled through the drifts, the dogs retreating before me, barking and growling, the fur erect on their necks.

A tall young woman with an open face and a chipped tooth came to the door. I could hear a child crying. I told her what had happened and asked if I could borrow a shovel. "Come in," she said.

The room was drab. Some chairs and a table, bare walls. She was calling into the kitchen for her husband. On top of an old file cabinet a black-and-white television was turned on. Suddenly I saw something familiar, out of the deepest past — covering the couch was a gray blanket, the dense gray of boyhood uniforms, with a black and gold border. I recognized it; it was a West Point blanket. Her husband was pulling on his shirt. *How fitting,* I thought, *one ex-regular bumping into another in the tundra, years after, winter at its coldest, life at its ebb.*

In a littered truck we drove back to the car and worked for an hour, hands gone numb, feet as well. Heroic labor, the kind that binds you to someone. We spoke little, only about shoveling and what to do. He was anonymous but in his face I saw patience, strength, and that ethic of those schooled to difficult things. Shoulder to shoulder we tried to move the car. He was that vanished man, the company commander, the untiring god of those years when nothing was higher; *privations mean little to him, difficulties cannot break his spirit. . . .*

Together we rescued the car and back at the house I held out some money. I wanted to give him something for his trouble, I said. He looked at it. "That's too much."

"Not for me," I said. Then I began, "Your blanket . . ."

"What blanket?"

"The one on the couch; I recognize it. Where'd you get it?" I said idly. He turned and looked at it, then at me as if deciding. He was tall, like his wife, and his movements were unhurried. "Where'd we get it?" he asked her. The ladies who come up in June . . . I thought. They'd been married in the chapel.

"That? I forget. At the thrift shop," she said.

For a moment I thought they were acting, unwilling to reveal themselves, but no. He was a tattoo artist, it turned out. He worked in Cheyenne.

SCOTT RUSSELL SANDERS

Wayland

FROM THE GETTYSBURG REVIEW

TWO BLACKTOP ROADS, broken by frost and mended with tar, running from nowhere to nowhere, cross at right angles in the rumpled farm country of northeastern Ohio. The neighborhood where they intersect is called Wayland — not a village, not even a hamlet, only a cluster of barns and silos and frame houses and a white steepled Methodist church. Just north of Wayland, the Army fenced in fifty square miles of ground for a bomb factory, and just to the south the Corps of Engineers built a dam and flooded even more square miles for a reservoir. I grew up be- hind those government fences in the shadows of bunkers, and on farms that have since vanished beneath those government waters. Family visits to church began carrying me to Wayland when I was five, romance was carrying me there still at seven- teen, and in the years between I was drawn there often by duty or desire. Thus it happened that within shouting distance of the Wayland crossroads I met seven of the great mysteries.

Even as a boy, oblivious much of the time to all save my own sensations, I knew by the tingle in my spine when I had bumped into something utterly new. I groped for words to describe what I had felt, as I grope still. Since we give labels to all that puzzles us, as we name every blank space on the map, I could say that what I stumbled into in Wayland were the mysteries of death, life, beasts, food, mind, sex, and God. But these seven words are only tokens, worn coins that I drop onto the page, hoping to bribe you, coins I finger as reminders of those awful encounters.

The roads that cross at Wayland are too humble to show on

the Ohio map, too small even to wear numbers. And yet, without maps or mistakes, without quite meaning to, I recently found my way back there from half a thousand miles away, after an absence of twenty-five years, led along the grooves of memory.

The grooves are deep, and they set me vibrating well before I reached the place, as the spiral cuts in phonograph records will shake music from a needle. I was heading toward Cleveland when I took a notion to veer off the interstate and see what had become of Akron, which led me to see what had become of Kent, which led me to Ravenna, the seat of Portage County. Nothing aside from stoplights made me pause. Not sure what I was looking for, I drove east from the county seat along a highway hurtling with trucks. Soon the rusted chain link fence of the Ravenna Arsenal came whipping by on my left and the raised bed of the Baltimore & Ohio tracks surged by on the right. Then I realized where I was going. My knuckles whitened on the steering wheel as I turned from the highway, put my back toward the trucks and bombs, and passed under the railroad through a concrete arch. Beyond the arch, the woods and fields and houses of Wayland shimmered in the October sunlight, appearing to my jealous eye scarcely changed after a quarter of a century.

I knew the place had changed, of course, if only because in the years since I had come here last — drawn in those days like a moth to the flame of a girl — the population of the earth had nearly doubled. Every crossroads, every woods, every field on the planet is warping under the pressure of our terrible hunger. So I knew that Wayland had changed, for all its pastoral shimmer in the autumn light. Yet I was grateful that on the surface it so much resembled my childhood memories, for in my effort to live adequately in the present, I had come here to conduct some business with the past. What had brought me back to Wayland was a need to dig through the fluff and debris of ordinary life, down to some bedrock of feeling and belief.

I left my car in the graveled parking lot of the church and set out walking. Without planning my steps, I meandered where memory led, and where it led was from station to station of my childhood astonishment. Not yet ready for the church, I went next door to the parsonage, where I had first caught a whiff of death. The white clapboard house, a two-story box with a porch across the front and a green hipped roof, could have belonged to any of the neighboring farms. That was appropriate, for the ministers who succeeded one another in the house often preached as though they were farmers, weeding out sins, harvesting souls.

The minister whom I knew first was the Reverend Mr. Knipe, a bulky man sunken with age, his hair as white as the clapboards on the parsonage, his voice like the cooing of pigeons in the barn. Much in life amused him. Whenever he told you something that struck him as funny, he would cover his mouth with a hand to hide his smile. Despite the raised hand, often his laugh burst free and rolled over you. I began listening to him preach and pray and lead hymns when I was five, and for the next two years I heard Reverend Knipe every Sunday, until his voice became for me that of the Bible itself, even the voice of God. Then one Sunday when I was seven, I shook his great hand after the service as usual, suffering him to bend down and pat my head, and I went home to my dinner and he went home to his. While his wife set the table in the parsonage, Reverend Knipe rested on the front porch in his caned rocking chair, drifted off to sleep, and never woke up.

When Mother told me of this, the skin prickled on my neck. To sleep and never wake! To be a white-haired man with a voice like a barnful of pigeons, and the next minute to be nothing at all! Since my parents considered me too young to attend the funeral, I could only imagine what had become of his body, and I imagined not decay but evaporation — the flesh dispersing into thin air like morning mist from a pond.

The following Sunday, while a visitor preached, I stole from church and crept over to the parsonage. I drew to the edge of the porch, wrapped my fingers around the spindles of the railing, and stared at the empty rocker. Reverend Knipe will never sit in that chair again, I told myself. Never, never, never. I tried to imagine how long forever would last. I tried to imagine how it would feel to be nothing. No thing. Suddenly chair and house and daylight vanished, and I was gazing into a dark hole, I was falling, I was gone. I caught a whiff of death, the damp earthy smell seeping from beneath the porch. It was also the smell of mud, of leaping grass, of spring. Clinging to that sensation, I pulled myself up out of the hole. There was the house again, the chair. I let go of the railing, swung away, and ran back to the church, chanting to myself: *He was old and I am young. He was old and I am young.*

Nights, often, and sometimes in the broad light of day, I still have to scrabble up out of that hole. We all do. Sometime in childhood, each of us bangs head-on into the blank fact we call death. Once that collision takes place, the shock of it never wears off. We may find ourselves returning to the spot where it occurred as to the scene of an accident, the way I found myself drawn, half a lifetime later, to the front steps of this parsonage. I was a stranger to the family who lived there now. Not wishing to intrude on them, I paused by the steps and surveyed the porch. Vinyl siding had covered the clapboard. An aluminum folding chair had replaced the rocker. I squatted by the railing, lowering my face to the height of a seven-year-old, closed my eyes against the shadows, and sniffed. From below the sill of the porch came the earth's dank perennial breath, fetid and fertile. Yes, I thought, filling myself with the smell: this abides, this is real; no matter the name we give it, life or death, it is a fact as rough and solid as a stone squeezed in the palm of the hand.

A dog yapped inside the parsonage. I stood up hurriedly and backed away, before anyone could appear at the door to ask me what in tarnation I was looking for under that porch.

Still following the grooves of memory, I crossed the road to stand in the driveway of another white frame house. It was not so much the house that drew me as it was the side yard, where, about this time each fall, we brought our apples for pressing. The old press with its wooden vat and iron gears used to balance on concrete blocks in the shade of a willow. We would pick apples in the military reservation, from orchards that had been allowed to go wild after the government bulldozed the farmsteads. Unsprayed, blotched and wormy, these apples were also wonderfully sweet. We kept them in bushel baskets and cardboard boxes in the cellar, their fragrance filling the house, until we had accumulated enough to load our station wagon. Then we drove here, parked beside the willow, and fed our fruit into the press.

On this mild October day, the willow looked as I remembered it, thick in the trunk and gold in the leaves. There was no sign of a press, but that did not keep me from remembering what it was like to squeeze apples. First we pulped them in a mill, then we wrapped them in cheesecloth and tamped them down, layer by layer, into the slotted wooden vat. To mash them, we spun a cast iron wheel. It was easy to begin with, so easy that my brother and sister and I could make the spokes whirl. Later, the cranking would become too hard for us, and our mother would take her turn, then our father, then both of them together. The moment that set me trembling, however, came early on, while my hand was still on the iron wheel, the moment when cider began to ooze through the cheesecloth, between the slats, and down the spout into a waiting bucket. Out of the dirt, out of the gnarled trunks and wide-flung branches, out of the ripe red fruit had come this tawny juice. When my arms grew tired, I held a Mason jar under the spout, caught a glassful, and drank it down. It was as though we had squeezed the planet and out had poured sweetness.

What came back to me, musing there by the willow all these years later, was the sound of cider trickling into the bucket, the honeyed taste of it, and my bewilderment that rain and wood and dirt and sun had yielded this juice. Amazing, that we can drink the earth! Amazing, that it quenches our thirst, answers our hunger! Who would have predicted such an outlandish thing? Who, having sipped, can forget that it is the earth we swallow?

Well, I had forgotten; or at least I had buried under the habits of casual eating that primal awareness of the meaning of food. And so here was another fundamental perception, renewed for me by my sojourn in Wayland. This image of cider gushing from a spout was my cornucopia, proof of the dazzling abundance that sustains us.

From the cider house I walked downhill to the crossroads. One corner was still a pasture, browsed by three horses, another was a scrubby field grown up in brush and weeds, and the other two corners were expansive lawns. Through the brushy field meandered a creek where I used to hunt frogs with a flashlight and bucket. As in all the Octobers I could remember, the maples in the yards were scarlet, the pasture oaks were butterscotch, and the sycamores along the creek were stripped down to their voluptuous white limbs. Yellow mums and bright red pokers of salvia were still thriving in flowerbeds. A portly older man on a riding mower was cutting one of the lawns, while from a stump beside the driveway an older woman observed his progress, a hand shading her eyes. I knew them from childhood, but their names would not come. I waved, and they waved back. That was conversation enough. I had no desire to speak with them or with anyone in Wayland, since I would have been hard put to explain who I was or why I had come back. Maybe I also wanted to keep the past pure, unmixed with the present.

Because the crossroads are laid out on the grid of survey lines, the blacktop runs due north and south, east and west. The roads were so little traveled that I could stand in the intersection, the tar gummy beneath my boots, and gaze along the pavement in each of the cardinal directions. I had just come from the south, where the church gleamed on its hill. My view to the north was cut off by the railroad, except for the arched opening of the underpass, through which I could see the rusted fence of the Arsenal. Memories of a girl I had courted were beckoning from the west; but less feverish memories beckoned from the opposite direction, and that is where I chose to go next.

A quarter mile east of the crossroads I came to a farm where the Richards family used to breed and board and train horses. Although the name on the mailbox had changed, ten or twelve horses were grazing, as before, in a paddock beside the barn. I leaned against the fence and admired them.

In boyhood I had raised and ridden horses of my own, a stocky mixture of Shetland pony and the high-stepping carriage breed known as hackney. They all came out of a single ornery mare called Belle, and they all had her color, a sorrel coat that grew sleek in summer and shaggy in winter. We used to bring Belle here to the Richards place for mating with a hackney stallion. Years before the voltage of sex began to make my own limbs jerk, I had been amazed by the stallion's urgency and the mare's skittishness. He nipped and nuzzled and pursued her; she danced and wheeled. Their energy seemed too great for the paddock to hold. Surely the fence would give way, the barn itself would fall! Then at length Belle shivered to a standstill and allowed the stallion to lift his forelegs onto her rump, his back legs jigging, hoofs scrambling for purchase, her legs opening to his dark pizzle, the two of them momentarily one great plunging beast. And then, if luck held, twelve months later Belle would open her legs once more and drop a foal. Within minutes of entering the world, the foal would be tottering about on its wobbly stilts, drunk on air, and it would be ramming its muzzle into Belle's belly in search of milk. What a world, that the shivering union of mare and stallion in the barnyard should lead to this new urgency!

Musing there by the paddock on this October afternoon, I felt toward the grazing horses a huge affection. Each filled its hide so gloriously. I gave a low whistle. Several massive heads bobbed up and swung toward me, jaws working on grass, ears pricked forward. Their black eyes regarded me soberly, then all but one of the heads returned to grazing. The exception was a palomino gelding, who tossed his white mane, switched his white tail, and started ambling in my direction. As he drew near, I stretched my right arm toward him, palm open. Had I known I would be coming here, I would have brought apples or sugar cubes. My father would have pulled a cigarette from his pocket and offered that. But all I had to offer was the salt on my skin. The palomino lowered his muzzle to my palm, sniffed cautiously, then curled out his rasping red tongue and licked.

I knew that sandpapery stroke on my hand as I knew few other sensations. Just so, my own horses had nibbled oats and sugar and sweat from my palm. The pressure of their tongues made my whole body sway. There by the fence, past and present merged, and I was boy and man, swaying. I reveled in the muscular touch, animal to animal. Contact! It assured me that I was not alone in the world. I was a creature among creatures.

When the palomino lost interest in my right hand, I offered my left. He sniffed idly, and, finding it empty, turned back to the greater temptation of grass. But the rasp of his tongue on my palm stayed with me, another clean, hard fact, another piece of bedrock on which to build a life.

*

The field across the road from the Richards place was grown up into a young woods, mostly staghorn sumac and cedar and oak. When I had seen it last, twenty-five years earlier, this had been a meadow luxuriant with grasses and wildflowers. Back where the far edge of the field ran up against the sinuous line of willows bordering the creek, there had been a cottage, low and brown, moss growing on the roof, weeds lapping at the windows, a place that looked from a distance more like a forgotten woodpile than a house. Today, no cottage showed above the vigorous trees. But near my feet I could see the twin ruts of the dirt track that used to lead back to the place. I followed them, my boots knocking seeds from thistle and wild rye.

I knew the meadow and the cottage because the woman who used to live here was my science teacher in high school. Fay Givens must have been in her early sixties when I met her in my freshman year. Many students mocked her for being so unthinkably old, for looking like a schoolmarm, for loving science, for trembling when she spoke about nature. She would gaze fervently into a beaker as though an entire galaxy spun before her. She grew so excited while recounting the habits of molecules that she would skip about the lab and clap her spotted hands. She would weep for joy over what swam before her in a microscope. Mrs. Givens wept easily, more often than not because of a wisecrack or prank from one of the students. Our cruelty was a defense against the claim she made on us. For she was inviting us to share her passionate curiosity. She called us to hunger and thirst after knowledge of the universe.

I would not join the others in mocking her. I supposed it was pity that held me back, or an ingrained respect for my elders. Only in the fall of my freshman year, on a day when Mrs. Givens brought us here to this field for a botany class, did I realize that I could not mock her because I loved her. She led us through her meadow, naming every plant, twirling the bright fallen leaves, telling which birds ate which berries, opening milkweed pods, disclosing the burrows of groundhogs, parting the weeds to reveal caterpillars and crickets, showing where mice had severed blades of grass. Much of the meadow she had planted, with seeds carried in her pockets from the neighboring countryside. Every few years she burned it, as the Indians had burned the prairies, to keep the woods from reclaiming it.

While Mrs. Givens told us these things in her quavery voice, students kept sidling away to smoke or joke or dabble their hands in the creek, until there were only three of us following her. I stayed with her not from a sense of obedience but from wonder. To know this patch of land, I dimly realized, would be the work of a lifetime. But in knowing it deeply, right down to the foundations, you would comprehend a great deal more, perhaps everything. As she touched the feathery plants of her meadow, as she murmured the names and histories of the creatures who shared the place with her, I came to feel that this was holy ground. And if the meadow was holy, why not the entire earth?

At one point, Mrs. Givens knelt amid the bristly spikes of a tall russet grass. "You see why it's called foxtail, don't you?" she said. "Livestock won't eat it, but you can twist the stalks together and make a fair rope. Farmers used to bind up corn fodder with hanks of foxtail." She grasped one of the spikes, and, with a rake of her thumb, brushed seeds into her palm. She poured a few seeds into my hand and a few into the hands of the other two students who had remained with her. "Now what do you have there?" she asked us.

We stared at the barbed grains in our palms. "Seeds," one of us replied.

"That's the universe unfolding," she told us, "right there in your hands. The same as in every cell of our bodies. Now *why*? That's the question I can't ever get behind. Why should the universe be alive? Why does it obey laws? And why these particular laws? For that matter, why is there a universe at all?" She gave a rollicking laugh. "And isn't it curious that there should be creatures like us who can walk in this beautiful field and puzzle over things?"

She asked her questions gaily, and I have carried them with me all these years in the same spirit. They rose in me again on this October afternoon as I followed the dirt track to the spot where her cottage used to be. Stones marked the cellar hole and the front stoop. Brush grew up through the space left by her death. The woods had reclaimed her meadow. Yet the ground still felt holy. Her marveling gaze had disclosed for me the force and shapeliness of things, and that power survived her passing. She taught me that genius is not in our looking but in what we

see. If only we could be adequate to the given world, we need
not dream of paradise.

Reversing my steps, I walked back to the crossroads and kept
going west for a hundred yards or so, until I fetched up before
the house where, as a simmering teenager, I had wooed a girl.
Let me call her Veronica. She and her family moved from Wayland soon after the Army Corps of Engineers built that needless
dam, and so on this October day her house was for me another
shell filled only with memory. The present kept abrading the
past, however, because during the few minutes while I stood
there a grown man in a go-cart kept zooming around the yard,
following a deeply gouged path. Every time he roared past, he
peered at me from beneath his crash helmet. I nodded, assuming the look of one who is infatuated with loud machines, and
that appeared to satisfy him.

Veronica had the face of a queen on the deck of cards with
which I learned to play poker, a face I considered perfect. Words
tumbled from her lush lips, impulsively, like rabbits fleeing a
burrow. Black wavy hair tumbled down her back, twitching
nearly to her slender hips. Having learned in marriage what it
means to love a woman, I cannot say that what I felt for Veronica
was quite love. Nor was it simply lust, although for much of my
seventeenth year the mere thought of her set me aching. At that
age, I would have been reluctant to see myself as the urgent
stallion and Veronica as the skittish mare. Later, I would realize
that horseflesh and humanflesh dance to the same ardent music,
even though our human dance is constrained by rules that
horses never know. During the season of our affection, Veronica
was a chased girl but also a chaste one, and I was a polite boy,
both of us keenly aware of boundaries.

In her backyard there was a sycamore tree that loomed high
over the house, its fat trunk a patchwork of peeling bark and its
crooked upper branches as creamy as whole milk. Wooden cross-
bars nailed to the trunk formed a ladder up to a treehouse.
Veronica and I often sat beneath the sycamore on a stone bench,
talking and falling silent, aware of parental eyes watching us
from the kitchen. With our backs to the house, our sides pressed
together, I could risk brushing a hand over her knee, she could

run a fingernail under my chin. But even a kiss, our mouths so visibly meeting, would have prompted a visit from the kitchen.

One October day, a day very like this one of my return to Wayland, Veronica and I were sitting on the bench, hunting for words to shape our confusion, when suddenly she leapt to her feet and said, "Let's go up to the treehouse."

"We'll get filthy," I said. I glanced with misgiving at my white knit shirt and chino pants, so carefully pressed. Her lemony blouse was protected by a green corduroy jumper.

"It'll wash out," she said, tugging me by the hand.

I stood. Without waiting for me, she kicked off her shoes and clambered up the wooden rungs, but instead of halting at the rickety platform of the treehouse, she kept on, swaying from limb to limb. I watched until the flashing of her bare legs made me look away. When she had gone as high as she dared, high enough to escape the view from the kitchen, she balanced on a branch and called to me, "Come on up! Are you afraid?"

I was afraid — but not of the tree. I stepped onto a crossbrace and started climbing, and as I climbed there was nowhere else to look but up, and there was nothing else to see above me except those white legs parted within the green hoop of her skirt. Her creamy forked limbs and the creamy forked limbs of the sycamore merged in my sight, as they merge now in memory, and I was drawn upward into the pale shadows between her thighs. My knowledge of what I was climbing toward would remain abstract for a number of years. I understood only that where her legs joined there was an opening, a gateway for life coming and going. When I reached Veronica I put my hand, briefly, where my gaze had gone, just far enough to feel the surprising warmth of that secret, satiny place. Then I withdrew my hand and she smoothed her skirt, neither of us risking a word, and we teetered there for a hundred heartbeats on those swaying branches, shaken by inner as well as outer winds. Then the kitchen door creaked open and her mother's voice inquired as to our sanity, and we climbed down. I went first, as though to catch Veronica should she fall, my eyes toward the ground.

The buzzing of the go-cart eventually wore through the husk of memory, and my lungs filled with the present. I became again what I was, a man long married, a man with a daughter the age

Veronica had been on that day of our climb into the tree. The sycamore still rose behind the house, twenty-five years taller, crisp brown leaves rattling in the wind, the pale upper limbs as pale and silky as ever.

I had a choice of returning to the church by the road or across the stubble of a cornfield. I chose the field. All the way, I could see the white steepled box gleaming on its rise. The only car in the parking lot was mine. Beyond a treeline to the southwest, beyond the annihilating waters of the reservoir that I could not bear to look at, the sun wallowed down toward dusk. The church might already be locked, I thought, so late on a weekday afternoon. Still I did not hurry. My boots scuffed the ridges where corn had stood. Raccoons and crows would find little to feast on in this stubble, for the harvester had plucked it clean. I recalled the biblical injunction to farmers, that they leave the margins of their fields unpicked, for the poor and the beasts. I thought of the margins in a life, in my life, the untended zones beyond the borders of clarity, the encircling wilderness out of which new powers and visions come.

A cornfield is a good approach to a church, for you arrive with dirt on your boots, the smell of greenery in your nostrils, dust on your tongue. The door would be locked, I figured, and the main door was, the broad entrance through which the Methodist women carried their piety and their pies, through which men carried mortgages and mortality, through which children like myself carried headfuls of questions. But the rear door was unlocked. I left my boots on the stoop and went inside.

The back room I entered had the familiarity of a place one returns to in dream: the squeaky pine boards of the floor, the dwarf tables where children would sit on Sundays to color pictures of Jesus, the brass hooks where the choir would hang their robes and the minister his hat, the folding chairs collapsed into a corner, the asthmatic furnace, and on a counter the stack of lathe-turned walnut plates for the offering.

Every few paces I halted, listening. The joints of the church cricked as the sun let go. Birds fussed beyond the windows. But no one else was about; this relieved me, for here least of all was I prepared to explain myself. I had moved too long in circles where to confess an interest in religious things marked one as a charlatan, a sentimentalist, or a fool. No doubt I have all three qualities in my character. But I also have another quality, and that is an unshakable hunger to know who I am, where I am, and into what sort of cosmos I have been so briefly and astonishingly sprung. Whatever combination of shady motives might have led me here, the impulse that shook me right then was a craving to glimpse the very source and circumference of things.

I made my way out through the choir door into the sanctuary. Cushionless pews in somber ranks, uncarpeted floor, exposed beams in the vault overhead and whitewashed plaster on the walls: it was a room fashioned by men and women who knew barns, for preachers who lived out of saddlebags, in honor of a God who cares nothing for ornament. No tapestries, no shrines, no racks of candles, no gold on the altar, no bragging memorials to vanished patrons. The window glass, unstained, let in the plain light of day.

I sat in a pew midway along the central aisle and looked out through those clear windows. My reasons for coming here were entwined with that sky full of light. As a boy I had looked out, Sunday after Sunday, to see corn grow and clouds blow, to watch crows bustle among the tops of trees, to follow hawks, unmindful of the Sabbath, on their spiraling hunts, and to sense in all this radiant surge the same rush I felt under my fingers when I pressed a hand to my throat. There was no gulf between outside and inside. We gathered in this room not to withdraw, but more fully to enter the world.

On this day of my return, I kept watching the sky as the light thinned and the darkness thickened. I became afraid. Afraid of dying, yes, but even more of not having lived, afraid of passing my days in a stupor, afraid of squandering my moment in the light. I gripped the pew in front of me to still my trembling. I wanted to dive down to the center of being, touch bedrock, open my eyes and truly, finally, unmistakably see. I shifted my gaze from the darkening window to the altar, to the wooden cross, to the black lip of the Bible showing from the pulpit. But those were only props for a play that was forever in rehearsal, the actors clumsy, the script obscure. I was myself one of the actors, sustained in my own clumsy efforts by the hope that one day the performance would be perfect, and everything would at last come clear.

One cannot summon grace with a whistle. The pew beneath me, the air around me, the darkening windows did not turn to fire. The clouds of unknowing did not part. I sat there for a long while, and then I rose and made my way down the aisle, past the organ, through the choir door and back room, out into the freshening night. On the stoop I drew on my boots and laced them up. The chrome latch of my car was already cool. I drove back through the crossroads with headlights glaring, alert for animals that might dash before me in the confusion of dusk.

There is more to be seen at any crossroads than one can see in a lifetime of looking. My return visit to Wayland was less than two hours long. Once again half a thousand miles distant from that place, making this model from slippery words, I cannot be sure where the pressure of mind has warped the surface of things. If you were to go there, you would not find every detail exactly as I have described it. How could you, bearing as you do a past quite different from mine? No doubt my memory, welling up through these lines, has played tricks with time and space.

What memory is made of I cannot say; my body, at least, is made of atoms on loan from the earth. How implausible, that these atoms should have gathered to form this *I*, this envelope of skin that walks about and strokes horses and tastes apples and trembles with desire in the branches of a sycamore and gazes through the windows of a church at the ordinary sky. Certain moments in one's life cast their influence forward over all the moments that follow. My encounters in Wayland shaped me first as I lived through them, then again as I recalled them during my visit, and now as I write them down. That is of course why I write them down. The self is a fiction. I make up the story of myself with scraps of memory, sensation, reading, and hearsay. It is a tale I whisper against the dark. Only in rare moments of luck or courage do I hush, forget myself entirely, and listen to the silence that precedes and surrounds and follows all speech.

If you have been keeping count, you may have toted up seven mysteries, or maybe seven times seven, or maybe seven to the seventh power. My hunch is that, however we count, there is only one mystery. In our nearsightedness, we merely glimpse the light scintillating off the numberless scales of Leviathan, and we take each spark for a separate wonder.

Could we bear to see all the light at once? Could we bear the roar of infinite silence? I sympathize with science, where, in order to answer a question, you limit the variables. You draw a circle within which everything can be measured, and you shut out the rest of the universe. But every enclosure is a makeshift, every boundary an illusion. With great ingenuity, we decipher some of the rules that govern this vast shining dance, but all our efforts could not change the least of them.

Nothing less than the undivided universe can be our true home. Yet how can one speak or even think about the whole of things? Language is of only modest help. Every sentence is a wispy net, capturing a few flecks of meaning. The sun shines without vocabulary. The salmon has no name for the desire that drives it upstream. The newborn groping for the nipple knows hunger long before it knows a single word. Even with an entire dictionary in one's head, one eventually comes to the end of words. Then what? Then drink deep like the baby, swim like the salmon, burn like any brief star.

ROBERT SHERRILL

The Truth About Growing Old

ONCE, not so long ago, they were scattered little patches on the family quilt — distinct, but of a piece. Now they are everywhere. You see them picking their way slowly along the sidewalks in your neighborhood, ones and twos. They infest the malls. They edge stubbornly up and down grocery store aisles. They ride the buses, taking forever and eternally to creak up and in or step fearfully out. Some drive great wheeled barges, strapped in, chins up, aloof from everything, keeping their slow, stately pace, horns and curses be damned.

They have that one distinguishing feature, from the little lady reeling across the busy boulevard with heart-stopping audacity to that tall, slender, craggy fellow in tweed, Celtic cow-flop cap, and houndstooth sport coat at the bar: They are old. And I am one of them. And you will be, too; it is just a matter of time.

I have been watching myself, and I have been collecting stuff — lies, propaganda, myths — that says that growing old is great, and have come to one dazzling and, I think, irrefutable conclusion: Growing old is spinach. Believe me. To paraphrase Sophie Tucker: I've been young and I've been old. Young is best. Screw old. Anyone who says old is gold is demented, a mindless optimist, under forty, or doing a study on it — old age, I mean. I'm sixty-seven. Old.

Attitudes toward old people haven't changed much in centuries, it seems to me, and they haven't improved lately; there are more of us. When you exist at all in the minds of others, especially the young, it is ambiguously, somewhere between saint and

Donald Duck, or one of those chestnuts with which the old are
disposed — old fart, dirty old man, blue hair, little old lady in
tennis shoes, geezer, and so on. Does it bother me? Yes. I love
the young — I've been one — but I've become wary of them.
They'd leave you behind for the wolves. And it seems to me that
old people are victims, victims of our own persistence in life, the
stupefying publicity we've received, and the times. The times: I
shall never forget the day I howled to the heavens when I caught
a silver strand of my mustache in a pop-top beer can and knew
with the clarity born of such insignificant events that I was the
twentieth-century victim. I am not ready for the twentieth century, much less the twenty-first, should I be here. Who is?

I've acquired a great heap of habits, turns of mind, prejudices,
but generally I find: I lie more easily, with relish, in fact. A kind
of fatalism takes over what I wryly call my judgment. With a
smile I am able to supplant annoying rationalization with: the
hell with it. I have grown a heap more cranky, more angry than
ever, more desperate to be heard; convinced, of course, I have
something to say, knowing how Cassandra felt, to know the truth
and not be heeded. And I am less tolerant, less tolerant of
movements and such, but more tolerant of people, individually.
Although I notice no one cares either way, he says wistfully.

It is too bad moments do not accrue, for they are the salutary
coin of growing old, such as when I slip into my thank-the-Lord-
for-small-favors mode: My God, that coffee smells good; it's a
great blue heron (flapping majestically into darkness, neck
cranked back, rapier bill outthrust, twiggy legs trailing); the bus
is on time; I didn't leave the stove on; it was a dream. I love big
winds and one came up at the brink of winter that stripped the
leaves from the branches of the trees, and my modest little house
in Durham, North Carolina, trapped, for a wink, a fierce, blind-
ing burst of sunshine. There was another bonus, a heavy shower
of pecans, and quick, I beat a gang of greedy gray squirrels to
them, filling my pockets to bulging. I had never noticed before
now this fugitive puff of keenest pleasure that comes unbidden
from some secret place and sweeps over me, ineffably and eerily
wonderful, and very suspicious. Be wary. Be wary.

The poet D. J. Enright wrote: "And, true, it helps to be old:
God looks slightly likelier." True. I am not quite that old yet, but
I'm getting there.

Is this monograph, screed, or whatever, solipsistic (to appropriate a word from the vast charnel house of reviewing)? Do I need a license? Is it instructive? Good God! I hope not. Onward. Sometime in my late fifties, the world inexplicably jinked, and I, as inexplicably, did not. Damn it! Hold still! Understanding and rapport began to break down, and miles of baling wire and friction tape couldn't hold the old heap together. That fatalism came in right handy: Screw that feckless world, too. It'll have to spin in without me. Events racketed on, battering me (us) silly with nary a clue from that Great Ouija Board of Life. Healthy skepticism yielded to suspicion, to paranoia, sputter, sputter. I needed explanations. I needed $8 million, a nice new body, tabula rasa. (Note: Elder writers are allowed twelve mixed metaphors per thousand words no matter how immiscible or risible. It's the rule.)

Neither you (you still there?) nor I want to wake up someday like my hero, François Villon, saying:

> How I regret my time of May.
> My days of riot, now no more,
> That unperceived stole away
> Till age was knocking at my door . . .
> How then? As quick as thought
> On eagle wings did soar
> My youth, and I am left with nought.

No, we do not want that, do we? Old-growing is gradual. Alex (Dr. Joy of) Comfort once wrote that the inexorable decline begins after twelve years of age (if that's any comfort), when life is at its peak, but you don't see anybody start to worry about a walker or foot warmers when he turns thirteen, or forty-five. The certain knowledge of Old creeps up on you, yes, but usually an event punctuates it, claps it into your consciousness, after which you know there is no retreat. The fifties are the incubating years, but the crucial ones come along with that event, such as my surprise induction into the Grand Sodality of Senior in a completely unrehearsed and highly unsecret roadside rite four or five years ago.

I am humming on down one of my favorite roads, U.S. 19, somewhere on those loamy plains south of that mess called

Atlanta, descending to the bottom of America in perfect pitch with the engine of my little MG, the moment, and the universe. Pale, pastel flowers (poppies?) and deep banks of sweet-smelling honeysuckle hem this lonely stretch of road. Intoxicating. The sun beats down hard and hot, and the wind, still laced with night-cool, whips and roils around me, achieving a kind of cosmic intersection, perfect balance, divine equipoise, right down there in that sweet spot directly behind the belly button. I feel good.

I ease down for a town and pull into the Pulley Bone Café yard — or was it one of those replicator restaurants that are right there where you least expect them, even in this kind of little lost hamlet? I leap from my lovely machine, hum into the place, truck right up to the counter, and ask for a cup of joe. Seeming a bit addled, the waitress looks at me and says, "Senior? Senior citizen?"

"No," I say quietly, fighting to hold down a swelling bubble of fury. "No. Old. Merely old, child. Forgive me, I am a Bob Sherrill . . . not, perhaps, the World's Champion Bob Sherrill, but a *contendah!* Heh, heh. Are you a junior, a junior citizen?" Those blank blue eyes skitter all over the place as she hands me my coffee, checking, doubtless, for the exit in case the old crock turns violent. I notice then the place is filled with those who have ratified their identity. Arise fogies! You have nothing to lose but your discounts!

So, I growl out of there thinking what a woeful performance that was — ill, ugly, graceless, ungentlemanly, boorish. How unsouthern of me, picking on that poor little old girl who had some vague notion, as well as orders, that to help a *senior* was her duty. She just happened to be the first target that got into my line of fire. For some time, I'd been armed cap-a-pie, bristling to storm the very palace redoubt of Golden Oldie land. Well, you got to start somewhere, and besides, she'll salve those sore feelings knowing weird Mr. Old is only a couple of clucks away from the cackle box. Age is youth's revenge. So, there I am, labeled, euphed, conscripted. . . .

Do what you want. Lock me up in the stockade. Shoot me, but do not call me Senior Citizen . . . or Pops. I shall not wear my toga senilis lightly. The fight is on, the battle joined . . . another lost cause, of course. This is, I fervently hope, a running story. Naturally, I want to see how it comes out.

Sometime back, a friend who is a right smart younger than I asked if I wanted to go to a Grateful Dead concert over at this big stadium in Raleigh. Well, *all reet*, as we used to say before the Dead were born. Couldn't wait. Last concert of the sort I'd been to I lost sight of Ike and Tina Turner in a fluffy bank of marijuana fog. Fine with me. Let the good times roll. Nobody asked, but I was old even then. Anyway, before you could say Jerry Garcia, I am sitting under the menacing muzzles of several thousand speakers that are bombarding us in a drizzling rain, greasy hot and digging it. Yes. Yes, yes! I am studying the way T-shirts cling to female, mostly very young female, torsi, and so on. I didn't come to meditate.

So what happens? A hand brushes my back (woo-woo?). I turn to see the source. It is a sallow, empimpled boy of sixteen, going on eighty — Billy the Kid. I turn back. I don't know him from Adam's house cat. I'm brushed again, a little more insistently. I turn.

"You," the boy says. "You got a problem."

"Me?" I say. "I got a problem? None I know of."

"With your crotch, I mean. Your crotch."

"My crotch? What *are* you talking about? I fear you're having delusions, if you're saying what I think you are. I ain't about to embarrass my friends, myself, or you. What pulled your chain? I won't pretend disinterest in the women here, but that's all I'm guilty of. I eschew bad form and trouble. And obviously, I am old."

"That's what I mean, old man. Old."

OOO*ooh*, so that's it. An old gaffer at a musical entertainment for the young is by definition a pervert, a dirty old man. Good Lord, I was a dirty *young* man, though I never quite made pervert. Why me? I hadn't worn my Burberry and made no gesture to suggest what this boy is accusing me of. Still, suppose he and his friends press this weird business, swearing that this obscene, drooling old booger is right out there playing pocket pool in front of forty thousand sensitive Christians?

The boy keeps up this line of talk until, finally, he mashes my

button. I push my face close to his and say: "You got the problem. Your mouth. Shut it the fuck up." (I beg your pardons.)

Well, he does. He says nothing else for the rest of the blast, but
he scowls sullenly at me with little pig eyes (I swear; I am not
exaggerating). I'd pray for him, if I prayed, this moral savage,
infant inquisitor, baby vigilante, unsavable soul. Mean. A lot of it
going around these days. Is there an antidote for this sort of
poison? Where did I get the idea Dead concerts were for loving?
Should the old grayheads be barred or kept in a special section
and watched? Can't we both live in the same world? Do I exist at
all? Maybe a good, hard kick in the ass would let them know you
are more than a hole in the scenery. That boy ruined my concert.
I bear up. What will happen when they roll me (and the Dead)
in for the concert in 2002? That little bastard better not be there.

I conceded, years ago, that my days of riot were no more, but
something more important had unperceived stolen away: wom-
en. Like a lot of other things, I'd noticed this but wouldn't let
the news sink in.

If you love women, do you have any idea what it is like to be
without? Being old, even moderately old, is hell; being old and
solo is hell times fourteen. By the time I let the news trickle in, it
had been so long since I'd entertained a beckoning smile, an
encouraging glance, I forgot how to answer, make a pass — like
a gentleman, of course. Or maybe not. So, I'd have to depend
upon grumpy, old lackadaisical hormones, fading memories,
and the need for the company of women to restore the natural
order — to score, I suppose you could say — should the opportunity arise. No chance. I was staring into the sexual abyss,
despairing, when one day what should I see in the *New York
Review of Books* but this ad: "STIMULATING, ULTRA-SYMMETRICAL,
discerning, independent NYC woman seeks quiet, serious, egre-
gious man 40+, with paradoxes. . . . His slippers await." *Wooo-
wee!* A hit, a very palpable hit. It's me through and through.
Who is more 40+ than I? I am 40 + 20, and Lord am I egre-
gious and got more paradoxes than you can shake a stick at. My
feet await. Flip-flops okay. Still, there was also a "WWF PRETTY
ECCENTRIC NYC PROFESSOR . . . seeks interesting man 40–59."
Interesting old Bob loves pretty eccentric professors but . . . oh,

pshaw, missed the cut. I let the urge to answer egregiously seep away and die in little velleitic daydream cameos, good for the nonce but not for the ages. Besides, she left an *m* out of symmetrical. Wonder what ultra-symmetrical Cindereddie got the slippers? Even now, I find myself thinking of EARNEST, VIVACIOUS, WITTY, ENERGETIC, SPIRITUAL, SENSUOUS BALL OF FIRE or something, who wrote poetry and gamboled about Machu Picchu on vacation. And what about those ads? If there are so many people swarming with such good traits, why is the world in such a fix?

The magazines and newspapers choke the press with stories about sex over sixty, and they all say yes. Resoundingly. But who? Some seem to suggest *how*, but we clamoring (fumbling) old fogies need a who or two before the insistent flame finally gutters out. Well, there's always *Penthouse*, dirty movies, one-handers, binoculars, Anaïs Nin, 1-900 numbers, and books. I was looking through a book catalogue sometime back when I ran across *The Complete Manual of Sexual Positions*. Oh, boy. Now we're talking. "Over Two Hundred Photos, Many in Full Color." Oh, boy, again. The blurb is relentless: "Graphic, step-by-step guide to various forms and means of sexual expression. Incl. tips on dressing and undressing for seduction, the orchestration of foreplay, 'the Grafenberg Orgasm.' " What? The orchestration of foreplay? The Grafenberg Orgasm? I've missed something somewhere. How many people are involved in this sexual expression? I remember the Big O, but the G.O.? Of course, I'd rather have an O named after me than a disease, like Alzheimer's. What depths of sexual imagination would the Grafenberg plumb? Maybe it's sexual platooning. Well, heck, I know all the positions anyway, and solitary practicing would be, as we say, counterproductive. To be honest, I'd settle for a little step-by-step, or even casual, nuzzling, holding hands, and maybe some kissing on the lips, tender talk and caresses, and a few exchanges of coy glances.

I am gaga — do old men go gaga? — mooning at the lovely fresh face caught by the candle flame in this dark place. There is music. She — Loreli — loves me, I think, in a way, though she is twenty-five years younger than I. We talk about nothing, friends, jobs, plans. I hold her hand, thrilled. She turns those usually laughter-filled eyes on me and says, "Why don't we get a house together, both of us?"

"I thought I heard you say, 'Let's get a house together.' "

"I did. I know a big one, but we could use yours. And my daughter, it might be good if there were a man around."

My mouth is working but nothing issues. I am flattered, ecstatic. I thought I'd died and gone to heaven. Please Lord, don't let this stop. She has thought about it. We talk on . . .

It is a gloomy saloon, perfectly suited to the Baptist ethos of the South. Swilling beer and whiskey is evil, a one-way ticket to hell, a terrible sin and thus much more enjoyable when it is done, as it is now, in a dark hole in the middle of a sunshiny afternoon. I am talking with the barkeep, who is telling me she is heading out to Hollywood to write music as soon as she finishes Duke, the university of Durham. So I begin telling her (seriously) how much fun, how exciting tha . . . tha . . . but she is already somewhere else, talking past my encouraging words of wisdom. Ah, well, I do not find this unusual. I was the tiniest, most fleeting blip on her screen, if there at all. It makes you uncomfortable — "Unhand me, graybeard loon." It is more, and less, than bad manners — if you prick us, do we not go *Ouch?*

"The retirees now are basically a gender-role traditional group," she says. "They are the baby-boom parents. For this cohort [group] to have house-husbands just doesn't work very well.

"It might change once you get the more so-called gender-role-modern generations retiring. . . .

"There needs to be a dialogue when they're forty-five or fifty. . . ."

— from *News and Record*, Greensboro, N.C.

Hey, you old basically gender-role cohorts, let's dialogue! With words, but what words? Dead words. Words that have been exhumed but not rejuvenated or invented by vacated minds. They spread like the plague and many are nearly as deadly. How little love and affection you find in the words of Old, how much contempt. Read 'em, old folks — and young — and weep: Young old, old old, nouveau old, muppy, AARP and AARPies (from American Association of Retired Persons), AGE

(Americans for Generational Equity [!]), savvies, luckies, OPALS, wooms, golden agers, gumpies, whoopies, rappies, suppies, golden mafia, Age Wave (that's a marketing company), notcher, fossil, relic, oldun, gramps, cove, gerio, geriatrics, geri-every-thing; retirement community, medigap (a horrible barbarism), medicare and medicaid (horribler barbarisms), long-term care, elder law, spend-down, retirement village, nursing home, rest home, grandparenting (why not olding?), shared group home, ageist, ageism, Alzheimer's (a word that once specifically meant premature senility but now means any senility or senile de-mentia. I prefer dementia or senility, thank you), and on and on and on. It'd gag a green fly. Reporters would rather be as-signed to sewer outfalls (which they would call sewer outfalls) than write and translate this Old doodah into good old colloquial English.

Newspapers, magazines, and radio and television strive might-ily to see who can peddle this alien sticky stuff, like, you know: the Gospel of the Golden Years, the Big Fib, the generational jive. There are publications, of course, exclusively generational, or that purport to be — for instance, *Longevity*, or *Modern Matu-rity*, the big one, published by AARP, and it is shaking the flin-ders out of the money tree. Old is a big business. But it isn't the exploitation of the aged that bothers me, it is how it is done — the telling and retelling of that persistent fib. Old began showing signs of chic when a *Time* magazine cover offered a handsome couple of nouveau fogies in expensive sweat suits (*sweats* to hip ancients), who are happy as hogs in slop, and the cover line goes: AND NOW FOR THE FUN YEARS. Honest.

The story steps off right smartly with President Reagan (sev-enty-seven at the time) and Dr. Jonas Salk, the polio doctor (seventy-three). And the writers tried to sex it up with Elizabeth Taylor (fifty-five) and Joe Niekro (forty-three), both still dewy athletes. Now if *Time* had given us Marlene and the Mongoose (Archie Moore), I'd have nodded sagely. This story, the usual business, is illustrated with a flock of fogies, all of whom are wildly happy at the luck of being so wonderfully old. Well, all right, there is a little meat in there, too, something about us Olds coming at a high cost to the nation, to balance off the whoopee of the rest of the article. In an accompanying story, Dr. Richard Besdine, director of the aging center at the University of Connecticut, says, "Aging doesn't necessarily mean a life that is sick, senile, sexless, spent, or sessile." Sessile!

The *New York Times* jumped in with a color advertising magazine called the *Best Years*. On its cover a perfectly groomed sort-of-old couple are cooing at each other amid impressive statuary — suggesting what? The cover lines were: GAME PLAN FOR A RETIREMENT, which is for perfectly groomed sort-of-old couples, but not for you and me. Another line went: SEX DOESN'T END AT SIXTY. Have you no decency, Old Gray Lady? A few years ago, Sophia Loren smiled at us (is that a *sincere* smile?) from the cover of *Parade* and said, "Getting older is wonderful." She was fifty-two. Ivana Trump gazes at you from the cover of a recent issue of *Longevity*. She was forty-two. The subtitle of *Longevity* is "A Practical Guide to the Art and Science of Staying Young." This art and science eludes me. It eluded old Tithonus too. According to reports from Greece, or somewhere over yonder, he was once a mortal. But then the goddess Aurora tumbled to the beautiful boy and got Jupiter (Zeus), an Olympus-class god, to grant him eternal life. It never dawned on her to stick in a clause giving Tithonus eternal youth too. So he went on living *and* aging. After a while Aurora could not abide the sight of the immortal old geezer and locked him away. But Tithonus kept calling, feebler and feebler, for death, until Aurora took pity and turned him into a grasshopper. A boffo act. What a sense of humor. This myth is de rigueur in any story on age and death with literary pretensions, but I put it in here, anyway, though I find it unimaginably cruel. Sorry. Still, what could be more cruel than the life of the Struldbrugs that Swift's Gulliver encountered in his strange travels? Gulliver was delighted with the idea of Struldbrug immortality until he learned they grew ever older, crazier, uglier — loathed by everyone else in the odd country of Luggnagg. Or consider what James Hilton did to Maria for merely trying to escape Shangri-la. What of Dorian Gray? Or the fate of the Savage's mother, Linda, in *Brave New World*? The Park Lane Hospital for the Dying, where she was sent for a comfortable death, smacks a little too much of the comfort of the present nursing home, rest home, hospice. I think Aldous Huxley, with his sense of the future, knew that. Old is punishment, a wacky, wacky joke.

*

No, younguns, olden isn't so golden. There is that Alzheimer's, you go bowlegged from lack of calcium, blood pressure rises, arthritis sets in, hearing goes bad, the chance of cancer soars, your eyesight dims, and you've got "most weak hams." A flock of annoying or deadly diseases awaits near the end of the line. TV, newspapers, and magazines will never let you forget. *Newsweek* published two cover stories on Alzheimer's that were chillingly alike. (Maybe they forgot?) One proclaimed Alzheimer's "the disease of the century." What an honor! Were flu, polio, AIDS, syphilis, or malaria in the running? And *Newsweek*, as well as other fonts of wisdom, kept harping on dignity, that old har-rumph, but gave us pictures of little old ladies afflicted by the disease.

It doesn't seem to matter how much weight the story has, it is disgorged willy-nilly, especially if it has that word *breakthrough* in it. Such a story appeared not long ago, saying a postmortem test had been developed for Alzheimer's. Now, there's a real help. The *Times* ran an article not long ago about a study showing the longer we live the sicker we get. Jay Olshansky, author of an article from which the report came, said, "We appear to be trading longer life for worsening health." Is there a barely lucid wrinkly-puss alive who doesn't know that? In another, earlier report the same researcher said eighty-five years is about as much as any of us can shoot for, even if all the deadly diseases miraculously go away. Well, it keeps them off the street, as we say these days.

A lot of the bad news comes from this strange critter himself. You, the critter, will find new kinks and aches and tics and twitches you wouldn't have dreamed of forty years ago — ten years ago. Stiffness creeps in, breathing a mite more labored. Plumbing soughs, glurps, and chokes. There is a certain light-ness in the head, even at Budless and boozeless times. You teeter a tad, but very carefully you can still pull on your trousers without holding onto the bedpost. There are funny, off-beat *thrumpteeteethrump-thrumpings* and worse. There are unprovoked tremors and fuzzy focusing and more trips to the bathroom, doctor, and hospital. There are dark warnings about high blood pressure and fat sludging up the arteries. The Old flesh is heir to something new and portentous every day.

My doctor, Pat Guiteras, over in Chapel Hill, said I was in fair shape despite benign prostate hypertrophy, senile dermatitis, seborrheic keratosis, chronic sinusitis, and degenerative arthritis. He was worried about my cholesterol (280) and drinking. Me, too.

So I stand in front of the mirror at the YMCA and flex my flab and gaze upon that marvelous sclerotic old carcass. Boy, who is that old cat standing there? He is a mess, a pure mess. The beard is scraggly gray, hair going that way. The crinkly old hide swags here and there. There are some interesting, if not pretty, squiggles crawling up the ancient calves and eloquently glyphic scars setting off the belly button, evidence left by happy surgeons as they gleefully plucked out my giblets. Well, I worked hard on my pecs (sixty years too late), and look at that definition! Of my dugs, I mean.

Remember, it is not all your fault. God was not much of an engineer. Heavens, it took real genius for Him to scrape together this little heap of dust and tease it into hair, bones, muscles, innards, and so on, and stuff it into one strange parcel with legs, arms, and eyeballs. It is a miracle that it works at all, much less after (in my case) an Amazon of booze has sluiced through it, and it has been battered and attacked by everything from beer bottles and brogans to those tiny little bugs we can't see. Must have been a speck or two of luck in that dust. Besides, these are my golden years.

I jot down the figures for the bills I've paid, and what ho! they add up to more than the good Uncle gives me. Well, I can give up food. Better start looking for a nicely located overpass or abandoned loading dock and maybe membership in the jungle out yonder beyond the switchyard with those boys who used to be called hoboes, but even they have been euphed: "Down a shady lane by the sugarcane, a dirty homeless person comes a-hiking. . . ." The Fogy Dole doesn't help a whole lot.

Last year I found I'd dug myself a deep hole fixing up my house, paying for a car and some other things, so when the chance came to do some copy-editing work part-time, I did, more than I intended to or was wise. Social Security will penalize you for working — that is, deduct from your benefits one dollar for every three you earn over $10,200 (how the hell did the SS arrive at that figure?). So I worked a lot and got paid well for it, but dear old Uncle Sugar will cut my benefits by $2,000 for this year.

I get more than most people my age, but let me tell you something. I keep hearing about disaster coverage in medical insurance, or whatever, but to most of us who have no sure source of income besides Social Security, a new commode is a disaster. A roof is not even ponderable, nor is a pair of new tires or a generator for the $300 LTD. Social Security is, as they used to say up in the North Carolina hills, better than a poke in the eye with a sharp stick, but not much. And so you, youthy pilgrims, hack hack, do not get killed in the rush to the gravy of age without studying the recipe closely.

Who among us musty old mortals is not at least a little aware of standing on the Big Trapdoor as the Master toys teasingly with the lever — even those with whom death has never seriously flirted? We are wallowing in death. This country has been on a death jag for twenty years and more, since the life went out of the sixties like air out of the bellows of an old church organ or one of those old blacksmith's forges, and the showers of sparks subsided and the coals finally died. What has happened? Death with dignity. Who started that hideous joke? Now, along with everyone else, when one of us old people with a feeble grip on life goes into the hospital, he is asked if he wants the plug pulled should he stop twitching. Nah, just put the gun to my right temple and . . . This "living will" reeks of perfectly proper politics, but whatever, death does not interest me. Fuck death.

Oh, life, where is thy sting? Or something like that. Why is *Final Exit*, a work on how to kill yourself, a best-selling book? Wisdom is a gloomy bird of prey. Maybe it is like the dancing madness of the Middle Ages, but the whole thing seems to have culminated in the figure of that ineffably screwy sawbones Jack Kevorkian, who invented a death machine for the convenience of those who figure they have had enough. He wanted to organize killing *teams* — when you see that word, singular or plural, off the sports pages, punt. These would dispatch the ailing or despondent. "O brave new world / That has such people in't." Go burn a flag, Jack. Leave life alone. Me? I want to die with my loafers on . . . I mean off.

*

My momma didn't raise her boy to be a mallbird. Of course, when she'd have advised the boy, there were no malls. I have no yen to don my Joseph's shirt and faux Nikes and lounge about under the rotunda skylight and flap my wattles at the callipygous miracles undulating up and down the corridors. Not my style, and no taste either for joining a toilet-paper-comb kazoo band, nor for interacting with a caregiver or a nurturer (and, Lord, please don't empower me) of a geriatric nite at Wrinkle Towers. Oh, I'll likely wind up in one of those Old storages, but, then, I shall have forgotten, surely, that melancholy Tennyson line, "As tho' to breathe were life." Still, I kind of like "Life piled on life."

So I head for the saloons (restaurants down here), hopes low. Maybe that pretty waitress at Devine's will yield to my charms. Even a blind hog finds an acorn every now and then. Like many another vagabond, I've ricocheted back and forth across the country, strewing friends — societies — behind, whipped on by work, hope, or curiosity, or some restless demon. After the sailors of yore, I have (or had) a society in every port. Saloons were where your societies were. I know almost no one my own age — few hang around bars — and that's sad, and that old debbil generational slips in, and the very youngest know thee not nor acknowledge thy wisdom, and they scorn thee. You are becoming the New Invisible Man, with only a boon buddy or two as witness. Isolation is setting in. Time has been at its sure work, picking off kin here, a friend there; a wife here, a lover there. It sends you down one fork of the road and those you love down another. First thing you know, the solo life is achieved.

There is a cluster of saloons in the Bull City known, with generous irony, as the Strip. I attend these occasionally and sup a couple at the elders' table, often with Scrapper Carswell, who works for a construction company; Bill Johnson, who works for a cleaner's; and Frankie Webster, whose business is, or was, ambulatory and aleatory. He made book.

Frankie is a little bitty fellow who has trudged around town for years using a cane, but somehow, he never seemed ill to me. Some years ago, he discovered the wonders of Las Vegas and rediscovered them frequently. Then the FBI discovered him and his little business by a wiretap that wasn't even on his own phone — after a perfect record, thirty years law-free. Not long after that, doctors discovered Frankie had lung cancer. He quit smoking. He takes chemotherapy and hates it, but when he says so, he sounds more like a boy hating that Saturday-night bath. The only change in his appearance is, he is a little sallow and his hair is gone, but he covers that with one of his 499 astonishingly beautiful baseball caps. Once I asked him how he was getting along, and he said, "Well, it's beginning to hurt a little." He laughed, his eyes alive and wily. He wears a jacket all the time because he gets "a little cold." He is talky, funny, and sixty-five. And he swears Scrapper can't wait to attain that magic age so he can get the discounts. Frankie is a credit to us all.

So, old man, what in the hell *are* you whining about?

Well, now, let's see. It's . . . it's just a sort of singing the blues, a lonesome lament about the whips and scorns of old age . . . I mean, the generational inequities . . . *Hey!*

Wake up, damn you!

Epidamnlogue: I almost forgot. Talk with Loreli, the young woman who suggested we get a house together, strayed from that wonderful idea. Evaporated. Several weeks later, sitting in the same place, Loreli looking as lovely as usual, I finally say, "Now about the house we were talking about. Why don't we —"

"I guess that wasn't such a good idea," she says . . . She's thought about it.

Shoofly, don't bother me. Get away old man, get away.

FLOYD SKLOOT

Trivia Tea: Baseball as Balm

FROM THE GETTYSBURG REVIEW

Question: Which fourteen players have hit thirty or more home runs in a season in each league?

I will give you the most recent one right off the bat. San Diego's Fred McGriff hit thirty-one homers last season, his first in the National League, after having hit over thirty each of the three previous seasons for Toronto. I have ulterior motives in starting with McGriff, because he leads me to talk about a book called *The Answer Is Baseball,* by Luke Salisbury (Vintage, 1989).

Salisbury's book is composed of questions, including the one above, and brief discussions of their answers. I felt annoyed to find my question already in print, having believed for years that I was the person who had thought it up. But then I felt relieved to see that Salisbury had the answer wrong. Or rather, incomplete. Excluding Fred McGriff, who had not yet hit his thirty-plus for San Diego when the book was written, Salisbury still fails to identify five players belonging on his list. Baseball statistics thus become yet another aspect of American culture for which we poets apparently must take responsibility.

The primary use I make of baseball these days is as a form of alternative medicine: its history and statistics are taken in like herbal remedies, its lore meditated on as a form of relaxation therapy, its long televised games approached as part of a natural healing process. Like a lot of natural healing, Harry Caray's voice and patter can be extremely difficult to take, but I am convinced they do me good. An herbalist once convinced me to take heaping tablespoons of something called Major Four, which had precisely the consistency of sand, so I have already proven myself willing to try almost anything.

I am a lifelong participant in games of ball. In a direct progression from a childhood spent playing punchball, stickball, and sandlot baseball, an adolescence playing high school baseball (in the same infield as that famed shortstop, Billy Crystal), and a young adulthood playing college baseball, until my mid-thirties I even dressed up twice a week in grotesque double-knit uniforms to play softball under the lights. But at thirty-five, having discovered long-distance running, I found myself turning away from the sport altogether. It was difficult learning to change my relationship to baseball; I had trouble finding new, more passive pleasures in it. But in the last few years, I have learned to tolerate its becoming a sport primarily read, thought about, and watched on TV — an indoor sport. My loss is in no longer seeing games outdoors and in person at Ebbets Field, Yankee Stadium, the Polo Grounds, and Shea Stadium. The benefit is that this change has helped me cope with having a disabling and chronic incurable disease.

A lifetime of baseball made me a numbers person. Stats are facts. I have been sick for 1,234 days.

In late fall of 1988, when I faced a hundred-mile-an-hour flu, I never imagined still being sick come spring 1992. It began on a business trip to Washington, D.C., with intense fatigue and weakness. I awoke in my hotel room unable to move. The covers held my arms down with such weight that I could not lift a hand to shut off the alarm. The room reeked; I thought I could smell the odors of everyone who had ever stayed there. Sliding from the bed, alarm still chirping, I walked into the bathroom doorjamb. For weeks I remained light-headed and dizzy.

I have Chronic Fatigue Syndrome, a disease in which an unknown viral trigger reactivates other long-dormant viruses in the body, creates deficiencies in the hormones that manage stress, and interferes with crucial chemical changes along the antiviral pathway in the immune system. Suddenly and irreversibly, the immune system is simultaneously in overdrive and inefficient, fighting everything from nonexistent viruses to the body's own tissue while failing to ferret out the original culprit. It took time to accept that while this disease might not flat-out kill me, it had snatched my life as a leaping shortstop might snatch a rising line drive.

Despite its name this is not an illness about tiredness, though fatigue is both a key and the most obvious symptom. Calling it Chronic Fatigue Syndrome is like calling emphysema Chronic Coughing Syndrome. My brain has been scarred. My immune system is in a state that might best be termed a kind of internal toxic spill. Its consequences, and those of the viruses still rampant in my body, are seen clearly in failures of the central nervous system.

If I see you scratch your head while we talk, chances are I will forget what I was trying to say. When preparing breakfast in the morning, I am as likely to pour my rolled oats into the lid as into the pot. At the grocery store, there is reason to doubt I will pick out what I am looking for. A stock clerk talked to me while I selected Santa Rosas, and I put my bag of plums into the recycling bin instead of our cart — an interesting variation on my usual theme of depositing goods into other shoppers' carts. My balance and strength are unpredictable now, as is my coordination. I break plates and glasses so often that I seldom risk cleanup duty. I see obstacles in my path and walk into them anyway. I do not drive.

Nothing is second nature to me anymore. I must think about every move. I can no more field a ground ball or hit a fastball than I can fly.

All of which says little about how I feel. Most often, I feel unplugged, as though the cables to my fuel sources have been shredded. At times I feel unmoored, the vessel of my self having slipped from its anchorage to my body. I feel detached from my past and uncertain of my future. I feel vulnerable, my emotional levees weakening as the waters keep rising. And although I resist it, sometimes I simply feel unhealthy, like a polluted stream. I have dreams in which a giant stalk of rotten celery grows out of my mouth. When I try to pull it free, I can sense it rooted deep in my belly; it feels as though I am uprooting my soul.

And the things I say! I ask my wife for a stick of decaffeinated gum, ask my doctor whether the blood tests show amnesia instead of anemia, talk about freeze-drying my new pants instead of hemming them. I call the car's antenna an umbrella; I say that film needs to be validated instead of developed and that my

mother-in-law's cookies are made of Rice Krispies and mushrooms instead of marshmallows. Close, but not correct, as
though my circuits had been rewired by Gracie Allen. The Xerox
machine apparently stands for all machines in my rearranged
brain: I ask my wife to reheat my coffee in the Xerox, ask my
son to Xerox the lawn, explain to my daughter that the doctor
will Xerox her injured arm. My spelling, like my math, has become utterly original.

In three and a half years, I have learned to adjust. One way
has been to reach into my past for baseball and, by redefining
my relationship to it, open a path to the future.

Having grown up in Brooklyn in the fifties, I learned early to
mark life's key moments according to the happenings in baseball.
My family moved away from Brooklyn in the fall of 1957, exactly
when the Dodgers left, and the two events are inextricably linked
in my mind. My father died in 1961, when I was fourteen, and
those last months of his life are woven together with Roger
Maris's pursuit of Babe Ruth's single-season home run record. I
remember talking with my father during late summer and early
fall about whether Maris had hit another that day, whether it
would be Maris or Mickey Mantle to reach sixty homers first. My
awe at the Mick's size limited my imagination, so I thought it
would be him. My father, stuck in history, did not think either of
them would do it. I actually got him to sit down and talk to me
about this stuff. Unprecedented attention. One night he even
came into my bedroom, picked up my bat from where it leaned
against the doorjamb, and showed me the famous Hack Wilson's
batting stance. My father, thick Havana cigar jutting from the
corner of his mouth, and reaching halfway to an imaginary first
base, shifted his weight and swung for the seats. Those were the
first real conversations we ever had, conversations in which he
seemed to consider my opinions. Also the last. In 1969, I met my
wife during the autumn of the Miracle Mets, that zany season
when New York's infamous losers turned it around and won the
World Series.

So it is not remarkable that I should have returned to baseball
when I got sick. But it seems remarkable to me that I should find
in it a way to help me adapt to being sick rather than another
way to sadden me over my losses.

I love this question about thirty-home-run seasons because it can be reasoned out well enough that I almost feel in control. Approaching it is like approaching most questions about my health — one can understand enough about viruses and the immune system to formulate reasonable answers, even though they may not prove correct. It flexes the brain. It gives a sense of comprehension.

I also love it because in baseball, statistics offer the illusion of meaning. Early in my illness, when so much happening to me was undiagnosable, when questions about why my body behaved as it did and how long it would continue were unanswerable, I developed a lust for facts. Viruses run from about 0.02 to 0.3 micrometers; a billion billion of them would fill one Ping-Pong ball. DNA mixes four simple chemicals, as a good major league pitcher mixes four different pitches. The brain weighs about three pounds. Mine felt as though it were petrifying, the way decaying wood does as it turns to solid stone, and it pressed me daily deeper into the bed.

Reason and facts, of course, are not enough. Certain principles need to be set down before the question can be approached properly. One is that baseball is divided into two utterly separate leagues, unlike other major American sports. Not conferences or divisions — artificial groupings ignored during the regular season when all teams in the sport play each other anyway — but two leagues with distinct identities. Players may do well in the American League, but fail utterly in the National. Catcher Lance Parrish comes to mind, an American League slugger who twice hit over thirty home runs for the Detroit Tigers, but suffered through two miserable seasons with the Philadelphia Phillies, and who thus is not a correct answer to the question. There are also historical principles. Nobody hit over thirty homers prior to 1920, when Babe Ruth hit fifty-four. The new policy about keeping a clean, new baseball in play rather than using the same ball throughout the game had a lot to do with that, as did the earlier elimination of the spitball and other so-called trick pitches. More important for the question before us is that there was no significant interleague trading until 1960. A player could move from one league to the other only via waivers, a process by which any other team in his league might claim him before he could switch to the other league. Nobody capable of hitting thirty home runs who played before the sixties was likely to clear waivers, so no pre-sixties players appear among the correct answers. Hank Greenberg came close, hitting twenty-five during his one National League season for the Pittsburgh Pirates after being sold to them for $75,000 by the Detroit Tigers in 1947. Finally, not a historical principle but a question: what kind of player, capable of hitting thirty home runs, would a team be willing to trade? Clumsy fielding power hitters mostly. Those first basemen or left fielders who become expendable because a team needs some real defensive help or pitching. Thus no shortstops or catchers appear on the list, no center fielders noted for their gloves. If those guys hit thirty home runs, teams keep them. Interestingly, all but two of the fourteen players on the list who were traded between leagues (four moved as free agents or were simply sold for cash) were traded for pitchers.

Answers from the sixties: Dick Stuart, Frank Robinson, Frank Howard.

The sixties was a decade of great home run hitters. It seems amazing to me that ten of the thirteen lifetime home run leaders in the history of baseball played in the sixties — sluggers such as Hank Aaron, Willie Mays, Harmon Killebrew, Reggie Jackson, Mickey Mantle, Ted Williams, Willie McCovey, Eddie Matthews, and Ernie Banks. The all-time, single-season home run leader, Roger Maris, played in the sixties; he spent seven of those years in the American League and two in the National. Yet none of these great home run hitters had seasons of thirty or more in both leagues.

Only "Dr. Strangeglove," "Robbie," and "Hondo."

It is difficult to find links among them. Lousy fielders? Frank Robinson, who — when not a designated hitter — played almost ninety percent of his games in the outfield, was not bad at all, with a lifetime fielding average of .984. His ex-teammate Paul Blair, considered a great fielder, had a lifetime fielding average only four thousandths of a percentage point better, .988, good enough to rank twelfth on the all-time list for outfielders. Slow runners? Robinson had several seasons in which he stole over twenty bases. They were not all troublemakers, they were not all losers (both Howard and Robinson appeared in World Series), and they were not all flakes. If they share anything, maybe it is firsts: Robinson became baseball's first black manager, Howard was the first Ohio State University basketball player to play for the Dodgers, and Stuart was the first American player to become a star in Japan.

I picked up these juicy tidbits looking through baseball books that friends brought as gifts. During the most acute phase of my illness, through the spring of 1989, I could not read anything. Even *People* magazine was too difficult to understand. So I listened to music. I slept. And in April baseball began appearing on television. I could watch parts of games, dozing to the drone of Harry Caray's voice, waking for the fourth through sixth innings when he would be replaced by Dwayne Staats, an announcer I could tolerate, and then dozing again to Harry's gravelly blabbering as the game ended.

Finally, in July 1989 I was able to read David Halberstam's *Summer of '49*. Baseball had brought me back — or so it seemed to me as I slowly emerged from the first phase of my illness. And reading Halberstam's book returned me to my earliest memories of baseball, from the fifties and early sixties. I remembered being at Yankee Stadium for a World Series game in which an outfielder fell into the stands trying to catch a ball. This, I was convinced, had to have been 1952, when I was five. I do not think I can tell you how important it seemed for me to find something this specific in my memory, which had grown so totally unreliable that I could neither place a close boyhood friend who had sent me a letter of good wishes nor remember my date of birth.

Yankee Stadium. I remembered my father working the top off a miniature bottle of rye with his pocketknife between pitches, the Havana as always jutting from his mouth. I remembered seeing a pile of salted peanut shells sucked flat and dark under his slatted seat. He folded his scorecard like a funnel and his gravelly voice rose clear with the line drive's thock. I knelt on my seat beside him, cheering a split second after he did.

After Halberstam's book, it was not long before I was leafing through *The Baseball Encyclopedia*, looking at its numbers the way I remembered seeing my mother leaf through magazines looking at the fashion photographs, not really absorbing anything, just feeling connected to something I valued, just passing time. I began to spend my two or three coherent hours a day at it.

According to the World Series section of this 2,781-page treasure, the game I saw in 1952 was number five, when Andy Pafko
fell into the seats snaring Gene Woodling's drive to right.

On one of these idle summer leafings through The Book, I
found myself gazing at Willie Mays's four-inch chunk of numbers. In 1957 he had done something that caught my attention — hit twenty-six doubles, twenty triples, and thirty-five
home runs. It took me almost three weeks of additional leafings
to conclude that the only other modern players to hit more than
twenty doubles, triples, and home runs in one season were Jim
Bottomley in 1928, Jeff Heath in 1931, and George Brett in
1979. Anyone who even came close — Kiki Cuyler, Lou Gehrig,
Goose Goslin, Rogers Hornsby, Joe Medwick, John Mize, Stan
Musial, George Sisler — is in the Hall of Fame or, in the case of
Ryne Sandberg, certain to be. Another day, I focused on the
listing for Frank Howard, whom I remembered playing for the
Dodgers after they had deserted me. Noticing that he had hit
over forty home runs for the Washington Senators three times, I
wondered if he had ever hit that many for the Dodgers (thirty-
one was his tops). This was how my question got started.

I posed it to everybody I knew. Soon word got out that I could
handle some light baseball reading. Also that I needed something other than the *Encyclopedia*, or else I would drive them all
nuts. My friends, many of whom had been steadfast for me
during these months, yearning to offer something helpful, at last
knew what they could bring for me.

Answers from the seventies: Dick Allen, Bobby Bonds, Reggie
Smith, Jeff Burroughs.

The only one of these players mentioned in *The Answer Is
Baseball* is Reggie Smith, who hit thirty for the Red Sox in 1971
and thirty-two for the Dodgers in 1977. I do not want to brag,
but even sick, even with holes in my brain that show up on
Magnetic Resonance Imaging tests, I got Allen and Bonds.

Nobody gets Burroughs. In a sixteen-year career, he hit 240
home runs, an average of just fifteen per year. But he exploded
in 1973, hitting thirty for the American League Texas Rangers,
and in 1977, hitting forty-one for the National League Atlanta
Braves in their friendly stadium. Almost a third of his lifetime
home runs came in those two seasons. Despite having won an

American League Most Valuable Player award (only Frank Robinson and Dick Allen from the list were also MVPs) and despite
his two explosive home run seasons, it turns out that Burroughs
was not a memorable player.

A quick look at the list from the seventies suggests that players
this productive who still get traded probably do so because they
are, er, difficult people. Allen was traded four times between
1970 and 1975. Bonds played for eight teams in his fourteen-
year career and Burroughs with five. Smith was widely regarded
as a moody, troublesome player and was with four teams between 1973 and 1982. Hell, if they were playing today instead of
in the seventies, they would be zillionaires, compounding their
fortunes with each move between teams.

Thinking about Dick Allen makes me consider how fragile the
human body is and how whimsical the fortune that holds it
intact. Even the powerful body of someone capable of hitting
351 major league homers, which places him among the fifty
greatest sluggers in the game's history. In 1966, still a sprightly
twenty-four-year-old, Allen dislocated his shoulder while sliding
and missed two dozen games (still hitting forty home runs). His
next season ended in late August when his right hand broke
through the headlight of an old car he was pushing. In 1968 he
had a groin injury and missed ten games; two years later he
missed forty games with an Achilles' heel injury and various
pulled muscles. In 1973 Mike Epstein, who was larger than Allen
and known affectionately as Superjew, stepped on Allen's leg
after Allen dove for a bad throw. Allen missed more than half
the season with a broken bone. Although he hit thirty-two home
runs in 1974, Allen missed thirty-four games with a sore shoulder and bad back. He retired in 1977, at thirty-five, after spending most of the previous two seasons on the disabled list.

Not only are bodies essentially frail, they are part of a system.
It is so easy for athletes to think of their bodies either as separate
from their essential selves — a kind of machine — or — at the
other end of the scale — as their entire selves. At forty-one, my
body was in its best shape ever and I was dangerously close to
seeing it as invincible. Running forty-five to fifty miles a week,
winning ribbons for races at anywhere between a mile and a
marathon, I was convinced — had proof — that the older I got

the better I got. I weighed less than I did in junior high school
and my percentage of body fat was under twelve. The more I
pushed myself, the stronger I seemed to get. Now I understand
that the kind of rigorous exercise I thrived on actually weakens
the body, rendering it vulnerable to viral attack. Stress compro-
mises the immune system. According to an article in the *New
England Journal of Medicine* for August 1991, "stress is associated
with the suppression of a general resistance process in the host,
leaving persons susceptible to multiple infectious agents." While
I do not believe I made myself sick by overexercising and failing
to heed my levels of stress, I was not helping myself either. My
body reminded me that it is part of an integrated system, neither
more nor less than my self. I have been on the Disabled List since
December 7, 1988.

There are several players you would swear had thirty-home-run
seasons in each league. People mention Orlando Cepeda among
the first half-dozen names, remembering his one season (1973)
swinging for Boston's Green Monster in left field. But he hit only
twenty homers that year. Tony Perez actually came closer than
Cepeda, hitting twenty-five homers for Boston in 1980, but few
people whom I have asked this question remember his playing
in Fenway. Lee May hit over thirty, three straight years for the
National League's Reds, but never more than twenty-seven for
Baltimore in the American League. Bobby Murcer came as close,
topping thirty for the Yankees, then hitting twenty-seven for the
National League's Cubs. Although it is difficult to remember he
was ever this productive, Joe Pepitone hit thirty-one for the
Yankees in 1966 and four years later hit twenty-six in a National
League season split between the Astros and Cubs. Johnny Mize
and Roy Sievers were sluggers in their heydays, just before interleague trading began; Graig Nettles, Rusty Staub, and Ken Sin-
gleton are among recently retired almosts.

    There are also a few active players with good chances to join
the list. Watching how they do will add to my pleasure in the
1992 season. Jack Clark keeps coming very close. In fact, he is
the closest of anyone in history, having hit thirty-five in 1987 for
the National League's Cardinals (despite playing in mammoth
Busch Stadium) and having hit twenty-eight last year for the Red

Sox. He also hit twenty-seven for the Yankees in 1988. Eddie
Murray hit over thirty homers five times for Baltimore in the
American League, but topped out at twenty-six for the Dodgers.
With the Mets now, he still has a chance to join the list, but at
thirty-six may be running out of time. I was thrilled when the
Seattle Mariners acquired Kevin Mitchell from the Giants earlier
this year; if he stays healthy, he ought to hit sixty-five in the
Kingdome to go with his two National League seasons of more
than thirty, or at least join Darrell Evans as the only players to
hit forty in both leagues. Dave Parker, bouncing around the
American League since 1988, needs to turn back time.

Then there is Nick Esasky, who hit thirty homers for the Red
Sox in 1990 before signing with Atlanta in the National League
for the 1991 season. Then a mysterious disease, spookily similar
to my own, stopped him at the peak of his career.

Esasky had come home; he had signed a three-year, $5.7
million contract with the Braves that would let him play just a
half hour from his suburban home in Marietta. In March of
1991, one week into spring training, came the weakness and
severe fatigue. "At first I thought it was the flu and that it would
go away," he told *People* magazine. "Then I began to get head-
aches and nausea, and I felt light-headed and dizzy."

Esasky saw more than thirty specialists in the first six months
without a definitive diagnosis. Ballplayers do everything big; I
saw only a dozen specialists in my first six months. Diagnosed
after he had reached the point of not caring what to call his
illness, the problem was damage to Esasky's inner ear caused by
a viral infection. I have Chronic Fatigue Syndrome as a remnant
of my viral infection. Esasky has vertigo as the remnant of his. It
is chilling to imagine him facing a major league curve ball or
catching a hard throw at first base. He told *Sports Illustrated* that
"it felt like I was in slow motion, and everything else was moving
very quickly around me." When I tried to run after my illness
began, I found out the hard way that I had lost the ability to
gauge my speed or direction; I fell off the margin of the wooded
trail I was on, rolling fifteen feet downhill before coming to rest
against the trunk of an old-growth red cedar.

Esasky also told *Sports Illustrated* about his quest for a cure. An
orthodontist removed his braces. He took infusions of antibiotics
for Lyme disease, which he did not have. An allergist tested him,

a psychologist talked with him, and a hypnotist tried "to see if we could just block it out by mind power. That didn't work. Hocus-pocus doesn't do it."

Well, no. Neither did eating sand. Esasky now works with the neurologist who directs the Dizziness and Balance Center in Wilmette, Illinois, retraining his balance system. He is trying to overcome vertigo by learning how not to feel sick whenever he moves, hoping eventually to play again for the Braves. But he can accept if it never happens.

"Either way," he says, "I will be taken care of. This has taught me that there are a lot of people out there with problems much worse than mine."

Sounds like jock-speak, the sort of innocuous thing players say to reporters all the time. Except I believe him. I used to think baseball was what connected me to these guys. Now, when I get the urge to heft my hand-carved cocobolo cane and cock it like a bat, I do it in honor of Nick Esasky's comeback attempt.

Answers from the eighties: Jason Thompson, Dave Winfield, Greg Luzinski, Dave Kingman, Darrell Evans, Larry Parrish.

In *The Answer Is Baseball*, Luke Salisbury forgot the last three of these players, even Evans, the one with forty in both leagues. Kingman will have the distinction of being the one player among the twenty greatest home run hitters in baseball history *not* to be elected to the Hall of Fame. Traded so often — shuttling from league to league, once even playing for four teams in one season — he did virtually nothing but hit home runs and strike out, and it is hard not to miss him as a candidate for this list. Missing Larry Parrish I can understand; he can be confused with Lance Parrish, who as I said before is the Parrish you would think ought to be on this list and is not.

It is hard to feel intimate with 1980s baseball, the era of escalating salaries, strikes and lockouts, of what Roger Angell writing in *The New Yorker* called an "omnipresent industry, with its own economics and politics and crushing public relations." Television coverage made fans familiar with teams throughout both leagues — the Cubs and Braves on giant cable stations, other teams through the saturation coverage provided by ESPN — even as familiarity with one's local team became prohibitively expensive.

Angell also says, "American men don't think about baseball as much as they used to, but such thoughts once went deep." He is probably right, and I realize that my own situation is unusual in that I have so much time at home, unable to function well and freed — in a sense — to think about baseball. I feel lucky still to have thoughts about it that run deep because I believe baseball has given me hope. It links my past, which damage to my brain threatened to pillage, with a present that I live in largely outside of time. The flow of my days, the accumulation of my weeks and months, is simply not like those of most people anymore. I often spend two-thirds or more of my time in bed and am disconnected from time in a way most people are not — time matters only when I have to see my doctor or eat lunch with a friend or watch a ballgame or call the editor of the *Gettysburg Review* to ask for two more weeks to finish this essay. Baseball also links my past and present with an uncertain future. I do not know how long my illness will last or where it will take me, but: Will Jack Clark for Boston or Kevin Mitchell for Seattle hit thirty home runs this year and join my list?

Don't get me wrong, this is not all I have to live for. I have love, family, friends, writing. But baseball provides an important and satisfying way for me to feel coherent in a world suddenly very different from what I thought it would be. Baseball moves me again.

It was the autumn of worst to best. The Atlanta Braves and Minnesota Twins, last-place teams in 1990, were challenging for the pennants in 1991. It seemed as though anything was possible: the Soviet Union was breaking apart, and I had been awarded a one-month writer's residency at Centrum, an artists' retreat on the grounds of Fort Worden State Park in Port Townsend, Washington.

Near the end of September, my friend Eric Hosticka drove up from Portland to take me on the one trip I was willing to make away from the gorgeous isolation of Centrum. We went by car and ferry to the Kingdome, where the Seattle Mariners were hosting the Texas Rangers and Nolan Ryan would pitch. Indoor baseball, the apotheosis of my redefined relationship to the sport.

I had been to the Kingdome before, in 1977, on a visit to show my nine-year-old son his first major league game. It took me nine years to get him to a game because 1977 was the first time a team played close enough to where we lived to make the trip viable. As soon as we walked into the stadium, I knew it would be hard to forgive myself — Matt, forget what you are seeing; this is not a baseball park. It was Picture Day, and we spent some time down on the carpet snapping pictures of such luminaries as Craig Reynolds and Jose Baez, hearing a kind of recirculated fan noise that could be described only as otherworldly.

We did not go back to the Kingdome. Fortunately, at least in terms of the family's baseball continuity, we moved to the Midwest for a while, close enough to St. Louis that I could make amends.

Yet in September of 1991, I felt delighted to be entering the Kingdome again. Nolan Ryan is six months older than I. I think I planned to wave my cane at him and yell that he should pitch till he is fifty. We got there early enough to watch Ryan warm up. The Mariners' pitcher, Rich DeLucia, was two years old when Nolan Ryan began his major league career for the Mets in 1966. DeLucia came out onto the carpet just after Ryan — to serious cheering from the crowd — began his slow walk toward the bullpen in left field. DeLucia immediately started throwing from the bullpen mound in right, his pitches snappy enough to hear. He was all business; I watched him for a while because Ryan was taking so long to make his way out. When I looked back, Ryan was sitting on the carpet stretching his legs. By the time DeLucia was through with his warmups, Ryan was finishing his stretches. Then he sashayed toward the left field wall and began casually flipping a ball toward the infield, where his catcher stood. His motion was like an outfielder's after catching a lazy fly ball with no one on base — a few trotting steps, a toss that used a minimum of arm and maximum of leg and upper body. After twenty minutes he approached the bullpen mound and began pitching, easy at first, not hard enough to pop the catcher's mitt until several more minutes had passed. The man was careful with his body.

We sat directly behind home plate. Peering through the chain-link safety screen took some getting used to, but by game time I was set. When the Mariners came up to hit in the bottom of the

first, I felt both excited and nervous, as though perhaps I would
have to hit against Ryan later in the game. I remember thinking,
Where did that come from? And thank you, baseball, for giving
it to me again.

What remains with me most clearly is the grunting sound Ryan
made as he delivered a fastball. There would be this *uhhhh*,
almost but not quite simultaneous with the sound of the ball
hitting Ivan Rodriguez's glove. I imagine Ryan did not worry too
much about tipping off his fastball with the noise, which he did
not make on curves or changeups.

He had already won twenty-nine games and struck out 493
batters — nine percent of both lifetime totals — by the time his
young catcher was born in the late autumn of 1971. (Jeez, I love
doing these numbers.) Did he really let the kid call his pitches?
Seemed to. Would he sit with him between innings to discuss
strategy? No, he went into the clubhouse between most innings,
probably to work out on the stationary bike.

This was a late-season game, meaningless in the standings, and
I wondered if Ryan would coast through five innings to get his
victory and then leave. He did not, bless his heart. I got to see
him strike out ten batters through eight innings and win the
314th game of his career, tying him with Gaylord Perry for
fourteenth on the all-time victory list. I got to see him bear down
against the Mariners's fine young star, Ken Griffey, Jr., pitching
to him with palpably greater intensity than he pitched to Omar
Vizquel, who was hitting .230, or Dave Valle at .194. Before his
second appearance against Ryan, I watched Griffey in the on-
deck circle, about twenty feet from where I sat. The kid looked
different from how he had looked before his first appearance,
when I had noticed him scanning the seats behind home plate to
check out the young women in their Indian summer finery.

It felt wonderful to be where I was, in the Seattle Kingdome
late on a Wednesday afternoon in September, watching indoor
baseball, letting numbers run through my head, telling Eric
about games I had seen as a boy, listening to his tales of watching
Roberto Clemente and Bill Mazeroski play at Forbes Field in
Pittsburgh. We did not eat hot dogs because I must be very
careful about chemicals in my food, but we had brought apples.
There is always a new way to see things.

SHELBY STEELE

The New Sovereignty

FROM HARPER'S MAGAZINE

TOWARD THE END of a talk I gave recently at a large midwestern university, I noticed a distinct tension in the audience. All re- spectful audiences are quiet, but I've come to understand that when there is disagreement with what's being said at the podium the silence can become pure enough to constitute a statement. Fidgeting and whispering cease, pencils stay still in notetakers' hands — you sense the quiet filling your pauses as a sign of disquiet, even resistance. A speaker can feel ganged-up on by such a silence.

I had gotten myself into this spot by challenging the orthodoxy of diversity that is now so common on university campuses — not the *notion* of diversity, which I wholly subscribe to, but the rigid means by which it is pursued. I had told the students and faculty members on hand that in the late 1960s, without much public debate but with many good intentions, America had em- barked upon one of the most dramatic social experiments in its history. The federal government, radically and officially, began to alter and expand the concept of entitlement in America. Rights to justice and to government benefits were henceforth to be extended not simply to individuals but to racial, ethnic, and other groups. Moreover, the essential basis of all entitlement in America — the guarantees of the Constitution — had appar- ently been found wanting; there was to be redress and repara- tion of past grievances, and the Constitution had nothing to say about that.

I went on to explain that Martin Luther King and the early

civil rights leaders had demanded only constitutional rights; they had been found wanting, too. By the late sixties, among a new set of black leaders, there had developed a presumption of collective entitlement (based on the redress of past grievances) that made blacks eligible for rights beyond those provided for in the Constitution, and thus beyond those afforded the nation's non-black citizens. Thanks to the civil rights movement, a young black citizen as well as a young white citizen could not be turned away from a college because of the color of his or her skin; by the early seventies a young black citizen, poor or wealthy, now qualified for certain grants and scholarships — might even be accepted for admission — simply *because* of the color of his or her skin. I made the point that this new and rather unexamined principle of collective entitlement had led America to pursue a democracy of groups as well as of individuals — that collective entitlement enfranchised groups just as the Constitution enfranchised individuals.

It was when I introduced a concept I call the New Sovereignty that my audience's silence became most audible. In America today, I said, sovereignty — that is, power to act autonomously — is bestowed upon any group that is able to construct itself around a perceived grievance. With the concept of collective entitlement now accepted not only at the federal level but casually at all levels of society, any aggrieved group — and, for that matter, any assemblage of citizens that might or might not have previously been thought of as such a group — could make its case, attract attention and funding, and build a constituency that, in turn, would increase attention and funding. Soon this organized group of aggrieved citizens would achieve sovereignty, functioning within our long-sovereign nation and negotiating with that nation for a separate, exclusive set of entitlements. And here I pointed to America's university campuses, where, in the name of their grievances, blacks, women, Hispanics, Asians, Native Americans, gays, and lesbians had hardened into sovereign constituencies that vied for the entitlements of sovereignty — separate "studies" departments for each group, "ethnic" theme dorms, preferential admissions and financial aid policies, a proportionate number of faculty of their own group, separate student lounges and campus centers, and so on. This push for equality among groups, I said, necessarily made for an inequality among individuals that prepared the ground for precisely the racial, gender, and ethnic divisiveness that, back in the sixties, we all said we wanted to move beyond.

At the reception that followed the talk I was approached by a tall, elegant woman who introduced herself as the chairperson of the women's studies department. Anger and the will to be polite were at war in her face so that her courteous smile at times became a leer. She wanted to "inform" me that she was proud of the fact that women's studies was a separate department at her university. I asked her what could be studied in this department that could not be studied in other departments. Take the case of, say, Virginia Woolf: in what way would a female academic teaching in a women's studies department have a different approach to Woolf's writing than a woman professor in the English department? Above her determined smile her eyes became fierce. "You must know as a black that they won't accept us" — meaning women, blacks, presumably others — "in the English department. It's an oppressive environment for women scholars. We're not taken seriously there." I asked her if that wasn't all the more reason to be there, to fight the good fight, and to work to have the contributions of women broaden the entire discipline of literary studies. She said I was naive. I said her strategy left the oppressiveness she talked about unchallenged. She said it was a waste of valuable energy to spend time fighting "old white males." I said that if women were oppressed, there was nothing to do *but* fight.

We each held tiny paper plates with celery sticks and little bricks of cheese, and I'm sure much body language was subdued by the tea party postures these plates imposed on us. But her last word was not actually a word. It was a look. She parodied an epiphany of disappointment in herself, as if she'd caught herself in a bizarre foolishness. *Of course, this guy is the enemy. He is the very oppressiveness I'm talking about. How could I have missed it?* And so, suddenly comfortable in the understanding that I was hopeless, she let her smile become gracious. Grace was something she could afford now. An excuse was made, a hand extended, and then she was gone. Holding my little plate, I watched her disappear into the crowd.

Today there are more than five hundred separate women's studies departments or programs in American colleges and universities. There are nearly four hundred independent black studies departments or programs, and hundreds of Hispanic, Asian, and Native American programs. Given this degree of entrenchment, it is no wonder this woman found our little debate a waste of her time. She would have had urgent administrative tasks awaiting her attention — grant proposals to write, budget requests to work up, personnel matters to attend to. And suppose I had won the debate? Would she have rushed back to her office and begun to dismantle the women's studies department by doling out its courses and faculty to long-standing departments like English and history? Would she have given her secretary notice and relinquished her office equipment? I don't think so.

I do think I know how it all came to this — how what began as an attempt to address the very real grievances of women wound up creating newly sovereign fiefdoms like this women's studies department. First there was collective entitlement to redress the grievances, which in turn implied a sovereignty for the grievance group, since sovereignty is only the formalization of collective entitlement. Then, since sovereignty requires autonomy, there had to be a demand for separate and independent stature within the university (or some other institution of society). There would have to be a separate territory, with the trappings that certify sovereignty and are concrete recognition of the grievance identity — a building or suite of offices, a budget, faculty, staff, office supplies, letterhead, et cetera.

And so the justification for separate women's and ethnic studies programs has virtually nothing to do with strictly academic matters and everything to do with the kind of group-identity politics in which the principle of collective entitlement has resulted. My feeling is that there can be no full redress of the woeful neglect of women's intellectual contributions until those contributions are entirely integrated into the very departments that neglected them in the first place. The same is true for America's minorities. Only inclusion answers history's exclusion. But now the sovereignty of grievance-group identities has confused all this.

It was the sovereignty issue that squelched my talk with the women's studies chairperson. She came to see me as an enemy not because I denied that women writers had been neglected historically; I was the enemy because my questions challenged the territorial sovereignty of her department and of the larger grievance identity of women. It was not a matter of fairness — of justice — but of power. She would not put it that way, of course. For in order to rule over her sovereign fiefdom it remains important that she seem to represent the powerless, the aggrieved. It remains important, too, that my objection to the New Sovereignty can be interpreted by her as sexist. When I failed to concede sovereignty, I became an enemy of women.

In our age of the New Sovereignty the original grievances — those having to do with fundamental questions such as basic rights — have in large measure been addressed, if not entirely redressed. But that is of little matter now. The sovereign fiefdoms are ends in themselves — providing career tracks and bases of power. This power tends to be used now mostly to defend and extend the fiefdom, often by exaggerating and exploiting secondary, amorphous, or largely symbolic complaints. In this way, America has increasingly become an uneasy federation of newly sovereign nations.

In *The True Believer*, Eric Hoffer wrote presciently of this phenomenon I have come to call the New Sovereignty: "When a mass movement begins to attract people who are interested in their individual careers, it is a sign that it has passed its vigorous stage; that it is no longer engaged in molding a new world but in possessing and preserving the present. It ceases then to be a movement and becomes an enterprise."

If it is true that great mass movements begin as spontaneous eruptions of long-smoldering discontent, it is also true that after significant reform is achieved they do not like to pass away or even modify their grievance posture. The redressing of the movement's grievances wins legitimacy for the movement. Reform, in this way, also means recognition for those who struggled for it. The movement's leaders are quoted in the papers, appear on TV, meet with elected officials, write books — they come to embody the movement. Over time, they and they alone speak for the aggrieved; and, of course, they continue to speak *of* the aggrieved, adding fresh grievances to the original complaint. It is their vocation now, and their means to status and power. The idealistic reformers thus become professional spokespersons for the seemingly permanently aggrieved. In the civil rights movement, suits and briefcases replaced the sharecropper's denim of the early years, and $500-a-plate fund-raisers for the National Association for the Advancement of Colored People replaced volunteers and picket signs. The raucous bra burning of late sixties feminism gave way to women's studies departments and direct-mail campaigns by the National Organization of Women.

This sort of evolution, however natural it may appear, is not without problems for the new grievance-group executive class. The winning of reform will have dissipated much of the explosive urgency that started the movement; yet the new institutionalized movement cannot justify its existence without this urgency. The problem becomes one of maintaining a reformist organization after considerable reforms have been won.

To keep alive the urgency needed to justify itself, the grievance organization will do three things. First, it will work to inspire a perpetual sense of grievance in its constituency so that grievance becomes the very centerpiece of the group itself. To be black, or a woman, or gay, is, in the eyes of the NAACP, NOW, or Act Up, to be essentially threatened, victimized, apart from the rest of America. Second, these organizations will up the ante on what constitutes a grievance by making support of sovereignty itself the new test of grievance. If the women's studies program has not been made autonomous, this constitutes a grievance. If the National Council of La Raza hasn't been consulted, Hispanics have been ignored. The third strategy of grievance organizations is to arrange their priorities in a way that will maximize their grievance profile. Often their agendas will be established more for their grievance potential than for the actual betterment of the group. Those points at which there is resistance in the larger society to the group's entitlement demands will usually be made into top-priority issues, thereby emphasizing the status of victim and outsider necessary to sustain the sovereign organization.

Thus, at its 1989 convention, the NAACP put affirmative action at the very top of its agenda. Never mind the fact that studies conducted by both proponents and opponents of affirmative action indicate the practice has very little real impact on the employment and advancement of blacks. Never mind, too, that surveys show most black Americans do not consider racial preferences *their* priority. In its wisdom the NAACP thought (and continues to think) that the national mood against affirmative action programs is a bigger problem for black men and women than teen pregnancy, or the disintegrating black family, or black-on-black crime. Why? Because the very resistance affirmative action meets from the larger society makes it an issue of high grievance potential. Affirmative action can generate the urgency that justifies black sovereignty far more than issues like teen pregnancy or high dropout rates, which carry no load of collective entitlement and which the *entire* society sees as serious problems.

In the women's movement, too, the top-priority issues have been those with the highest grievance potential. I think so much effort and resources went into the now-failed Equal Rights Amendment because, in large part, it carried a tremendous load of collective entitlement (a constitutional amendment for a specific group rather than for all citizens) and because it faced great resistance from the larger society. It was a win-win venture for the women's movement. If it succeeded there would be a great bounty of collective entitlement; if it failed, as it did, the failure could be embraced as a grievance — an indication of America's continuing unwillingness to assure equality for women. *America does not want to allow us in!* — that is how the defeat of the ERA could be interpreted by NOW executives and by female English professors eager to run their own departments; the defeat of the ERA was a boon for the New Sovereignty.

I also believe this quest for sovereignty at least partially explains the leap of abortion rights to the very top of the feminist agenda on the heels of the ERA's failure. Abortion has always been an extremely divisive, complex, and emotionally charged issue. And for this reason it is also an issue of enormous grievance potential for the women's movement — assuming it can be framed solely in terms of female grievance. My own belief is that

abortion is a valid and important issue for the women's movement to take up, and I completely support the pro-choice position the movement advocates. However, I think women's organizations like NOW have framed the issue in territorial terms in
order to maximize its grievance potential. When they make
women's control of their own bodies the very centerpiece of their
argument for choice, they are making the fact of pregnancy the
exclusive terrain of women, despite the obvious role of men in
conception and despite the fact that the vast majority of married
women deciding to have abortions reach their decisions with
their husbands. Framed exclusively as a woman's right, abortion
becomes not a societal issue or even a family issue but a grievance
issue in the ongoing struggle of the women's movement. Can
women's organizations continue to frame pro-choice as a grievance issue — a question of a right — and expect to garner the
votes in Congress or in the state legislatures, which is where the
abortion question is headed?

I don't think this framing of the issue as a right is as much
about abortion as it is about the sovereignty and permanency of
women's organizations. The trick is exclusivity. If you can make
the issue exclusively yours — within your territory of final authority — then all who do not capitulate are aggrieving you. And
then, of course, you must rally and expand your organization to
meet all this potential grievance.

But this is a pattern that ultimately puts grievance organizations out of touch with their presumed constituencies, who
grow tired of the hyperbole. I think it partially explains why so
many young women today resist the feminist label and why the
membership rolls of the NAACP have fallen so sharply in recent years, particularly among the young. The high grievance
profile is being seen for what it mostly is — a staying-in-business
strategy.

How did America evolve its now rather formalized notion that
groups of its citizens could be entitled collectively? I think it goes
back to the most fundamental contradiction in American life.
From the beginning America has been a pluralistic society, and
one drawn to a radical form of democracy — emphasizing the
freedom and equality of *individuals* — that could meld such di-

versity into a coherent nation. In this new nation no group would lord it over any other. But, of course, beneath this America of its ideals there was from the start a much meaner reality, one whose very existence mocked the notion of a nation made singular by the equality of its individuals. By limiting democracy to their own kind — white, male landowners — the Founding Fathers collectively entitled themselves and banished all others to the edges and underside of American life. There, individual entitlement was either curtailed or — in the case of slavery — extinguished.

The genius of the civil rights movement that changed the fabric of American life in the late 1950s and early 1960s was its profound understanding that the enemy of black Americans was not the ideal America but the unspoken principle of collective entitlement that had always put the lie to true democracy. This movement, which came to center stage from America's underside and margins, had as its single, overriding goal the eradication of white entitlement. And, correspondingly, it exhibited a belief in democratic principles at least as strong as that of the Founding Fathers, who themselves had emerged from the (less harsh) margins of English society. In this sense the civil rights movement reenacted the American Revolution, and its paramount leader, Martin Luther King, spoke as twentieth-century America's greatest democratic voice.

All of this was made clear to me for the umpteenth time by my father on a very cold Saturday afternoon in 1959. There was a national campaign under way to integrate the lunch counters at Woolworth stores, and my father, who was more a persuader than an intimidator, had made it a point of honor that I join him on the picket line, civil rights being nothing less than the religion of our household. By this time, age twelve or so, I was sick of it. I'd had enough of watching my parents heading off to still another meeting or march; I'd heard too many tedious discussions on everything from the philosophy of passive resistance to the symbolism of going to jail. Added to this, my own experience of picket lines and peace marches had impressed upon me what so many people who've partaken of these activities know: that in themselves they can be crushingly boring — around and around and around holding a sign, watching one's own feet fall, feeling the minutes like hours. All that Saturday morning I hid from my father and tried to convince myself of what I longed for — that he would get so busy that if he didn't forget the march he would at least forget me.

He forgot nothing. I did my time on the picket line, but not without building up enough resentment to start a fight on the way home. What was so important about integration? We had never even wanted to eat at Woolworth's. I told him the truth, that he never took us to *any* restaurants anyway, claiming always that they charged too much money for bad food. But he said calmly that he was proud of me for marching and that he knew *I* knew food wasn't the point.

My father — forty years a truck driver, with the urges of an intellectual — went on to use my little rebellion as the occasion for a discourse, in this case on the concept of integration. Integration had little to do with merely rubbing shoulders with white people, eating bad food beside them. It was about the right to go absolutely anywhere white people could go being the test of freedom and equality. To be anywhere they could be and do anything they could do was the point. Like it or not, white people defined the horizon of freedom in America, and if you couldn't touch their shoulder you weren't free. For him integration was the *evidence* of freedom and equality.

My father was a product of America's margins, as were all the blacks in the early civil rights movement, leaders and foot soldiers alike. For them integration was a way of moving from the margins into the mainstream. Today there is considerable ambivalence about integration, but in that day it was nothing less than democracy itself. Integration is also certainly about racial harmony, but it is more fundamentally about the ultimate extension of democracy — beyond the racial entitlements that contradict it. The idea of racial integration is quite simply the most democratic principle America has evolved, since all other such principles depend on its reality and are diminished by its absence.

But the civil rights movement did not account for one thing: the tremendous release of black anger that would follow its victories. The 1964 Civil Rights Act and the 1965 Voting Rights Act were, on one level, admissions of guilt by American society that it had practiced white entitlement at the expense of all others. When the oppressors admit their crimes, the oppressed can give full vent to their long repressed rage because now there is a moral consensus between oppressor and oppressed that a wrong was done. This consensus gave blacks the license to release a rage that was three centuries deep, a rage that is still today everywhere visible, a rage that — in the wake of the Rodney King verdict, a verdict a vast majority of all Americans thought unfair — fueled the worst rioting in recent American history.

By the mid-sixties, the democratic goal of integration was no longer enough to appease black anger. Suddenly for blacks there was a sense that far more was owed, that a huge bill was due. And for many whites there was also the feeling that some kind of repayment was truly in order. This was the moral logic that followed inevitably from the new consensus. But it led to an even simpler logic: if blacks had been oppressed collectively, that oppression would now be redressed by entitling them collectively. So here we were again, in the name of a thousand good intentions, falling away from the hard challenge of a democracy of individuals and embracing the principle of collective entitlement that had so corrupted the American ideal in the first place. Now this old sin would be applied in the name of uplift. And this made an easy sort of sense. If it was good enough for whites for three hundred years, why not let blacks have a little of it to get ahead? In the context of the sixties — black outrage and white guilt — a principle we had just decided was evil for whites was redefined as a social good for blacks. And once the formula was in place for blacks, it could be applied to other groups with similar grievances. By the 1970s more than 60 percent of the American population — not only blacks but Hispanics, women, Asians — would come under the collective entitlement of affirmative action.

In the early days of the civil rights movement, the concept of solidarity was essentially a moral one. That is, all people who believed in human freedom, fairness, and equality were asked to form a solid front against white entitlement. But after the collaboration of black rage and white guilt made collective entitlement a social remedy, the nature of solidarity changed. It was no longer the rallying of diverse peoples to breach an oppressive group entitlement. It was the very opposite: a rallying of people within a grievance group to pursue their own group entitlement. As early as the mid-sixties, whites were made unwelcome in the civil rights movement, just as, by the mid-seventies, men were no longer welcome in the women's movement. Eventually, collective entitlement *always* requires separatism. And the irony is obvious: those who once had been the victims of separatism, who had sacrificed so dearly to overcome their being at the margins, would later create an ethos of their own separatism. After the sixties, solidarity became essentially a separatist concept, an exclusionary principle. One no longer heard words like "integration" or "harmony"; one heard about "anger" and "power." Integration is anathema to grievance groups for precisely the same reason it was anathema to racist whites in the civil rights era: because it threatens their collective entitlement by insisting that no group be entitled over another. Power is where it's at today — power to set up the organization, attract the following, run the fiefdom.

But it must also be said that this could not have come to pass without the cooperation of the society at large and its institutions. Why did the government, the public and private institutions, the corporations and foundations, end up supporting principles that had the effect of turning causes into sovereign fiefdoms? I think the answer is that those in charge of America's institutions saw the institutionalization and bureaucratization of the protest movements as ultimately desirable, at least in the short term, and the funding of group entitlements as ultimately a less costly way to redress grievances. The leaders of the newly sovereign fiefdoms were backing off from earlier demands that America live up to its ideals. Gone was the moral indictment. Gone was the call for difficult, soulful transformation. The language of entitlements is essentially the old, comforting language of power politics, and in the halls of power it went down easily enough.

With regard to civil rights, the moral voice of Dr. King gave way to the demands and cajolings of poverty program moguls, class action lawyers, and community organizers. The compromise that satisfied both political parties was to shift the focus from democracy, integration, and developmental uplift to collec-

tive entitlements. This satisfied the institutions because entitlements were cheaper in every way than real change. Better to set
up black studies and women's studies departments than to have
wrenching debates within existing departments. Better to fund
these new institutions clamoring for money because who knows
what kind of fuss they'll make if we turn down their proposals.
Better to pass laws permitting Hispanic students to get preferred
treatment in college admission — it costs less than improving
kindergartens in East Los Angeles.

And this way to uplift satisfied the grievance-group "experts"
because it laid the ground for their sovereignty and permanency: You negotiated with *us*. You funded *us*. You shared
power, at least a bit of it, with *us*.

This negotiation was carried out in a kind of quasi-secrecy.
Quotas, set-asides, and other entitlements were not debated in
Congress or on the campaign trail. They were implemented by
executive orders and Equal Employment Opportunity Commission guidelines without much public scrutiny. Also the courts
played a quiet but persistent role in supporting these orders and
guidelines and in further spelling out their application. Universities, corporations, and foundations implemented their own
grievance entitlements, the workings of which are often kept
from the public.

Now, it should surprise no one that all this entitlement has
most helped those who least need it — white middle-class women
and the black middle class. Poor blacks do not guide the black
grievance groups. Working-class women do not set NOW's
agenda. Poor Hispanics do not clamor for bilingualism. Perhaps
there is nothing wrong with middle-class people being helped,
but their demands for entitlements are most often in the name
of those less well off than themselves. The negotiations that
settled on entitlements as the primary form of redress after the
sixties have generated a legalistic grievance industry that argues
the interstices of entitlements and does very little to help those
truly in need.

In a liberal democracy, collective entitlements based upon race,
gender, ethnicity, or some other group grievance are always
undemocratic expedients. Integration, on the other hand, is the

most difficult and inexpedient expansion of the democratic ideal; for in opting for integration, a citizen denies his or her impulse to use our most arbitrary characteristics — race, ethnicity, gender, sexual preference — as the basis for identity, as a key to status, or for claims to entitlement. Integration is twentieth-century America's elaboration of democracy. It eliminates such things as race and gender as oppressive barriers to freedom, as democrats of an earlier epoch eliminated religion and property. Our mistake has been to think of integration only as a utopian vision of perfect racial harmony. I think it is better to see integration as the inclusion of all citizens into the same sphere of rights, the same range of opportunities and possibilities that our Founding Fathers themselves enjoyed. Integration is not social engineering or group entitlements; it is a fundamental *absence* of arbitrary barriers to freedom.

If we can understand integration as an absence of barriers that has the effect of integrating all citizens into the same sphere of rights, then it can serve as a principle of democratic conduct. Anything that pushes anybody out of this sphere is undemocratic and must be checked, no matter the good intentions that seem to justify it. Understood in this light, collective entitlements are as undemocratic as racial and gender discrimination, and a group grievance is no more a justification for entitlement than the notion of white supremacy was at an earlier time. We are wrong to think of democracy as a gift of freedom; it is really a kind of discipline that avails freedom. Sometimes its enemy is racism and sexism; other times the enemy is our expedient attempts to correct these ills.

I think it is time for those who seek identity and power through grievance groups to fashion identities apart from grievance, to grant themselves the widest range of freedom, and to assume responsibility for that freedom. Victimhood lasts only as long as it is accepted, and to exploit it for an empty sovereignty is to accept it. The New Sovereignty is ultimately about vanity. It is the narcissism of victims, and it brings only a negligible power at the exorbitant price of continued victimhood. And all the while integration remains the real work.

LEWIS THOMAS

Crickets, Bats, Cats, & Chaos

FROM AUDUBON

I AM NOT SURE where to classify the mind of my cat Jeoffry. He is a small Abyssinian cat, a creature of elegance, grace, and poise, a piece of moving sculpture, and a total mystery. We named him Jeoffry after the eighteenth-century cat celebrated by the unpredictable poet Christopher Smart in a poem titled "Jubilate Agno," one section of which begins, "For I will consider my cat Jeoffry." The following lines are selected more or less at random:

> For he counteracts the powers of darkness by his electrical skin
> and glaring eyes.
> For he counteracts the Devil, who is death, by brisking about
> the life . . .
> For he is of the tribe of Tiger . . .
> For he purrs in thankfulness, when God tells him he's a good
> Cat . . .
> For he is an instrument for the children to learn benevolence
> upon . . .
> For he is a mixture of gravity and waggery . . .
> For there is nothing sweeter than his peace when at rest.
> For there is nothing brisker than his life when in motion.

I have not the slightest notion what goes on in the mind of my cat Jeoffry, beyond the conviction that it is a genuine mind, with genuine thoughts and a strong tendency to chaos, but in all other respects a mind totally unlike mine. I have a hunch, based on long moments of observing him stretched on the rug in sunlight, that his mind has more periods of geometric order, and a better facility for switching itself almost, but not quite, entirely off, and accordingly an easier access to pure pleasure. Just as he is able to hear sounds that I cannot hear, and smell important things of which I am unaware, and suddenly leap like a crazed gymnast from chair to chair, upstairs and downstairs through the house, flawless in every movement and searching for something he never finds, he has periods of meditation on matters I know nothing about.

While thinking about what nonhumans think is, in most biological quarters, an outlandish question, even an impermissible one, to which the quick and easy answer is nothing, or almost nothing, or certainly nothing like *thought* as we use the word, I still think about it. For while none of them may have real thoughts, foresee the future, regret the past, or be self-aware, most of us up here at the peak of evolution cannot manage the awareness of our own awareness, a state of mind only achieved when the mind succeeds in emptying itself of all other information and switches off all messages, interior and exterior. This is the state of mind for which the Chinese Taoists long ago used a term meaning, literally, no-knowledge. With no-knowledge, it is said, you get a different look at the world, an illumination.

Falling short of this, as I do, and dispossessed of anything I could call illumination, it has become my lesser satisfaction to learn secondhand whatever I can, and then to think, firsthand, about the behavior of other kinds of animals.

I think of crickets, for instance, and the thought of their unique, very small thoughts — principally about mating and bats — but also about the state of cricket society. The cricket seems to me an eminently suitable animal for sorting out some of the emotional issues bound to arise in any consideration of animal awareness. Nobody, so far as I know, not even an eighteenth-century minor poet, could imagine any connection between events in the mind of a cricket and those in the mind of a human. If there was ever a creature in nature meriting the dismissive description of a living machine, mindless and thoughtless, the cricket qualifies. So in talking about what crickets are up to when they communicate with each other, as they unmistakably do, by species-unique runs and rhythms of chirps and trills, there can be no question of *anthropomorphization,* that

most awful of all terms for the deepest error a modern biologist
can fall into.

If you reduce the temperature of a male cricket, the rate of his
emission of chirping signals is correspondingly reduced. Indeed,
some of the earlier naturalists used the technical term "ther-
mometer crickets" because of the observation that you can make
a close guess at the air temperature in a field by counting the rate
of chirps of familiar crickets.

This is curious, but there is a much more curious thing going
on when the weather changes. The female crickets in the same
field, genetically coded to respond specifically to the chirp
rhythm of their species, adjust their recognition mechanism to
the same temperature change and the same new, slower rate of
chirps. That is, as John Doherty and Ronald Hoy wrote on observing the phenomenon, "warm females responded best to the
songs of warm males, and cold females responded best to the
songs of cold males." The same phenomenon, known as temperature coupling, has been encountered in grasshoppers and tree
frogs, and also in fireflies, with their flash communication system. The receiving mind of the female cricket, if you are willing
to call it that, adjusts itself immediately to match the sending
mind of the male. This has always struck me as one of the neat-
est examples of animals adjusting to a change in their environment.

But I started thinking about crickets with something quite
different in mind, namely bats. It has long been known that bats
feed voraciously on the nocturnal flights of crickets and moths,
which they detect on the wing by their fantastically accurate
ultrasound mechanism. What should have been guessed at, considering the ingenuity of nature, is that certain cricket species,
green lacewings, and certain moths have ears that can detect the
ultrasound emissions of a bat, and can analyze the distance and
direction from which the ultrasound is coming. These insects
can employ two separate and quite distinct defensive maneuvers
for evading the bat's keen sonar.

The first is simply swerving away. This is useful behavior when
the bat signal is coming from a safe distance, twenty to thirty
meters away. At this range the insect can detect the bat, but the
bat is too far off to receive the bounced ultrasound back to its

own ears. So the cricket or moth needs to do nothing more, at least for the moment, than swing out of earshot.

But when the bat is nearby, three meters or less, the insect is in immediate and mortal danger, for now the bat's sonar provides an accurate localization. It is too late for swerving or veering; because of its superior speed the bat can easily track such simple evasions. What to do? The answer has been provided by Kenneth Roeder, who designed a marvelous laboratory model for field studies, including instruments to imitate the intensity and direction of bat signals.

The answer, for a cricket or moth or lacewing who hears a bat homing in close by, is *chaos*. Instead of swerving away, the insect launches into wild, totally erratic, random flight patterns, as unpredictable as possible. This kind of response tends to confuse the bat and results in escape for the insect frequently enough to have been selected by evolution as the final, stereotyped, "last-chance" response to the threat. It has the look of a very smart move, whether thought out or not.

So chaos is part of the useful, everyday mental equipment of a cricket or a moth, and that, I submit, is something new to think about. I don't wish to push the matter beyond its possible significance, but it seems to me to justify a modest nudge. The long debate over the problem of animal awareness is not touched by the observation, but it does bring up the opposite side of that argument, the opposite of anthropomorphization. It is this: Leaving aside the deep question as to whether the lower animals have anything going on in their mind that we might accept as conscious thought, are there important events occurring in our human minds that are matched by habits of the animal mind?

Surely chaos is a capacious area of common ground. I am convinced that my own mind spends much of its waking hours, not to mention its sleeping time, in a state of chaos directly analogous to that of the cricket hearing the sound of the nearby bat. But there is a big difference. My chaos is not induced by a bat; it is not suddenly switched on in order to facilitate escape; it is not an evasive tactic set off by any new danger. It is, I think, the normal state of affairs, and not just for my brain in particular but for human brains in general. The chaos that is my natural state of being is rather like the concept of chaos that has emerged in higher mathematical circles in recent years.

As I understand it, and I am quick to say that I understand it only quite superficially, chaos occurs when any complex, dynamic system is perturbed by a small uncertainty in one or another of its subunits. The inevitable result is an amplification of the disturbance and then the spread of unpredictable, random behavior throughout the whole system. It is the total unpredictability and randomness that makes the word "chaos" applicable as a technical term, but it is not true that the behavior of the system becomes disorderly. Indeed, as James P. Crutchfield and his associates have written, "There is order in chaos: underlying chaotic behavior there are elegant geometric forms that create randomness in the same way as a card dealer shuffles a deck of cards or a blender mixes cake batter." The random behavior of a turbulent stream of water, or of the weather, or of Brownian movement, or of the central nervous system of a cricket in flight from a bat, are all determined by the same mathematical rules. Behavior of this sort has been encountered in computer models of large cities: When a small change was made in one small part of the city model, the amplification of the change resulted in enormous upheavals, none of them predictable, in the municipal behavior at remote sites in the models.

A moth or a cricket has a small enough nervous system to *seem* predictable and orderly most of the time. There are not all that many neurons, and the circuitry contains what seem to be mostly simple reflex pathways. Laboratory experiments suggest that in a normal day, one thing — the sound of a bat at a safe distance, say — leads to another, predictable thing — a swerving off to one side in flight. It is only when something immensely new and important happens — the bat sound at three meters away — that the system is thrown into chaos.

I suggest that the difference with us is that chaos is the norm. Predictable, small-scale, orderly, cause-and-effect sequences are hard to come by and don't last long when they do turn up. Something else almost always turns up at the same time, and then another sequential thought intervenes alongside, and there come turbulence and chaos again. When we are lucky, and the system operates at its random best, something astonishing may suddenly turn up, beyond predicting or imagining. Events like these we recognize as good ideas.

My cat Jeoffry's brain is vastly larger and more commodious than that of a cricket, but I wonder if it is qualitatively all that different. The cricket lives with his two great ideas in mind, mating and predators, and his world is a world of particular, specified sounds. He is a tiny machine, I suppose, depending on what you mean by "machine," but it is his occasional moments of randomness and unpredictability that entitle him to be called aware. In order to achieve that feat of wild chaotic flight, and thus escape, he has to make use, literally, of his brain. When Int-1, an auditory interneuron, is activated by the sound of a bat closing in, the message is transmitted by an axon connected straight to the insect's brain, and it is here, and only here, that the swerving is generated. This I consider to be a thought, a very small thought, but still a thought. Without knowing what to count as a thought, I figure that Jeoffry, with his kind of brain, has a trillion thoughts of about the same size in any waking moment. As for me, and my sort of brain, I can't think where to begin.

We like to think of our minds as containing trains of thought, or streams of consciousness, as though they were orderly arrangements of linear events, one notion leading in a cause-and-effect way to the next notion. Logic is the way to go; we set a high price on logic, unlike E. M. Forster's elderly lady in *Aspects of the Novel,* who, when accused of being illogical, replied, "Logic? Good gracious! What rubbish! How can I tell what I think till I see what I say?"

But with regard to our own awareness of nature, I believe we've lost sight of, lost track of, lost touch with, and to some measurable degree lost respect for, the chaotic and natural in recent years — and during the very period of history when we humans have been learning more about the detailed workings of nature than in all our previous millennia. The more we learn, the more we seem to distance ourselves from the rest of life, as though we were separate creatures, so different from other occupants of the biosphere as to have arrived from another galaxy. We seek too much to explain, we assert a duty to run the place, to dominate the planet, to govern its life, but at the same time we ourselves seem to be less a part of it than ever before.

We leave it whenever we can, we crowd ourselves from open green countrysides onto the concrete surfaces of massive cities, as far removed from the earth as we can get, staring at it from behind insulated glass, or by way of half-hour television clips.

At the same time, we talk a great game of concern. We shout at each other in high virtue, now more than ever before, about the befoulment of our nest and about whom to blame. We have mechanized our lives so extensively that most of us live with the illusion that our only connection with nature is the nagging fear that it may one day turn on us and do us in. Polluting our farmlands and streams, even the seas, worries us because of what it may be doing to the food and water supplies necessary for human beings. Raising the level of CO_2, methane, and hydrofluorocarbons in the atmosphere troubles us because of the projected effects of climate upheaval on human habitats. These anxieties do not extend, really, to nature at large. They are not the result of any new awareness.

Nature itself, that vast incomprehensible meditative being, has come to mean for most of us nothing much more than odd walks in the nearby woods, or flowers in the rooftop garden, or the soap opera stories of the last giant panda or whooping crane, or curiosities like the northward approach, from Florida, of the Asiatic flying cockroach.

I will begin to feel better about us, and about our future, when we finally start learning about some of the things that are still mystifications. Start with the events in the mind of a cricket, I'd say, and then go on from there. Comprehend my cat Jeoffry and we'll be on our way. Nowhere near home, but off and dancing, getting within a few millennia of understanding why the music of Bach is what it is, ready at last for open outer space. Give us time, I'd say, the kind of endless time we mean when we talk about the real world.

PHILIP WEISS

How to Get Out of a
Locked Trunk

FROM HARPER'S MAGAZINE

ON A HOT SUNDAY last summer my friend Tony and I drove my
rental car, a '91 Buick, from St. Paul to the small town of Waconia, Minnesota, forty miles southwest. We each had a project.
Waconia is Tony's boyhood home, and his sister had recently
given him a panoramic postcard of Lake Waconia as seen from a
high point in the town early in the century. He wanted to dupli-
cate the photograph's vantage point, then hang the two pictures
together in his house in Frogtown. I was hoping to see Tony's
father, Emmett, a retired mechanic, in order to settle a question
that had been nagging me: Is it possible to get out of a locked car
trunk?

We tried to call ahead to Emmett twice, but he wasn't home.
Tony thought he was probably golfing but that there was a good
chance he'd be back by the time we got there. So we set out.

I parked the Buick, which was a silver sedan with a red interior, by the graveyard near where Tony thought the picture had
been taken. He took his picture and I wandered among the
headstones, reading the epitaphs. One of them was chillingly
anti-individualist. It said, "Not to do my will, but thine."

Trunk lockings had been on my mind for a few weeks. It
seemed to me that the fear of being locked in a car trunk had a
particular hold on the American imagination. Trunk lockings
occur in many movies and books — from *Goodfellas* to *Thelma and
Louise* to *Humboldt's Gift*. And while the highbrow national news-

papers generally shy away from trunk lockings, the attention they receive in local papers suggests a widespread anxiety surrounding the subject. In an afternoon at the New York Public Library I found numerous stories about trunk lockings. A Los Angeles man is discovered, bloodshot, banging the trunk of his white Eldorado following a night and a day trapped inside; he says his captors went on joyrides and picked up women. A forty-eight-year-old Houston doctor is forced into her trunk at a bank ATM and then the car is abandoned, parked near the Astrodome. A New Orleans woman tells police she gave birth in a trunk while being abducted to Texas. Tests undermine her story, the police drop the investigation. But so what if it's a fantasy? That only shows the idea's hold on us.

Every culture comes up with tests of a person's ability to get out of a sticky situation. The English plant mazes. Tropical resorts market those straw finger-grabbers that tighten their grip the harder you pull on them, and Viennese intellectuals gave us the concept of childhood sexuality — figure it out, or remain neurotic for life.

At least you could puzzle your way out of those predicaments. When they slam the trunk, though, you're helpless unless someone finds you. You would think that such a common worry should have a ready fix, and that the secret of getting out of a locked trunk is something we should all know about.

I phoned experts but they were very discouraging.

"You cannot get out. If you got a pair of pliers and bat's eyes, yes. But you have to have a lot of knowledge of the lock," said James Foote at Automotive Locksmiths in New York City.

Jim Frens, whom I reached at the technical section of *Car and Driver* in Detroit, told me the magazine had not dealt with this question. But he echoed the opinion of experts elsewhere when he said that the best hope for escape would be to try and kick out the panel between the trunk and the backseat. That angle didn't seem worth pursuing. What if your enemies were in the car, crumpling beer cans and laughing at your fate? It didn't make sense to join them.

The people who deal with rules on auto design were uncomfortable with my scenarios. Debra Barclay of the Center for Auto Safety, an organization founded by Ralph Nader, had certainly heard of cases, but she was not aware of any regulations on the matter. "Now, if there was a defect involved —" she said, her voice trailing off, implying that trunk locking was all phobia. This must be one of the few issues on which she and the auto industry agree. Ann Carlson of the Motor Vehicle Manufacturers Association became alarmed at the thought that I was going to play up a non-problem: "In reality this very rarely happens. As you say, in the movies it's a wonderful plot device," she said. "But in reality apparently this is not that frequent an occurrence. So they have not designed that feature into vehicles in a specific way."

When we got to Emmett's one-story house it was full of people. Tony's sister, Carol, was on the floor with her two small children. Her husband, Charlie, had one eye on the golf tournament on TV, and Emmett was at the kitchen counter, trimming fat from meat for lunch. I have known Emmett for fifteen years. He looked better than ever. In his retirement he had sharply changed his diet and lost a lot of weight. He had on shorts. His legs were tanned and muscular. As always, his manner was humorous, if opaque.

Tony told his family my news: I was getting married in three weeks. Charlie wanted to know where my fiancée was. Back East, getting everything ready. A big-time hatter was fitting her for a new hat.

Emmett sat on the couch, watching me. "Do you want my advice?"

"Sure."

He just grinned. A gold tooth glinted. Carol and Charlie pressed him to yield his wisdom.

Finally he said, "Once you get to be thirty, you make your own mistakes."

He got out several cans of beer, and then I brought up what was on my mind.

Emmett nodded and took off his glasses, then cleaned them and put them back on.

We went out to his car, a Mercury Grand Marquis, and Emmett opened the trunk. His golf clubs were sitting on top of the spare tire in a green golf bag. Next to them was a toolbox and what he called his "burglar tools," a set of elbowed rods with red plastic handles he used to open door locks when people locked their keys inside.

Tony and Charlie stood watching. Charlie is a banker in Minneapolis. He enjoys gizmos and is extremely practical. I would describe him as unflappable. That's a word I always wanted to apply to myself, but my fiancée had recently informed me that I am high-strung. Though that surprised me, I didn't quarrel with her.

For a while we studied the latch assembly. The lock closed in much the same way that a lobster might clamp on to a pencil. The claw portion, the jaws of the lock, was mounted inside the trunk lid. When you shut the lid, the jaws locked on to the bend of a U-shaped piece of metal mounted on the body of the car. Emmett said my best bet would be to unscrew the bolts. That way the U-shaped piece would come loose and the lock's jaws would swing up with it still in their grasp.

"But you'd need a wrench," he said.

It was already getting too technical. Emmett had an air of endless patience, but I felt defeated. I could only imagine bloodied fingers, cracked teeth. I had hoped for a simple trick.

Charlie stepped forward. He reached out and squeezed the lock's jaws. They clicked shut in the air, bound together by heavy springs. Charlie now prodded the upper part of the left-hand jaw, the thicker part. With a rough flick of his thumb, he was able to force the jaws to snap open. Great.

Unfortunately, the jaws were mounted behind a steel plate the size of your palm in such a way that while they were accessible to us, standing outside the car, had we been inside the trunk the plate would be in our way, blocking the jaws.

This time Emmett saw the way out. He fingered a hole in the plate. It was no bigger than the tip of your little finger. But the hole was close enough to the latch itself that it might be possible to angle something through the hole from inside the trunk and nudge the jaws apart. We tried with one of my keys. The lock jumped open.

It was time for a full-dress test. Emmett swung the clubs out of the trunk, and I set my can of Schmidt's on the rear bumper and climbed in. Everyone gathered around, and Emmett lowered the trunk on me, then pressed it shut with his meaty hands. Total darkness. I couldn't hear the people outside. I thought I was going to panic. But the big trunk felt comfortable. I was pressed against a sort of black carpet that softened the angles against my back.

I could almost stretch out in the trunk, and it seemed to me I could make them sweat if I took my time. Even Emmett, that sphinx, would give way to curiosity. Once I was out he'd ask how it had been and I'd just grin. There were some things you could only learn by doing.

It took a while to find the hole. I slipped the key in and angled it to one side. The trunk gasped open.

Emmett motioned the others away, then levered me out with his big right forearm. Though I'd only been inside for a minute, I was disoriented — as much as anything because someone had moved my beer while I was gone, setting it down on the cement floor of the garage. It was just a little thing, but I could not be entirely sure I had gotten my own beer back.

Charlie was now raring to try other cars. We examined the latch on his Toyota, which was entirely shielded to the trunk occupant (i.e., no hole in the plate), and on the neighbor's Honda (ditto). But a 1991 Dodge Dynasty was doable. The trunk was tight, but its lock had a feature one of the mechanics I'd phoned described as a "tailpiece": a finger-like extension of the lock mechanism itself that stuck out a half inch into the trunk cavity; simply by twisting the tailpiece I could free the lock. I was even faster on a 1984 Subaru that had a little lever device on the latch.

We went out to my rental on Oak Street. The Skylark was in direct sun and the trunk was hot to the touch, but when we got it open we could see that its latch plate had a perfect hole, a square in which the edge of the lock's jaw appeared like a face in a window.

The trunk was shallow and hot. Emmett had to push my knees down before he could close the lid. This one was a little suffocating. I imagined being trapped for hours, and even before he had got it closed I regretted the decision with a slightly nauseous feeling. I thought of Edgar Allan Poe's live burials, and then about something my fiancée had said more than a year and a half before. I had been on her case to get married. She was

divorced, and at every opportunity I would reissue my pro
posal — even during a commercial. She'd interrupted one of
these chirps to tell me, in a cold, throaty voice, that she had no
intention of ever going through another divorce: "This time, it's
death out." I'd carried those words around like a lump of wet
clay.

As it happened, the Skylark trunk was the easiest of all. The
hole was right where it was supposed to be. The trunk popped
open, and I felt great satisfaction that we'd been able to figure
out a rule that seemed to apply about 60 percent of the time. If
we publicized our success, it might get the attention it deserved.
All trunks would be fitted with such a hole. Kids would learn
about it in school. The grip of the fear would relax. Before long
a successful trunk-locking scene would date a movie like a fedora
dates one today.

When I got back East I was caught up in wedding preparations.
I live in New York, and the wedding was to take place in Philadelphia. We set up camp there with five days to go. A friend had
lent my fiancée her BMW, and we drove it south with all our
things. I unloaded the car in my parents' driveway. The last
thing I pulled out of the trunk was my fiancée's hat in its heavy
cardboard shipping box. She'd warned me I was not allowed to
look. The lid was free but I didn't open it. I was willing to be
surprised.

When the trunk was empty it occurred to me I might hop in
and give it a try. First I looked over the mechanism. The jaws of
the BMW's lock were shielded, but there seemed to be some kind
of cable coming off it that you might be able to manipulate so as
to cause the lock to open. The same cable that allowed the driver
to open the trunk remotely . . .

I fingered it for a moment or two but decided I didn't need to
test out the theory.

Biographical Notes

MARCIA ALDRICH is an assistant professor in twentieth-century poetry at Michigan State University. "Hair" is part of a larger manuscript of prose pieces, inspired by letters of the alphabet, called *The X-Woman*. She is also working on *Lethal Brevity: Louise Bogan, Modernism, and the Feminine Lyric*.

JOSEPH BRODSKY, exiled from the Soviet Union in 1972, is Andrew Mellon Professor of Literature at Mount Holyoke College. His books include two collections of poetry, *A Part of Speech* and *To Urania*, and *Less than One*, a volume of essays. He received the Nobel Prize for Literature in 1987. His most recent book is *Watermark*, a long essay about Venice.

ANTHONY BURGESS is the author of some fifty books of fiction and nonfiction as well as children's books, translations, and screenplays. His novels include *A Clockwork Orange, Earthly Powers, The Kingdom of the Wicked,* and, most recently, *Any Old Iron*. He has published two volumes of autobiography, *Little Wilson and Big God* and *You've Had Your Time*. He was a professional musician and composer before turning his attention to writing. The essay in this volume was adapted from his most recent book, *On Mozart: A Paean for Wolfgang*.

JACOB COHEN is chairman of the American Studies Department at Brandeis University. He has written widely about allegations of government conspiracy throughout American history. A book in progress, *The Performance of Innocence*, considers the performances of Sacco and Vanzetti, Bruno Hauptmann, Alger Hiss, Ethel and Julius Rosenberg, and John Demjanjuk.

GERALD EARLY, professor of English and director of the African and the Afro-American Studies Program at Washington University in St.

Louis, is the author of *Tuxedo Junction: Essays on American Culture* and the editor of numerous books, including *Lure and Loathing: Essays on Race, Identity, and the Ambivalence of Assimilation*. His latest collection of essays, *The Culture of Bruising*, will be published in the fall of 1993.

JEAN ERVIN, the author of two books on the Twin Cities and the editor of an anthology of Minnesota prose, has published stories and essays in a number of magazines. She is at work on a book about growing up in New England during the Great Depression and World War II.

LAWRENCE OTIS GRAHAM is the author of ten nonfiction books and numerous essays. A graduate of Princeton and Harvard Law School, he is a corporate attorney, a business consultant, and an adjunct professor at Fordham University. His articles have appeared in the *New York Times, Essence, Good Housekeeping*, and *New York*. His new collection of essays, *Member of the Club*, will be published early in 1994.

DANIEL HARRIS is an essayist and book critic whose work appears in the *Los Angeles Times, The Nation, Salmagundi*, and elsewhere.

BARBARA GRIZZUTI HARRISON, a contributing editor of *Harper's* and *Mirabella*, is the author of *Italian Days, The Islands of Italy, The Astonishing World* (a collection of essays), *Visions of Glory: A History and a Memory of Jehovah's Witnesses*, and *Foreign Bodies* (a novel). She has contributed essays, articles, and short stories to many publications, including the *New York Times Magazine, New Republic, Vanity Fair, Paris Review, Condé Nast Traveler*, and *Esquire*.

DIANE JOHNSON is the author of seven novels, the most recent of which are *Persian Nights* and *Health and Happiness;* two biographies; and a collection of travel pieces, *National Opium*, of which "Rolex" is one. Her essays and criticism appear in the *New York Review of Books*, the *New York Times Book Review*, and elsewhere. She is the coauthor, with Stanley Kubrick, of the scenario for his film *The Shining*, and she is working on a scenario for Francis Ford Coppola on the subject of AIDS.

WARD JUST lives in Vineyard Haven, Massachusetts. He is the author of nine novels and three collections of short stories. A new novel, *Ambition and Love*, will be published in the spring of 1994.

PAUL R. MCHUGH is a psychiatrist and neurologist. He was born in Lawrence, Massachusetts, graduated from the Harvard Medical School in 1956, and has been the director of the Department of Psychiatry and Behavioral Sciences at the Johns Hopkins School of Medicine since 1975. He received the William C. Menninger Award from the American College of Physicians in 1987 and was elected to the Institute of Medicine, National Academy of Science, in 1992. He is the author (with Phillip Slavney) of *The Perspectives of Psychiatry* and *Psychiatric Polarities*. These books represent, as does the essay in this volume, his current work in delineating how the methods of thought that provide psychiatrists with their skills can also, if misemployed, lead them astray.

SHAUN O'CONNELL is a professor of English at the University of Massachusetts at Boston, where he has taught American and Irish literature since 1965. He is the author of *Imagining Boston: A Literary Landscape,* and he is writing a book on literary New York City.

CYNTHIA OZICK is the author of three novels, *Trust, The Cannibal,* and *The Shawl,* and several collections: *The Pagan Rabbi and Other Stories, Bloodshed and Three Novellas,* and *Levitation: Five Fictions.* She has published *Art and Ardor: Essays* and *Metaphor and Memory: Essays,* and written *Angel,* a play currently in development.

THOMAS PALMER is the author of two novels, *The Transfer* and *Dream Science.* He writes that his essay "is an attempt to come to terms intellectually with the emotional turmoil anyone with 'green' sympathies must suffer as the old disappears and the new takes its place." The essay is adapted from *Landscape with Reptile: Rattlesnakes in an Urban World,* a natural and cultural history of the Boston area's last timber rattlesnakes. Palmer is currently working on a novel about race in the suburbs.

JAMES SALTER is the author of *Dusk and Other Stories,* which won the 1989 PEN/Faulkner Award, and the novels *Light Years, A Sport and a Pastime,* and *Solo Faces.* His work appears frequently in *Esquire* and the *Paris Review,* and he is finishing a memoir, from which "You Must" is taken.

SCOTT RUSSELL SANDERS is the author of more than a dozen books, including *The Paradise of Bombs, The Invisible Company, Secrets of the Universe,* and *Staying Put.* "Wayland" is the final chapter in the last of these books, a personal account of the effort to make a home in a restless world. With the aid of a Guggenheim fellowship, Sanders is at work on two new books, a collection of stories about an urban coyote he calls Gordon Milk and *Writing from the Center,* about living, working, and making a community in the Midwest. He teaches literature and writing at Indiana University, in Bloomington, where he lives with his wife and two children.

ROBERT SHERRILL is a reporter, writer, and editor who has worked for eight or so newspapers and two magazines. He was an associate editor and contributing editor at *Esquire* for twelve years. He writes, or rewrites, all the time and thus has several works in progress, none of which are spoken for.

FLOYD SKLOOT is the author of two novels, *Pilgrim's Harbor* and the forthcoming *Summer Blue*. His collection of poetry, *Music Appreciation*, will be published in the fall of 1993. He is writing a novel to be called *Patient 002*, based on his experiences as a human medical research subject.

SHELBY STEELE is a professor of English at San Jose State University. He is the author of *The Content of Our Character*, which won the National Book Critics Circle Award for nonfiction in 1991. His essays have appeared in *Harper's Magazine*, the *American Scholar*, the *New Republic*, the *New York Times Magazine*, and many other publications. He is currently at work on a new collection of essays on the workings of identity in America, to be published in the winter of 1994.

LEWIS THOMAS, a physician and medical researcher, has published five collections of essays: *The Lives of a Cell, The Medusa and the Snail, Late Night Thoughts on Listening to Mahler's Ninth Symphony, Et Cetera, Et Cetera,* and *The Fragile Species*. In addition to numerous scientific papers, he is also the author of a memoir, *The Youngest Science: Notes of a Medicine Watcher*.

PHILIP WEISS is a contributing editor at *Harper's Magazine* and *Esquire*. He lives in New York and is at work on a novel.

Notable Essays of 1992

SELECTED BY ROBERT ATWAN

JAMES SLOAN ALLEN
Reflections at the Edge of the World.
Sewanee Review, Fall.

ROGER ANGELL
Early Innings. The New Yorker,
February 24.

WILL BAKER
The Gulf of Unknowing. Georgia
Review, Spring.

HELEN BAROLINI
My Mother's Wedding Day. Southwest
Review, Winter.

JOHN BERGER
Disappearing. Harper's Magazine,
December.

SAUL BELLOW
Mozart. Bostonia, Spring.

SVEN BIRKERTS
The Woman in the Garden. Agni, No.
35.

DAVID BRADLEY
Malcolm's Myth Making. Transition,
No. 56.

ROSEMARY L. BRAY
So How Did I Get Here? New York
Times Magazine, November 8.

NICHOLAS BROMELL
Family Secrets. Harper's Magazine,
July.

FREDERICK BUSCH
Reading Hemingway Without Guilt.
New York Times Book Review,
January 12.

MARYLOU CAPES
Silence. Georgia Review, Winter.

TOM CARSON
To Disneyland. L.A. Weekly, March
27–April 2.

CHRISTOPHER CLAUSEN
Dialogues with the Dead. American
Scholar, Spring.

BERNARD COOPER
Picking Plums. Harper's Magazine,
August.

JIM W. CORDER
Lessons Learned, Lessons Lost.
Georgia Review, Spring.

MICHAEL DIBDIN
The Pathology Lesson. Granta, No.
39.

JEANNE DIXON
Deep in the Heart of It. Northern
Lights, Vol. 8, No. 1.

MICHAEL DORRIS
The Quest for Pie. *Antaeus,* Spring.

BRIAN DOYLE
Letterature. *Portland,* Winter.

BETTINA DREW
Bradford Market. *Virginia Quarterly Review,* Autumn.

DAVID JAMES DUNCAN
A Mickey Mantle Koan. *Harper's Magazine,* September.

LOWELL EDMUNDS
Choosing Your Names. *Raritan,* Winter.

GRETEL EHRLICH
Time on Ice. *Harper's Magazine,* March.

LARS EIGHNER
Phlebitis. *Threepenny Review,* Spring.

LOUISE ERDRICH
Foxglove. *Georgia Review,* Fall.

MELODY ERMACHILD
The Death of Ian Freedman. *New Letters,* Vol. 58, No. 2.

BRUCE FLEMING
On Becoming Human. *Sewanee Review,* Summer.

RICHARD FORD
An Urge for Going. *Harper's Magazine,* February.

ROBERT ELLIOT FOX
Afrocentrism and the X-Factor. *Transition,* No. 57.

ROBIN FOX
Fatal Attraction: War and Human Nature. *National Interest,* Winter.

BRIGITTE FRASE
The Past Too Is Unfinished. *Hungry Mind Review,* Summer.

STEPHEN FRIED
Just Visiting. *Philadelphia,* March.

BETTY FUSSELL
On Murdering Eels and Laundering Swine. *Antaeus,* Spring.

DON FUTTERMAN
I Never Compete with My Brother. *Tikkun,* September/October.

JANE GALLOP
Knot a Love Story. *Yale Journal of Criticism,* Fall.

GEORGE GARRETT
Locker Room Talk: Notes on the Social History of Football. *Witness,* Vol. 6, No. 2.

PHILIP GARRISON
Meditation. *Iowa Review,* Spring/Summer.

ALEXANDER GEORGE
Ruminations of a Vegetarian. *Massachusetts Review,* Fall.

HERBERT GOLD
A Blazing Incident. *Partisan Review,* Winter.

ALBERT GOLDBARTH
Dual. *Georgia Review,* Fall.
To Write of Repeated Patterns. *Iowa Review,* Fall.

STEPHEN JAY GOULD
The Most Unkindest Cut of All. *Natural History,* May.

C W. GUSEWUELLE
A Great Current. *Missouri Review,* Vol. 15, No. 1.

ALEX HALEY
Malcolm X Remembered. *Playboy,* July.

DONALD HALL
Going, Going, Gone. *Yankee,* March.

MARTHA HEYNEMAN
The Mother Tongue. *Parabola,* Fall.

LAWRENCE HOFFMAN
Being a Jew at Christmas Time. *Cross Currents*, Fall.

ANDREW HOLLERAN
A Good Long Steady Soaking Rain. *Christopher Street*, No. 175.

WILLIAM HOWARTH
Putting Columbus in His Place. *Southwest Review*, Spring/Summer.

DAN HOWELL
Cowards. *The Sun*, December.

PAT C. HOY II
Imagining Lives of Our Own. *Virginia Quarterly Review*, Winter.
Leadership. *Sewanee Review*, Summer.

ROBERT HUGHES
The Fraying of America. *Time*, February 3.

ADA LOUISE HUXTABLE
Inventing American Reality. *New York Review of Books*, December 3.

GEOFFREY JOHNSON
Love, Death, Superman. (Chicago) *Reader*, December 4.

ALFRED KAZIN
Cry, the Beloved Country. *Forbes*, September 14.

JAMES KILGO
Coming Off the Back of Brasstown Bald. *Oxford American*, Vol. 2.

JAMAICA KINCAID
Biography of a Dress. *Grand Street*, No. 43.

FLORENCE KING
A WASP Looks at Lizzie Borden. *National Review*, August 17.

WILLIAM KITTREDGE
Lost Cowboys (But Not Forgotten). *Antaeus*, Autumn.

HERB KOHL
On Not-Learning. *Threepenny Review*, Summer.

LEONARD KRIEGEL
Flying Solo. *Sewanee Review*, Summer.
Pursuing Women, Meeting Myself. *Southwest Review*, Autumn.
A Loaded Question. *Harper's Magazine*, May.

JAKE LAMAR
The Problem with You People. *Esquire*, February.

LEWIS LAPHAM
Who and What Is American? *Harper's Magazine*, January.

NORMAN LAVERS
Yours Sincerely, Wasting Away. *North American Review*, January/February.

DAVID LAZAR
The Coat. *Mississippi Valley Review*, Fall.

SYDNEY LEA
Father and Son: Toward a Theory of Fortunate Fall. *Prairie Schooner*, Fall.

DAVID LEHMAN
Deconstruction After the Fall. *AWP*, December.

MONTY S. LEITCH
Driving by Water. *Shenandoah*, Fall.

FRANK LENTRICCHIA
En Route to Retreat. *Harper's Magazine*, January.

DORIS LESSING
Women's Quests. *Partisan Review*, Spring.

PHILLIP LOPATE
In Search of the Centaur: The Essay-Film. *Threepenny Review*, Winter.

BARRY LOPEZ
The Rediscovery of North America.
  Orion, Summer.

GLENN C. LOURY
Free at Last? *Commentary,* October.

BIA LOWE
Bats. *Kenyon Review,* Summer.

NICK LYONS
No, No, a Thousand Times No. *New
  York Times Book Review,* July 26.

THOMAS MALLON
The Last Rocket Club. *Southwest
  Review,* Spring/Summer.

DAVID MAMET
The Rake. *Harper's Magazine,* June.

GREIL MARCUS
Notes on the Life and Death and
  Incandescent Banality of Rock 'n'
  Roll. *Esquire,* August.

ANNE MATTHEWS
Humidity. *Southwest Review,* Spring/
  Summer.

FRANCIS MAYES
The Walking Rain. *Virginia Quarterly
  Review,* Summer.

JAMES MCCONKEY
My Life with the Other Animals.
  Hudson Review, Spring.

COLIN MCENROE
Faerieland. *Northeast,* June 21.

TOD MCEWEN
My Mother's Eyes. *Granta,* No. 39.

DONALD MCQUADE
Living In — and On — the Margins.
  *College Composition and
  Communication,* February.

N. SCOTT MOMADAY
New Mexico: Passage into Legend.
  *New York Times Magazine
  (Sophisticated Traveler),* October 18.

DAVID MORSE
The Rat Historian. *Boulevard,* Fall.

DERVLA MURPHY
Reflections on Travel Writing. *Wilson
  Quarterly,* Summer.

KATHLEEN NORRIS
Is It You, Again? A Discourse on
  Monasteries. *Gettysburg Review,*
  Autumn.

NAOMI SHIHAB NYE
Newcomers in a Troubled Land.
  Southwest Review, Spring/Summer.

S. OSO
Lessons. *Hudson Review,* Summer.

KEVIN ODERMAN
Writing the Living Daylights.
  Northwest Review, Vol. 30, No. 33.

ALICIA OSTRIKER
The Interpretation of Dreams.
  Kenyon Review, Summer.

DAVID OWEN
One-Ring Mud Show. *The New Yorker,*
  April 20.

CYNTHIA OZICK
Of Christian Heroism. *Partisan
  Review,* Winter.

GEORGE PACKER
Class Interests, Liberal Style. *Dissent,*
  Winter.

ADAM PHILLIPS
First Hates. *Raritan,* Fall.

SAMUEL F. PICKERING
Fall. *Missouri Review,* Vol. 15, No. 2.
Sweet Auburn. *New England Review,*
  Fall.

ADRIAN PIPER
Passing for White, Passing for Black.
  Transition, No. 58.

DAVID QUAMMEN
Death at a Peculiar Age. *Outside,*
  November.

ALASTAIR REID
Waiting for Columbus. *The New Yorker*, February 24.

WILLIAM REWAK
Three Graves. *Commonweal*, December 4.

DAVID RIEFF
Original Virtue, Original Sin. *The New Yorker*, November 23.

MARILYNNE ROBINSON
Hearing Silence: Western Myth Reconsidered. *Northern Lights*, Vol. 8, No. 2.

MARK ROZEMA
Coming Home. *Puerto del Sol*, Summer.

OLIVER SACKS
A Surgeon's Life. *The New Yorker*, March 16.

JAMES SALTER
When Evening Falls. *GQ*, February.

REG SANER
Swiss Wilderness. *Gettysburg Review*, Autumn.

ARTHUR SCHLESINGER, JR.
Was America a Mistake? *Atlantic Monthly*, September.

LYNNE SHARON SCHWARTZ
Help. *Michigan Quarterly Review*, Spring.

FRED SETTERBERG
Zora Neal-Hurston in the Land of 1000 Dances. *Georgia Review*, Winter.

LOUIS SIMPSON
Going Back. *Gettysburg Review*, Summer.

W. D. SNODGRASS
Love and/or War. *Georgia Review*, Spring.

GARY SNYDER
Exhortations for Baby Tigers. *Zyzzyva*, Spring.

DEBRA SPARK
The Lure of the West. *Ploughshares*, Spring.

HARRY STEIN
Presumed Guilty. *Playboy*, June.

ROBERT STONE
Havana Then and Now. *Harper's Magazine*, March.

WILLIAM STYRON
Nat Turner Revisited. *American Heritage*, October.

ELIZABETH TEMPLEMAN
The Chaos Theory. *High Plains Literary Review*, Spring.

DAVID THOMSON
Happiness. *Film Comment*, September/October.

SALLIE TISDALE
Talk Dirty to Me. *Harper's Magazine*, February.

DAVID UPDIKE
The Colorings of Childhood. *Harper's Magazine*, January.

ANDREW WARD
The Little Big Horn. *American Heritage*, April.

GEORGE WATSON
Confessions of a Streetwalker. *Virginia Quarterly Review*, Autumn.

PAUL WEST
The Concorde Pilot's Other Life. *Witness*, Vol. 6, No. 1.

DOUGLAS WHYNOTT
My Mother's New Heart. *Boston Globe Magazine*, October 11.

JOHN EDGAR WIDEMAN
Dead Black Men and Other Fallout
  from the American Dream. *Esquire,*
  September.

PETER WILD
Lost on the Ranch: Reassembling the
  Whole. *North Dakota Quarterly,* Fall.

JOHN P. WILEY, JR.
How Far *Is* Far? *Smithsonian,*
  September.

JANET WOLKOFF
Erica Counts. *Iowa Woman,* Spring.

C. VANN WOODWARD
The Aging of Democracies. *Southern
  Humanities Review,* Winter.

GEOFFREY WOLFF
Boy Racer. *TriQuarterly,* No. 83
  (Winter).

CATHY YOUNG
Victimhood Is Powerful. *Reason,*
  October.

TRACY YOUNG
A Few (More) Words about Breasts.
  Esquire, September.

Interested readers will also discover many fine essays in the following special magazine issues that appeared in 1992:

Antaeus, "Not for Bread Alone," edited by Daniel Halpern. Spring.
Georgia Review, "Love and/or War," edited by Stanley W. Lindberg. Spring.
Gettysburg Review, "Travel and Exotic Places," edited by Peter Stitt. Autumn.
Sewanee Review, "Fields of Memory," edited by George Core. Summer.
Southwest Review, "American Places," edited by Willard Spiegelman. Spring/
    Summer.
Witness, "Sports in America," edited by Peter Stine. Vol. 6, No. 2.